Where to Buy Property Abroad

An Investor's Guide

David Cox | Ray Withers

This edition published in Great Britain in 2007 by
Crimson Publishing
Westminster House
Kew Road
Richmond
Surrey
TW9 2ND

First published 2006
Second edition 2007

A catalogue record for this book is available from the British library.

ISBN 978-1-85458-391-8

Printed in Turkey by Mega Printing.

Contents

Part I
UNDERSTANDING WHERE AND WHAT TO BUY ABROAD

PART II
INVESTMENT POTENTIAL OF INDIVIDUAL COUNTRIES

Foreword

Until now, there have been few comprehensive books catering for international property buyers whose primary motivation is investment. There are books on buying property in France or Spain, and many other countries, all of which may pay some attention to the investment aspect of buying property in those specific markets. But there is no book on the general subject of international property investment; discussing its principles, the required tools and techniques and providing analysis and comparisons of a broad range of markets across the globe. The purpose of this book is to fill that gap, to provide people with an accessible overview of many of the most exciting international property markets and how to purchase safely.

This book is also about guidance and access to information. Even when you have made a decision about where to buy, working out how the buying process works can be a complex and unrewarding task and there are a lot of unscrupulous agents that give the industry a bad name. In order to invest in property with confidence, you need access to the best possible information that is up-to-date and reliable. And it is here that people looking further than the UK and traditional markets tend to suffer. There just isn't enough written about markets beyond the historical holiday home hot-spots and a few books based purely on Buy-To-Let and property investment.

Surprisingly, although property is one of the largest of all the asset classes it is among the most misunderstood. Investment banks plough millions into the research of debt and equity markets and analyse them on a daily basis. This has not been the case within the international property market and there have been no unified and reliable sources for investors on international property markets.

That doesn't mean that the required information doesn't exist, simply that it doesn't exist in a format readily accessible to ordinary investors. Our advantage is that we are not professional writers but actual practitioners of property investment. In our professional capacity at Property Frontiers we analyse and assess international property investment opportunities on a daily basis. As such we have a good understanding of both the methods of assessing opportunities and the sourcing of the data that our decisions rely upon.

The range of property investment opportunities around the globe makes it physically impossible to discuss them all in a book with a practical weight limit. But we have drawn on our own experience and the expertise of our colleagues to provide information on 33 of the most interesting and popular investment markets in the world today.

The first half of the book looks at where and what to buy, providing the tools and background understanding necessary to analyse property markets and investment opportunities. After introducing the international property market, its history and an overview of global trends, we move on to look at market analysis starting with a discussion of how markets work. We look at the different forces that cause property price movements and look at some detailed case studies on the impact of factors such as EU accession, hosting the Olympics and low cost air travel.

In the second chapter of this book, *Where to Buy Abroad*, we introduce some tools for assessing the relative value of a property market and finally look at some specific considerations when buying in the city or countryside; in ski resorts or by the beach.

Chapter three, *What to Buy*, provides a basis for developing an investment strategy and gives some simple tools for assessing the attractiveness of a specific property investment opportunity. This chapter also considers the pros and cons of old property, new build and off-plan. We also deal with the potential risks of buying abroad and ways in which those risks could be minimised through collective investment schemes such as funds and real estate investment trusts (REITs).

Chapter four, *Making a Profit from Property*, looks at the various ways you can profit from your investment; in particular Buy-to-let purchases, and helps you calculate potential return before looking into the different aspects you should consider when purchasing a property to ensure you are able to exit and liquidate your property and release your profit.

Chapter five, *Good Advice and Information*, discusses the role of an agent and how to find one you can rely on. It also highlights some good sources of information and other resources that you will need.

Chapter six, *Financial Considerations*, examines the financial considerations of buying abroad including mortgages, currency exchange, closing costs and taxation.

Finally, Part II looks at 33 of the most popular markets. Each set of country details includes information on the best areas to buy, the type of property to look for, and the buying process.

Above all we aim to equip people with the knowledge they need to identify good investment markets for themselves. Forgive the analogy, but this book is more fishing rod than fish. Tell someone where to invest and they may make money, teach someone how to identify good investments for themselves and its 'hello Aston Martin'. Perhaps not quite, but knowledge and self-reliance are two of the most valuable assets around. Good luck.

David Cox and Ray Withers
September 2007

The recommendations and advice given in this book are the considered opinions of the authors, however other commentators may take a different view of individual markets. Changes of government policy or economic climate, or natural disasters in a particular area, can result in positive or negative fluctuations in property values. As with stocks and shares, prices can go down as well as up.

The authors and publishers have every reason to believe in the accuracy of the information given in this book and the authenticity and correct practices of all organisations, companies, agencies etc. mentioned. Situations may change though, and telephone numbers, websites, regulations and exchange rates can alter. Readers are strongly advised to check facts and credentials for themselves.

Acknowledgements

The Authors would like to thank all of our colleagues at Property Frontiers who have made outstanding efforts to support the production of this book. All of the country experts have given extensive amounts of their time in supporting our research.

In particular a special thank you must go to Judi Williams, Emma Holifield and the research team for the production of the country profiles and many hours of editorial support. Without their efforts this book would be much poorer in detail and facts.

We would also like to thank the publishing and editorial team at Crimson Publishing for their expert guidance and support.

Website

www.aninvestorsguide.com

Where to Buy Property Abroad – An Investors Guide has a dedicated website www. aninvestorsguide.com. Please visit for more information on additional countries, updated market news and new features for investors.

PART I

UNDERSTANDING WHERE AND WHAT TO BUY ABROAD

INVESTING IN PROPERTY

WHERE TO BUY ABROAD – ANALYSING MARKETS

WHAT TO BUY – ASSESSING OPPORTUNITIES

MAKING A PROFIT FROM PROPERTY

THE MOST VALUABLE TOOLS – GOOD ADVICE
AND INFORMATION

FINANCIAL CONSIDERATIONS

1 Introduction

No matter which part of the English speaking world you live in, you will undoubtedly be familiar with dinner party conversations regarding either property investment or real estate investment. Whatever the terminology, property is a national obsession in Britain, the USA, Australia and Ireland. Home ownership in these countries is extremely high by international standards, but more importantly from the point of view of this book, so is the level of property investment.

Over the last 30 years, more and more people have purchased a second home, some for their own personal enjoyment and some purely for investment. In the US this led to the evolution of prime second home destinations such as the Gulf Coast of Florida and the snowy peaks of Aspen. For those of us that live in the less geographically diverse British Isles, we have tended to head to the sunnier climes of the Mediterranean. By dint of geography then, the international property industry is much more developed in the UK as people wanting a second home in the sun have had no choice but to buy abroad. However, motivations are changing. Recent decades have seen significant domestic property booms in the UK, USA, Australia and Ireland. A coincidence of circumstances (mainly related to easily accessible mortgage financing due to heavy competition in the banking sector) has democratised the ownership of real estate. Ordinary families have become landlords; re-financing their own homes to build a portfolio of properties that generate a healthy return.

As a result of these recent booms, property investment has overtaken investing in equities in terms of popularity (particularly in the UK and Ireland), but it is no investment panacea. Real estate is most certainly part of a market place; subject to the same peaks and troughs as any other asset market. It is true that property markets tend to be more stable, partly due to the lack of liquidity (property isn't as easy to dispose of as other types of asset) and partly due to the fact that no matter how much prices drop, people still need a home. But the reality remains that prices may go down as well as up. The real estate markets in the USA, Spain and Australia have all experienced a slow down in recent years and in some areas prices have actually fallen. But in today's age of international travel and the internet, people are very aware that there is a world beyond their doorstep and that world is full of places where property markets are just beginning to boom.

The fact that we are writing this book is evidence enough that international property investment is a very popular topic. Brits have been buying property abroad for many years, but today around 60% of those doing so state investment (rather than a holiday home) as their main motivation. According to Moneycorp, by 2006 80,000 Britons owned homes overseas. Barclays Bank have predicted that some 2.2million Brits will invest in overseas property over the next 5 years whilst the Bank of Scotland International have gone one step further and showed that an incredible 42% of Britons are interested in buying property abroad. Research carried out at the end of 2006 by Moneycorp also declared that "59% of first-time buyers may buy their first property abroad". In the US, the story is slightly different. US holiday home owners have mostly purchased in other parts of the country meaning that the market for holiday homes abroad was small. However as a result of the recent downturn in the US home market, a rapidly growing international real estate industry has sprung up in the US looking to service the requirements of investors looking for better returns overseas.

The Different Motives of Buyers

Many international property buyers may be investors, but there are still many other buyers whose primary motivation is different; perhaps they are looking for a holiday home or even to relocate. Whatever the motivation though, the investment considerations discussed in this book play an important part in the decision making process. Even people whose main motivation is to enjoy a holiday home in the sun must consider whether or not their purchase is a sound investment. Few people can afford to buy a holiday home that is a bad investment. The concepts discussed in this book are therefore as relevant to holiday homers and relocators as they are to hard-nosed investors.

When buying a property abroad, for any purpose, there are many questions to answer. Should you buy in somewhere like Spain or France where there is a long history of foreigners buying property, or an emerging market where prices may be much lower and potential returns much higher, but where the process is more complicated and the investment potentially riskier? Is an off-plan development better than an older house? Are rentals for ski chalets higher than for beach houses, and how do you find out about banking, taxes, fees or how to find the notary or estate agent who can give you the best service?

In the UK, overseas property programmes, exhibitions, articles and magazines seem inescapable, but despite the ubiquity of coverage there is a lack of clear information on countries other than the traditional holiday home favourites of Spain, France and Italy. Understanding the property market and buying process in less well trodden destinations can seem like one of the labours of Hercules. And that is what makes this book different; the breadth and depth of information given. Recognising that people's motivations are different, and that they are buying more adventurously, this book aims to explain how to buy property in Malaysia as well as Canada, Brazil as well as Turkey, Slovakia as well as Mongolia.

Growing numbers of people have the incentive and budget to invest in property abroad, but are uncertain about where to spend their money. The information in this book is provided for all those people. If you are interested in buying property but unsure where and what to buy we will help you to understand the basic concepts of international property investment, to understand why prices rise in a certain area and where they should rise over the next two or three years.

The Great Global Property Boom

The Rise in House Prices

Why is property investment a topic of such broad appeal? Well there are several reasons but one of the most significant is that the western world has just been through the biggest property boom in history. This means that there is a whole generation of people who have experienced what a good investment property can be. They also have a great deal more funds available to invest as the values of their own properties have risen so dramatically. In fact, over the past decade house prices have boomed in almost every developed market with the exception of Germany and Japan. House prices in Australia, Britain, Ireland, the Netherlands, Spain and Sweden have all risen by more than 50%.

The Economist Research Unit calculates that the value of residential property in developed economies has increased by three quarters since 2000 to almost $75 trillion (that's twelve zeros). The increase is equivalent to more than 100% of those countries' national incomes. This is a rocketing rate of growth; so much so that in the UK and US, house prices have become a staple of conversation. The rising value of property has made a whole generation of people feel financially secure and encouraged consumer spending which benefits the wider economy. During periods of economic instability household spending has proved surprisingly resilient – and the reason for this resilience has been linked to rising property values and lower costs of mortgage borrowing.

The last set of housing indices, published by BIS National Statistics suggests that, since 1997, house prices have risen internationally as below.

Whilst this boom has created a generation of potential property investors, it has also left them feeling that they have missed the boat. With developed economy markets at their current high, is now a sensible time to start investing? There is no simple answer to that question. Some developed property markets or areas within developed markets still present a good opportunity (despite recent levels of growth) whilst others do not. What is certain though is that there are many property markets across the globe that have not yet reached these levels of growth and it is these emerging markets that are rightly catching investors' attention.

Fig 1. Real House Price Change (1996–2006)
(* 2001–2006)

Country	Percentage change 1997–2005
Estonia	306
Ireland	180
UK	167
Spain	115
Sweden	110
South Africa*	103
Norway	102
France	101
Denmark	97
Australia	96
Finland	74
New Zealand	72
Greece	69
Netherlands	69
US	61
Italy	54
Canada	22
Thailand	10
South Korea	4
Switzerland	3
Malaysia	-2
Germany	-10
Taiwan	-12
Austria	-13
Hong Kong	-27
Singapore	-30
Japan	-32
Indonesia	-44
Philippines	-53

How Property Has Outperformed Shares

The debate between investing in stock and property is one which has been ongoing for a substantial amount of time. Property investment greatly increased in popularity between 2000 and 2003, corresponding with a 40% fall in the value of shares. This fall in the stock market dented investor confidence and raised concerns over the reliability of pension funds. In a world of fiscal uncertainty, the tangibility of property becomes extremely attractive.

'Whereas stock markets are vulnerable to the whims of the investor and the slightest dip in confidence, property values are much harder to shake'

Property is perceived as a reliable investment, and will often be used by serious investors as a low risk venture suitable for balancing the distribution of risk in a portfolio of investments. Whereas stocks and shares are vulnerable to the whims of the investor, the world financial system and to the slightest dip in confidence, property values are much harder to shake. It is easier to borrow money to finance a property purchase than it is to borrow to play the stock market. And for most people, following the daily or even hourly fluctuations of the stock market is a practical impossibility, too complex, too hard, and too reliant on having prior information. In contrast, as well as being an investment, property is something that most people encounter as part of their daily lives. For most people, property is familiar and easier to understand than other, less tangible, investments. The fact that a property investment is an investment in something real also gives added security. Generally, a house stays where you have left it. In the worst case the value of a house may decline, but leaving aside the possibility of earthquake or fire, it is unlikely to vanish overnight like fairy-gold or an investment in Enron.

International Support for the Right to Buy Overseas Property

As we saw above, the level of property prices in developed markets has led investors to examine international markets at an earlier stage in their growth cycle. However, there has also been another driver behind the growth of international property investment and that is the increasing level of international support for investors to be able to safely buy in different countries. Today, countries recognise the value of outside investment. Over the last decade, barriers have been lowered and the right to buy extended to foreign nationals by many countries. As an example of the general trend towards greater freedom, the Turkish government redrafted legislation in July 2003 to allow foreigners to buy in Turkish villages as well as towns and the tourist areas of the coastal strip.

With the WTO (World Trade Organisation) upholding investment rights there is more security for money being sent abroad. The WTO also plays an important role in ensuring international commitment to enforcing property ownership, and systems of law and government which uphold reciprocal rights.

Governments benefit from the international property industry and have an incentive to provide as much protection to buyers as possible. Taxes and fees provide money for governments to spend on infrastructure and development but the property market also brings work; employment for solicitors and translators and of course construction workers. Foreign buyers can also help to preserve older housing stock. In Morocco crumbling riads have been lovingly restored by foreigners with the time and inclination to bring these lovely courtyard houses back to life and in the Far East, many of the few remaining colonial villas have been restored by foreign buyers.

'Ten years ago, buying outside of France or Spain without detailed personal knowledge of the country meant leaping in to the dark. This is no longer the case'

The opening up of the former Eastern Bloc countries and certain areas of the Far East has presented a whole new range of opportunities. The economies of these countries are only just beginning to experience the full benefits of the open market and many are set to experience very high levels of economic growth. Property prices in such countries have historically been held at artificially low levels and are likely to rise dramatically as the wealth of the local population increases. Many of these countries are very receptive to foreign investment as a means of providing the funds required for rapid development.

All of these advantages ensure that governments have an incentive to treat international buyers and developers well, working together to ensure that cross-border investment is both safe and straightforward.

Example – The Valencia Land Grab

A good example of the international commitment to reciprocal property rights has been provided by the co-ordinated response of governments and international organisations to recent property seizures in Valencia, Spain.

Badly drafted legislation in the Valencia region enabled developers to take land away from homeowners, under the cover of development. The 1994 *Ley Reguladora de la Actividad Urbanistica* states that all land can be converted for property development unless it is protected on historical, cultural or ecological grounds. Under the LRAU developers can request that land should be reclassified from rural to urban land without asking for the owner's permission.

They can then compulsorily purchase the land, paying compensation which can be far below market value and even forcing the property owner to pay for infrastructure improvements such as water installation or road building.

The Valencia land grab laws have been one of the most embarrassing problems in international property over the last two decades, but the case has also shown the amount of support available for property owners. After 15,000 complaints to the European Parliament the EU is (at the time of writing) in the process of taking the Spanish government to the European Court of Justice. Ensuing negotiations between MEPs (Members of the European Parliament) and Spanish politicians are expected to result in new European legislation to protect property owners and there are hopes that a mechanism for compensation may be established.

The Valencia case has shown that governments are prepared to campaign internationally for the rights of buyers. The quality of information now available internationally was another key element helping to create co-ordinated opposition. The higher standard of information, not least the way that journalists now regularly cover stories about issues affecting buyers overseas, is one of the changes that have made people feel safer.

Ten years ago, buying outside of France or Spain without detailed personal knowledge of the country meant leaping into the dark. This is no longer the case. There are still countries where buying can be a challenge – property title in the Turkish Republic of Northern Cyprus, is for example, distinctly dubious, and although there have been some heavily publicised cases and many debates, at the time of writing there is still no definitive answer as to whether buying property in certain areas of Northern Cyprus is 100% secure.

The problems in Valencia and Northern Cyprus have been all the more unusual because modern economists and governments recognise the value of encouraging foreigners to buy houses. Foreign investment is good for a country, bringing in money and rejuvenating economies. This money disappears the moment people begin to feel that their investment may not be safe.

As word spread about the unjust laws in Valencia property sales noticeably declined and prices plummeted for land considered to be at risk. According to the European foreign residents association, *Ciudadanos Europeos,* 1.5 million properties have been bought by families from outside Spain over the last 40 years. Towards the end of 2006 Bloomberg reported that foreigners had reduced their investments in Spain to around 400 million euros per month – a great deal of money to risk losing in this way.

International Property Investment: Coming of Age

As property prices have rocketed across the western world, investors have begun to look elsewhere for potential gains. This has led to a coming of age for international property investment. Buying property abroad is not new, as we see below, but never before has buying property in another country been so accessible or driven by people whose primary motivation is pure investment.

This new breed of international property buyer is both the child of the 'great international property boom' and of a tradition which stretches back much further into the past.

Buying Property Abroad: Early Beginnings

The appeal of a second home in the sun is by no means a notion restricted to modern tastes; even the Romans had their villas at Baie! The origins of the international property market as we know it lie in the expansion of tourism in the nineteenth century. English travellers who had developed a taste for the southern sun began to buy property in Europe, either wintering abroad or swapping Brighton for Cap Ferrat on a permanent basis.

The moneyed beneficiaries of the industrial revolution quickly developed a preference for the promenades of Europe over the dark, dank mills of home. This influence is still reflected in place and hotel names across Europe. The hotel names Carlton, Majestic and Bristol reflect the importance of British customers to their proprietors. To top this off, the Brits invented winter sports tourism by flocking to the Swiss resort of Zermatt. By 1901 half a million travellers crossed the English Channel every year.

The next key development was the extension of affordable air travel. In the 1960s air travel was combined with the affordable package tour and a world of tourism was born. The World Travel and Tourism Council estimated at the beginning of 2007 that tourism and related industries would contribute 10.4% of world GDP and be responsible for 231 million jobs worldwide during the course of the year. With the development of affordable international travel people could divide their time between a working life at home and relaxation abroad. The second home market in France and Spain opened up in the 1960s, a decade that also saw the launch of the first international property magazines in the UK. From the beginning of the 1970s pioneers began to explore Italy and then, in the late 1980s and 1990s Portugal, Greece and Florida joined the market, and buying overseas property became a desirable end in itself. The markets in Spain, Italy and France exploded and a secondary interest in winter sports destinations developed.

The Opening Up of Eastern Europe

In the 1990s the fall of communism opened up vast new markets in the east of Europe and contrary to the picture held by many people of grey crumbling walls and Soviet era tower blocks, the majestic beauty of the mountains and lakes of Eastern Europe has proven very popular.

An important part of this success has been prices which, to Western eyes, look ridiculously low. Houses in Bulgaria or Romania can sell for a few thousand euros. The prices available in Eastern Europe have helped to democratise the international property market; buying a home overseas is no longer the preserve of the wealthy. In 2004 42% of Britons buying overseas property reported incomes of £40,000 or less.

The lower costs in Eastern Europe have been a pleasant surprise for many buyers, who still raise finance off the back of their homes. The average amount of money that people expect to spend on a second home is close to £160,000 – an amount which would fall nearly £20,000 short of a one-bedroom flat in Barcelona, but would buy a newly built three bedroom house with two bathrooms, a private swimming pool and a sea view in even the most popular corner of Turkey. In August 2005 the national median price for property sold to overseas buyers in Spain was €250,000, while in Bulgaria the average price was close to €30,000, leaving more money for buying elsewhere and increasing your portfolio.

Finally, with buyers realising the sheer range of possibilities and prices available, the number of viable markets has exploded. Britons spent £20 billion on overseas property in 2006, and countries which are now fair game for investors include Malaysia, Brazil, Morocco, Grenada, Argentina, Poland, India, Mongolia and many others.

Emerging Markets

Over the last three years, interest in emerging markets has blossomed. The traditional markets of France and Spain still attract 50.5% of potential buyers. However other markets are growing fast.

People are travelling further and becoming familiar with new parts of the world. The primacy of France, Spain and Italy is being rapidly overtaken by new destinations. Italian machismo took a knock in 2004 as China ousted the country from fourth place in the list of most popular destinations, and Turkey entered the top ten destinations a year later. The World Tourism Organisation forecasts that by 2020 Europe will still be the world's first choice for tourism, but that the region's share of the market will have dropped dramatically. Rather than catching the ferry to France or taking a flight to the Florida Keys, tourists will be more likely to hop on a long-haul flight to Hainan or Brazil. Long-haul holidays are one of the fastest growing segments of the tourist industry, taking a share of the market which will have increased from 18% in 1995 to 24% by 2020.

This roaming spirit contributes to the emergence of property markets further overseas. As people see more of the world and destinations once seen as exotic become familiar and therefore feel safe, the traditional markets can look rather tame. You do not have to travel half way round the world to find exciting new property investment destinations. For example the coasts of Morocco and Spain are so close that a 39km tunnel is being planned to link the two countries, yet a two bedroom apartment which would cost £135,000 on the south coast of Spain costs from £30,000 in Morocco.

'The prices available in Eastern Europe have helped to democratise the international property market; buying a home overseas is no longer the preserve of the wealthy'

The threshold to get into emerging markets is much lower, extending appeal beyond the typical 40-something investor or holiday home buyer to younger people and even first time buyers hoping to get onto the property ladder but priced out of the market in their home country.

A good example of a market where investors have recently become active and successful is **Shanghai.** Shanghai is at the forefront of the international economy handling most of the wealth which is pouring into China. The next five to ten years are shaping up to be memorable for Shanghai. The Shanghai World Financial Centre will be able to claim a place as the world's tallest building (until the Burj in Dubai is completed) and the city will host events for the 2008 Beijing Olympics. This blistering growth in reputation and financial success has been translated into the property market, with an average property price growth of 25% in 2003 and 20.4% in 2005. Concerned that these growth rates would cause a bubble, in 2006 the Chinese government introduced measures to slow the residential real estate market down, reducing the rate of growth substantially. At the time of writing, it is still not possible for foreigners to invest in property in China. However, we see this as a short term measure, and predict that growth be strong for foreseeable future. According to the 'Emerging Trends in Real Estate Asia Pacific 2007' report from the Urban Land Institute and PriceWaterhouseCoopers, Shanghai is one of the most exciting cities in the entire region for both property investment and development.

With property in Eastern Europe, Latin America and beyond available for the price of a new car in the West, it can be easy to get carried away. Ultimately, rather than a ramshackle farmhouse which costs €5,000 but is 200 miles from the nearest town, research suggests that the properties which do best are attractive developments in areas with strong fundamentals of demand i.e. city centres or emerging tourist resorts where people are likely to travel. With a little thought, it is possible to find a property which will provide a solid rental return while appreciating in value by up to 20% per year. And this is what investors should look for. Low prices alone do not indicate that prices are on the way up.

Overview of the World Property Markets

The areas where people buy are changing. This is partly due to the emerging pre-eminence of the profit motive amongst buyers and partly because even holiday homers are trying to get more for their money. This can be seen as both a positive and a negative development. From one perspective there is more choice and therefore more opportunity. From another, greater choice creates greater confusion.

Whatever viewpoint you hold, the reality remains that developed western markets are not necessarily the best place to invest in property. For example, property in much of Western Europe is very expensive and offers low rates of return, especially once rental yields are swallowed up in management costs and taxation. Overbuilding in favourite areas helps supply to outweigh demand, creating competition for rental business and putting deflationary pressure on property prices. The dangers of over-building are particularly apparent in Spain, which holds the crown for using more concrete than any other country in the EU – laying down more than 50 million tonnes every year. In 2006 close to 150,000 holiday homes were built along the coast, and up to one-third of Spain's Mediterranean coast is now under concrete.

Overdevelopment on this scale has a big impact on the market. Around 65,000 Britons buy property abroad every year. In 2003, 55% of these buyers headed straight for Spain, attracted by the near perfect climate of the Mediterranean coast, but by 2006 the number had declined to 31.6%, with most of the missing 23.4% attracted to the better investment opportunities available in Eastern Europe and Asia.

Eastern Europe

The main factor pulling buyers towards Eastern Europe is initial cost. Low prices make investment in property more widely accessible. But it isn't all about low prices. Many parts of Eastern Europe have delivered excellent returns for the investors that arrived on the scene early. Some parts of Bulgaria saw price rises of almost 50% in one year whilst capital cities across the region have also proven to be good choices. The opportunities in Eastern Europe are tied to two key factors; first of which is domestic economic growth. Burgeoning local economies are increasing the wealth of local residents, thus creating greater demand for housing. Additionally this economic growth has the benefit of attracting foreign companies and their workers which contribute positively to the local economy and create further demand for property. This factor will be most obviously felt in major commercial centres and capital cities.

The second factor is increasing tourism. The natural heritage of many Eastern European nations is set to make them extremely popular with tourists. Investing in areas where tourism is likely to grow can be a good choice as more tourists mean more tenants and more development means increasing property values. A word of caution though; timing is even more important when buying in tourist resorts. Rampant speculation and over development can lead to the creation of a property market bubble. It is important therefore that you consider the sustainability of the resort which is primarily dependent upon the existence of underlying factors that make it an attractive destination to holiday. To put this into a practical example, we wouldn't personally invest in a resort such as Sunny Beach in Bulgaria. The Bulgarian coast simply doesn't have an attractive enough climate to compete with resorts in the Mediterranean. This doesn't mean that investors haven't made profits in Sunny Beach; they have, but that statement is in the past tense.

Despite this, Eastern Europe does present interesting opportunities within tourism locations. The states of Eastern Europe have some extremely important historical and cultural attractions as well as good skiing, all of which attract tourists. Our tip is therefore to buy in cities that will attract short-break visitors such as **Budapest** and **Krakow** or in **ski resorts** with reliable snowfall.

Asia and the Pacific

Beyond Eastern Europe lie other areas which have shown impressive growth in recent years. Investment buyers have been attracted to the high profits in expanding economic centres such as **China** and **Dubai**. There has also been considerable growth in investment purchasers in key tourist and second home destinations such as **Malaysia**. Many of these countries are actively pursuing foreign property buyers as they realise the obvious economic benefits of converting tourists into buyers.

Investing in paradise is not always as cheap as people expect. Prices in Thailand for example reflect just how desirable a location this has become. Even the most modest of one bedroom apartments in **Phuket** will cost £60,000 ($120,000).

Whilst we all recognise Asia's exotic appeal, it is its economic performance which should be of most interest to investors. **China** is one of the most exciting economies and its rapid level of development and internationalisation make it very interesting from a property investment perspective. At the time of writing, the Chinese government has imposed temporary measures to restrict foreigners from buying property in China. We see this as a positive effect to cool the market and once restrictions are lifted see China as a good prospect for long term growth. With a little searching, apartments can still be found in Shanghai from £40,000, and often come with rental guarantee schemes which provide some security against the risk involved in investing in such new markets.

'The choice of where to buy depends on the degree of risk that you are willing to accept and your rationale for buying'

Outside of China, the Asian economic growth story extends to many nations in the region and brings with it excellent investment opportunities. Two examples of markets to watch are the Malaysian capital of **Kuala Lumpur** and Thailand's second city **Chiang Mai**. Both these cities demonstrate strong underlying growth drivers which should see property prices rising significantly in the near future.

A more unusual Asian market which is currently creating a buzz in the property investment world is Mongolia. The country is attracting a great deal of mining interest (**Mongolia** has the largest copper deposits in Asia), and large numbers of expatriate workers are moving into the capital, Ulaanbataar. Accommodation in the region is generally poor with a large percentage of the population still living in traditional yerts. As a result there is a severe shortage of executive standard accommodation and the few high quality developments which are under construction sell out extremely quickly. Investors who enter the market early should see substantial profit.

Australia and **New Zealand** are still two of the most popular with younger buyers yearning to emigrate, although Australia is now considered to be one of the only countries in the world further through the housing cycle than the UK. Average house prices doubled between 1996 and 2004 but then began to fall. According to *The Global Property Guide*, prices in Sydney fell by 4.8% between June 2004 and December 2005, with *The Australian* citing Melbourne prices as falling 11% in 2004. However according to the Knight Frank Global House Price Index the situation improved between the end of 2005 and the final quarter of 2006 with prices rising again by 8.3%. Australian house prices in many cities are still considered to be overvalued, meaning that the price correction may not be over yet.

Africa

In Africa, overseas buyers have tended to concentrate on only a few specific markets. **South Africa** is one of the strongest second home markets in the world. At the other end of the continent **Cape Verde** and **Morocco** are creating a new challenge.

South Africa has seen some of the fastest increasing property prices in the world. According to the global house price indices tracked by *The Economist*, house prices in South Africa grew by 351% between 1997 and 2006, a rate of growth second only to Ireland.

Northern Africa, Morocco and the Cape Verde Islands are becoming popular with buyers keen to find an emerging tourist hotspot within reasonable travelling distance of Northern Europe. The historic cities of Morocco began to capture the attention of trend-setters after World War II and the designer Yves St Laurent credited Morocco with introducing him to colour. Winston Churchill was a famous fan describing himself as 'captivated by Marrakech'.

The Cape Verde Islands are a newer market; this group of nine islands lies off Africa's west coast, following the curve of the continent beyond the Canary Islands. A host of articles and travel programmes in early 2005 testified that Cape Verde was gaining a reputation as one of the hot new markets. The islands were first colonised by Portugal in the fifteenth century and now have one of the most stable governments in Africa. The Cape Verde islands have become a haven for ex-patriots, to the point that foreigners may now outnumber native Cape Verdeans. The strange, wild beauty of the islands combined with property prices from £27,000 ($54,000) means that the Cape Verde Islands were one of the most talked about new destinations in 2006.

South America

South America is home to some examples of "true emerging markets" in the economic sense of the term. Many of the countries carry the characteristics of newly emerging economies and this means that problems with stability remain across the continent. However, this doesn't mean that opportunities do not exist. There are places in South America though where only the hardest nosed investor would consider buying. One example that springs to mind is **Colombia**. The property market in Colombia has grown rapidly over recent years, but as the country is commonly referred to as one of the most dangerous places on earth it may be a place where profit comes at too high a price.

More stable options exist in **Brazil** and **Argentina** as well as in Central American states such as **Mexico**, **Belize**, **Honduras** and **Panama.** In areas such as the north coast of Brazil, developers are taking advantage of the verdant rainforest, stunning beaches and sense of space to work on luxury developments. In the first quarter of 2007 alone, tourism to Brazil increased by 9.6%. With a cost of living around one fifth of that of the UK or US, property analysts suggest that Brazil may have a bright future.

There is also much excitement about parts of the Caribbean where prices have been rising by as much as 20% per annum. **The Dominican Republic** has a reputation for some of the most affordable property in the Caribbean. Land ownership restrictions have been removed, residency is easy to obtain and there is no property tax, making the island a healthy bet (although the rental potential and prohibitively high income taxes for non-nationals outside certain tourist areas make it best as a second home or retirement option rather than a buy-to-let destination). Another option is **Grenada**, which is yet to experience the levels of development seen on other Caribbean islands and therefore has lower prices and greater potential for growth.

Conclusion

The inescapable conclusion is that investors are looking further afield for their profits. And whilst the markets above are some of the more popular options, there are very few limits on investing anywhere overseas. Overseas property agents now receive daily enquiries about buying in **Ghana**, the **Ukraine** and **Vietnam**.

The choice of where to buy depends on the degree of risk that you are willing to accept and your rationale for buying. If you are interested in a specific country, maybe one of those mentioned above, the country information in the second part of this book should help to get you started. Alternatively, for buyers more concerned with the amount of profit to be made than the country in which they make it, the chapters below should help you to work out which opportunities to consider.

2 Where To Buy Abroad: Analysing Markets

How Property Markets Work

Before we can understand which property markets offer the best opportunities, we must have an understanding of how property markets work. Don't worry, we are not about to launch into an extended monologue on economic theory. We don't need to. The reality is that understanding property markets is less about technical knowledge than about understanding the behaviour of people; you certainly don't need a PhD in economics.

THE VALUE OF PROPERTY: SUPPLY AND DEMAND

Just like the price of any asset or commodity, the value of property is based upon the concept of scarcity. Simply put, the supply of any resource is finite (there will be a limited amount of land and therefore properties within a city). Thus the more market demand there is for it, the more its price will rise. This is the principle of supply and demand; the two concepts that make market economies work. Supply and demand determine the availability of every commodity or asset (including properties) and the price at which it is sold. This principle is fundamental to the analysis of property markets; if you want to know how any event will affect the property market you must consider the implications of that event on the supply of property and the demand for property.

Essentially, when supply and demand are balanced, prices are stable. When supply exceeds demand prices fall. And when demand exceeds supply, prices rise.

Without becoming too concerned with the theory, the levels of supply and demand are dependent upon the behaviour of market participants – people; how will a particular event make people feel and act? It is judging the behaviour of people and their response to certain events and actions that stops economics from being a pure science. The genius of people such as Warren Buffet and George Soros is not their in-depth understanding of finance and economics, but more their ability to predict how people will react to certain events. After all, it is people that make up markets and the actions of people that determine whether prices rise or fall.

The market reaction to some events is easy to predict. For example, when interest rates rise, so does the cost of mortgage repayments and therefore the cost of property ownership. In a real estate market where many of the participants rely on mortgage financing to purchase a property, this will reduce demand for property and therefore have a deflationary impact on prices. It is important to remember though that the effect will be relative. In this example, higher interest rates may reduce demand, but demand may still exceed supply (albeit by less than it did before). In this scenario prices will continue to rise but at a lesser rate.

Other events may have a less obvious effect on a market because the reaction of people is harder to predict. For example, a change of government could either increase or decrease demand for property. The reaction to the event depends on people's opinions of whether the new government will make property ownership more or less desirable as a result of their policies on tax for example. A further complexity is that some market participants will base their decision not on whether they think the change in government will have a positive or negative effect on the market, but on their opinion of what other market participants will feel about the change. Some people may personally believe that the new government will be positive for the housing market but may not buy because they believe the other market participants will have a contrary belief. In situations where the consequences of an event are not clear, you often see a slowdown in market activity as people wait to see the response of other market participants.

What then allows us to assess property markets and make predictions is our understanding of the factors at work within the market; otherwise known as market forces. Whilst supply and demand are market forces in themselves it is the market forces that affect supply and demand that need to be understood if you are to successfully assess a property market. The problem is that no market is 'perfect.' Perfect markets are essentially fictional economic models used to explain the principles of how markets work. No market in the real world is perfectly predictable as people will make irrational as well as rational decisions.

'Irrational behaviour' is what makes markets difficult to predict. In addition, property markets have their own peculiarities that need to be born in mind. Firstly, people don't buy property purely on financial motivations. Whether or not a property market is falling or rising, people need somewhere to live. Shelter is a basic human requirement. Additionally, people often choose a house because they like it rather than because it has good investment potential. A key influence on people's buying decisions is taste and as the saying goes, there is no accounting for it. Personal perceptions of where is a desirable place to live mean that markets can be so subjective that prices which are acceptable in one town are regarded as outrageous in the next. That doesn't make property markets unpredictable; it simply means that we need to be aware of the factors that make one location a more desirable place to live than another. The question then is; what do people find attractive when choosing somewhere to live?

Secondly, property is not a liquid asset. Property doesn't lend itself to the easy tradability of assets such as stocks and shares. Properties take longer to sell and have high transaction costs (costs of buying and selling). This means that people hold on to real estate even when prices are falling. It also means that property markets react slowly to market forces and events. From an investor's point of view, this is one of the most attractive characteristics of property investment; markets are relatively slow moving and stable. A property price crash is a very different beast to a stock market crash. Global stock markets have been known to lose 15% or more of their value in a single day. A property market crash that wipes 15% off property values is likely to take a matter of years to bottom out.

'No market in the real world is perfectly predictable as people will make irrational as well as rational decisions'

From an economist's perspective the biggest problem with property markets is that they are so localised. Property markets are more influenced by local factors affecting supply and demand than they are by broad economic trends. According to The Economist, 'Fluctuations in property prices can arise not only owing to cyclical movements in economic fundamentals, interest rates and the risk premium, but also as a result of the intrinsic characteristics of the property market itself.' This is perhaps the real key to understanding property markets; they move to their own rhythm. For all the importance of economic factors, the really significant factors are things like local supply. Research carried out for the International Monetary Fund suggests that 'almost three fifths of the overall variation in housing prices can be explained by innovations in the housing market itself. The combined effect of other explanations, such as GDP, interest rates, bank credit and equity prices, accounts for the rest.'

The largely independent nature of individual property markets therefore makes generalisations and broad projections dangerous. However, it also means that uniform increases and falls in value are unlikely. A statement such as 'over the last three years property prices in South Africa have risen dramatically' is invariably misleading. It is much more likely that certain towns or neighbourhoods in South Africa have seen dramatic increases in prices, whilst others have been stagnant or even dropped. The truth in the statement is that the average value of property across South Africa has risen dramatically, but this doesn't mean that any South African property would have been a good investment.

The fact that property markets are localised and relatively independent of one another doesn't mean that local property markets have not been subject to the impacts of globalisation. The fact that you are reading this book proves that they have.

For example, the real estate market in the Costa Del Sol will be closely related to the economic health of the UK and Ireland whose residents make up a major proportion of property owners (market participants) in the area.

If there were an event in the UK which reduced the ability or desire of UK based buyers to buy in the Costa Del Sol, this would reduce demand and have a deflationary impact on prices. This means that one of the most important steps in analysing a property market is to identify who the market participants are. Only once you have done this are you able to consider the market forces which may impact upon their behaviour.

The important point to take away is that to understand what is happening in a property market and, more importantly, to predict what will happen, requires an analysis of all of the factors affecting supply and demand at a local, national and international level. In other words, you need to consider both the microeconomic and macroeconomic influences on supply and demand.

Below we consider some of the most common microeconomic and macro-economic influences on supply and demand in a property market. The factors discussed here are not intended to be exhaustive, but merely illustrative. The intention is that these examples will help you to understand what other events may impact on supply and demand in a property market that you are assessing.

Some Potential Events Causing Price Movement in Property Markets

The below diagram lists just a few of the factors that could stimulate movement in a property market. When evaluating the result, or potential result, of any one or more of these events on a market we must proceed with caution. The impact of one event on another is never direct or simple in the real world. We can not say that EU membership directly causes property prices to rise. This would, at the very least, over simplify the situation. In the real world, events happen in chains of events linked to one another by causality. Also, there may be other, omitted variables that have an effect. Relationships between real life events are neither isolated nor linear; unidirectional nor normative.

	Will Influence Supply	Will Influence Demand
Macro	Law Changes (e.g. increasing the amount of land that can be built on)	Income growth (GDP)
		Cost of ownership – tax
	Taxation incentives for developers	Finance availability
	National or regional level infrastructure	Change in law
		Membership of trade organisations
Micro	Building restrictions	Local population growth and immigration
	Local business activity (perhaps factory closures may open brown field sites)	Local infrastructure developments
		Tourism
	Price of land	Local level of employment

We couldn't possibly hope to map and understand every variable at work within a property market, but we can use past experience and common sense to work through potential scenarios highlighting the most logical chain of events. Sticking with the EU example, why is it that people believe that membership leads to property boom? Much of this belief comes from past experience of other members joining the Union such as Ireland (see below), but there are many potential chains of events which logically link this cause and event; for example;

EU entry → More trade with other members → Increase in levels of employment and rates of pay → Increase in wealth of the local population → Increased demand for privately owned housing → Increases in house prices.

This example remains oversimplified and is just one of a vast range of possibilities. We could create an equally logical argument to suggest that EU membership will cause property prices to fall;

EU entry → Ability for local workers to migrate to other parts of the EU in search of higher paid jobs → Decreases in local population → Less demand for housing → Decreases in house prices.

In reality both of these series of events may occur at once. Certainly Poland is an example where the local population is falling due to emigration whilst at the same time Gross Domestic Product (the wealth of the country) is rising. What, therefore, will be the net impact on the property market?

This is neither a simple nor easy question to answer. The above example shows why the international property industry employs experts to analyse these situations. Whilst it might not be possible for ordinary investors to work through all these scenarios or stay abreast of all the events that may impact on property markets across the globe, it is important that you are aware how complicated markets can be and are able to be more questioning when someone suggests that a particular event will have a direct and certain impact on property prices.

Despite the conflicting possibilities above, we do believe that it is possible to make an educated assessment of what is happening in most markets. Whilst it might not be possible to evaluate every cause, effect or scenario we can rely on past experience and common sense to come to an opinion on what is likely to happen in the future.

Financial advisors always tell us that past performance is no indicator of future performance, but it is a good place to start. You will see in a later case study what EU membership did to property prices in Ireland and why, therefore, many people expect the same results in current and future entrants. EU entry provided Ireland with investment in infrastructure and increased its levels of trade. Both these effects will also be felt by more recent entrants. However, whilst the Irish experience suggests that Eastern Europe will experience significant growth, we can not simply map the Irish experience onto other countries.

Picking up one of the international property magazines it is easy to identify a number of factors used almost as a synonym for capital appreciation. First among these is European Union entry, followed by the hosting of international sporting or commercial events. For example, Beijing has been one of the most popular investment buys of the past couple of years and much of its popularity has been related to its selection as host of the 2008 Olympic Games.

The excitement about the ways in which single events can impact on property prices is sometimes justified. Ukraine's prospects before and after the Orange Revolution of 2004, for example, could not be more different. Yet it often pays to be slightly cynical about the impact of any single factor on the market. As a general rule, big name events like the Olympics justify a rise in property prices only if backed by other factors such as investment in infrastructure development.

The Benefits of European Union Accession

Anyone considering buying property in Eastern Europe will be well used to predictions that property values will grow at a rate of 5-10% every year until accession, followed by an immediate doubling of values on the day that integration is formalised. Working on the principle that any prediction taken so seriously and allotted such attention is always worth questioning, the section below examines the true benefits that lie behind EU accession, helping you to work out just how much of a difference it will make to property prices.

Accessions are planned a long time in advance – Turkey began preliminary membership negotiations in October 2005 but isn't expected to join the Union before 2015. Beyond this, Croatia, Bosnia and Herzegovina, Serbia, Montenegro, the former Yugoslav Republic of Macedonia, Albania and potentially even the Ukraine and Georgia may also join the EU. Beyond the geographical limits of Europe, Cape Verde is also interested in joining.

If some of the claims made by agents are correct then all of these countries should see prices rising, but the 'magic effect' of joining the EU may not appear. The idea that countries joining the European Union will see an automatic and impressive climb in prices owes a great deal to the Irish experience.

THE IRISH EXPERIENCE

When Ireland joined the EEC in 1973 GDP per head was 63% of the EU average. By 2001 this had climbed to 126%. This economic success has been matched by increasing real estate prices. Over the last eight years alone the value of property has climbed by 196%.

Unfortunately, Ireland may be the exception rather than the rule. More recent accession states have seen a slower pace of growth. Greece joined the EU in 1981, but in the years of Ireland's greatest triumph, had an economy which remained almost stagnant at around 69% of the Union average.

It looks very much as though the rules of enlargement are changing. Ireland succeeded so dramatically because it is a small country and, as one of the first and best value entrants, enlargement caused foreign investment to flood in.

Limits to the Impact of EU Accession

EU accession isn't quite the magic solution that some agents believe. The key to price rises in Eastern Europe is more often economic development than EU entry, though often the two go hand in hand. Some highly developed countries have opted to stay out of the Union – for example, Norway – but few property agents would argue that EU accession would have any impact on property prices there. Given that fact that they remain out of the EU Norwegian property has increased 102% over the last 10 years.

In the Baltics, wages have risen by 10% in a single year. Outside investors have been able to make profits by betting on this rise. The average price of property in Latvia rose 45.3% between the second quarter of 2005 and that of 2006 and Bulgaria was not far behind with growth of 20.5%.

'The key to price rises in Eastern Europe is more often economic development than EU entry, though often the two go hand in hand'

The most recent wave of accessions has been in the Mediterranean and Eastern Europe, in areas where prices were naturally going to rise anyway. Cyprus and Malta have benefited from the rising numbers of people retiring to the sun. The price rises in Bulgaria and Romania have arguably more to do with artificially low property prices after the end of communism than with the effects of accession.

What EU membership does do is make buyers feel more secure. In order to be invited into the Union, countries need to have stable economies, removing the risk of a currency crash or profit eroding inflation. The European Union also provides 'fundamental freedoms,' including free movement of people and money.

Citizens have the right to live and work anywhere in the EU and no limits will be placed on investment.

In some ways the benefits of EU accession are more symbolic. This is especially important where countries were part of the communist sphere but have now embraced market economies and are keen to turn towards Western Europe. European Union entry carries real prestige – shown by the long list of often slightly surprising countries who see accession as an eventual aim.

ACCESSIONS IN EASTERN EUROPE

If nothing else, the increasing numbers of entrants (10 in 2004) means that the 'magic effect' of joining the EU may not appear. Believing that ten countries can all see a simultaneous increase at the levels predicted by some commentators slightly stretches credibility.

Enlargement has now turned towards the larger populations and vast geographical area of Eastern Europe. With such a variety of new markets and so many areas in which to invest, there may not be enough of the old EU accession magic to go around.

The 2004 accessions increased the surface area of the EU by a quarter and the total population by a fifth. The accession of Bulgaria and Romania on 1 January 2007 further increased the total number of people living within the EU to 490 million, and another generation including Croatia and Turkey waits in the wings.

Economic Benefits of Membership

With the Union growing at such a rate, the pace of economic growth linked only to accession will be limited. This doesn't mean that EU accession states don't have a bright future, only that expecting EU entry to act as a universal panacea is unduly optimistic.

Having set out the reservations and the provisos, the limits and the reasons for a degree of pessimism, it is only fair to balance the picture by noting that EU entry is very good for any fledgling economic power. Far from being conferred from the outside by EU entry, this is the result of hard work within the country.

The complex economic criteria required for accession are designed to establish a 'stable market economy.' This sounds straightforward enough, but in reality means bringing fledgling economies up to the standard where they can compete on equal terms with the original EU 15. Finally there is the long process of adopting the whole body of EU law, known as the *acquis communautaire*. Candidate countries are required to step into line with the EU; and this can mean anything from eliminating corruption in Romania to altering water standards across vast swathes of Eastern Europe.

In return for this considerable effort, large amounts of money are transferred to the candidate countries. Since 2000 Romania, for example, has received substantial financial assistance from the EU, with pre-accession funds exceeding

€1 billion and allocated post-accession funds amounting to €19,688 billion between 2007 and 2013. The money can be used for infrastructure improvements or for projects such as developing education, improving employment opportunities and promoting tourism. These factors all have an indirect impact on property prices.

The advantages of entry also include higher rates of foreign investment. Outside investors feel more confident about the security of their funds and the standard of treatment that they will receive at the hands of local government. More importantly, accession states get to join the free-market, greatly improving potential for economic performance. The conditions for investment are also improved. As economies fall into line and financial markets are opened, interest rates fall sharply. Low interest rates encourage people into the housing market and are one of the best preconditions for rising prices.

THE IMPORTANCE OF TIMING

If you do want to buy hoping to take advantage of price rises around accession, timing is important. Property prices go up when buyers feel at their most confident. This is not necessarily at the actual moment of accession, but is generally months or even years before. Buyers who wait until the date is set may miss the boost effect.

The Czech Republic joined the European Union in 2004. In 2003 prices rose by 20%-25% in expectation of joining, just prior to entry prices faltered, with people feeling that they had been over optimistic. Then, after entry, prices began a slower but more sustained rise based on greater internal wealth.

As a local businessman interviewed in the Prague Post said 'There is no immediate impact on the real estate market, because all participants have already projected it in their expectations a long time ago'.

Impact of Future Accessions on Property Prices

The next country to join will probably be Croatia. At the time of writing, Croatia's candidacy has been resumed after the EU accepted that the Croatian government was making genuine efforts to co-operate with the UN War Crimes Tribunal at The Hague. The country looks set to be granted membership in 2009 or 2010, providing that the criteria for membership are met and that the treaty of accession is ratified by the parliaments of the other member states.

From October 2005 membership talks have also been opened with Turkey, an official candidate from 1987 – seven years before applications were received from Poland and Hungary. Turkey has been making progress on human rights and other requirements, but membership is unlikely to occur before 2015 at the earliest.

Turkey's candidacy has caused concern in some of the EU countries because of the size of the population as well as a number of other factors (some of which have been seen more as xenophobia than legitimate objection). Opening talks in 2005 signalled that these concerns have been overcome and that Turkey will eventually be welcomed into the Union. However, the conditions set on Turkey's candidacy are extremely stringent. For the first time, there is a criterion that the EU must have the capacity to absorb a new country. Turkey's membership, which has been seen by some as a step too far, is by no means assured yet.

Opinion polls taken at the time of the establishment of the European constitution showed a noticeable cooling regarding further accession. Turkey's official candidacy has been delayed too long for the EU to fob Turkey off, but we may now see a couple of years of consolidation before the EU begins to consider the next wave of accessions.

Having said this, there are definite signs that Montenegro is on the way to joining the Union since independence was gained from Serbia in 2006, although the country is currently experiencing ecological, judicial and crime-related problems that may hinder its bid. Other countries recognised as 'potential candidate countries' (the EU specialises in this kind of coy language) are Albania, the Federal Republic of Macedonia, Serbia and Bosnia and Herzegovina.

Of the recent and future member countries, Turkey's popularity as a second home destination means that accession is unlikely to make much of a difference to property values in the second home resorts along the Mediterranean coast. Of all the potential new member states the best opportunity of all is in Montenegro, a small coastal state next to Croatia on the Adriatic.

Before the war in the former Yugoslavia disrupted tourism in the region, Montenegro was a popular destination with the yachting crowd – a position it is rapidly regaining.

Timeline of European Accession

Year	Country
1952	Founding members included Belgium, France, West Germany, Italy, Luxembourg and the Netherlands
1973	Denmark, Ireland and the United Kingdom
1981	Greece
1986	Portugal, Spain
1990	East Germany reunites with West Germany and becomes part of the EU
1995	Austria, Finland and Sweden
2004	Cyprus, Czech Republic, Estonia, Hungary, Latvia, Lithuania, Malta, Poland, Slovakia, Slovenia
2007	Bulgaria, Romania
c.2008 – 10	(Potentially) Croatia, Montenegro
c.2012 – 15	(Potentially) Turkey, FYR Macedonia, Albania, Bosnia & Herzegovina, Serbia

The Impact of Low-Cost Airlines

There is a close relationship between cheap flights and second home ownership; so much so that the growth of the second homes market can hardly be imagined without the no-frills airlines. Research suggests that most owners of second homes visit their property six times a year.

As long as you are fairly relaxed about the area where you hope to buy, identifying a region set to attract cheap flights is a sure-fire way to find a property on the way up. The link between flights and homes is so close that airlines now often advertise property in their in-flight magazines.

The Open Skies Agreement in the European Union has done a great deal to promote cheap flights. Figures released by the UK Civil Aviation Authority show that the numbers of Britons visiting the Czech Republic rose by 59% in 2004, an additional 770,000 people. Visits to other new EU states, including Hungary, Poland, Slovakia and the Baltics, almost doubled. Tour operators also noted that bookings for 2005 showed an increase of 96% for Poland.

'The growth of the second homes market can hardly be imagined without the no-frills airlines'

According to an article published by Jenny Knight in *The Times* 'One day I'll fly away' (19th April 2005), since 2001 property prices in the French towns of Montpellier and La Rochelle had risen by 144% and 126% respectively. In the equally attractive Saint-Etienne, which was not served by a budget airline, prices had risen by only 44%. A landmark survey by Savills Research and Holiday-Rentals.co.uk in 2006 found that the average price of a property located within 10 miles of an airport served by a low-cost airline is 39% higher than for properties within the same distance from an airport without a low-cost carrier. Rents were also found to be up to 30% higher for properties within 10-20 miles of airports.

How to Find Out About New Routes

By importing such vast numbers of visitors, cheap flights can have a radical impact on house prices and rental potential. This makes new destinations one of the factors most closely monitored by house buyers. Working out where flight routes are going to open up is easy. Airlines announce future routes in the news sections of their websites and announcements are also often placed in the national press.

Risks of Buying to be Close to Destinations Served by Budget Airlines

Buying solely because of the introduction of another cheap flight destination is, however, a risky strategy. The value airlines can be ruthless about cancelling routes that are not proving sufficiently popular or if airport costs rise. This creates a danger that the airlines may pull out and anticipated appreciation vanish like the morning mist. Some analysts have also registered concern about flight costs rising if an area is over dependent on a single carrier.

Impact of hosting the Olympics and other International Events

Part of the arguments put forward for hosting the Olympics are the benefits that accrue to the host cities. These include employment and tourism growth as well as the vast amounts of money visitors spend whilst the games are on. The area will also benefit from what economists call the 'Multiplier effect,' with the money then being spent and re-spent in the city.

A survey by Halifax Building Society, which coincided with the announcement of London's successful Olympic bid, suggests that there is a correlation between hosting the games and house prices rising. The survey found that in the five years prior to the 1992 games, Barcelona saw a 131% increase in prices compared with an average across Spain of 83%. Athens, the host in 2004, saw a 66% increase in prices over the four years and nine months before the games, compared with a 47% price increase across Greece. Halifax's research suggests the average increase among host cities has been 66%.

The table below shows how house prices changed in Olympic cities in the five years prior to holding the Olympic Games

Games	5 year increase in host city	5 year increase in host nation
1992 Barcelona	131%	83%
1996 Atlanta	19%	13%
2000 Sydney	50%	39%
2004 Athens*	63%	55%
Average	66%	47%

* Data is for 4.75 years not 5 years.

Other benefits of the Olympics are harder to measure. Research by Price Waterhouse Coopers suggests that the 'extensive media exposure during the Games may enhance the reputation of the city as an attractive business centre, further attracting new investment and trade from global companies'. This investment may also be supported by the fact that local people may be encouraged to learn valuable new business skills, for example being given training in languages and customer service.

Hosting the Games can also galvanise governments into proceeding with long meditated infrastructure improvements. This is expected to be the primary benefit of the 2012 Games for London. Already an internationally famous tourism destination, the chief advantage of the games will be in the improved transport links and lasting developments to be constructed in east London.

The building projects and infrastructure developments linked to international events are the real reason that prices rise. Barcelona, Athens and Sydney all saw significant work on the urban environment. In Barcelona 78km of new roads were created, the city also saw a 78% increase in green zones and beaches and a 268% increase in the number of ponds and fountains. In Beijing, a dozen Olympic sports centres, a new cross-city underground railway, a host of office towers, a massive airport terminal and a colossal French-designed theatre are all due to be completed before next year's 2008 Olympics. A report by The Economist in March 2007 stated that Chinese officials estimate that the Olympics have been contributing more than 2% to Beijing's annual growth since 2003.

Olympic Opportunities

All of the analysis on the Olympics suggests that countries benefit most if they don't have a high profile before holding the Games. The evidence suggests that cities which already have an international reputation may benefit less from the Olympics than the less well known. The next cities to hold the games will be Beijing in 2008 and London in 2012, with winter games in Vancouver 2010. Apart from Beijing, the Olympic Committees seem to have chosen a selection of cities where the opportunities for property investors will be limited.

The difference between the impact on Olympic cities and across the host country suggests that it is also important to be specific. To take advantage of the Olympic factor you need to buy as close to the events as possible, right down to looking for something next to the Olympic villages. Prices in Beijing are rising fastest between the third and fourth Ring Roads – where the Olympic stadium is being built.

Other Sporting Events

Buying ahead of the Olympics works because the sheer size and prestige of the Games guarantees heavy investment. But they may be more the exception than the rule. Sporting events generally have a short shelf life. And there may just be too many sporting events around. The number of World Cups, championships, games and contests means that an event will have to be fairly special to justify the build up.

However, smaller scale events can have some benefit in the right circum-stances. For example, prior to the 1995 Rugby World Cup, Johannesburg

International Airport was severely under funded, after the event it was world class. The Rugby World Cup may only have lasted for a couple of months but it made a lasting contribution to the city.

Perception or Reality? Knowing When Growth is Sustainable

Within any property market, there are three general types of buyer; end users (people that want to live in their property all or some of the time), investors (people that want to let their property out for profit) and speculators (people that buy in the anticipation that prices will rise). Thinking about market participants in this way allows us to make better judgements as to whether the market we are analysing is experiencing growth based on economic fundamentals or whether it is a bubble.

The underlying concept is that sometimes price growth is based on fundamentals (supply is exceeded by genuine and sustainable demand) and sometimes growth is self-perpetuating, i.e. price growth attracts buyers, which makes prices rise further. In such a scenario speculators believe prices will grow and therefore buy property. If enough speculators buy property, demand increases and prices go up. Such a market is based entirely on fragile human confidence and when the speculators lose their confidence and stop buying or start selling prices plummet as there are no genuine end users in the market.

'Problems arise when rampant speculation takes over a market. Price rises become more dependent on speculative investment than they do on demand'

Speculation is essentially second guessing how other market participants will respond to certain stimuli and then gambling on it. Speculation is a valid investment strategy used by many different types of investors and is not harmful to a market *per se*. The problems arise when rampant speculation takes over a market and price rises become more dependent on speculative investment than they do on fundamentally driven demand. An excellent example of speculation leading to a bubble followed by a crash is the Asian Economic Crisis of 1997. This particular economic phenomenon was only partly related to real estate investment but it did play a part. Once speculators lost faith in the markets of South East Asia they pulled their money out. As a result stock markets in the region crashed, currencies plummeted in value and the real estate markets went into free fall.

What does this mean for international property investors? It means that when deciding whether or not to invest in a market, you must decipher whether any price rise or fall is the result of underlying fundamentals or whether it is down to the second guessing of speculators.

Sunny Beach in Bulgaria

It is our opinion that an excellent example of a speculative market is Sunny Beach in Bulgaria. Due to Bulgaria's accession into the EU and the Bulgarian government's attempt to bring tourism to its Black Sea Coast, investors made the decision that Sunny Beach would be a good place to invest. Those who got in early were right. Prices in the town have risen dramatically. However, at the time of writing holiday apartments in Sunny Beach and on the Black sea coast are being sold off-plan to investors at over €1,500 per square metre and in some cases over €2,000 per square metre. The question is; do the fundamentals support this price? Our opinion would be no, for the following reasons.

As a tourist destination, Sunny Beach could have two kinds of end-users for the types of apartments and villas that are being built there; holiday home owners and holiday let landlords. With the massive development that is happening in the town and competing resorts along the Black Sea Coast, we would need to see a reasonable number of holiday home buyers and more importantly a massively expanding tourist base to create demand for holiday lets. If there isn't enough demand for the number of hotel rooms and holiday apartments owned by investors then yields (net annual rental income as a percentage of the total purchase price) will be below the level which is attractive to investors. If this is the case then investors will not want to buy.

Our view for Sunny Beach is that due to the local climate, it will not be able to compete with the resorts of the Mediterranean in attracting tourists. The summer season in Sunny Beach is only 4 months long and the climate is too cold to attract even low paying guests for the rest of the year. Because investors' apartments will be empty for much of the year, they would have to achieve extremely high rents during the summer season in order to achieve an attractive yield. However, as the supply of holiday accommodation is likely to exceed the demand for it, rents are likely to be low even in the summer months.

In our opinion the driver behind the spectacular growth in Sunny Beach property prices has been speculation. People are buying because prices are rising. It is likely that many buyers in Sunny Beach have purchased with the intention of letting their property and would therefore consider themselves investors rather than speculators. However, the reality is that the demand fundamentals may be not there and whether buyers are aware of it or not, their purchases have been speculative. This may ultimately lead to a significant correction as off-plan properties are completed and investors struggle to generate respectable rental incomes. As people realise that the price of property is not justified by the available rental income there will be a slowdown in demand. Equally, as those who have already purchased fail to see a return they may begin to sell leading to an increase in supply. Supply will outstrip demand. If this happens the correction could be significant, although prices are unlikely to drop below a point that bears a sensible correlation to the rental income (see the section below on price to earnings ratios).

Deciding Whether a Market is Overvalued or Undervalued

It goes without saying that the best property investment is in a property which is currently undervalued and set to increase in price. The difficult part is knowing whether a market is undervalued, overvalued or valued correctly. Knowing whether a market is valued correctly is a good starting point when considering where to invest. Undervalued markets will not always increase in value but normally will. Overvalued markets may not necessarily fall. Just because a formula says that a market is overvalued it doesn't mean that people will stop buying. However, an overvalued market does not make a good investment.

There are formulas which help us to identify anomalies, compare markets and to make a decision on whether a market is ripe for investment or may be about to crash. Two key tools discussed below are the price to earnings ratio and the affordability ratio. It is also important to look at vacancy rates and the ownership ratio. We have focused on these because they are measures which allow us to connect a property's price with its underlying value as an asset and its underlying affordability as a home.

The Price to Earnings Ratio

The price to earnings ratio (the P/E) is a measure used by investors when considering many forms of investment. A quick flick through the stock market indices will show a column giving the P/E for each stock. The P/E can also be used as a tool to evaluate and compare house prices.

In the case of a property, its net earnings is the amount of revenue received through letting minus costs (maintenance, property management, mortgage financing etc). The P/E is the purchase price of the property divided by the net earnings.

$$\text{House P/E} = \frac{\text{Property price}}{\text{Earnings after costs}}$$

The house P/E provides a direct comparison to P/E ratios used to analyse other uses of the money tied up in a property investment. This means that you can use this measure to compare two property investment opportunities or compare a property investment opportunity against an alternative use of the money.

The P/E is effectively the inverse of yield. Therefore what it is assessing is the value of the property based upon its income. In a property market where average net yields are 10%, the P/E would be 10; or in other words, the value of the asset (the property) is ten times its net annual profit (rent). When comparing markets, therefore, we want to see a low P/E ratio which means that rental yields are high. When the P/E ratio is high, say 25, yields would be unattractive for investors and we could say that the asset is overvalued compared to returns.

Rents, just like corporate and personal incomes, are generally tied very closely to supply and demand fundamentals; one rarely sees an unsustainable "rent bubble" (or "income bubble" for that matter). Therefore a rapid increase of house prices combined with a flat renting market can signal the onset of a bubble. This would be highlighted by an increase in the P/E ratio.

Occupancy Rate

The *occupancy rate* (opposite of *vacancy rate*) is the number of occupied units divided by the total number of units in a given region (in commercial real estate, it is usually expressed in terms of area such as square metres for different grades of buildings). A low occupancy rate means that the market is in a state of oversupply brought about by speculative construction and purchase. In this context, supply-and-demand numbers can be misleading: sales demand exceeds supply, but rent demand does not. This scenario would lead to falling yields compared to property prices (an increase in the P/E ratio) and may signify the beginnings of a bubble.

OWNERSHIP RATIO

The ownership ratio is the proportion of households who own their homes as opposed to renting. The ownership ratio gives a good indication of the relative levels of demand for renting and home ownership. Markets with low ownership ratios can offer low price property with high yields. Germany is currently a good example of this. The ownership ratio can partly depend on culture, but it also tends to rise steadily with incomes. Governments can sometimes play a role by enacting measures such as tax cuts or subsidized financing to encourage and facilitate home ownership. If a rise in ownership is not supported by a rise in incomes, it can mean either that buyers are taking advantage of low interest rates (which must eventually rise again as the economy heats up) or that home loans are awarded more liberally, to borrowers with poor credit.

The interesting point regarding ownership ratios is that they tell us where purchase demand may be set to rise. A country with a growing economy combined with a low ownership ratio would be a very good bet for price growth.

The Affordability Ratio

The affordability ratio is the ratio between property prices and household earnings. As an example, analysts believe that a healthy ratio is 1:4; in this case an average household income of £25,000 should mean that the average cost of a home should be £100,000. The cost of a house in the UK and US is now out of kilter with this equation – one of the reasons for fears that a property bubble may have formed. Even Alan Greenspan, the famously cautious former chairman of the Federal Reserve, has been moved to issue warnings about the 'frothy housing market' in the US. Prices in the US rose 15.8% over the year between September 2004 and September 2005. The affordability ratio has been used to identify areas at most severe risk. In Las Vegas, Los Angeles, Miami, New York, Seattle and others, the gap between average household incomes and price was wider at the beginning of 2006 than at the end of the 1980s, when the price of property was far above its genuine value.

If house prices become too out of line with household incomes then prices will probably stagnate if not fall. Market growth where there is already a ratio of 1:6 or 1:7 is unlikely to be sustainable. This now appears to be beginning in the US, as shown in The Economist's March 2007 house-price index. The latest price rises compared with the fourth quarter of 2005 went down from 13.2% to 5.9%, the lowest annual rate for seven years and a dramatic slowdown.

This tool is more useful when evaluating a market where the primary market players are local residents as the relationship between earnings and prices in a holiday home market will be very different.

Market Cycles: Does Boom Lead To Bust?

Researching property markets in general, you may come across a couple of forums dedicated to discussing the worldwide property crash which should be coming any day now. These forums tap into a slightly puritanical streak in some market analysts. The reasoning is that with property prices having risen so fast over the last ten years, something has to give. The global property market is soaring Icarus-like towards inevitable decline.

As with any asset class, over heated property markets do sometimes fall. However, government research suggests that there is little relationship between boom and bust. A report by the Federal Deposit Insurance Corporation, (*US Home Prices: Does Bust Always Follow Boom?* April 8, 2005) concluded that '*our answer must be no*'; in the cases looked at by the FDIC only 17% of boom markets turned into bust within five years.

The report found that rather than turning to bust, property markets tend to stagnate. Prices rarely fall, although they may decline against inflation: '*for 83% of our post-boom cities, nominal home prices rose by an average of 2% per year during the five years after the boom ended*'.

This is good news for worried property owners in the UK, US, Australia or Ireland and part of the reason that economists see property as a fundamentally safe way to invest money. It also accords with common sense. People always need houses, and without serious over-supply, there is a limit to how far property values can fall before people decide to tighten their belts and hang on for higher prices.

'It takes a lot for property prices to start falling, making property one of the safest investments imaginable'

While stock markets may swing wildly with investor confidence, the higher cost of buying and selling property means that in a falling market, most people will continue to pay their mortgages, and hold on for better days. One of the other advantages of property is that the markets are fundamentally local and therefore protected from contagion. It takes a lot for property prices to start falling, making property one of the safest investments imaginable.

When prices do fall, the slump in the market can usually be predicted. Prices may have become wildly unrealistic or external factors, such as high interest rates, will have had an impact. Soaring interest rates were the primary cause of rampant negative equity in early 1990s Britain. House prices in the South-east of England fell 27% and more than 1.7 million households suffered negative equity after interest rates climbed to 15%.

RAMPANT SPECULATION

The biggest predicator to a bust is rampant speculation. When property prices become so out of line with underlying fundamentals, like affordability, or their price bears no resemblance to their earnings potential, trouble may be imminent. Outside of the real estate world, we can look at the internet bubble of the late nineties and early noughties. In this case investors saw the internet as an entirely new business model that changed the parameters of the game. As a result, over excitement among investors caused them to invest in internet companies whose shares were very highly priced yet were earning no profits. The P/E ratio should have told people that the price of the shares was out of kilter with their underlying value. The internet did not change the rules of the game; even in the new e-world, businesses still have to make money.

Ultimately the bubble burst and share prices dropped to more realistic levels. A lot of people lost money and got burned but this doesn't mean that they have learned their lesson. It is a strange fact of human nature that people will buy into an investment once they have seen other people doing well. This is what happened with the internet boom. Everyday people watched the bull market rising and rising until they could resist it no more. They invested their nest egg just before the bubble burst and then watched the value of their investment plummet.

When a market's success is compounded by other people jumping on the band wagon due to that very same success, there should be warning bells. Regardless of whether you are investing in equities or properties, you should tread very carefully in a market where prices cannot be justified by underlying returns.

The answer to the question 'does boom lead to bust?' is a resounding 'not necessarily'. The fact is that property markets are generally very stable, but when there is rampant speculation a bust may well follow. Markets don't need speculation to boom. Ordinary homebuyers may enter into fierce competition for properties, but when the number of speculators outstrips the number of investors and home owners, there are fewer people to hold on for better days. Speculators have no ties to the market and are liable to cut their losses and move on elsewhere.

If you do get caught in a falling market and decide to hang on for happier times, research suggests that the waiting period will be limited to an average of just over four years before prices recover. If you do decide to sell, remember that falling markets often create a vicious cycle. People are reluctant to buy in case prices fall further, sellers have to drop prices again in order to tempt buyers in, but then buyers become even more reluctant. This means that if the market starts to fall and you are in a position to sell out, prompt action is essential. However, if you can afford to hold on through the hard times (which should be possible if the investment generates a positive cash flow), then this might be the most financially rewarding scenario in the long run.

Specific Considerations for Different Types of Markets

Considering a property investment is a very different process to deciding on where to buy a holiday home. Investment is a financial decision and must be made with the head, not the heart. Just because you love that beautiful old farmhouse in the heart of the French countryside, it doesn't mean that you will make any money out of it. The question of whether you want sun drenched beaches or an equally sun-drenched terrace overlooking a medieval old town, ceases to be relevant. The real question is: is it better to invest in a city, the countryside or a tourist resort?

City or Country

Research suggests that over the long term, the rental and resale potential of properties in cities outperforms that of properties in the countryside. The following table, taken from The Economist, shows the national average price rises for a selection of countries compared to price rises in major cities within those countries between 1980 and 2001.

Country	National average % increase	City	City average % increase	Percentage difference
Spain	124	Madrid	149	25
Ireland	95	Dublin	207	112
UK	89	London	103	14
Netherlands	66	Amsterdam	103	37
Belgium	23	Brussels	58	35
US	20	New York	112	92
France	15	Paris	58	43
Japan	15	Tokyo	30	15
Australia	10	Sydney	83	73
Sweden	6	Stockholm	54	48

Prices in cities are however often more volatile than in the countryside, partly because the supply of land is more limited and partly because of higher rates of population mobility.

What attracts investors to countryside properties, particularly in emerging markets, is price. However, low prices don't necessarily suggest that prices are going to rise. You may be able to buy a run down village house in Romania for a few thousand pounds, but part of the reason that these properties cost so little is that nobody wants to live there. Even if your country house investment is close enough to new infrastructure, entertainment or commercial developments to increase demand, prices have got to go a long way before you make any significant profits in absolute terms. Our tip: stick to cities and major towns.

Buying in Resorts: The Impact of Tourism

Many property companies focus on selling properties in resort areas. This is partly due to the fact that many people buying abroad are buying a holiday home, but it is also partly a result of increasing investor interest in resort properties.

Increasing levels of tourism bring increased wealth and demand for short-term holiday accommodation. In theory, with more people comes more demand. However, it is the intentions of those people that are important to decipher. Genuine resort investment opportunities exist in places where there will be considerable tourist demand for holiday accommodation and where buyers are landlords or holiday home purchasers rather than speculators.

Determining the longevity of an investment in a resort area is based on simple common sense. There must be genuine, fundamental reasons why people would choose to holiday in the resort and even buy a holiday home there. For example; will the Black Sea coast of Bulgaria with its short summer

---

'Investment is a financial decision and must be made with the head, not the heart'

---

season actually be as popular a holiday and second home destination as Spain? The answer is probably not.

Climate and local attractions are important. People will always want to holiday and live in the Mediterranean area because of the climate. Equally, people will also always want to holiday or live near Disneyworld. Florida and Spain might be very mature markets, but there is a reason that prices have reached the levels that they have; there is genuine demand. When looking for emerging resort markets we have to look out for the same demand motivators.

There is also a potential, non-financial benefit to having a property that you can use yourself in a resort. In a holiday resort, your property is likely to be used for short term visitors rather than long term tenants and it is therefore likely that it will be available for you to use at least some of the time. On many purpose built resorts, developers offer packages where they let your property for you for most of the year but keep it open for your personal use at set times. This can be a good investment in your lifestyle as well as your financial future.

When considering a resort investment, we need to consider the main driver of rental and purchase demand; the number of tourists. As a starting point, the ten countries forecast by the World Travel and Tourism Council to show the highest levels of real growth up to 2015 are as follows:

Country	Predicted Annual Growth 2006–2015
Montenegro	9.9
China	9.2
India	8.6
Reunion	8.3
Croatia	7.8
Sudan	7.7
Vietnam	7.7
Laos	7.6
Czech Republic	7.5
Guadeloupe	7.2

These countries offer real opportunities.

Montenegro, in the top place for tourism growth, has often been named as the single best destination when trying to find a holiday home. Like neighbouring Croatia, Montenegro has a stunning coastline dotted with islands and a wooded interior studded with lakes which are largely UNESCO protected (reducing the likelihood of mass, overdevelopment). Both countries gained a reputation as high class holiday resorts in the 1960s and 70s. In Montenegro's upmarket Sveti Stefan Resort, Elizabeth Taylor and Richard Burton are said to have disturbed other guests with their arguing, whilst Sofia Loren gave the chef lessons in how to cook pasta.

'Research suggests that over the long term, the rental and re-sale potential of properties in cities outperforms that of properties in the countryside'

The tourist market in the region fell off during the 1990 war in the Balkans, unfairly in the case of Montenegro which had little involvement. There are no restrictions on foreigners buying property in Montenegro and prices have been relatively low but are increasing rapidly. The average price for a new, off-plan one bedroom flat is £73,700 going up to £250,000 for a 3 bedroom house. This is one of the reasons that Montenegro may be a better bet than Croatia, a favourite with German and Italian buyers for many years. Prices in **Croatia** start from a higher base with two bedroom apartments in an off-plan development with sea views costing over £100,000. In luxury new developments this sum might just stretch to a one-bedroom apartment.

The other European country on this list, the **Czech Republic**, is already one of the great success stories of the last ten years. The market for city centre property in Eastern Europe was practically invented in Prague and it is a model copied in many European capitals since. There is arguably too much existing competition for the market to prove particularly profitable. Opportunities do however exist outside the capital. The Czech government is making greater efforts to attract visitors to spa towns and destinations outside Prague, and is seeking millions of euros in extra development funds from the European Union. The money will be put towards tourism growth and improvement of infrastructure throughout the country. Spa towns such as Karlovy-Vary are attractive areas for second homes; property here is good value for money and prices are now likely to increase faster than in Prague.

India is an interesting nomination: high levels of interest have been sparked after a loosening of restrictions on foreign investment. Like China, India should be seen as a long term investment with the chance of significant long term capital appreciation.

Turning to other areas of South East Asia, **Vietnam** is one of the countries generating a real buzz at the moment. Construction has started on several prestigious second home developments on the coast. Designed to appeal to those who have fallen for this exotically beautiful country when travelling, these developments could also prove popular with the second home market drawn from China and Japan.

Ski Property

Second homes might generally be associated with escaping to the warmth and the beach, but rental yields in ski resorts can be higher. The supply of ski resorts is still far below that of beach holiday destinations, meaning that demand for accommodation can be high.

Skiing holidays are becoming increasingly popular. The Ski Club of Great Britain's analysis now estimates UK visits to ski resorts at over 1,205,000 – an 8.5% growth since the 2000/2001 season. However, with an average cost of over £600 for a week in the Alps, the cost of such holidays may be prohibitive. This gives the new resorts in central and Eastern Europe an opportunity to break into the market.

The rental season for ski property may also be longer. Resorts are often in areas which can appeal to people throughout the year. For example, the Alps now have a thriving summer market with people enjoying walking holidays and adventure sports.

Ski Destinations. Four key markets still dominate world skiing, accounting for two-thirds of the world market: Austria (56 million visits) France (57.6 million), the US (52.2 million) and Japan (52 million) but the market share of these countries is shrinking fast. The number of visits to Japan has declined by 40% over the last ten years (2006 figures).

Eastern Europe. There is a strong perception that the Eastern European markets offer the best value for money. A week in a Romanian or Bulgarian resort, including costs such as a week's lift pass, can cost a third of the price in France or Switzerland. The facilities in Eastern Europe are not bad either – **Bulgaria** put in a bid to host the 2014 Winter Olympics, and although the country was not shortlisted, the improvements made to the resorts of Borovets, Bansko and Pamporovo to support the bid make it a world-class skiing destination.

The Tatras, the range of mountains bordering Poland and Slovakia, also merits a look. **The High Tatras in Slovakia** is a particularly notable region, providing the only real competition for Alpine skiing in Eastern Europe. Skiing here is Olympic standard, with reliable snow and good facilities. The best known resort is Strbske Pleso, which is also a centre for adventure sports including paragliding and bungee jumping.

The High Tatras are a good bet because the high standard of skiing is backed up by a very solid housing market. With 19% flat income tax, a burgeoning economy and a tourist industry ranked 36th for long term growth by the WTTC in 2007, Slovakia presents an interesting opportunity.

Emerging Markets. Eastern Europe appeals to skiers from the West of Europe because of the comparatively low prices and reasonable flight times. There is, however, evidence that dedicated skiers are prepared to travel further and further for good snow.

Skiing in exotic locations is easier to arrange than people realise. Buyers looking for something further abroad could try looking at **Chile, Japan** or even **China**.

Skiing is one of the biggest trends to hit China in years. A decade ago, less than 200 people in China were believed to have tried skiing; now it's one million. The market is expected to grow to twelve million. The best resorts are in the northerly province of Heilongjiang. Yabuli, the site of the third Asian Winter Games, has excellent facilities and one of the longest toboggan runs in the world. Buying here could be the equivalent of investing in Whistler twenty years ago.

Renting Ski Property. As with beachfront property, it is possible to agree rental contracts with holiday companies. You may want to look for a development with a leasing agreement or guaranteed rental scheme already in place. More than 60% of ski holidays are sold as inclusive packages. The six key companies to look for are Airtours, Crystal, Inghams, Thomson, First Choice and Neilson. Renting directly should also be possible. Figures from the Ski Club of Great Britain show that people arranging independent trips now make up almost 25% of the market; a rise of more than 300% over the last five years.

Beach Destinations

The sheer number of beach resorts, everywhere from the Americas to the Black Sea, means that the relationship between supply and demand is not nearly as favourable as with ski property. Nonetheless, 18.7% of buyers still say that they are looking for a property close to the coast. The majority of these buyers are looking for personal use rather than investment property. Prices are often higher on the coast and in most countries the number of second homes at the coast will ensure intense competition for holiday lets.

For those people determined to buy on the coast, the most favourable conditions are often in emerging markets where there is little competition. Prices may be low on the Black Sea coast, but with the number of people buying in Bulgaria and Turkey, rental yields are going to be low. In **Brazil** or **Goa**, the numbers of apartments built to the standard expected by Western tourists is lower, meaning that rental yields on high quality property are likely to be more satisfactory.

Another policy is to buy near a beach, but in an area which also has other strengths. The Costa del Sol in Spain has benefited from proximity to

Barcelona; **Dubai** attracts tourists to the beach, but also for the shopping and nightlife. Prices have risen much more quickly in these markets than in straightforward beach towns.

Some of these 'beach extra' markets are still in their infancy and provide a good opportunity for buyers. **Gdansk**, for example, is a beautiful Hanseatic town in Poland which attracts high numbers of tourists. Attractive beaches lie just outside the city limits, but with the relatively short summer season it is the city's other attractions which provide a basis for demand. The south of **Italy** and **Sicily** also combine historical attractions and beautiful cities with glorious beaches.

The newer markets in the Middle East can also be good places to look. **The Middle East** is becoming more and more fashionable. Travel agents report that in 2006, the number of UK visitors increased by 41% to Egypt, 9% to Morocco and 7.2% to Dubai. Cities such as Doha and Muscat may be the next big tourist destinations to look out for.

Another good place to look is in **Kenya** and **East Africa**. Kenya has beautiful beaches, with proximity to Zanzibar and other island resorts. People visiting Kenya on safari also book a few days at the coast. Mombasa and Malindi have good transport links, large expat communities and visitors who return year after year.

3 What To Buy: Assessing Opportunities

If you are buying a home, or even a holiday home, deciding what to buy is reasonably straight forward. If you need three bedrooms, you buy a three bedroom house and if you are a beach lover, you will buy a home in the sun and near the sea. Knowing what to buy for investment is decidedly trickier.

What makes a good investment is dependent on so many different things which relate not only to the property itself, but also to events in the local, national and international market place. In chapter two we looked at the issues of where to invest. In this chapter we narrow our analysis down to examining what type of property to invest in. There is no one answer to this and the range of good property investment opportunities out there is equalled only by the range of bad opportunities.

Best to Invest: Old or New Build

Research suggests that more than three-quarters of potential international buyers want to buy either an off-plan or new-build property. Whether to look for new-build or older property is a question that depends on your reasons for buying. Putting aside the question of personal preference, this is about working out which type of property will be the best investment in any given area.

Older Property

In France, for example, the market is calibrated to older property and buyers tend to look for something with charm rather than novelty. This is partly also a case of buyers adapting to availability. With an ample supply of older housing and strict planning laws, something older may be easier to find and provide better value for money.

Italy is another country where the market is adapted to older properties. It is not insignificant that these countries are among the most sophisticated and developed of second home markets. A link can often be made between the youth of the market and the youth of desirable housing. People prefer new developments in Eastern Europe because the quality of existing housing is not good.

The key to the appeal of new-builds is the confidence that they instil in the buyer. The thought of older houses, with the potential for dry rot and rising damp, can put off even the most determined buyer. And whilst coping with a leaking roof and fragmenting walls is possible if you are living in a house, coping with the manifold disasters that may beset your paying tenants several thousand miles away can be spectacularly daunting.

Newer property can sometimes also seem better calibrated to social and cultural developments. This is not a case of 'all mod cons', but of the growing demand for smaller properties across the world. The trends for later marriage, higher divorce rates and more single households ensure that prices for apartments often climb faster than for houses.

New-Builds

New properties may also be easier to maintain than older buildings – an important consideration if you are stuck a thousand miles from a building with a flooding washing machine. If you buy on a new development the developer may even have made arrangements for management before completing the project.

For people looking for a second home, there is often some comfort in numbers. Master planned communities can include facilities which older housing can't match. This doesn't just mean swimming pools integrated into the design of the house but can extend to golf courses, shopping centres and water parks.

A sense of community can add value to a rental property, especially if you are aiming for holiday lets. If a development is well placed, close to the sea or a ski resort, and attractively planned, you will hold a competitive advantage over other properties in the area which lack these benefits. With new builds the reputation and prior experience of the developer is often a useful guide. Large developers have to run their businesses on very professional lines and this gives the buyer a chance to demand good service. Asking to look at references, to look at completed developments or even to talk to people who have bought before are all valid requests. You won't get this level of service from someone selling their family home; but then, you can explore a completed house at leisure, whereas a new-build may not be completed for two years after purchase.

There is also a less positive side to newer builds. Just as the presence of developers can be an advantage, showing you that an area is very much on the way up, in areas where a great deal of new building is underway, there is a danger of over-supply.

The Joy of Off-Plan

A number of structures have been developed to cater for the investment market. By far the most popular is off-plan property. Buying off-plan means purchasing a property before the building is complete; instead of touring a property the buyer works from images, plans and computer simulations. At best, this arrangement benefits both developer and purchaser. Off-plan property is sold at a discount in order to compensate buyers for the inconvenience of waiting for completion. On some projects prices rise in three or four stages. As the development nears completion the developer's risk exposure lessens and they raise prices.

Off-plan property does cost less, and often carries other advantages; for example, people buying a property before completion may be able to influence the design. However, there is also some risk attached and it is a good idea to make sure that the developer is able to deliver the property that is promised.

Selecting a Development

The primary reason for selecting a development is that you believe it is a good investment. Perhaps there is a five star hotel on site to help attract paying tenants, or perhaps you feel that the off-plan prices are undervalued compared to comparable properties. Whatever the investment rationale, you also need to ensure that the off-plan promise is going to translate into reality when the development is finished.

There are simple measures that you can take to ensure that you are making the right choice of development. Ask the developer for some information on their track record; see what developments they have done before. This will provide a good indication that the developer is credible and should give some confidence in their build quality. In emerging markets, however, you may find that you come across many first time developers. This doesn't automatically mean that they won't be good. In this scenario, check that the promoting agent has completed sufficient due diligence, that the contract paperwork is in order and that the developer has sufficient finances to deliver the project.

'Developer insurance, taken out by the company and guaranteeing at least your money back if the project falls through, will help keep your investment safe'

You also need to look at floor plans with a critical eye. Look at the shared areas as well as the design of your individual property. Is the swimming pool generous enough to cope with fifty families? Does the design look crowded and where are restaurants and recreation facilities in relation to your apartment?

It is also important to ask about completion dates – something that a surprising number of buyers seem to be relaxed about. Off-plan property is most likely to be sold in areas where demand out-strips the existing housing stock. But if demand is high, developers will be tempted to take on as many projects as possible, cranes may be booked up, there may be a shortage of qualified construction staff. With the best intentions in the world, they can fall behind schedule.

A good contract will include penalty clauses for every day beyond the scheduled completion date that handover is delayed. For example, developments have been found which offer refunds of a small percentage of the purchase price for every single day of delay, and if delivery is held back for more than 90 days the buyer is offered their money back. With this kind of penalty in place, delay can be quite profitable. If nothing else, you will be saved the frustration of seeing your money tied up in a project that seems to be going nowhere.

SAFEGUARDING YOUR INVESTMENT

Think also about what lies beyond the edge of the development plans. Is more building planned in the area and do you have guarantees that high-rise buildings won't spring up around the charming low-density development on the plans? This is something that a lawyer can help with (another reason to have a good professional enlisted before beginning your hunt for property). Ask your lawyer to conduct a search as soon as possible, looking at plans and regulations on surrounding sites. This is particularly important for properties with a sea view – you'll pay a premium for this and the property value will fall if developers squeeze another property in between you and the coast.

The staged payments common with off-plan property are themselves a form of guarantee. The points at which instalments will be needed differ under various jurisdictions; a typical schedule in Europe would be a reservation deposit – which will be legally binding in most jurisdictions, and then four instalments on completion of foundations, the shell of the building, roof and finish.

In some markets, developers should have a sheaf of independent guarantees and should be falling over themselves with eagerness to present these to customers. Developer insurance, taken out by the company and guaranteeing at least return of your money should the project fall through, will help to keep your investment safe. Developers sometimes also offer bank guarantees which offer similar protection. However, many emerging markets do not have these systems of guarantees in place and so you need to be even more certain that the developer can and will deliver on their promises.

Finally, check the contract for clauses limiting your right to resell before completion. This is called flipping and is extremely common in markets like Dubai. When markets grow at an unsustainable rate, local governments may encourage or require developers to take action by inserting contractual clauses making flipping illegal. This can be good for the market, encouraging stability and preventing markets from spiralling out of control, but if there is any chance that you will need to resell prior to completion of the property, you need to be sure that this right is specified before buying.

Off-Plan: Too Good to Be True?

The excitement of flipping leads us to the second problem with buying off-plan, the dangers of the 'too good to be true' stories of instant capital appreciation and instant profit. Search 'off-plan property' on the internet and you will find a hundred 'true stories' starring ordinary folk who put down a deposit on an off-plan development and then re-sold it before completion for enormous profit. It's an appealing story and, where people have made a clever choice of development, sometimes true. Property sold in the first stages of development on the Palm in Dubai for £90 per square metre now sells at £4,207 – over 4000% profit. But this isn't always the case and buying property purely in the expectation of such swift capital appreciation and resale is a dangerous policy.

In some areas, buyers have been so confident that the real estate markets are rising, that they have taken loans in order to buy several properties, even if they depend on resale in order to meet the final instalments. Others have leveraged in order to buy more than one apartment or house, hoping to make profit on as many properties as possible.

When buying off-plan you have to be sure that there are underlying reasons why someone will want to rent or buy your property from you when it is completed. In some cases where markets are dominated by off-plan property, you may find that new market entrants only want to buy direct from the developer as well. This is a very typical scenario in a market dominated by speculators. If the growth drivers in the market are genuine, people will be desperate to buy your completed property off you in order to live in it or rent it out. If you don't believe that there is a queue of people waiting to buy completed property, then you should avoid any off-plan developments and probably avoid the market altogether.

Reducing Risk

Firms dealing with the emerging markets will often encounter clients worried about the security of their rights to purchased property. Spain and China are two of the most common countries of concern. The opportunities for capital growth in China are enormous but potential buyers worry about the constitutional protection of property. Chinese law says that the government can confiscate land for other uses, provided that they pay fair compensation.

What many buyers don't realise is that similar laws are in place in many other countries where property rights are considered perfectly safe. The US government has similar powers to confiscate private property and is now in the middle of a debate about these rights, which are known as *eminent domain*.

The truth of the matter is that most risk lies in ignorance. Investing in almost any part of the world can be safe provided that you know what you are doing and that you take due care and consideration. At a property level, the risks are rather limited, beyond the obvious dangers of buying something which is falling down or that you don't actually own. Most risks exist at a market level; some are predictable and therefore avoidable; others aren't. Some risks just have to be accepted; who knows if there will be a natural disaster which could ruin a particular property market for years.

At a property level you can manage your risks by using a lawyer, commissioning a survey and by taking time to make a logical and considered decision about what to buy. This, however, will not protect you from market level events which could strike at any time. To manage risks at this level there are two main options; diversifying by buying in more than one area or country; or, if you don't have the resources for this approach, investing through collective investment schemes.

Diversifying and Building a Portfolio

Diversifying is simply a matter of hedging your bets. You may find a development that seems guaranteed to double in price, but to buy up as much as possible of a single development or area is risky. Any unexpected change in the market will endanger the whole, rather than a small proportion, of your investment.

The ideal approach is to split your investment and buy as large a range of property as possible. At some stage this may mean commercial and industrial property as well as residential. These markets are more complicated however, and price entry thresholds are higher. Most new property investors will prefer a first venture into commercial property to be in their home country.

For those people taking their first step into property investment, look instead for different kinds of residential property, and in different countries or different continents even. Because property markets are often localised (usually at a national level), buying in a range of countries helps to reduce your risk. Buying on different continents will reduce your risk exposure even more, by limiting the impact of regional events on your portfolio. In the late 1990's property prices plummeted across the whole of South East Asia. Property investors who had all of their investments in the region suffered significant losses. For those who owned South East Asian properties as part of a broader portfolio, the events of 1997 were less of a concern.

Even if you are absolutely devoted to a single market and determined to pick up as much as possible in the country of your choice, there are ways to diversify risk by buying different kinds of property. Dubai has been one of the favourite investment destinations of the last few years. In Dubai apartments have traditionally been more desirable than villas. This has caused many investors to concentrate exclusively on building a portfolio of apartments. In 2005 the market shifted slightly and villas became more desirable. One study suggests that between 2005 and 2006 villas appreciated up to 15% faster than apartments, a trend which is likely to continue. Those investors who have had the foresight to diversify will therefore benefit.

> ## 'Buying on different continents will reduce your risk exposure even more, by limiting the impact of regional events on your portfolio'

If your first property is in a sunny holiday resort, try to balance this with something in a city. If you have been busy buying up houses with five or six bedrooms, then balance your portfolio with a couple of one-bedroom apartments or studio flats. After all, the size of the family is shrinking and more people are living alone than ever before.

Part of this diversification is trying to put together a portfolio where the properties carry different levels of risk and will react differently as an investment in different circumstances. Put simply, it is the old adage of not putting all of your eggs in one basket.

Whilst diversifying your investment helps to reduce your risk, over stretching yourself can be equally damaging. If you only have enough money to buy one property, the best option is to buy something generating significant yields and then save that income towards your next property in a different market. Over time you will end up building a healthy, sustainable, low risk and diversified portfolio.

Collective Investment Schemes: Property Funds and Reits

For those with limited budgets, there are ways of investing in a portfolio of high quality properties without mortgaging everything you own. There are a range of collective investment schemes available which offer the opportunity to participate in large scale property investments for a relatively small amount of cash. Collective investment schemes operate like funds in which investors' money is put together to purchase a range of properties.

Collective investment funds have numerous benefits, not least of which is that someone with only £20,000 ($35,000) to invest could gain access to the sort of returns only usually available with larger scale investments. Another benefit of collective investments is that they let people duck out of the process of researching markets, assessing when to buy and when to sell and all of the difficulties of finding and keeping tenants. They also allow people to invest in commercial and industrial property, the thresholds of which are set too high for most investors.

Different investment funds will have different objectives. Some might have the purpose of developing a resort or tower block allowing investors to make the same kinds of returns as developers, others may buy a range of off-plan properties from across the globe and flip them before completion. Whatever the purpose of the fund, its objectives will be laid out in a prospectus for investors to examine prior to committing their funds. The actions of the fund managers will be governed by the parameters set out in the prospectus, so you can be certain how your money will be invested.

BENEFITS OF COLLECTIVE INVESTMENT SCHEMES

- Opportunity to benefit from property without the hassle of organising buying, letting or arranging sales
- Your investment will be managed by experts
- Opportunity to expose even small investments to a broad portfolio of properties and countries
- Funds can use their buying power to arrange bulk discounts
- Some funds have tax benefits. In the UK, investors can invest in many types of funds with money held in ISAs and even SIPPs (self invested personal pensions)
- No sleepless nights over letting, tenants, vacancy rates and so on…

Types of Funds

The types of funds on offer vary dramatically in their structure and their investment objectives. In the US and Australia, readers will be familiar with Real Estate Investment Trusts (REITs) which are regulated funds managed by major financial institutions which operate in a similar way to unit trusts. The UK launched REITs in January 2007, and they took South-east Asia by storm in 2005 and 2006. In the United States, REITs recently celebrated their fortieth birthday.

Other forms of investment trust do however already exist. From the informal syndicate of friends to collective property funds, people are buying property through a variety of different instruments.

The rules and regulations surrounding investment funds make describing their various forms difficult here, but in outline there are several different forms which are usually made available to different types of investor.

Onshore or Offshore

Often funds will be referred to as offshore or onshore funds. This typically refers to the country they are domiciled in and therefore the jurisdiction which regulates their activity. In the UK for example, an onshore fund would refer to one that is regulated by the UK's Financial Services Authority (FSA). Onshore funds need to meet certain criteria and the greater level of regulation usually allows them to be offered to a broader range of investors.

Onshore funds will often be structured differently to offshore funds due to regulatory requirements. Often onshore funds will have greater liquidity making it easier for investors to sell their interest in the fund when they want to (see open ended investment vehicles vs. close ended investment vehicles below).

Maintaining the UK example, an offshore fund would not be regulated by the FSA. The fund would, however, be regulated by the financial regulator in the country in which it is domiciled. The domicile of an offshore fund will usually be in a jurisdiction with low taxation and a reliable financial system which investors have confidence in. Typical locations for offshore funds include Jersey, Guernsey, The Isle of Man and the British Virgin Islands.

Whilst offshore funds are not regulated directly by the onshore regulator, the sale of shares in those funds is a regulated activity. In the UK, FSA regulations state that offshore funds can only be offered as an investment to 'sophisticated' or 'high net worth' investors. Investors need to self declare themselves as being in one of these categories before a qualified financial advisor can hand over details of the fund.

Open Ended Investment Vehicles vs. Close Ended Investment Vehicles

Open ended investment vehicles are funds which allow investors to sell their units or shares almost without restriction. This makes these funds very similar to unit trusts which hold a range of equities. In order to facilitate the movement of cash in and out of the fund as new investors buy units and other investors sell units, the fund needs to maintain a certain level of liquidity.

In other words a fund which allows investors to take their money out of the fund as and when they wish, needs to have the cash available to pay them what they are owed. This would be difficult if the fund only owned property as property is not a liquid asset. Instead therefore, these funds have to hold more liquid assets like shares in other companies (usually property companies of some sort to maintain the theme) and even cash.

Most onshore, regulated funds will by order of the financial regulator be open ended. As a result these funds are open to all investors, including those who are viewed as neither 'sophisticated' nor of 'high net worth'.

Close ended investment vehicles do not allow investors to sell their shares in the fund when they want. Instead, investors commit their money to the fund for a fixed time period in which the fund managers invest in properties to generate a return and then dispose of them to liquidate the assets and release cash back to the investors.

The 'lock-in' time on these funds will vary, but will always be set within a band as laid out in the investment prospectus offered to investors before they commit. Because these funds do not have the liquidity requirements of open ended vehicles, the fund manager is able to invest all of the investors' money in property. The lack of liquidity in this type of fund is one of the primary reasons that the FSA only allow them to be offered to self-declared sophisticated and high net worth investors.

Real Estate Investment Trusts

Buying into a REIT is just like buying shares in any other kind of fund, with the exception that the security of the property market makes REITs less volatile. Whilst they have the advantage of being based on property investment, they enjoy the liquidity of equity based funds. Another appealing factor is the tax advantages that most governments package up as part of the deal. In the US and UK REITs escape corporation tax by distributing up to 90% of the income derived from rents or capital appreciation on real estate sales as dividends. The money is then taxed as income against individuals.

There are different forms of REITs, some of which look more like a financial than a property investment. Equity REITs invest in and own properties taking income primarily from rents. Mortgage REITs deal in investment and ownership of property mortgages, lending money for mortgages to owners of real estate. Income is earned primarily through interest charged on mortgage loans; this type of REIT accounts for less than 10% of the total.

Choosing a REIT. There are a couple of considerations to bear in mind when choosing a REIT. First is diversification. This is one of the great strengths of a REIT and if you are placing money into property through this kind of investment structure why not go the whole hog and pick a fund which enables you to invest in the full range of property including commercial buildings?

Secondly, because REITS are different from the common run of equities, assessing the relative success of any trust can be a complex task. Experts recommend judging a REIT according to 'funds from operations' a figure on the balance sheet which doesn't include depreciation. Property rarely depreciates – quite the reverse! And calculating success by funds from operations may therefore give a more accurate picture of performance.

Costs. Investing in a REIT can seem comparatively expensive. Initial charges can account for up to 5% of the value of the investment and a yearly management fee will be charged. But compared to the annual growth targeted by property funds, often between 15% and 20%, this looks reasonable. A good fund should return up to 15% annual growth and 6% yield; given the amount of research and administration necessary to identify and invest in growth areas, the fees begin to look comparatively reasonable.

In most jurisdictions, REITs have replaced ordinary property companies as the favoured way of holding property. However, there are some bonuses to staying outside this system in the UK. Here, REITs are restricted in how much they can borrow and how much development they can do, and overseas property owned through foreign subsidiaries is not eligible for tax-free status. As a result, most will be UK-focused and act more as landlords than developers, although they may still build new schemes. Many investors may therefore prefer the higher risks and potential gains of direct investment in foreign property or development.

Making a Profit from Property

What Makes a Good Investment?

The Oxford English Dictionary defines an investment as *'a thing worth buying because it may be profitable in the future'.* This is often the interpretation taken by most people, but a better financial definition is 'the purchase of an asset which produces a financial return in the form of income.'

In countries like the UK and the US, people often think of their homes as their biggest investment. This point of view is based upon the assumption that your home is an asset because it may increase in value. This is not only wrong, it is the exact opposite of what is actually the case; your home is a liability.

To understand this statement, we need to be clear of the difference between assets and liabilities. Assets are things that we own which produce cash. Liabilities are things that we own which drain cash. In the case of your home, you will need to pay the mortgage, the utility bills, taxes and maintenance costs. It costs you money to live in your house. The capital value of your house may rise but this 'profit' is a myth. You cannot realise that profit. You still need somewhere to live and if your house has risen in value, so will the cost of other houses you may choose to live in.

If we look at an example of a buy to let property, we can see that it is an asset. A buy to let property should generate positive cash flow and potentially increase in value. The capital appreciation on an investment property can be realised and reinvested or spent elsewhere as you do not need it to live in. There will (or at least should) be a positive difference between the costs of owning the property and the rental income. This net income is passively generated by the asset and is available to you to be reinvested or spent as you wish.

It is clear that owning assets is a good thing. However, building up your assets is a means to an end for an investor. The actual goal of investment is to generate enough income from your assets to support your lifestyle. Once you have done this you are freed from the toils of work. Income is therefore the ultimate investment goal. If you only had assets and you had to keep selling them to generate enough cash to live, you would eventually run out of assets and therefore cash. However, if your assets consistently generate income, that income can be sustained forever.

Therefore, in answering the question of what to invest in, we can clearly say, invest in assets. In the context of property this means investing in property which generates a net cash inflow which can be reinvested into more assets that also generate cash. This is the virtuous investment cycle. If you keep reinvesting income from your assets into more assets, you will eventually be generating enough cash to live on.

For a more detailed explanation of the concepts we have discussed here, you should refer to the Rich Dad Poor Dad series of books by Robert Kiyosaki. These provide an excellent grounding for developing an investment philosophy and are a useful resource for investors in any field. More details can be found on the website www.richdad.com.

Investment Versus Speculation

For most people starting out in international property investment, or investment of any kind for that matter, it is important to focus on buying assets and generating income. This is the basis from which to build a portfolio. This isn't to say that investing purely for capital growth is not a viable approach. In fact when selecting an investment property, the ideal scenario is to find one that generates cash and increases in value but the rental yield will always be the bottom line and the possibility of capital appreciation a bonus.

The danger for investors with a small portfolio comes when you invest in property purely for capital growth. If you are investing in a property which only breaks even in terms of income, or even worse costs you money every month, but you expect it to increase in value over time, you are not actually investing; you are speculating. These capital growth oriented investments have a place in an investment portfolio, but the cash generated by other assets in your portfolio should comfortably generate sufficient income to fund your outgoings on any speculative investment.

'If most players in the market are speculating on future capital appreciation and are not generating yield on their investment, then it is likely to be a bubble'

Understanding the difference between speculation and investment is also important from the point of view of analysing markets. If most players in the market are speculating on future capital appreciation and are not generating yield on their investment, then it is likely to be a bubble. On the other hand, a market where all the property owners are investors generating attractive amounts of rental income on their properties will be sustainable.

One of the most important aspects in ensuring you will make a secure and profitable investment is to research the market. Many agents and developers offer additional incentives such as "discounted property" or "guaranteed rental yields" but many are inflating the initial price to offer headline grabbing discounts. Simple internet research will enable you to tell whether the prices are in line with the local market.

When deciding what type of property to buy, you need to consider how you intend to profit from the investment. Below, we look at the three main ways in which property can generate a return on investment; rental yield (buy-to-let), capital appreciation and profit.

Buy to Let

Rental Yield

Buying for rental income is probably the best long term investment strategy available. Not only can the cash generated from the investment be used to re-invest into additional assets, it can also be more profitable than buying and selling property. There is an old Farsi saying which goes 'hold the property and it will hold you'. This simply means that when you buy property it is better to keep it. This is true for several reasons. Firstly, historically speaking, property prices always go up over time. There may be peaks and troughs at different points but the price trend is always upward. Secondly, when a property you own increases in price, you make money. If your property increases in value from £100,000 to £200,000, you have made £100,000. In most countries this profit is entirely tax free until you sell it. In theory therefore you could make a million pounds a year or more and not pay a penny in tax. Additionally, when you realise your profit by selling you will incur a variety of transaction costs.

If you keep a property, over time it will increase in value as will the amount of income you make from it. The value of your assets will grow and you will incur no tax or costs for the privilege.

Letting a Property. Letting a property abroad can be a hard slog. Setting up websites, finding tenants, arranging advertising, taking enquiries, finding some-one to take day to day care of the property. The anxiety of trying to control events from a distance can be difficult. However, this doesn't have to be the case. If you take the time to select the right property and instruct the right professionals to maintain and let your property, you should be able to sit back, and enjoy the income. On new developments built specifically for the holiday or second home markets, the management company may be as much part of the development as the swimming pool. Communal and management fees are spec-ified in the initial contract and cover services such as ground maintenance, local rates and sometimes also electricity and water costs. It is, however, potentially more difficult for people buying an older property with no built-in letting and management system.

'Buying for rental income is probably the best long term investment strategy available'

Another recent and popular scheme that many developers and hotel operators are now offering is the ability to purchase a room or suite within a fully managed hotel. This can be a secure way of ensuring you maintain a steady and sufficient income from your investment with the additional benefit that many schemes offer one to four weeks free usage per year. Many operators are starting to offer either a guaranteed rental scheme or a split of the revenue generated. With the right location, using a management company with a good track-record, the purchase price may be higher than a standard apartment, but you are likely to benefit from long term and secure rental potential. This is especially true when you buy through a large or respected hotel chain.

Fees. Management fees will usually be charged whether you rent out a property on a development or not. However, you should be particularly aware of these when renting as they will impact upon your returns. Management fees are often expressed as a charge per square metre or square foot. The charges can however vary significantly and you will need to read the contract carefully to ensure that fees are realistic.

When letting your property, the management company will also charge a percentage of rental income for the services that make rentals feasible such as finding tenants and maintenance. The level of management fee will often depend on whether you are renting to long term or short term (holiday) tenants. Management fees for holiday lets are usually higher because there will be more cleaning involved for changing over tenants on a weekly basis. In most places you should expect to pay between 5% and 20% of the rental income.

Calculating Rental Potential. Rental potential is a simple equation based upon the daily, weekly or monthly rental price (depending on the time periods you are letting the property for) multiplied by the occupancy rate. For example, an apartment with a monthly rent of £500 would deliver an annual rental income of £6,000. However, you may only be able to find tenants for 6 months of the year. The actual rental income would therefore be £6,000 x 50% = £3,000.

After the gross rental income, you will then need to deduct costs which will usually include management fees, rental management fees, maintenance costs and taxation.

Working Out Occupancy Rates. One of the most important determinants of your rental income is occupancy. The agent and developer should both be able to give a realistic idea of occupancy rates but you should also check this from an unbiased source. In relation to holiday lettings, you need to consider the length of the letting season; information on this can usually be found on the internet or from the local tourist board.

When assessing likely occupancy try not to be unduly cynical, or to automatically disbelieve people who tell you that the letting season is comparatively long. Cities are a cert for year round letting and there are areas of the countryside which also attract people in summer and winter. The Alps attract high numbers of summer visitors for walking holidays and the mountain resorts of Eastern Europe look like developing in the same way.

Whether to Rent to Locals or Try for the International Short-Let Market. Part of working out the expected occupancy is deciding whether you will market to locals or to holiday lets. The two markets are very different. Renting a house to the local market will provide a more reliable income, with tenants often booking an apartment for a year or more. (This is typically the case in city centre locations.) It is also sometimes possible to rent to businesses or international organisations. In Brussels for example, apartments are sold with a rental agreement with the European Union already in place. The EU uses your apartment to house politicians or diplomats and you receive a regular and generous income. In Mongolia, yields are high due to the number of companies that have partnered with developers to offer long term rented accommodation for their international workers.

As we keep reiterating, it is important to conduct research on the local market. Certain countries and regions have a culture of renting (e.g. Germany) whereas others are focused on home ownership (e.g. the UK).

In some countries, rents have not always kept up with the increase in property prices, giving compressed yields. This has certainly been the case in many Eastern European cities where there has been an over supply of property put onto the markets by investors.

If you have already purchased overseas without any management contracts in place, there are a number of ways to find tenants for your property:

1. Local agents
2. Advertising in the local press
3. Large or international companies in the area who may be looking for accommodation for their staff
4. British embassies who may be looking to relocate new arrivals to a country
5. The internet – there are many local and international portals (www.holiday-rentals.com) who list property for rent

LONG TERM VERSUS SHORT TERM RENTALS

Long Term Lets

Renting long term is the simplest and often one of the most profitable ways of renting, especially when the property is let to tenants all year round. Long term lets are often easier to find in city centres rather than holiday resorts. There is no need to arrange for tenants to be met at the airport, no need to clean between lets or to arrange for the garden to be maintained. Your tenants will also expect less; you won't have to put in a swimming pool or worry about access to an airport if you are renting to local business people. Of course, what your tenants expect will be determined by local norms so you need to make sure your property is competitive. On the other hand, your rental on a daily basis will be much lower than for holiday lets and you won't be able to holiday in the property yourself.

The advantages of long term lets include:

- Reliable long-term income.
- The possibility of agreeing long-term contracts with businesses or international organisations.
- Hassle free.
- Lower management costs.

Short Term Lets

Short-term lets can offer a greater financial reward, but there is less security. If you invest in a holiday resort, you are more likely to let your property to people staying in your property for only one week who will expect to pay a relatively high price for that week compared to someone renting an apartment for a year - an apartment that generates £400 a month if let yearly could generate £50 a night from tourists. However, with short term lets, you will always have void periods. How long the void periods are depends upon the length of the letting season (often dictated by the climate) and local competition in the letting market. It should be emphasised that short term letting is not just restricted to holiday destinations. Many European cities such as Barcelona, Prague, Krakow and Gdansk have opened up to cheap, direct flights and are proving popular long weekend destinations, meaning higher yields are now attainable.

The advantages of short term lets include:

- Higher rental value.
- Opportunity to book the property for your own use and to occupy it during the low season.

Disadvantages:

- Possible void periods making income less reliable.
- High rental management costs.

Guaranteed Rental Schemes. An increasing number of developments offer the potential of guaranteed rental returns. Guaranteed rental is exactly what it suggests. When you buy the property, you sign a contract with either the developer or a management company to lease the property from you for a fixed annual amount for a set number of years. The management company will then use your property to let to tenants and take the risks and rewards from doing so. Whatever happens, you receive your pre-agreed rental. Yields tend to be 6 to 7% or more of your initial purchase price and the term can last from 1 to 20 years. These schemes can take much of the stress and effort out of investing abroad. It is however important to remember that the guaranteed income you hold is only as good as the company guaranteeing it. You should also be cautious. These schemes may seem very attractive but we have seen and heard of developers increasing the purchase price to compensate or cover the yield. A simple way of checking this is to look at the price of comparable developments in the area.

'Remember that the guaranteed income you hold is only as good as the company guaranteeing it'

It is also prudent not to be blinded by the initial guaranteed rental period. Many of you will be buying for investment so it is essential that you consider what will happen once the guaranteed rental period has elapsed. Is it likely that you (or the person you sell your apartment to) will be able to rent it out and generate a good yield? Often, in areas where there is a lot of development (such as the Black Sea coast in Bulgaria) many developers offer schemes to differentiate themselves. You have to remember that your apartment will be competing with other apartments in the vicinity once the guaranteed rental period is over, so you will need to be confident that there is sufficient demand.

Personal Use. A common advantage of guaranteed rental schemes is that they often allow owners to use the property for free for a set number of days each year (typically from 1 week to 1 month per annum). Many of these schemes are associated with hotel complexes, which means that owners also get use of the hotel facilities when staying in their property.

Capital Appreciation

Research suggests that most people evaluate potential investments primarily on the capital appreciation that they offer. In fact many people specify that they are more interested in capital appreciation than rental income. For example, research in Ireland suggested that seven out of ten buy-to-let mortgages are not covered by rental income, but that this is a price that people are willing to pay for potential capital appreciation.

On the basis of the points made earlier, this means that the majority of 'investors' are in fact 'speculators'.

For small or new investors, the pursuit of pure capital appreciation is a dangerous strategy. This is primarily because property ownership incurs expenses and if the property isn't generating cash then you have to fund the expenses from elsewhere. It sounds obvious, but it is always worth remembering that you can only pay for things in cash. It doesn't matter if your property has increased in value by £30,000; if you have not got the cash to pay the mortgage you will lose the property. Therefore, a good property investment should generate sufficient cash to cover expenses, and cash can only be generated through rental income. For those who want to build a portfolio, every investment should generate enough cash to cover expenses and leave a profit which you can use towards further investments in your portfolio.

'Whether you are a speculator or an investor buying for the long term you should always consider how easy it will be to liquidate your asset'

Having said all this, capital appreciation is important and is often the single biggest contributor to your overall profit from the property. The ideal investment is therefore one which pays for itself through rental yield whilst appreciating at a healthy rate. The two objectives of yield and growth are not mutually exclusive; both objectives can be met in one investment.

Many investors' demands for capital appreciation are unrealistic and it is worth noting that a property which appreciates in value by only 7% per year will almost double in value over ten years. This is growth which, compared to other asset classes, is both generous and sustainable.

Exit Strategy

In order to realise the capital appreciation from your property investment you need to sell and liquidate it. Whether you are a speculator buying for short term gain or an investor buying for the long term you should always consider how easy it will be to liquidate your asset.

Often people are (and we have both been ourselves) blinded by the attractiveness of a new build resort that is offered for sale and do not think about how attractive the property will be in a few years time. This is especially important in areas of fast touristic and economic growth. You must consider what competition there is (or is likely to be) in the area and how likely it is that you will be able to sell to either another investor or an end user of the property.

Resale

When the time comes to sell your property, there will be several options. A private sale through a newspaper or internet site is the first, although this will be a time-consuming and difficult process.

A better idea is to talk to the agent who sold you the property in the first place. Most agents will be prepared to help people who bought through them, even if the company does not specialise in re-sales. They will also already be familiar with the area and development, and should have marketing materials to hand. Finally, if you are selling on a particular development, your agent should already be linked in buyers' minds with the property. They may even keep a list of people waiting to buy re-sales in the property. And even if the agent can't sell the property themselves, they should have enough of a relationship with the developer and other agents to be able to find someone that specialises in re-sales locally. Approaching the developer will pay similar dividends with the additional bonus that developers often keep sales offices on the site of the development. The sales office may receive enquiries about buying into the development and they can pass these potential clients on to you. For a list of some key agents please refer to part II of the book.

Profit

The third means of making money from property is profit. Whilst in general terms profit can refer to any money made, it does have a specific meaning which is money made as a result of discount purchasing or renovations. Profit in this sense is the money made by buying and selling a property, not including capital appreciation. This shows that you can make money from property even if prices in the market are not rising. As an example, if you were able to buy a property for 10% under market value and then sell the property at market value, you will have made a profit, even if the market value has not risen.

There are two basic strategies for generating profit from property. The first is discount buying and the second is adding value. It is possible to buy property below market value when buying off-plan as developers often give genuine discounts to get early sales before construction starts. Bulk buyers can also buy below market value as they are likely to negotiate a discount for buying a number of properties in one development. However, these bulk discounts can also be available to people even when they only buy a single property. This is usually achieved through bulk buying as an organised group. This could be as informal as getting together with some friends to buy a number of properties, or could involve joining a property club or syndicate where the club arranges bulk buy discounts on behalf of its members. Buying through clubs like this can prove very profitable, as long as the discounts being offered are genuine. Before buying through a club, check that the savings stack up as you will usually pay some form of fee for the privilege of receiving the discount.

Profiting by adding value to a property usually involves renovation and modernisation. This is a good strategy in your home market, but very difficult to organise when the property is abroad. Unless you are doing it on a large scale and therefore able to employ a turnkey project management company, it is best to steer clear of this approach to international property investment.

5 The Most Valuable Tools: Good Advice and Information

Buying property is complicated. Even in well established markets like the UK or US, the process of purchasing a property isn't a straightforward transaction like buying a car. No matter how experienced an investor you are, you will always need professional advice; unless of course, you are a qualified lawyer, surveyor, financial advisor and real estate broker. Without this unlikely cocktail of qualifications and experience you will need help and advice when buying a property, and especially when buying a property overseas.

When considering investing in overseas property, the first place you will start is research. It is recommended that you undertake thorough independent research before you approach an agent to at least get a feel for the area you want to invest in. Agents can play many roles in assisting your purchase; one of these is providing information and expert opinion. In most markets there will be many agents selling property and it is worth speaking to several of them, even if you have already chosen an agent to work with.

The first section below provides guidance on where and how to gather information on international property markets. This chapter then goes on to describe the role that agents and other professionals play and how to get the best out of them.

Sources of Information

Rather than wondering where to find information about international property, the question exercising many people's minds may be how to escape it. Property television shows, newspaper articles and even radio shows have proliferated almost to the point of ubiquity. A number of magazines are now targeted at international property buyers; most tabloid and broadsheet newspapers carry at least weekly sections on overseas property and most libraries will have a shelf-full of books telling you how to buy. The available information is, however, rather lopsided, with most books and articles dealing with the traditional markets in Spain, France, Italy and Florida etc – although a number of more useful books have been published recently, focused mainly on buy-to-let markets.

In addition, much of the information available has a very 'lifestyle' angle to it and tends to skate over the surface, looking at individual properties or attractive local vistas and leaving you little wiser about how the market works. However, most of the information available does have some value to investors as many articles will contain information on some aspect or other of the buying process. It becomes somewhat of a jigsaw, but collecting articles can help you achieve a good level of knowledge.

Despite the usefulness of this form of 'light' coverage, there is a gulf between information absorbed passively from light reading and the research that will really help you understand where and how to buy. The fact is that it will take a lot of short articles to be able to deliver the specific, often very local information that will help you to make the optimum investment. You need to source information on the numbers; how prices, taxes and demand are operating; and what market forces are at work.

Buying a house touches on a lot of subjects, with some of them, for example taxation, having the potential to be very dry. Professional property investors will make a decision based almost entirely on the financial detail of an opportunity and the surrounding market forces. Consider the value of understanding where domestic interest rates are in their cycle; are they going to rise or fall?

This means that you need to look beyond the core property media to develop a deeper understanding of the market. In fact, the UK is very well served with reliable sources of information and thanks to the wonders of the world wide web, so is everyone else.

Newspapers and Magazines

A good place to start is with broadsheet newspapers like The Financial Times or The Wall Street Journal. Not only do these publications often carry property specific news, but they will undoubtedly refer to social, political and economic developments around the globe which will affect local property markets. If interest rates are set to rise in China or property law is about to change, newspapers like this will report it in reasonable detail. Almost all good broadsheets also have excellent websites.

Additionally, most countries will have an online edition of the local English language newspaper. From the Baltics to Shanghai, a local English language newspaper is now published almost everywhere and there is no more absorbing topic than the local property market for local newspapers. Searching within the property section of a local newspaper's website will also often dredge up translations of government statistics which would otherwise lie buried in thousands of results returned by Google.

News magazines can also be useful. One of the best sources is The Economist, which regularly publishes comment on the state of the global property industry as well as more localised information. The Economist in particular is useful as it actually collates data on global property markets and many of its articles carry in depth leadership pieces on what is happening to property markets internationally. Other magazines which may be useful include weekly business journals and investment magazines.

There is also a plethora (in the UK at least) of specialist magazines on the topic of overseas property. These magazines often have a more holiday home appeal but can be useful because they publish articles on a whole range of countries and also carry adverts. Scanning through these will give you an idea of local prices and provide contacts for agents covering the area you are interested in.

NEWSPAPERS AND MAGAZINES

- The Financial Times – www.ft.com
- The Times – www.timesonline.co.uk
- The Wall Street Journal – www.wsj.com
- The International Herald Tribune – www.iht.com
- The Real Estate Journal – www.realestatejournal.com
- The Economist – www.economist.com
- Homes Overseas – www.homesoverseas.co.uk
- A Place in the Sun – www.aplaceinthesunmag.co.uk
- International Property Investor – www.ipimagazine.com
- Property Investor News – property-investor-news.com
- International Homes – www.international-homes.com

Organisations with Online Resources

There is, unfortunately, no single worldwide authority distributing information on property markets. However, many multinational institutions publish property related information, albeit at a very macroeconomic level. Nevertheless, useful information can be gathered from the World Bank (www.worldbank.org), the International Monetary Fund (www.imf.org) and the Organisation for Economic Cooperation and Development (www.oecd.org).

Other useful resources include the CIA (https://www.cia.gov/library/publications/the-world-factbook/index.html) whose fact book is always a reliable source of information on prevailing economic and social conditions and trends in a country. The US Heritage Foundation(http://www.heritage.org/research/features/index/) publishes an index of economic freedom which includes a useful country by country assessment of property rights and investment conditions. Finally, the Mercer cost of living index (www.mercer.com) gives an idea of comparative costs in different counties.

Europe is better served in terms of research than many parts of the world. The Royal Institute of Chartered Surveyors produces the annual European Housing Review which covers countries including Western Europe, Austria, Hungary and more. The RICS report draws an unimpeachably accurate picture of the property markets in each country and is available online at www.rics.org.

Government statistical websites can also be a useful source of information on the property market within a country. The National Statistical Institute of Bulgaria, for example, leads the way in Eastern Europe by analysing and translating price statistics which are then published at their website on www.nsi.bg. This degree of information is however slightly unusual and other countries may leave statistics un-translated or even uncollected.

Other excellent resources can be found by using a little lateral thinking. There are many organisations involved in various professions within the property industry and their websites can often prove useful. These include industry bodies, investment banks and financial services companies. Just because a magazine or website is aimed at people working in the real estate industry, it doesn't mean that it isn't relevant to potential investors.

Websites to check include the National Association of Realtors (www.realtor.org), and the Overseas Property Professional (www.opp.org.uk). Investment banks invest billions in global property markets and therefore conduct excellent in-depth research. Try the websites of companies such as Merrill Lynch, JP Morgan or UBS Warburg.

Last but not least, international real estate companies also publish extensive market research and analysis. This information is usually targeted and comprehensive, making it an excellent starting point for your research.

Property Investment Shows and Presentations

The UK has a number of international property shows. Each brand hosts a number of events every year and aims to cover the different areas of the UK. Details of up-coming events are available on the internet and you can also often apply for free tickets. The top events are:

The Homebuyer Show	www.homebuyer.co.uk
The Property Investors Show	www.propertyinvestor.co.uk
A Place in the Sun Live	www.aplaceinthesunlive.com

If you do decide to attend a show, try to make time for a seminar or two. The teaching sessions are run by property professionals and as well as providing useful information, there will often be time for asking questions.

Other parts of the world are less well served with international property shows but this is changing fast. It is also worth looking out for road shows and training seminars held by international property firms. Many real estate agents and property clubs also hold useful seminars which invariably have the dual objective of educating attendees as well as presenting the company's latest investment opportunities.

Next Steps

Carry out research in sufficient depth and no matter which country you are interested in, there shouldn't be anything in the transaction that takes you too much by surprise. But research will only take you so far. Ultimately you will need the support of a professional or more likely professionals. Whilst there is no logical end to research and there is no such thing as too much knowledge when you are considering spending thousands of pounds, there is a limit to the amount of information that you will be able to access as a non-professional and, in most cases, without fluency in the local language. There is also something known as 'analysis paralysis'; the condition of having so much data and information that it is impossible to know what to do. At this point, seeking out, and listening to, good independent advice is essential.

Working with Property Agents

Why Buy Through an Agent?

The authors of this book work for one of the leading international real estate companies and it is therefore unsurprising that buying through an agent is highly recommended here. However, the truth of the matter is that dealing directly with a developer or vendor carries far greater risks and has no real benefits. In the majority of cases, the services of an agent are free to purchasers. Agency fees are usually paid by the developer or seller and are not usually an addition to the price of the property. Typically, the price of a property is fixed by the vendor and if they use an agent, the cost comes out of the vendor's profit. Even in markets where buyers do contribute towards agency fees, a good agent is more than worth the cost.

THE ROLE OF ESTATE AGENTS

The role of an agent is to bring buyers and sellers together. They therefore put a great deal of effort into attracting buyers and this includes offering a wide range of services from research to after-sales care; all of which are of significant value to investors. Technically speaking, when the seller of a property pays the agent's fees, the seller is actually the customer. However, it is impossible for an agent to make money and survive without buyers, which means that they should be very keen to turn you into a loyal customer.

The concept of customer loyalty in the real estate industry is, in many ways, tied in with the investment market. With the primary residence and even holiday home markets, people complete transactions very occasionally and are more interested in the specific property than the agent they buy through. In this market, customer loyalty isn't such an issue, although every agent realises the value of reputation.

In the investment market, especially with agents that cover many countries and multiple investment options, customer loyalty is a much bigger issue. Investors will undertake many transactions throughout their lifetime and if they are confident that a particular agent is capable of providing top-notch advice and finding them the best investment opportunities, they will come back time and time again. The role of an international property agent in the investment market is somewhat akin to that of a stockbroker; helping clients make the best investments on an ongoing basis.

'The research teams of good agents will have put more resources, time, money, effort and expertise into locating the best investment properties than any lone investor could ever do'

If nothing else, agents provide access to properties that would otherwise be difficult or impossible to find. You may be able to find a project promoted directly by the developer, but you should ask why there is no agent representing them. Agents are commercial operators. The more properties they sell, the more money they make. It is a foolish agent that makes enormous effort to sell a bad property. Investors are savvy and even if an agent succeeded in selling second rate properties for a while, their reputation would soon catch up with them.

The key to a successful international agency is the ability to identify and source the best properties. Good properties sell themselves and it is far more financially rewarding for an agent to invest his effort into analysing markets and sourcing good properties than employing a hard core sales team. This may seem like a sidetrack but it is a critical point. The research teams of good agents will have put in more resource, time, money, effort and expertise into locating the best investment properties than any lone investor could ever do.

This approach has nothing to do with altruism, simply good business sense. An agency dealing in international investment properties wants to source excellent investments and sell them to their loyal customer base of property investors. Honest agents will take a long term view and will do most of the leg work to find the best property for you while making a profit for themselves.

The last few paragraphs have sung the praises of international real estate agents, and in most cases this is well deserved. However, it is a sad and unavoidable fact that some companies out there are not up to the challenge, have a short-term 'sell anything quick' attitude or are just plain dishonest. Thankfully though, they represent a minority. Property Frontiers (www.propertyfrontiers.com) is not the only international agent to operate in a way that benefits investors. There are many organisations in the marketplace whose services are also of great value. They vary from the likes of large multi-nationals such as Savills (www.savills.com) or websites like that run by E-quity (www.e-quity.com), to smaller, boutique agencies like Some Place Else (www.someplaceelse.co.uk).

We have made our argument for using a good agent, but what should an investor expect from an agent and how should you choose which agency to buy through?

What to Expect From an Agent

As discussed above, the most important thing that an agent should do is source the best investment properties. This involves conducting research into which countries, regions, cities and even streets present the best opportunity. It also involves undertaking comprehensive due diligence on the developer and answering questions such as: does the developer own the land? do they have the right licenses? do they have sufficient financial backing? and what is their track record or experience? You would be surprised the number of agents who would be unable to answer these fundamental questions.

As a result of the agent's research and background checks on a developer they will be able to provide you with detailed information on the market, the location, the property and the buying process. A good agent will provide you with this information. If they don't, ask for it. This is absolutely within the rules; any salesman worth his salt should never make you feel that you are being demanding or asking for too much information. In the UK we can be overly diffident about asking for information. American buyers have no such qualms, reasonably regarding information as a right instead of a privilege and expecting information on how comparative property is priced, local growth rates, standard of build and all of the things that are required to make you feel confident about a decision.

Your agent should also be capable of providing a packaged service. This includes being able to support and guide you through the purchase process as well as recommending or even organising currency exchange services and mortgage financing. As an example, Property Frontiers has a large "aftersales" department whose sole role is to help investors through the paper work involved with buying property and a separate division specialising in overseas mortgages. A packaged service means that you will not be abandoned as soon as you have signed on the dotted line. It is also a strong sign that your agent has the necessary connections, experience and expertise that you would expect.

WHAT TO LOOK FOR IN AN AGENT

You should also expect a good agent to give you options. They should listen to your requirements and then offer a range of suitable properties or countries, depending on your enquiry. An agent promoting a single project has a motive and indeed a need to convince you that it is the best property for you. This may well be the case, but it is difficult to judge without comparison.

Similarly, an agent focusing on just one country is more likely to skip over any negatives surrounding the market. Every market has its pros and cons and an agent who covers multiple countries will be more likely to discuss them with you openly. This doesn't mean that single country focused agents are unreliable; it simply means that they believe in the market they are selling and are going to push the benefits. An agent covering multiple countries is more able to offer a balanced review of each market. It's the difference between having markets to fit the customer and making the customer fit the market. It is a fact that different markets offer a different balance between reward and risk.

If you are looking at investing in a number of properties over a period of time, the logical step up from a packaged service is a relationship. An agent is going to want to build a relationship with you and present you with the best opportunities that come onto their books. A good agency will be able to offer you someone to effectively act as your account manager; a dedicated point of contact who will answer ongoing questions as well as present you with new opportunities.

Some agents will also offer portfolio services; effectively a formalisation of the account manager service but paid for. An agent with whom you have a good relationship will offer you the best opportunities first, but if you want them to provide advice and guidance even when you are buying a property through another agent, you will normally need to pay. Whichever level of relationship suits you, a good agent will be able to offer a service to meet your needs.

Selecting an Agent

In some cases, the agent you use is dictated by which agent is selling the property you want. However, the reliability of the agent should play as much of a role in your decision as the attractiveness of the investment opportunity as it will have an equal impact on the success of the venture.

Checking That Your Agent is Reliable. Do your research and you will be able to test whether an agent really knows their market or whether slick internet marketing is making a company seem more competent than is really the case. Can your agent answer specific questions about the country and area where you are looking? Do they know about taxes, fees and can they advise on whether you will be able to resell a property easily?

You can't reasonably expect an agent to know the answer to everything, but if they are a quality company, they will admit what they don't know, commit to finding the right answer and do so quickly.

> *'You can't reasonably expect an agent to know the answer to everything, but if they are a quality company, they will admit what they don't know'*

A good idea is to look for an agent selling a range of properties, or working in more than one country. An agent could be linked to only a few developments, and will be responsible for marketing those developments in the UK or US. If the company is focused on too limited an offering they will be forced to push you toward what they have available. It is much better to use a company offering a range of options so they can find the one that suits you.

In many countries, estate agents are regulated and it is worth looking at letterheads and other paperwork for membership of a professional body. You can also ask for details of a firm's liability insurance. A good idea in the UK is to look for an agent registered with the newly formed Association of International Property Professionals (AIPP) or the Federation of Overseas Property Developers, Agents and Consultants; an organisation which rejoices in the acronym FOPDAC.

Whether to Work with a Local or International Agent

Contacting estate agents and developers in the country where you hope to buy has some advantages. They are likely to have in-depth knowledge of the country and what is happening with the local market. Being locally based, they will also be available to show you around the area if you choose to visit the country.

On the other hand, using an agent operating from the UK, US, Ireland or your home country may have advantages. Firstly and most importantly, buyers have the potential for legal redress if an agent breaks the law or can be proved negligent. A firm based in the UK or your home country is easier to deal with – simple things such as telephone calls and receiving papers will take less time and energy.

Working from a distance can also give an agent a useful sense of perspective. An international company will be able to look at a local market with a critical eye, and if the market begins to drop, will be able to turn to an alternative area or country. In contrast, an estate agent with close links to a particular region will naturally tend to be biased. The really international companies, those that operate in several countries at a time can also advise buyers on the countries and conditions that will best suit their needs.

Inspection Trips

Advantages and Disadvantages

At their best, viewing trips offer you the chance to look at the property in context, to measure for yourself how far it is to shops and airports and to work out whether the property really does have the rental potential that the estate agent has rhapsodised about. At worst, you can feel under immense pressure to buy and may spend an acutely miserable weekend fending off a salesman trying to flog a property which is unappealing and not appropriate for your needs.

In either case, inspection trips are arranged to encourage people to buy. Companies will arrange flights and accommodation at rock bottom or subsidised prices and arrange for you to be met by a salesman or local representative based in the country you are interested in; you will then be taken on a tour of properties that fit your criteria.

INSPECTION TRIPS ARE NO HOLIDAY

While in the country you will spend almost every moment in the company of a salesman who will earn a commission if you buy. It is emphatically not worth considering an inspection trip because you feel like a cut price holiday. Quite apart from having no time for the beach, you may be lucky to have the evening meal unaccompanied. The busier the market, the worse this will be. Real estate agents in Florida have a reputation for lurking in hotel foyers hoping to lure away clients from rival companies!

Avoiding Pressure to Buy

It stands to reason that companies would not arrange viewing trips if they didn't stand to benefit. To avoid the pressure to buy, it may be better to arrange your own flights and accommodation and make up your mind in a more relaxed setting. By all means meet vendors, but arranging the trip on your own should be straightforward and may just make for a more comfortable experience as well.

If you have enough confidence in a country to buy there, you should presumably also have the confidence to explore on your own. Doing so allows you to see the less attractive areas of a country, building a three-dimensional picture. Hiring a car at the airport and finding a ski resort in the middle of the

---

'It is emphatically not worth considering an inspection trip because you feel like a cut-price holiday'

Carpathian Mountains is a daunting thought – but then, if you can't find the house or apartment, it will also be difficult for tenants.

Weaken during a buying trip, however temporarily, and you will have a contract placed in front of you. It's almost a certainty that you will get some form of hard sell. You will be told that properties are running out, that time is running out, that you have to make a decision now! Nine times out of ten, this will be an exaggeration.

When You Want to Sign a Contract on the Spot

If you have been convinced by a property whilst at home and seeing the site adds that final grain of conviction, or if there really is a queue of people clamouring to buy, you may wish to sign a contract while you are in the country. In this case you will usually be offered one of the following kinds of contract:

- A reservation contract: under this you reserve the right to buy the property for a certain period in return for payment of a relatively small deposit. If you do not sign a full contract within the specified period – usually three weeks – you will lose your deposit. This is similar to the option contracts used in the UK.
- Preliminary purchase contract. This commits you to the purchase come what may – unless, for some reason, the seller is unable to proceed. Even in that situation, whilst you will be legally entitled to recover the deposit paid, it might in practice be difficult or not cost effective to do so.

This is where having a lawyer waiting makes sense. Even in the most rushed buying conditions you can fax or email a copy of the contract to your lawyer and have them examine it for evidence that the transaction is not quite what it seems. Firms specialising in international property transactions will commit to this service whenever you need them. Of course, it's better not to allow yourself to feel hurried into a transaction in the first place, but in those rare circumstances where there really is a queue of people keen to buy – if, for example, you happened to be in Dubai during the first release of property after legal title was granted to foreigners – it's good to be prepared.

Professional Advice

Lawyers

Before choosing a property and getting caught up in the buying process, you should try to have some arrangements in place. Better to have mortgage funding in place than to find a property with fabulous investment potential and then watch it being snapped up as you stand by waiting for your bank manager to make a decision. Making preliminary contact with a lawyer will also save time and preserve you from hours spent deep in the European countryside trying to find a lawyer through the local language version of the yellow pages.

The process of seeking advice should begin before you find a property. And of all the advisors that you will need, an English speaking solicitor familiar with local conditions should be top of the shopping list. A good solicitor will ensure that the property title is sound, that you will not be liable for unpaid taxes or charges on the house and that the purchase runs smoothly.

A good lawyer should be seen as an investment, not an unnecessary indulgence. In particular, you should never sign anything until an official translation has been checked by your lawyer. Although the majority of agents are honest, if you sign a contract while unsure of the contents you may be committed to arrangements that you don't understand, which may impose unfair terms and will not be designed for your benefit.

To paraphrase Mae West, a good solicitor is hard to find. If you are looking for a lawyer in the country where you hope to buy, at the very least you should try to find someone on personal recommendation. Use an untrustworthy or negligent lawyer abroad and you may find yourself stuck with large financial liabilities, no house, and a lack of legal redress. The laws governing solicitors vary widely. In some jurisdictions lawyers may not even be obligated to keep money entrusted to them separately from their own!

International Law Firms

As a more expensive but secure alternative, a number of solicitors in the UK specialise in international property transactions; companies such as Bennett & Co (www.bennett-and-co.com) or The International Law Partnership LLP (www.lawoverseas.com) employ bilingual lawyers but are based in the UK and governed by UK law. This gives you redress under UK law should anything go wrong; firms will carry heavy indemnity insurance to protect buyers in case of any negligence. The Law Society maintains a database of English-qualified solicitors working abroad and foreign lawyers working in the UK. This can be found at www.lawsociety.org.uk; follow the link to 'choosing and using a solicitor.'

Whether you opt for a home or locally based law firm is very much a matter of preference. As is often the case, the decision boils down to the relationship between cost and risk. A local lawyer will probably be cheaper – but local law may allow you no redress in case of incompetence or negligence. How much risk you are prepared to accept is entirely up to you.

Deciding where to look for your lawyer should also be influenced by the level of risk in the market where you are looking and the amount that you are preparing to spend. As a general principle, any purchase above £50,000 may warrant using a lawyer at home, or at least using a local lawyer recommended by a credible agent. It is sometimes said that lawyers in any EU country should be reliable. Unfortunately, the distinction isn't this easy. For some reason, problems are most often reported in Spain, although this may reflect the number of transactions rather than the relative competence of Spanish lawyers.

'A good lawyer should be seen as an investment, not an unnecessary indulgence'

Aside from the greater feeling of security, international firms may offer a service better tailored to the needs of people buying across borders. Lawyers will either be bilingual or qualified translators will be kept on hand. Either way, no room will be left for ambiguity about the meaning of legal terms and responsibilities. International firms are also better placed to understand which aspects of a legal system are apt to confuse or mislead overseas buyers, and will be used to explaining the process from beginning to end.

Against this, an international firm will lack the close personal knowledge of an area that a local solicitor will provide. However, close personal knowledge can be too close and too personal; you should avoid using a lawyer recommended by or associated with a developer. One of the developments in international property has been the increased number of developers offering legal services as part of a comprehensive package. Nine times out of ten, this service is honestly meant and carried out, but no one wants to be the tenth person. Whether you look for a lawyer abroad or at home, you want to find someone who has your best interests, rather than those of the developer, at heart.

Surveyors

Taking independent advice should also extend wherever possible to having a full survey of your property. Your agent should be able to find you a surveyor working in the area. Alternatively, the Royal Institute of Chartered Surveyors publishes a database of surveyors working around the globe at www.ricsfirms. co.uk. Using the RICS database will find a qualified surveyor anywhere from Croatia to Mexico.

Surveys on new build properties are rare as few buyers choose to have them. This is often because new build properties come with a range of guarantees from the developer. In most cases these guarantees should be sufficient, but if you have any doubts a surveyor will be able to assess the materials and build standards on your behalf.

In new markets a surveyor can also be an invaluable way to learn about the market. If you are considering an off-plan purchase for example, you may feel over-dependent on the estimated completion price given by the developer. And developers looking for sales may be unduly optimistic. A qualified surveyor should be able to give you a more accurate idea of the resale value of the property. If this sum is half the price that you have been told to expect, you may want to think again.

Translators

Most international property agents will arrange notarised translations as part of the service they provide. Should you need to have contracts translated, the translated version should be notarised as an accurate copy. In most legal domains the original version will be legally binding.

Financial Advice

A surveyor can stop you buying a twenty bedroom French chateau which is actually close to becoming a twenty bedroom French heap; a translator can prevent you from signing a document which says 'I, the buyer, give all my money to the owner of this heap and expect absolutely nothing in return'. Yet there is one more advisor who may prove equally invaluable – a financial advisor.

Financial planning is an integral part of buying property and can be a complex topic. Few people will be able to pay for a property with a single lump sum, leaving the majority of buyers at the mercy of stage payments, international mortgages, currency fluctuations, varying tax regimes and more.

Financial and taxation regimes vary widely and taking advice based on your individual circumstances is critical. This is something to think about before beginning to look seriously; deciding how to share the tax burden and under whose name to register the property have significant financial implications. Most financial advisors will be able to help you plan for your domestic financing options and liabilities, but there are also firms specialising in the international market of which Blevins Franks (www.blevinsfranks.com) is the best known.

6 Financial Considerations

Part of the appeal of investing in overseas property is that it is interesting, exciting, even 'sexy.' However, when it comes down to it, it is the relatively dull aspects of finance which determine the success of the venture. Considerations of financing, exchange rates and taxation can make the difference between profit and serious financial headaches.

The reality is, however, that with a little forethought the financial aspects of investing abroad can be taken care of quickly and simply. The three areas that need consideration are; being aware of the additional costs involved (both in terms of upfront costs and taxation); making adequate provisions for currency risks; and selecting the best financing option.

Calculating the Final Rather Than the Asking Price

Most experts advise adding 10% to your budget in order to cover taxes, fees and unexpected expenses. However, making general assumptions of the cost is dangerous. Underestimating the costs could mean that you have to find extra money for the purchase once you have committed. This could be difficult, especially if the amounts involved are in the thousands. Equally, overestimating the costs could mean that you pass up an excellent opportunity because you assumed the purchase costs were higher than they were in reality.

Broad percentage estimates are simply not good enough and aren't actually necessary. Any agent will be able to give you an accurate breakdown of the costs involved and you should request this if it is not volunteered. Some of these costs, such as stamp duty will often be derived from a fixed percentage of the property value. Others however will be fixed fees, regardless of the property price.

The best approach is to have a list of all potential, additional costs and write down the actual figures for the property in question. If you have access to Microsoft Excel or another spreadsheet programme use this as it will enable you to easily calculate the absolute values of percentage costs and to add all of the costs together. Holding the information in a spreadsheet makes it easier to compare the total costs of several investment opportunities at once.

As a guideline, the list below shows many of the potential additional purchase costs that you may encounter.

- Stamp duty/purchase tax
- Agent's fees
- Lawyer's fees
- Translation fees
- Survey fees
- Mortgage arrangement fees
- Notarisation fees
- Travel costs
- Bank set-up fees
- Currency transaction fees

Financing Your Purchase

When it comes down to it, you only have two options for financing your overseas property investment; use your own money or someone else's, such as the bank or even the developer themselves. As we saw earlier in the book, gearing your investment by using the bank's money to finance your investment is the ideal situation as it reduces your cash requirements and actually improves your return on investment from a capital gains perspective. If you decide not to use your own money to finance your purchase then there are three options available.

1. To raise a mortgage on the property you want to buy.
2. To re-mortgage against another property that you own in your own country.
3. To find a property where the developer is offering delayed stage payments.

International Mortgages: Raising a Local Mortgage Against your Investment

In many ways, raising a local mortgage for your property is ideal. One of the main benefits of financing your purchase this way is that your borrowing and repayments will be in the same currency as your rental income meaning that currency fluctuations will have no impact on your ability to make repayments.

Having the mortgage abroad will also make you feel more secure as your home assets will be left out of the equation. This creates a balance between assets (the property) and liabilities (mortgage debt) which is important. If you fall behind on payments the investment property is the only asset placed at risk.

However, in many countries the mortgage market simply won't be developed enough for you to be able to get a mortgage there. Mortgages might not be available to foreigners (or even at all). If mortgages are available they may have restrictive lending criteria or prohibitive interest rates.

Outside the Eurozone, where interest rates are around 4.5%, most places have higher rates than the UK or US. In places such as South Africa and Ghana rates are often around 11%. Rates like this will heavily erode any rental income. Lending conditions are also tighter. The amount that will be lent will often be less than in more established markets. Typically, banks will lend no more than 80% of the property value, although this is changing as the overseas mortgage market becomes more established. Repayment terms will also be shorter than the 25 to 30 years that many investors are used to. Often, repayment terms will be between 10 and 15 years – again, though, this is changing as overseas property investment becomes more common. This significantly increases the cost of monthly repayments. There are often restrictive age limits on lending, making it difficult for anyone over the age of 60 to borrow.

As a general rule, the more 'emerging' a market, the less likely it is to have a developed mortgage system. Buyers can easily borrow in order to buy in Western Europe, the US, Australia and parts of the Caribbean, but in countries outside of these areas it can often be a different story. A first step to finding out whether mortgages are available in the country you want to purchase in is to ask an agent dealing with that area. Agents realise the value of mortgage financing to investors and will be very keen to let you know when it is available.

Alternatively, there are some financial services companies which specialise in arranging mortgage finance overseas. It is worth speaking to them as they sometimes manage to arrange special deals on mortgage financing in countries where it is not usually available to foreigners. Frontiers Financial Services can organise financing in over thirty countries including Australia, Canada, the Caribbean, Cyprus, France, Greece, Ireland, Italy, Malta, New Zealand, Portugal, South Africa, Spain and the US. You can find out more by visiting their web site at www.frontiersfs.com.

Countries where it is possible to borrow locally include:

Albania, Andorra, Australia, Austria, Belgium, Bosnia, Bulgaria, Canada, Caribbean, China, Croatia, Cyprus, Czech Republic, Estonia, Finland, France, Germany, Ghana, Greece, Holland, Hong Kong, Hungary, India, Ireland, Israel, Italy, Latvia, Malaysia, Malta, Montenegro, Morocco, New Zealand, Panama, Philippines, Poland, Portugal, Romania, Serbia, Slovakia, Slovenia, South Africa, Spain, Sweden, Switzerland, Turkey, UAE, USA. There are more being added all the time.

Advantages of a Developing Mortgage Market

A developing mortgage market is one of the most reliable indicators that a country is on the way up. Without a developed mortgage market there is a limit to how far prices can climb. Where there is no mortgage market, the majority of transactions are in cash, purchasing power remains low, and prices stay artificially low.

There are still many countries where interest rates are prohibitive and there is little legislative backup for a mortgage market. In Brazil, for example, interest rates can be as high as 38% and repayment terms are generally short enough so that monthly instalments are higher than rental income. Little wonder that so many buyers choose alternative financing methods! Some developers are beginning to introduce developer financing, however, and a mortgage market is likely to be introduced within the next few years, so those who are able to buy through other means will benefit greatly from the additional demand which this will create.

Turkey is another good example of a mortgage market which is about to take off. Previously, interest rates have been as high as 22.5% and repayment terms were 60 months for loans in lira and 180 months for loans in foreign currency. Only 3% of purchases in Turkey are currently made with the help of residential loans. However, in January 2008 a new mortgage law is due to come into force which will open up the market to new types of investor with mortgages now available over 30 years.

Re-Mortgaging to Finance an Overseas Investment

Another option is to re-mortgage your home or other properties that you own in your country of residence. This has become relatively common practice in countries like the UK and US where house prices have risen dramatically giving people access to large amounts of equity.

The advantages to this approach are that you will be able to arrange finance before you find a property abroad, meaning that you will be ready to proceed when necessary. You are also likely to have an established credit rating and be familiar with the borrowing process making it far less complicated than raising finance abroad. There is also the issue of interest rates which in the UK and US are relatively low. Because you will be borrowing against the value of an existing property, you may also be able to finance 100% of the purchase cost of the overseas property, giving you 100% gearing.

The downside of borrowing at home is that you may be exposing your main residence to risk if you fail to meet your repayments. There is also the currency risk. If you are letting out the overseas property, you will most likely be receiving rental income in the local currency. However, your repayments will be in your domestic currency. As the values fluctuate between the two, your rental income may drop relative to your mortgage repayments, making it harder to meet the repayments.

Whether you raise finance domestically or internationally is a personal decision which should be made in light of careful consideration of all of the benefits and risks. If you are unsure which option suits your needs best, speak to a professional financial advisor who can help ensure that you make the right decision.

Developer Financing

A potential alternative to mortgage financing to watch out for is developer financing. In areas where finding a mortgage can be difficult, some larger developers may offer financing or deferred payment schemes. Confident developers may agree to take money in regular instalments, bringing apartments and villas within the reach of more people. To all intents and purposes developer financing works like a mortgage although developers don't always charge interest.

Deferred payment schemes are different from stage payments. Stage payments are a limited form of financing where you pay for the property in stages until it is completed and you take ownership. Deferred payment schemes include stage payments but the stages continue well beyond the completion of the building. A typical deferred payment scheme would allow you to pay chunks of the property price at regular intervals over a seven year period even though the property is completed and you are given ownership within two years.

Developer financing is of course a marketing strategy that helps the developer sell more properties. In instances where the developer doesn't openly charge interest on the deferred payments, you may find that they have added a premium to the purchase price. Check this by comparing similar properties without developer financing. Adding a premium for this form of payment plan is perfectly reasonable and should be expected, just make sure that the premium isn't excessive and you are not paying over the odds.

TIPS FOR FINANCING A PROPERTY

1. If you are arranging finance on the property, ensure that this is stated in any contract and you have an 'opt-out clause' if the loan is not agreed (which will ensure any deposit paid is refunded).
2. Have mortgage financing arranged before agreeing to purchase, or before signing contracts and paying a deposit. This will help you to avoid delays and difficulties should your application be rejected.
3. Open a bank account in your chosen country and ensure you get a Certificate of Importation for the money you bring in from your home country. This will make repatriation of funds much easier.
4. Set up standing orders in a local bank account to meet bills and taxes. Failure to pay your taxes in some countries, such as France, Portugal and Spain, could lead to court action and possible seizure of your property.
5. Consider using a specialist overseas mortgage broker – this will be invaluable when dealing with the red tape associated with foreign banks and as previously mentioned they will be able to negotiate better rates and terms.

Currency and Foreign Exchange

People often underestimate the impact of currency fluctuations, but it is worth remembering that movements in exchange rates can turn profit into loss very quickly. However, it is also worth remembering that it can equally turn a loss into a profit.

Currency markets are an investment opportunity in themselves and you should always consider the impact of currency movements when evaluating a property investment. As an example, between July 2006 and June 2007, the pound rose from €1.4500 to over €1.5120 euros and then back again to €1.4680. This meant that a property costing the euro equivalent of £200,000 in July 2006 fluctuated in value by almost £13,000 in less than a year, purely as a result of currency movements.

'Always remember that movements in exchange rates can turn profit into loss very quickly'

An extreme example of a currency where investors have made substantial profits is the Chinese currency, the RMB. For some years the RMB was pegged to the US dollar at a rate which kept the value of the currency artificially low. This made Chinese goods significantly cheaper in global markets than would otherwise be the case. In July 2005 the Chinese government removed the peg, associating the RMB instead with a basket of currencies composed of euros, yuan, other Asian currencies and the dollar and allowing the value of the currency to float based on market supply and demand. As of May 2007, the RMB was trading at over 7 yuan to the dollar, a 7.5% increase since the removal of the peg. It is still frequently suggested that the currency is undervalued, and analysts initially predicted rises of up to 40% relative to other currencies in ten years. This would present an excellent opportunity to international property investors who invest in property in China, with a possibility of seeing the value of their property rise in value by up to 40% in pound or dollar terms even if the price in RMB doesn't change at all.

Knowing where currencies are going to move would be an extraordinary gift, but international money markets are complicated and it would be very difficult for ordinary investors to predict currency movements. These sorts of considerations are best left to the experts, but the good news is that there is an entire industry whose job it is to monitor currency movements and their services are readily available to international property investors.

When you purchase abroad you will need to transfer currency from your home country to the country you are buying in. You could use your bank to do this but you are unlikely to get a good rate of exchange. The sensible option is to use a currency broker such as HIFX (www.hifx.co.uk), Currencies Direct (www.currenciesdirect.com) or Moneycorp (www.moneycorp.com). Not only will these companies be able to save you thousands of pounds by offering a better exchange rate at the time of transfer, they will also be able to offer a range of associated services from advice on future currency movements to hedging currency risk.

Currency Brokers publish research on potential currency movements and will be able to help you understand what is likely to happen to the currency of the country in which you want to buy a property. They will also help you plan the best means of transferring money between your home country and the country in which you are investing. Depending on which way the currency you want to buy is moving, they will recommend when to buy the currency that you need. They will also provide the option of a forward contract where you book the currency now at an agreed exchange rate using a deposit of around 10% of the amount of currency you want to buy. This can be a very good option when you have stage payments to pay. For example, imagine that you are buying a home in Thailand and that the value of the Baht is rising against the pound – meaning that the price of your property will cost more in sterling. The purchase price has to be handed over in three months time. Under a forward contract you could agree to buy the Baht at today's exchange rate, or tomorrow's, or whenever your broker thinks the optimum exchange rate is available. After paying the deposit, whether the Baht continues to rise is a matter of supreme disinterest as in three months time the money will be delivered at the rates agreed. You can fix exchange rates in this way up to two years in advance.

If you are transferring money between countries regularly, for example for mortgage payments, transfer fees can be an unpleasant surprise. Bank fees can be as high as £50 for a single transfer and with little regard for the size of the transaction. In this case it may be worth looking at a regular transfer plan. HIFX offers regular transfer plans which reduce the transaction costs and can be used for mortgage payments or even for transferring your state pension payments overseas if you live abroad.

Taxation of Overseas Property

Taxes vary widely from country to country and unless you are planning to make a permanent move overseas, owning property abroad may have implications for your taxation liabilities at home. Tax filing dates, procedures and requirements may vary widely and penalties for making a mistake can be severe.

This makes the need to seek specialist advice doubly important. Wherever you buy, you will need to take advice on local taxation and the implications for your tax status at home. The information below highlights some potential issues, but professional advice from a qualified tax expert should always be sought.

'Taxation can make the difference between a rewarding investment and a pocket-emptying plunge'

Taxation can make the difference between a rewarding investment and a pocket-emptying plunge. This means that the level of taxation is one of the invisible driving forces behind the dispersal of buyers across different property markets. For example, higher rate income tax in Germany is 45%; Slovakia has a flat tax of 19%. Investment conditions in Germany would have to be very strong to compensate for the tax burden.

MAIN TAX CONSIDERATIONS

- How will any gain on the property be taxed in the country you wish to invest in?
- How will rental income be taxed? Is there a minimum tax on rental income? Is there a withholding tax?
- What is the level of inheritance tax?
- Are there any other local taxes to consider? These could include purchase taxes, annual rates (for example, the UK council tax) and annual wealth tax (countries with this include France, Spain and Greece – although many countries are now in the process of abandoning the wealth tax).
- Will any profits be taxable in your home country?

Forms of Taxation

There are several forms of taxation with the potential to make life seem very rosy or very blue for property investors. Some taxes are easy to calculate and your estate agent should be able to give you a good idea of the fees attached to buying in any particular country. Stamp duty, for example, is calculated as a percentage of the purchase price and is correspondingly easy to work out.

Other taxes are harder to calculate. Capital gains and income tax on renting can swallow up money like a starved boa constrictor but these taxes will depend on the amount of money made during the period of ownership. Reporting taxes in a foreign jurisdiction and working out which allowances apply is a matter for a specialised accountant. This is something else that will have to be factored into your costs.

Taxes can also impact on people in a way that they don't expect. Some countries operate a withholding tax, where a tenant is obliged to keep back tax on the payment of rent when the landlord is overseas. This can be levied at rates of over 20% creating problems for landlords dependent on rental income for interest payments or mortgages. Other jurisdictions, Spain for example, levy a wealth tax. In Spain this is collected annually on a sliding scale between 0.2% and 2.5% depending on the value of your property.

Capital Gains

Capital gains are a charge on profit made whenever a company or individual sells an asset to someone else and makes a profit. Capital gains are levied on all sorts of goods, from paintings to stocks, although many countries operate a dispensation on homes used as a primary residence. In the UK capital gains depends on your status as a tax-payer. Capital gains tax is charged at whatever your highest rate of tax is, up to 40%, and everyone has a capital gains allowance. In the tax year 2007–8 this is £9,200.

However, if the property you own abroad is an investment, the dispensation given on primary residences will not be available to you. This means that when you sell the property you may be liable for some form of capital gains tax.

The rate of capital gains tax and how it is calculated can vary significantly from country to country. Some countries offer taper relief which reduces the amount of capital gains owed for each year that you own the property. These sorts of schemes are often in place where governments are trying to stop rampant speculation in the property market.

Capital gains tax is usually charged against profit, but what is defined as profit will vary. Some countries may define the capital gain as the difference between the purchase price and selling price, whilst others may make allowances for other costs incurred such as purchase costs, selling costs and even property maintenance.

Income Tax

Income tax will be charged against rental income. The rate of tax will vary from country to country and may also vary according to the amount of income you make. In many countries, foreigners will be entitled to the same income tax allowances as locals. This means that you pay no income tax on some of your rental income, but then pay increasingly higher levels of tax on amounts of income above and beyond pre-defined thresholds.

You will also need to understand any allowances on offer to off-set against your income. Some tax departments will tax you on your gross rental income, whilst others will allow you to deduct some costs such as mortgage interest, maintenance and even travel before taxing you on the net remaining income.

Inheritance Tax

Inheritance or death taxes can be particularly problematic for overseas property holders. Some countries have very high death taxes and it is also worth considering inheritance laws as in many countries, property doesn't automatically pass to your next of kin. You will almost certainly find that your existing will is insufficient and that you will need to make a local will for all the assets you own abroad.

For countries where inheritance rules for property are against your interest, the usual response is to buy through a wholly-owned company. Even if this overcomes local inheritance and taxation issues, you should also be aware of the taxation of your estate in your home country. For everyone domiciled and resident in the UK, inheritance tax may be payable on your total worldwide assets.

Double Taxation

Many people select a country in which to invest based upon its attractive tax environment. However, this approach often overlooks the fact that whilst there may be no taxation in the country in which you are buying, it doesn't mean that you don't owe tax at home. A classic example of this is Dubai, where there are no capital gains or income taxes of any kind. People buy in Dubai for this very reason, perhaps choosing it as a preferential place to invest over a country such as Bulgaria where capital gains tax is 15%.

The problem that many people don't realise is that their total tax liability is likely to be the same in both circumstances. If you are domiciled in the UK or US, the Revenue is likely to want to take a slice of any capital gains you make in Dubai or Bulgaria at your usual rate. If your usual rate of capital gains tax is 40% then you will pay 40% capital gains tax on the gain you make in Dubai or Bulgaria. The only difference being that, as long as a double taxation treaty between your country of domicile and Bulgaria exists, you would pay 15% capital gains tax in Bulgaria for which you would be given a tax credit in your own country to reduce your liability there to 25%. Either way you end up paying the full 40%.

DOMESTIC TAX LIABILITY

Many international investors are entirely unaware of their domestic tax liabilities resulting from overseas property. This is very dangerous as a failure to accurately declare your interests could be seen as evasion. It is essential that you take appropriate advice and report all of your activities as necessary, both at home and abroad.

For all that has been said above, it is important to be aware of the existence of double taxation treaties. These treaties are formulated between governments to ensure that you are not taxed twice on the same slice of income. If you invest in a country where there is no double taxation treaty you may find yourself paying both local tax and domestic tax. If there is a double taxation treaty in place you will be given a tax credit for paying the tax locally and therefore only need to pay the difference in your home country.

The UK has more than 100 bilateral double-tax treaties, the largest network in the world and agreed with countries from Uzbekistan to Myanmar. Worldwide, there are more than 1300 double-taxation treaties. The treaties work to the advantage of countries as well as individuals. Companies are more confident about trading overseas if they know that they won't be taxed twice.

If the UK doesn't have a double-taxation agreement with the country where you own property, UK tax payers may be entitled to special relief called 'unilateral relief' or to something called a foreign tax deduction. Your local tax office should be able to give you more advice about whether you are eligible for this relief.

PART II

INVESTMENT POTENTIAL OF INDIVIDUAL COUNTRIES

Introduction

Readers should now have a range of ideas and frameworks for analysing both markets and investment opportunities. In Part II we examine 33 different property markets to make assessments of their attractiveness as property investment destinations.

Each country profile looks at the range of specific factors which make that country a good investment option or, in some cases, a bad investment option. Whilst we comment on the opportunity in each country, telling people where or where not to invest is not the objective. These 33 examples are practical applications of the theory discussed in Part I. The idea being to show by example what to look for in a market so that similar characteristics can be identified when analysing any market of your choice. It is also worth emphasising that we are not tipping every country we discuss. Featuring in this section is not necessarily an endorsement.

We have not hidden our opinions on each of the markets we discuss. If we believe there are good investment opportunities we say so. If we believe the market has had its day, we say that too. The commentary on each country therefore reflects our own opinions. Some may disagree. After all, in most cases our opinions are based on economic analysis and it is well known that finding two economists with the same opinion on anything is a difficult challenge. We are confident in our opinions nevertheless. There are of course no certainties and we do not carry crystal balls, but the following comments have been written from the point of view of where we would invest our own money. We can do nothing more than that.

Omissions

Many readers may look at the 33 countries chosen to feature here and wonder why some countries are missing. We are aware that there are some 'obvious' omissions. However, this book like any other has practical limitations and cannot cover everything. The final list was chosen not because the countries are the most popular with investors, but because they give a good range of examples. As was stated at the beginning of the book, its aim is to be more fishing rod than fish; to provide a basis of understanding that allows you to make your own analysis of your country of interest whether it is featured here or not.

Future Editions and More Information

The information contained herein will date quickly. Laws change, events happen and markets move. Therefore, there is a practical lifetime to the accuracy of the information in each of the country profiles. To overcome this, updates to the book will be published by way of future, updated editions and also through the book's website **www.aninvestorsguide.com** and on The Property Frontiers Website **www.propertyfrontiers.com**. Both the websites and future editions will expand the range of countries covered as well as the depth of information on each of those countries.

If the country or area of a country you are interested in is not covered in this edition, you may be able to purchase a profile online or request its inclusion in the next edition of *Where to Buy Property Abroad – An Investor's Guide*, by emailing info@propertyfrontiers.com

Guide to the Risk and Opportunity Ratings

At the end of each country profile, we have given a risk rating and an opportunity rating. These ratings are a summary of our analysis indicating the levels of risk when investing in a market and the level of opportunity to profit from it.

The ratings themselves are simple. Both work on a scale of one to five. The opportunity rating is indicated by the $ symbol. A single $ equals a low opportunity whilst 5 of them ($ $ $ $ $) equals the highest opportunity ranking.

For risk we have used the △ symbol. A ranking of △ equals a low risk rating whilst △ △ △ △ △ equals the highest risk rating.

Contacts

For contact telephone numbers and websites of financial advisors, lawyers, currency services, media resources and for general information on individual countries see the Contacts List in the Appendix.

Albania

CURRENCY
Leke (ALL)

Exchange rates:
1000 ALL = £5.50
£1 = 180.84
1000 ALL = US $11
US $1 = 88.88ALL

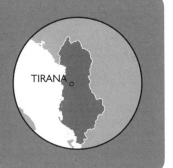

TIRANA o

Introduction

Albania has a rich and complex history and its people are believed by academics to be descended directly from ancient Illyrian tribes. It is a country of beautiful and relatively untouched natural landscapes, with vast sand beaches along its Mediterranean coastline, dramatic mountain ranges, lakes and thickly wooded countryside. Heritage sites dating back to Roman, Ancient Greek and Illyrian civilisations can be found throughout and grace the country with an authenticity and rich cultural history.

An independent nation since 1912, Albania has a population of 3.2 million people bordered by Greece, Kosovo, Macedonia and Montenegro. In the mid 1900s, the government decided to become self-sufficient and refused to take any further aid or interact with other developing nations. As the country became more isolated the reforms began to founder. Technology became dated, the economy failed and by the late 1980s much of the population was living in poverty. The country became increasingly backward in relation to its European neighbours and both governmental and social infrastructures had begun to break down.

A series of reforms implemented after the collapse of the Soviet system in 1990 brought limited investment from overseas, gave more freedom to the population and allowed political expression. At this time a quarter of the Albanian workforce, including many professionals, emigrated abroad. Several years of instability followed as the country struggled to come to terms with these new systems and it wasn't until 1992 that things began to change. The first democratically elected government took power, this was quickly followed by the opening up of the country's economy and overtures towards western nations for help with reconstruction. Since then, funding from prosperous countries has allowed Albania to move towards a more developed economy.

> *'Undoubtedly risky markets can be areas in which the greatest gains can be made and early investors could do well if the economy develops'*

Though there is still work to be done, the country has seen increased investment from overseas companies and public bodies and is experiencing a construction boom. The European Bank for Reconstruction and Development has secured at least €1bn for development and there are plans for improvement of infrastructure, including new roads, ports and the modernisation of Tirana International airport. The government has also agreed to tackle corruption, strengthen the public sector and complete an overhaul of financial systems. Standards of living have improved markedly, GDP rose by just over 5% in 2006 and the country is working towards EU entry in 2014.

Tourist numbers are still low but were expected to show growth of just over 5% in 2007. Tourism accounts for over 13% of the country's expected GDP and is predicted to continue to grow by at least 5% year on year until 2017.

Is This a Good Place to Buy?

Whether Albania is a good investment really comes down to your attitude to risk. It is a new and untested market in a country that has only seen a short period of social and political stability and democracy. Unemployment is still high at around 15% and around 10% of the population still live on less than $2 per day. The present government was elected somewhat controversially and a black market economy thrives, as does organised crime. The recent introduction of mortgages to Albania is partially responsible for sparking the current construction boom but, so far, less private foreign investment than predicted is entering the country. It may not, therefore, suit those who have a more cautious attitude towards investment.

Undoubtedly, risky markets can be areas in which the greatest gains can be made and early investors could do well if the economy develops as well as other eastern European countries have done. However, Albania is starting from a lower base a long-term view is needed. Prices are generally still low by developed, and even many emerging market standards and there is great untapped commercial and tourist potential in the country. The prospect of EU membership is already bringing a great number of benefits but there is still a lot to be done.

Price History

Historically property was owned collectively due to the Communist government directive and much of what was available would not suit a contemporary investor. There is, therefore, no reliable data as yet on price fluctuations, though there are claims by property agents that prices have risen by as much as 30% per annum in the past three to four years. Currently property in new and off-plan developments is selling from around €24,000 and average prices of land are around €50 to €150 per square metre, depending on location and whether planning permission has been granted. Prices in Tirana were forecast by some professionals to continue to increase by as much as 30% in 2007.

Which Type of Property Should You Go For?

Very little exists for the overseas investor outside of new-build. There is not the historic or rural housing stock present in other countries. This leaves two areas of investment: new-build developments and land. For those interested in speculation or longer-term investment, land may be the better option, though a shortage is starting to be seen in and around Tirana and prices are rising.

INSIDER TIP

New apartments are becoming targets for investors hoping to cash in on early growth. They mainly take the form of buy-to-lets for local residents and foreign workers in the capital or accommodation aimed at tourists nearer to the coast.

Hotspots

Tirana

Once a sombre Communist cradle, Tirana has woken up and is becoming more lively as former citizens return from overseas and employees of multinationals and official organisations move in. It does not have the picturesque charms of many other European capitals but it is home to some imposing grand public spaces, large open boulevards, squares and parks. It is also surrounded by beautiful mountains and the Saint Prokopi national park.

Tirana is a university town and has a large, low-cost workforce that may prove attractive to western employers. The range and quality of shops, restaurants and bars has improved greatly in recent years, which should help the rental market. Some developers expect this to provide at least 5% yields in the future.

Currently, there is a construction boom in progress as developers and investors anticipate global interest in property. According to some sources, appreciation is expected to reach around 30% per annum, though more conservative agents are predicting 10-15%. Prices are generally low by capital city standards, with property selling on average around €40,000 for one bedroom and €55,000 for two-bedroom apartments in the new business districts. Prices can be as low as €27,000 depending on style, quality and location of build but in more sought-after residential suburbs costs are higher, with price per square metre averaging around €1,500. In such areas, one should expect to pay upwards of around €120,000 for a two-bedroom apartment. Some developers are predicting the market will offer buy-to-let owners a return of at least 5%.

Vlore

Vlore is the second most important port in Albania and the site of a great deal of excitement among Albanian agents and developers. Orikum Bay is one main area of tourist development and the town is the gateway to the coastal road, also being called the Albanian Riviera, which takes you through quaint villages and along the largely unspoilt Mediterranean coastline. There are large numbers of old-style high-rise blocks, but new hotels and restaurants are appearing. Property for sale in new apartment blocks ranges from around €25,000 to €60,000 for one or two bedrooms with sea views. Currently the tourist trade comes mainly from locals and people from the border areas of Kosovo and Macedonia.

Durres

A busy port city that also has large, golden sand beaches, it is currently being touted as a new holiday resort. Some new-build is happening here and one or two resort-style developments are in the planning stages. Prices are higher than other areas and start at around €50,000. Villas are more common here too with prices for some off-plan property fixed around €207,000.

The Purchase Process

There are no restrictions on foreign ownership, however, non-nationals may not own land registered as agricultural and will only be approved to buy building land if they intend to construct a property that will triple the value of the initial purchase. These rules do not apply to companies however, meaning some buyers set up their own companies in order to open up their investment options.

It is important to insist that your lawyer shows you all documentation relating to the condition, situation and ownership of the property in your first language, especially confirmation that the title to a property is clean. The first step of the sale is to draw up a contract between buyer and seller. This is known as a purchase or notary deed, stipulating all the conditions of sale, including the purchase price, a definitive explanation of the property being bought and completion date. The deed is signed by both parties in the presence of a notary. A certificate from the Real Estate Registration Office, which certifies that the vendor is offering the property with clean title deeds must also be presented. Unless a future date is requested, the property changes hands on the date of the signing of the purchase deed and the full purchase price is transferred to the vendor. The new ownership of the property should then be registered with the Real Estate Registration Office.

Unless buying land, the majority of overseas purchases are likely to be off-plan through developers, and individual contracts and payment plans may vary. There is no transfer tax or stamp duty in Albania but you will need to allow for notary fees of up to 1%.

Mortgages

Albania is a developing market so mortgages too are in their early stages. 80% LTV mortgages are currently available over a term of 20 years at interest rates of 9%. Interest only options are also available for up to 3 years.

Key Risks and Opportunities

Despite the movement of the market being generally upward, buyers should exercise caution with regard to investing in Albania at present. It is still a heavily rural and underdeveloped country. The legal system is not subject to European regulations and investors are not necessarily scrutinised by the government. Organised crime and a black market economy still thrive, despite government attempts to crack down. Property buyers should ensure that their developer has a history of good trading.

There are also issues with land ownership as not all land is available for foreign ownership. Often there is no clear owner and no standard framework for settling a dispute legally. In urban areas land plots have been designated for building purposes and buyers, or their lawyers, should check town plans carefully to ensure the plot has permission for building. In addition, due to the country's Communist status, all property was state owned until 1992 meaning much of the property and land that passed into private hands has still not been registered with the Real Estate Registration Office.

Under Communism much of Albania's industry operated outside UN regulations. As a result inspectors have allegedly issued warnings that certain plants and surrounding areas need cleaning up as they are posing a threat to public and environmental health.

The neighbouring state of Kosovo, a home to many ethnic Albanians, is seeking independence from Serbia and, though not directly involving Albania, the unstable situation may lead to unrest in this region of the Balkans.

On the plus side, the country offers 250 miles of Mediterranean coastline and a rich collection of historic monuments. With tourists now seeking increasingly unusual and exotic destinations, Albania may soon become a more established location for tourists. Many observers liken areas of the country and coast to Greece or Croatia and according to the World Travel and Tourism Council, Albania is a 'middle-tier, middle-income' destination. Tourism demand is expected to grow steadily at 5% per year until 2017 – not an especially high figure but considering that tourist infrastructure is not yet in place and there is a lack of familiarity with the region, visitor numbers have the potential to increase dramatically in the future.

Opportunity Rating

Much of the growth in Albania today could be fuelled by speculation, despite there being a great deal of foreign investment in the country. Prices are low compared to other developed nations, which is an appealing prospect for many buyers. However, entry level to the market seems high in relation to what local people earn and to some observers it may seem overpriced for such a young and untested market.

This doesn't mean there is not the potential for reasonable, steady returns. For the right investor, Albania offers an excellent opportunity for someone to buy into a growing economy at ground level. Should EU membership be granted it could be a very canny investment but prices are rising fast so the window of opportunity may already be narrowing.

Rating: $$

Risk Rating

The political and economic situation offers uncertainties that may make it too much of a risk for some investors. In addition, the lack of registration of land titles, the corruption that may be present in certain industries and an untested market for tourism should make investors take advice before buying.

Rating: ⚠ ⚠ ⚠ ⚠

The Baltics

LATVIA: Currency: Lat
Exchange rates
100 Lats = £95.86   £1 = 1.04 Lat
100 Lats = US $191   US $1 = 0.52 Lats
LITHUANIA: Currency: Litas
EXCHANGE RATES
100 Litas = £19.51   £1 = 5.12 Litas
100 Litas = US $38.90   US $1 = 2.57 Litas
ESTONIA: Currency: Kroon
EXCHANGE RATES
100 Kroon = £4.30   £1 = 23.23 Kroon
100 Kroon = US $8.58   US $1 = 11.64 Kroon

Introduction

The Baltic states (Latvia, Lithuania and Estonia) are one of the most sought after investment markets of the moment.

The capital cities of Riga, Vilnius and Tallinn are particularly popular with buyers looking to combine capital appreciation with regular rental income over the medium to long term.

Part of the Baltics' appeal is that they combine all of the preconditions for a strong property market. The Baltics compete with Slovakia to be crowned as the greatest economic success of the 2004 accession states; the population is getting richer, mortgages are available on attractive terms and fees and taxes are low. The quality of build is also extremely high.

As well as long-term lets to locals, the three capitals also have a strong short let market. The historic centres of all three Baltic capitals are listed as Unesco world heritage sites and are on the short-breaks circuit. Vilnius is due to be the European City of Culture in 2009.

Vilnius has Gothic, Renaissance and Baroque buildings whilst Riga stands out for art nouveau architecture and Tallinn has an astonishingly attractive medieval old town. Ryanair and EasyJet both fly to the Baltics from the UK and visitor numbers are rising steadily. The Baltic States are described by The World Travel and Tourism Council as each being a 'fast growing travel and tourism economy'. During 2007, tourism rates were expected to grow by an average of 5.36% across the region and between 2008 and 2017, by an average of 6.26% per annum in real terms.

This combination of factors translates into high demand: so much so that developers have been known to raise prices 30% between the two releases of the same development.

Is This a Good Place to Buy?

The Baltics offer rewards and economic growth comparable to Asia, but in a safe and cleverly regulated environment. For investors, this means capital appreciation without risk, and as a result, foreign investment has increased dramatically.

The Baltics can be pretty and the capitals of Vilnius, Tallinn and Riga very attractive indeed, but economic factors are what usually induce people to buy.

Such advantages include European Union and NATO membership and currencies already pegged to the Euro, thereby preventing the risk of currency fluctuations. Financially the conditions in the Baltics are generally good with healthy GDP growth and low interest rates (e.g. Riga 4.5%). In Latvia there is no capital gains tax on a property held in private hands for more than a year and in Lithuania capital gains tax is exempt after three years.

'The Baltics offer rewards and economic growth comparable to Asia, but in a safe and cleverly regulated environment. For investors, this means capital appreciation without risk.'

Locals have been able to buy apartments since the beginning of the 1990s, and property prices subsequently increased 1000% by 2000 and are continuing to rise at staggering rates. Riga topped Knight Frank's Global House Price League for the second year in a row in early 2007 with an annualised price growth of an amazing 61.2%. But Latvia was not alone at the top of the league table with Estonia (Tallinn) taking second place with an annualised price growth of 24.5% and Lithuania (Vilnius) commanding third place with growth of 21.7%. Indications suggest that this high growth rate is not sustainable in the long term and transactions although still very high have begun to slow.

Research departments at the larger real estate companies find that demand in the Baltics is still climbing. This confidence is echoed in the markets. Because prices are rising fast, developers will occasionally raise their asking prices. This practice is likely to stop with the slowdown of the market. Some of the valuations are unrealistic and will price locals out of the market. Developments offering units at elevated prices often differ little, if at all, from cheaper developments. It is therefore important to look around and choose something that offers genuine value.

Although the Baltics are still considered by some to be a hot residential investment, the extensive capital appreciation which has characterised the market in recent years means apartment ownership in the capital cities is now as expensive as in Copenhagen, Helsinki and Stockholm. While the Baltics' continued GDP growth is only positive, (Latvia showed a very healthy GDP of 10.7% in the first quarter of 2007) one trend is worrying for investors – rental yields are falling.

In Tallinn property prices rose from Dec 2004 to Dec 2006 at an amazing 79% yet in the same period rents did not increase proportionally, rising only 18% (according to Global Property Guides estimates). Tallinn's average rental yields have therefore fallen significantly from about 8.47% to an average of only 5.77%. This same pattern can be seen in Riga where prices rose from Aug 2004–Dec 2006 138%, yet rents increased only 54% giving an average fall from 7.85% return to 5.04%. In Lithuania where the country's growth started later, the price increase from Jan 2005 to the end of 2006 was 83.5%, yet rents only grew by 27% so reducing the yield from 6.45% pa to 4.39%.

Price History

The market in the Baltics opened up in 2003, with prices for central apartments rising more than 10% and significantly more in Riga. In 2004 the market picked up with prices asked for new build property increasing 25%. During 2006 prices rose 30% alone with city centre developments selling for between €2,700 and €5,100 per sq m and in the historic Old Town for €3,500 to €6,000 per sq m.

By 2007 prices in Latvia were increasing across the board at staggering rates. The greatest growth was in Teika, where prices rose 56%, while Vecmilgravis, Imanta and Bolderaja saw rises of 46%. This growth is now beginning to taper to more sustainable levels, but given the strong economic performance of the Baltics as a whole the opportunities for long term capital appreciation still looks good.

Which Type of Property Should You Go For?

There is a slight risk that the level of development in the capitals may lead to an over-supply of new build apartments, however this is unlikely in the short term as demand is still increasing for residential, commercial and retail developments, with supply still falling short. The greatest demand remains for renovated apartments in higher quality city centre buildings. Good quality townhouses are also likely to do well.

The majority of new developments are one or two bedroom apartments and the average size of a new apartment has increased from 65sq m to 77sq m in Latvia and Estonia. The reverse is true in Lithuania where the average area of a newly constructed apartment is around 62sq m. Buying smaller properties here is seen by locals as a way onto the housing market which has been escalating in price far faster than incomes.

Some Soviet era property is of poor quality but new builds are generally well put together and prices will continue to reflect this with the gap widening between new build and the traditional housing stock. New property in the Baltics is often sold as a unit without tiles, flooring, lighting, bathroom or kitchen, so it is important to know how you expect the finished apartment to look and allow an extra €200 per sq m to complete the refurbishment.

Hotspots

Of the three states, **Estonia's** chances for long term capital appreciation look to be the strongest. A 2005 survey by Jones Lang LaSalle ranked Tallinn as the first city in the world for development potential. Since then Estonia has climbed higher and higher in house price indexes. Like the rest of the Baltics, demand in Estonia is being fuelled by easy credit, growing wages and an increase in the number of households per capita. By the end of 2006 more than 92% of all flats available in **Tallinn** had been sold and with limited construction capacity (due to the lack of local skilled labour) there can only be slow future supply growth. In short, growth may slow but should continue for many years to come, especially if Estonia continues to attract high levels of foreign direct investment. Estonia has the strongest economy of the Baltic States based on expanding electronics and telecommunications industries and close trading links with Finland, Sweden and Germany. Tallinn also ranks well for tourism. Estonia's travel and tourism is expected to generate $4,688.3m in 2007, an increase of 5.5%.

Those wanting to buy-to-let to holidaymakers in the Baltics should pick Lithuania where the travel and tourism industry was expected to generate $5,106.7m in 2007, an increase of 5.8% on the previous year.

Not only does Estonia seem to offer the best long term growth but at present property here is cheaper than Lithuania and Latvia and rental yields are higher. The latest Global Property Guide gives average prices in Vilnius as €3,792 per sqm, in Riga at €3,020 per sq m and in Tallinn at €2,383 with a gross rental yield of 4.04%, 4.97% and 6.13% respectfully.

There have been warnings that the market might be becoming overheated, with speculators driving prices up. Still property on the edges of Tallinn is likely to prove a good investment (most of the new residential developments are in the suburbs), as are new beachfront developments just outside the city limits.

The Purchase Process

As with other civil law countries, employing the services of a notary is the key to buying property in the Baltics. After making an offer to buy a deposit or reservation fee is paid. The parties then sign the contract in the presence of the notary who then registers the change of ownership with the authorities. State duty amounts to 2% of the purchase price, stamp duty is currently €15 and notary fees are normally between 0.5% and 1% of the purchase price.

Mortgages

Mortgages are available for up to 70% of the purchase price with a maximum term of 20 years. Latvia now has the most mortgaged homeowners in Europe – mortgage loans total 35% of annual GDP, whilst Estonia has total mortgage lending equalled to 32%. Although this is still below western EU member state levels (48% of GDP), mortgage growth is expected to slow in line with actual income growth.

Key Risks and Opportunities

The level of building in Riga and Tallinn may point to potential oversupply of apartments marketed to international buyers but at the moment, this seems unlikely. The sheer confidence of developers also means that they are sometimes prepared to leave apartments vacant rather than accept lower offers.

Baltic citizens usually prefer to own, rather than rent, property. However, with the area developing a reputation as one of the cheapest and most tax efficient places to do business in Europe, large numbers of expats are moving into the cities and looking for rented accommodation. Monthly rent for a 70 sq m typical three-room new apartment in Tallinn city centre ranges from €757 (unfurnished) up to €765 (furnished). In 2006 there was a 20% jump in rental rates and demand was a lot higher than the three preceding years – this indicates that out of the three countries Estonia is bucking the downwards rental yields trend.

Europe

THE BALTICS

Opportunity Rating

The climate in the Baltics means that none of these countries are going to become tourist hotspots beyond the city-break market. However, their success is more closely related to their economic growth and excellent position as trading hubs between Europe and Russia. Many international businesses are opening up in the Baltic States, bringing with them investment and an expatriate work force. With prices at their current levels and excellent access to capital, prices should continue to perform well.

Rating: $ $ $ $

Risk Rating

In markets like these, over speculation and over development is always a risk. Beyond this, though, the Baltic States are very stable.

Rating: ⚠ ⚠ ⚠ ⚠

Bulgaria

CURRENCY
Lev

EXCHANGE RATES
100 Lev = £34.54   £1 = 2.90 Lev
100 Lev = US $69.60 US $1 = 1.43 Lev

SOFIA

Introduction

At present Bulgaria is one of the least populated European states, approximately the size of England, but with a population of only eight million people. As well as 11 blue flag beaches, Bulgaria has 354km of Black Sea coastline, 37,000km of hiking paths in the mountains and a series of almost unpublicised Roman, Greek and Thracian historical attractions, including nine Unesco world heritage sites.

As one of the most rapidly advancing nations in Europe, Bulgaria has become a byword for international property investment. In fact, Bulgaria is now one of the most popular property investment destinations for British buyers, who between them invest in thousands of properties in Bulgaria each year. Many of these early investors have done well, enjoying an average property price increase in 2004 of 47.5%. According to the Bulgarian government some 30,000 Britons already own homes in Bulgaria and an increasing number are starting to retire there now that British pensions can be drawn locally.

Figures from the Bulgarian National Bank (BNB) show that foreign buyers purchased real estate totalling €310 million in the first quarter of 2007 – a 63% increase over the €190 million purchased in the same period in 2006. Foreigners spent a total of €1.13 billion on Bulgarian real estate in 2006 – led by the British who accounted for 16.4% of the total spend, followed by Luxembourg (11.3%), US (9.2%) and Greece (7%).

In a bid to preserve the beauty of its landscape and protect itself from over-development, Bulgaria is focusing on developing only top quality properties. Planning permission is only granted to the highest calibre projects and steps have been taken to protect the national parks and natural resources which have proved such an attraction.

2006 saw 15 million visitors enter Bulgaria (up 15% on 2005) and while tourism will continue to increase, it is not expected to grow at this level long term. Growth is expected to fall to 4.6% per annum, in real terms, between 2008 and 2017. However, First Choice still votes Bulgaria as its number one destination and online travel specialists Opodo considered Bulgaria its top emerging destination for 2007.

Since accession to the EU in January 2007, Bulgaria has been benefiting from simply billions of euros in EU funding, which will improve the country's transportation infrastructure. Sofia airport has recently opened new facilities, Varna Airport has doubled its capacity by adding a new terminal in mid 2007, Burgas has a new terminal scheduled, whilst more and more low-cost airlines are planning new routes to the area.

The Bulgarian economy seems also to be on the up: unemployment was down to 74% in 2007, average monthly income rose to €300 in May 2007, and GDP had risen to 6.1% by 2006. This new wealth is creating a growing middle class and Bulgaria now has one of the fastest-growing mortgage markets in Europe, almost doubling to €2.04 billion in April 2007 from €1 billion in January 2006.

Is This a Good Place to Buy?

After emerging from Communism in 1989, Bulgaria existed under a series of weak coalition governments, a situation which persisted until the election of a government devoted to free-market principles in 1997, a year which also saw the creation of a currency board that tied the Bulgarian lev first to the German mark and then to the Euro. This move has contributed greatly to economic stability.

The recent strength of Bulgaria's economic indicators mean that the international community now sees the country in a very positive light. Inflation has decreased to almost 0% and privatisation programmes are moving quickly. The World Bank's director for Romania and Bulgaria has identified Bulgaria as 'a good place for investment', noting that in three years, Bulgaria rose from being the Bank's lowest-rated country in the region to the highest. Increased economic prosperity in the country has created strong local demand for property and a new corporation tax at an all time low of 10% is helping to attract increased international investment.

Bulgaria's history of communism, combined with the slow start to the market economy in the 1990s meant that property prices in Bulgaria were significantly below realistic values. It was partly these extremely low prices combined with Bulgaria's EU entry that stimulated the demand for investment property in Bulgaria.

Bulgaria enjoys miles of beautiful coastline, clean beaches and some excellent skiing in the mountains. Whilst investors were primarily drawn to the coast, more recent interest has focused on the mountains, as investors realise Bulgaria's potential as a holiday hotspot of the future. Although many investors have done well from initial speculation, prices on some parts of the coast have soared way beyond realistic levels. Prices in Sunny Beach for example, one of the most popular investment locations, are well beyond the means of locals and there is such enormous supply that it is questionable whether there will be enough tourists to fill the empty beds.

'Although many investors have done well from initial speculation hyping the Bulgarian coast, prices on some parts have soared way beyond realistic levels'

Opportunities for profit on the Bulgarian coast are mainly achieved through holiday lets. But despite its potential, Bulgaria is not the new Spain. Tourism is certainly growing but the coastal climate allows only a four month summer holiday season (the area is too cold for the rest of the year). This means that for potential landlords to do well, they need to command very high prices during the short season; an objective which will be difficult to meet considering the competition and the fact that Bulgaria's biggest attraction for holidaymakers is its low prices. Over-supply has become a considerable issue with a total of almost 35,000 units available on the Black Sea Coast at the end of 2006 – equating to a 54% jump in just 6 months. The average price of one and two bedroom apartments in Sunny Beach dropped by 4% in the 12 months to July 2007.

This doesn't mean there are no good investment opportunities on the Bulgarian coast, rather it means that it is critical to buy well if you want to invest here. If you do decide to buy on the coast, remember that good properties are more likely to be found away from the traditional hubs of Sunny Beach and Golden Sands where prices will also be a lot cheaper. Consider towns like Sozopol, Dyuni (Dunes), Primorsko, Kiten and Lozenets. In Lozenet an average one bedroom apartment will cost £27,000, in Sunny Beach £37,000, in Varna £44,000 and in Golden Sands as much as £47,500. It is also critical that you buy a property with a differentiator; a standard apartment in an apartment block will be up against thousands of similar offerings and may be hard to rent or sell.

Better opportunities exist in some of the Bulgarian ski resorts. These resorts are slightly newer to investors and so prices haven't yet reached those achieved on the coast. More importantly, the market fundamentals are stronger here. Whilst the coast doesn't boast a climate anything close to the Mediterranean, the mountains are at least comparable to the alpine skiing of France and Italy. The letting season is also year round as the mountains offer a range of summer activities from hiking to golf. For potential landlords this means fewer void periods and the opportunity to generate a better year round yield.

Price History

The property market in Bulgaria remained strong in 2006, with growth of an impressive 20.5% – second only to Latvia (45.3%) in the Knight Frank Global House Price Index. Those entering the market three years earlier however, would have seen an average increase of a staggering 47.5% (2003–2004). Whether these price growths are sustainable remains to be seen and whilst some can be put down to economic growth and market catch-up, a lot are considered to be a result of speculation.

Despite significant price increases in the mountains, prices remain higher on the coast with apartment prices averaging 1,232 leva per square metre (£424).

Which Type of Property Should You Go For?

There is an old phrase which says 'if you can see the boat you've missed it' and Bulgaria may well be a missed boat, at least on the coast. Many buyers piled into the market because prices were low and the potential for capital appreciation was strong. Indeed the early investors have seen this capital appreciation, but mainly because their investments prompted even more people to buy for the same reasons. The fundamentals in many Bulgarian resorts however simply don't add up and for this reason, we would suggest that many coastal resorts be avoided. If, however the Bulgarian coast still appeals, we would recommend buying into high quality, multipurpose resorts which feature a combination of beach and golf amenities. Anything with an associated hotel will often have the types of facilities to differentiate itself from the many run of the mill holiday apartments that have recently been built.

Hotspots

Better opportunities lie in the mountain resorts of **Borovets, Pamporovo** and **Bansko.** Of the three Bansko is the largest, longest established and the fastest growing in Europe but prices are higher here. As on the coast, potential holiday landlords will face stiff competition so it is important to identify a property with clear differentiators. Like the Black Sea Coast there has been mass construction in Bansko and stories abound of apartments left empty even in the ski season. Again, developments associated with a hotel and spa and ski-in ski-out access will present the best opportunities. If such a development can be found with nearby golf facilities, it is more likely to offer year round rental opportunities.

Pamporovo and Borovets offer better value for money but the resorts themselves are smaller and less developed. However, this does improve the potential for capital appreciation. In any of the ski resorts it is worth looking out for chalets or lodges rather than apartments as these are often what appeal most to tourists used to the Alpine resorts of Western Europe (see picture 19 in the colour section).

INSIDER TIP **The most prestigious mountain location is Pampovoro which is at the centre of the £174 million Perelik Project, encompassing new pistes, ski lifts, hotels, car parking, artificial snow equipment, a new 100 km highway and possibly even a golf course. The Perelik is due for completion by the end of 2007 and some predict it will boost tourist arrivals by an impressive 40% ready for the 2007/2008 ski season. As the most upmarket ski resort in Bulgaria it will pay to buy the best quality you can afford here and on-piste stand-alone chalets are likely to command much higher rental yields than apartments.**

Another area to consider is **Sophia** the capital of Bulgaria. As one of the fastest emerging cities in Europe – just behind Prague and Budapest – growth is fuelled by the buoyant stock market, its multinational population and a growing student community. Choose locations close to the airport, city centre or the New Bulgarian University which opened in 1991, for the best investment opportunities.

The Purchase Process

The purchase process varies in Bulgaria depending on whether you buy an apartment or a landed property. Currently, foreign ownership of land is illegal (although the law was amended in 2007 to allow some ownership if the purchaser is resident in Bulgaria). Generally therefore, investors wanting to buy a house or villa must first set up a Bulgarian registered company. This costs around €600, but it is also necessary to deposit a further €2,600 in a company bank account whilst the company is registered. Once the registration process is complete, it is possible to withdraw the €2,600 capital or use it for any other purpose.

'Opportunities for profit on the Bulgarian coast are mainly achieved through holiday lets, but despite its potential, Bulgaria is not the new Spain'

Once your Bulgarian company is registered, the process is the same as when buying an apartment. On paying a deposit, you will be asked to sign a preliminary sales contract between you and the developer which can be checked by a lawyer either in your home country or Bulgaria. Once you have begun the purchase process, you will need to gain a Bulstat Number from the local government and whilst the developer will do this for you in most cases, your lawyer or agent can also help. The Bulstat Number is an official requirement as it is needed for the legal contracts which are stamped and legalised by a Notary Public in Bulgaria.

The official exchange of contracts is managed by the notary who works for the government and represents both the buyer and seller. The presence of a notary does not however reduce the need for a lawyer who should review all of the contracts prior to exchange and notarisation.

In total, the purchase costs in Bulgaria should amount to no more than 4–5% of the property value depending on whether you need to establish a company or not. Municipality tax (equivalent to stamp duty) is charged at 2% and the notary fee is 0.4% of the property value. Other costs include legal fees and company set-up, both of which should amount to around €1,000 each.

Mortgages

Bulgaria now has a burgeoning mortgage market but the industry is new – only 8 years ago mortgages where not even available for locals, let alone non-nationals. There are now 5–7 banks offering mortgages to foreign buyers and this competition has made loans more flexible. Interest rates are now available for between 6.5% and 7.5% and buy-to-let loans are widely available for foreign buyers.

Key Risks and Opportunities

Bulgaria has almost become a victim of its own success and this is the country's greatest problem at the moment. Prices have risen dramatically in recent months and are now somewhat precarious with experts wholly unsure of how sustainable they may be. For those investing in Bulgaria today then, the biggest risk is that the market is overvalued and prices are about to drop. This event is by no means certain but there is a clear potential risk.

Over-development in some key areas such as Sunny Beach and to a certain extent Bansko then, presents a risk of over-supply in the letting market. It also means that it will be difficult to re-sell a property if you are up against a number of new developments being sold off-plan by the developer. The rampant construction in some coastal towns has also been quite poorly planned and there are many unattractive developments. A glossy marketing brochure can easily mask a property's true aesthetics so those buying in an area they have never visited need to find a way of checking that their property is not an eyesore.

With the enormous infrastructure improvements planned for Bulgaria's ski resorts it will be the mountain resorts offering the country's biggest property investment opportunities.

Opportunity Rating

Investing in Bulgaria is now a well trodden path meaning many of the risks associated with buying in an emerging market have been overcome. Although prices on most parts of the coast are now very high, bargain properties with good potential for capital investment and rental returns can still be found in the country's less developed ski resorts.

Rating: Coast $ $
Ski resorts $ $ $ $

Risk Rating

Many people see Bulgaria as the biggest international property investment opportunity around. This may have been the case a few years ago, but today this assumption is somewhat inaccurate. The days of instant gains are over and significant price rises on the coast are out of touch with the country's fundamentals. Another big risk is the lack of clear exit strategy due to over-supply. Bulgaria then, should be viewed as a long term holiday home investment option rather than a market likely to provide immediate gains over the short term.

Rating: Coast ⚠ ⚠ ⚠ ⚠
Ski resorts ⚠ ⚠

Croatia

CURRENCY
Kuna HRK

EXCHANGE RATES
1000 Kuna = £92.00
£1 = 10.8 Kuna
1000 Kuna = US $182
US $1 = 5.5 Kuna

ZAGREB

Introduction

Steeped in centuries of colourful history, home to one of the world's most well preserved fortified cities and blessed with an idyllic Adriatic coastline, Croatia's appeal is extensive. Its borders brush the slopes of the Alps, plunge deep into the Pannonian Valley and overlook the Danube and Drava rivers. Its interior comprises verdant forests, deep gorges, a collection of magnificent lakes and rich vineyards as well as smatterings of quaint villages, romantic castles and stately manors. Named 'the Pearl of the Adriatic' by George Bernard Shaw, and enjoying a blend of Mediterranean, Southern European and Balkan cultures, Croatia is one of Europe's best kept and most beautiful secrets. With 1,185 islands lying just off its coastline, Croatia offers a host of secluded beaches with tranquil island living.

Travel and tourism now accounts for around 19% of the country's GDP and for 21.6% of its total employment. The tourism industry is expected to grow 7.8% in 2007 and by 7.9% per annum in real terms between 2008 and 2017 which is over 50% more growth than the average predicted increases for the rest of the world.

Before the dissolution of Yugoslavia, the Croatian Republic was one of its most prosperous and industrialised areas, with a per capita output around one third above the Yugoslav average. After a mild recession in 2000, the economy stabilised, and growth has averaged 4–5% for the last few years. This should be accelerated by the country's expected accession to the EU, scheduled for 2010. Where foreign investment is concerned, the government has introduced several measures to make the climate more attractive, including the establishment of the Agency for Trade and Investment Promotion which has a mandate to assist potential investors in Croatia. Foreign investors have the same rights and status as domestic investors (providing a condition of reciprocity is satisfied with their country of residence) and may invest in nearly every sector of the economy, although it is necessary to seek permission from the Ministry of Foreign Affairs before making any property purchases.

Is This a Good Place to Buy?

Croatia is becoming increasingly popular with foreign buyers, with 34% of its properties in the hands of non-Croatians by 2005. The country has a number of natural advantages as a tourist destination, including an average of 2,600 hours of sunlight a year, brilliant sandy beaches, a large number of Venetian-style towns and Dubrovnik, one of the world's best-preserved fortified cities. In addition there are plenty of direct flights from the UK with a number of low-cost carriers now flying to all five coastal airports as well as the capital. The travelling time is only two and a half hours, and flights to Zadar can be found from as little as £60 return.

'Enjoying a blend of Mediterranean, Southern European and Balkan cultures, Croatia is one of Europe's best kept and most beautiful secrets'

Renting or ownership of a property here is enough to obtain a residence permit and there are restrictions on development which mean that the country should never become as overdeveloped as the Costa del Sol in Spain: houses must not be more than three stories high or built within 300m of the sea, and there are targeted financial incentives to avoid creating concrete jungles. These factors therefore increase Croatia's appeal as a second home or retirement market. However, the main reason cited for purchasing property in Croatia is pure invest-ment, both for rental and for capital growth. Potential for each is high, with annual capital appreciation of property in Zagreb increasing by 10% per annum.

The beauty of Croatia lies in its under-development. Land is cheap compared to other European destinations, and is in good supply. Property is also inexpen-sive, although prices have been rising and the market has enjoyed price increases of between 20–30% per annum in recent years. The potential EU accession which should be achieved by 2010 is bolstering the country's increase in popu-larity, and it has been predicted that prices will rise by as much as 200–300% in the next few years. Such levels of growth are almost certainly overstated however.

Price History

As stated above, property prices in Croatia have been rising quickly, and compared with other Eastern European countries, they are high. However, Croatia is a well-placed and attractive country, sometimes dubbed as 'the new Mediterranean', and when compared to equivalent properties in Spain, France and Italy, prices here are consistently 30% to 40% cheaper. One-bed apartments built in new developments on popular islands such as Brac and Korkula are available at around £45,594 ($91,700), whilst a two-bedroom apartment in a central off-plan development with sea views can be found for £90,553 ($182,111). Dubrovnik, which is said by some to be overpriced, has small apartments from £32,322 ($65,000) and 3 bed villas from £124,315 (€250,000).

Which Type of Property Should You Go For?

Property in Croatia varies from beachside and city apartments to spacious, detached villas in acres of rambling countryside. The real estate market here is still in its infancy, and land and house prices are favourable, especially on the islands where there are beautiful stone houses built in the traditional style. The Croatian government is committed to protecting the country's coastline and natural beauty, and the restrictions on building which this commitment entails means that seafront properties will be at a premium, although there is still no shortage of opportunities.

The buy-to-let market is buoyant, and a central property in Zagreb will cost between £1,352–£1,892 ($2,719–$3,805) per square metre whilst providing an estimated 6–7% gross yield. Rental yields on the coast tend to be around 5%. The ideal property to go for would therefore be one with good rental potential in a popular area.

Hotspots

British buyers generally focus on more upmarket areas, such as **Tucepi, Brela, Porec** and **Rovinj**. Prices in these areas are beginning to reflect this popularity (properties on the Dalmatian coast typically have price tags of between £600,000/$1,206,580 and £900,000/$1,809,938) and it may therefore be wise to focus elsewhere.

Istria, in the north-west of Croatia, is one area which has yet to suffer the consequences of increased foreign investment. The region has tranquil towns, clean beaches and acres of countryside, comparable to Italy. Istria was in fact part of Italy at one time, and Venetian architecture and the Italian language are present in many towns and villages, a fact which has led to the region being dubbed 'the new Tuscany'. The area is easily accessible – budget flights operate to both Ljubljana and Trieste – and has traditionally attracted visitors from Italy, Germany, Slovenia and Austria. Thanks to this tourism, Istria has a more established property market than the rest of the country, and a number of high-quality developments are being produced. This, combined with the amount of land available, makes Istria a very good region in which to buy. Two-bed apartments 500m from the beach are available from £62,000 whilst a three-bed villa with a pool is available from £146,200 ($294, 014). In **Dubrovnik** and the surrounding area, the investment market is also in its infancy, and capital appreciation is rapid. Three golf courses are being built in the area, a fact which will likely attract British buyers. A two-bed apartment in the centre of Dubrovnik is available from £60,000 ($120,665). Lower end properties here are available for as little as £40,000 ($80,443), although luxury villas can also be found in the area for those with a higher budget.

The Purchase Process

If you choose to buy in Croatia, it is a good idea to open a foreign currency account in the country, as it is important to have easy access to funds. Property in Croatia can be bought in three ways: buying through a Croatian company, buying in your own name with a 10% pre-contract, or buying in your own name via the full payment method.

The easiest and fastest way to purchase real estate is to form a Croatian company for the specific purpose of real estate acquisition. Opting for this method bypasses the lengthy process buyers encounter seeking approval from the Ministry of Foreign Affairs. Domestic companies in Croatia can be entirely owned and controlled by a foreign person and also allow for the most tax efficient way to buy and sell real estate in Croatia. Additionally, when purchasing through a company there is no restriction on what type of land you can buy giving you the freedom to purchase anything from forested to coastal to agricultural land. The company method is also the best way by which to purchase larger properties, invest in several properties, or use your property for business purposes. You will, however, need to register your company in the same district as the property you are purchasing which can take anywhere from a week to a month, depending on the court backlog.

The process of incorporating in Croatia is quite straightforward, and by signing a Power of Attorney, your lawyer will be able to handle the majority of the paper chase for you. It is important to note, though, that the cost of incorporating in Croatia can run to as much as £2,486 ($5,000). Plus you'll need a capital reserve of about £1,840 ($3,700) in a Croatian bank account, in your name, during the incorporation process. However, on the day that your company is listed in the corporate register you can withdraw all the start-up capital if you wish.

Once you have completed all the legal and contractual formalities associated with both the incorporation of your company and of the sale of the real estate, you can register your property immediately in the Land Registry. In Croatia, the actual physical signing of the Land Registry ledger is the final and most significant step of the process of land ownership, and it is the means by which title is claimed. You should also remember that as a company your corporation will have to submit annual accounts and adhere to various legislative regulations.

Another means of attaining property as a foreigner is to do it in your own name, which will involve applying to the Ministry of Foreign Affairs for permission to purchase the land. Although Communism has ended in this part of the world, the dregs of its slow and inefficient bureaucracy still reign here. Purchasing property in your own name can take anywhere from three weeks to 12 months or more. It is also important to note, that the system by which the Ministry of Foreign Affairs operates in Croatia is not uniform. In the southern part of the country things tend to go a lot slower because they still rely heavily on manual systems for the processing of the applications, and they don't necessarily have the required manpower dedicated to the task.

The overarching benefit of waiting for the Ministry of Foreign Affairs means the purchase is subject to a myriad of checks meaning there is a much slimmer chance of running into any problems with title or validity of the sale at a later date. Considering that a third of the population fled the country during the war, rather a large possibility exists that the 'owner' may not be the legal owner (especially if the rightful owner happens to be a Serb). The government does not allow purchase of properties with unclear ownership so it is advisable to establish the rightful ownership of the property, before getting to the pre-agreement stage. However, being paperwork-obsessed, if there is one paper or formality that is missing or incorrect, the Ministry of Foreign Affairs will send your whole application back. You may even find that you have to start again, from the beginning, which can be extremely frustrating.

'Renting or ownership of a property here is enough to obtain a residence permit and there are restrictions on development, so Croatia should never become as overdeveloped as the Costa del Sol in Spain'

There is also a statute of limitations on the age of your documents in Croatia. If any document is over six months old at the time of submission, it will be rejected and a new one will be required. Discovering that you have outdated paperwork at the time you submit your application could set you back by up to a year.

Buying using your own name with the 10% pre-contract method requires that you put down at least a 10% deposit, in order to have the property removed from the market. Whilst 10% is traditionally all that is required, the burgeoning enthusiasm currently being shown in the Croatian real estate market means that many vendors now demand that the entire amount be held on deposit. Unless you speak Croatian, do not sign or turn over any money until you have had the agreement translated and notarised. In fact, by law in Croatia, as a non-Croatian speaking person you will need to have all documents translated. Notary fees, though constant, will be minimal (to the tune of only a few dollars per visit), as the Notary Public will only be verifying the names of yourself and the seller in his presence.

The next step is to apply to the Ministry of Foreign Affairs (MoFA) in order for them to approve the purchase. To succeed with this application, it is necessary to supply the following documents: the purchase agreement, the seller's proof of title (land registry certificate: *ZK izvadak*), certificate confirming that the property is within the construction zone envisaged by the zoning plan (*Uvjerenje o namjeni*), proof of citizenship for the buyer, proof of citizenship for the seller and power of attorney, if an attorney is involved. It is from this point that the waiting then begins. Once the approval from the MoFA is granted and the final contracts and other assorted documents are checked, translated and notarised, the documents are then submitted to the land registrar to convey the title. Once the ledger is signed, the property is officially yours.

You will have some protection while you wait for the MoFA. For example if the seller breaks the contract, he must pay you double the 10% deposit. This occurs quite frequently, and is of not too great an inconvenience to the seller, due to the rapidity with which property prices are rising. And it is often beneficial for them to do so, with property prices appreciating at up to 30% a year.

In light of this eventuality, it is often safer to go in with a higher deposit of at least 20% or 30%.

Two impracticalities of the 10% pre-contract method are that you cannot occupy the premises while you are waiting for the MoFA (as you would with the full payment method outlined below), and you will not be able to obtain financing in Croatia.

You can, of course, pay for the property in full and by doing so, move in straight away and live on the property while you wait for approval from the MoFA. There is nothing illegal about this, but remember the house or property does not belong to you in the eyes of the Croatian authorities, as you have not signed the land register. As a result you are not entitled to any utilities or any building permits.

A significant boon of buying outright is that while you are waiting for approval, you are authorised to start refurbishing and renovating any buildings or structures, providing the renovations are within the footprint of the pre-existing structure.

Ensure that your lawyer puts markers on the deeds so that it is apparent that you have applied for ownership. You may find that an unscrupulous vendor could mortgage or even sell the property from under your feet while you're applying for MoFA permission.

With the accession to the EU forecast to occur in 2009–2010 however, a relaxation on the restrictions of foreign ownership are expected, which should significantly facilitate the whole purchase process.

VAT is imposed on new dwellings, and is paid by the seller, who usually passes it on to the buyer through an increased purchase price and you should budget for an extra 8–10% to cover legal fees, notary costs, taxes and land registry fees. Shop around for an estate agent, as their fees vary from 3–10%. The corporate rental income tax rate is 10% (or 0% for companies operating in the Free Zones) and 25% for individuals. As long as you have either occupied the real estate whilst you owned it, have held the property for more than 3 years, or are selling the property to your spouse or member of your immediate family, you will pay no capital gains tax. Croatian corporations pay standard corporate income tax at a single rate of 20%.

Mortgages

Up to 70% LTV mortgages are available in Croatia at interest rates from 8%. Typical repayment is over a 20 year term. Be aware that when transferring money to Croatia, banks usually charge a fee on incoming transfers.

Key Risks and Opportunities

It is important when investing in any emerging market to seek legal advice both in Croatia and at home before making any commitments. Croatian property has previously been sold by a simple contract between local people, and never recorded in the Land Register. This means that people who are deceased or not involved in the sale can still be registered as owning the land concerned, and to secure a clean title, your solicitor may have to trace everyone involved with the property since the last record to obtain each of their signatures. Another problem incurred with many older properties is the possibility that records are out of date and inconsistent, with poor linkages between property registers and Land Registry records. If there are problems with the title, permission to buy can be refused, incurring legal fees and expenses. The same goes for changes which have been made to the property previously – always check for records of planning permission. A good local solicitor who is familiar with the intricacies of the legal system is vital, and is likely to charge 1–2% in fees.

It is also important to shop around when buying in Croatia, both for properties and estate agents. It may be that the same property is listed on different web sites for different prices. Also very few properties are advertised and the property market on the whole is relatively unregulated, meaning that there is no consistency in values. Agents don't value properties themselves, but tend to market them at a price named by the owner plus their fee, meaning that prices of very similar properties can differ by thousands of pounds.

To find a reputable estate agent, look for a company registered as *nekretnine*, under a name ending with the letters 'd.o.o.' All fees should be outlined before any involvement is decided, as different agents will charge for different things – even for inspection trips in some cases.

Opportunity Rating

Before the Yugoslav war in the early 1990s, Croatia was one of the most important tourist destinations in Europe – and the country is fast regaining this appeal. Property prices remain low in many regions, and the potential both for holiday rentals and capital growth is therefore high.

Rating: $ $ $

Risk Rating

With the property market in Croatia largely unregulated, investors need to be especially scrupulous when buying here. Problems with title may materialise and it is wise to shop around to find the best prices as they can vary dramatically depending on agents' fees.

Rating: ⚠ ⚠

Cyprus

CURRENCY (SOUTH)
Cyprus £

EXCHANGE RATES
10 CYP£ = £11.55
£1 = CYP £0.87
10 CYP£ = US $23.00
US $1 = CYP £0.43

Introduction

The birthplace of Aphrodite goddess of love, Cyprus is an island with a cultural and romantic history. Its intriguing past is wrapped in mythology and has resulted in a unique culture with its own characteristic traditions and customs. The country features a number of sites particularly important to the early Christian period including sacred tombs and medieval mountain churches of world heritage status. Cyprus is a land of beaches, mountains, castles and villages, with a real sense of days gone by. With its perfect climate, stunning beaches and rich heritage it is a prime holiday destination, with tourist facilities to suit everyone. The country has influences from North Africa, the Middle East and south-eastern Europe and is a rich tapestry of varying peoples and cultures. From sandy beaches to unspoilt villages and fertile orchards to pine forests, Cyprus is strikingly beautiful and proves eternally popular with a variety of tourists. Indeed the country's economy is almost completely reliant on tourism. An EU report released recently concluded that the island has the cleanest beaches in Europe and of the 100 beaches tested, each one scored 99% or higher in terms of compliance with European beach hygiene and bathing water quality regulations.

Cyprus has suffered a north/south divide since the Turkish invasion of 1974. It now comprises the internationally recognised 'Republic of Cyprus' in the South and the 'Turkish Republic of Northern Cyprus' (TRNC). The Turkish-occupied area north of the 'green line' accounts for about a third of the country. Political instability in the region means that the tourist market fluctuates frequently, and there is still a 'front line', which, contrary to expectations, has proved to be a draw for tourists. GDP growth in the Republic of Cyprus has been between 3.7% and 3.8% since 2004 which is well above the EU average. In the TRNC, thanks to economic growth, reduced unemployment and growth in the construction and education sectors, GDP growth stood at 10.6% in 2006. There are opportunities for investment in the TRNC, however the risk is currently very high due to the volatility of its economic and political situation as well as acute difficulties in attaining clean title. With 45% of the per capita GDP of its southern counterparts, the Turkish Cypriots suffer relative isolation, a bloated public sector, a relatively small market and a reliance on the Turkish lira. As a result, it does not offer a particularly secure investment option. Having said this, house prices are currently half that of the south and less than a third of the price of Spain and are therefore attracting a lot of local investors.

'The market potential for capital growth is strongest over the medium term rather than the short term. This means that for those looking for a quick sell, Cyprus may not be the best place to invest'

Accessibility is also due to open up in the near future thanks to the new Ercan International Airport Talks between TRNC, Richard Branson and British and American governments mean the likelihood of direct flights to the north is also strong. Add to this Turkey's determination to gain access to the EU, and a political settlement resolving the conflict between the two zones should be imminent. If this occurs however, it will induce Greek Cypriot refugees formally of the North to reclaim their land which may cause difficulties for those who have bought in the North and not secured legal title. Despite the negativity surrounding parts of the northern market, house prices are predicted to double over the next 3 years. Having noted the north's potential and associated risk, the rest of this chapter will deal mainly with investment in the Republic of Cyprus (hereafter just Cyprus).

Cyprus is currently experiencing a property boom and is especially popular with British buyers who already own 60,000 properties on the island. New developments offering a variety of apartments and villas are appearing across the country and should continue to support the strong investment environment. House prices were up year on year in 2007 by an impressive 9.1% and British tourist visitor numbers reached 1.5 million in 2006. The island's low crime rates, pleasant climate and low cost of living are just some of the aspects drawing foreigners to the island. According to Buysell, a couple with a house and car can enjoy a high standard of living for just £500 a month, significantly less than on many of its European counterparts. The legal system, especially the sector dealing with property sales, is very similar to the UK and English is widely spoken throughout. Personal taxation is encouragingly low especially for pensioners and British state pensions can be paid out directly on the island. There is also a robust land registry system which means unlike Spain or Portugal, working out who owns what, (at least in the south) is relatively quick and easy.

Is This a Good Place to Buy?

With expectations that capital growth will increase by 20% this year, that GDP will grow by up to 4% and that tourist visits will reach 3.5m by 2010 it is easy to comprehend the popularity of the island's investment market. Cyprus became a member of the EU in 2004, making it easily accessible and reducing the paperwork involved in buying property there. As of January 2008, Cyprus will join the euro which should take its economy from strength to strength and help to lower interest rates from 4% down towards the typical Eurozone level. EU nationals are now permitted to own more than one property and as a result the number of foreign home owners has grown by an incredible 240% since 2004. This was expected to rise at an even higher rate during 2007 as numerous investors rushed to beat the imposition of a new 15% VAT land tax applicable from January 1st 2008.

The island is very easy to get to, with 260 flights from 40 airlines including BA, Cyprus Airways, Olympic and KLM flying each week. The government's aim to promote the island as a top flight destination has provoked the construction of a new €650m terminal at **Lancarna** airport, planned to open in 2008. This will increase the airport's capacity from 5m to 7.5m initially and up to 9m by 2013. Ryanair are rumoured to be in talks to establish low cost flight routes there within 6 months, a supposition that is more than likely considering Panos Englezos's (the chairman of the Cyprus Tourism Organisations) recent announcement that he will seek to increase the number of budget carriers with routes to the island.

To complement the recent growth in the number of five-star hotels, a number of marina and golf developments are being planned including the construction of 10 new golf courses. Steps are being taken to foster a strong tourism market, not least because this sector is a significant contributor to the Cypriot economy. It currently brings in around £1.3billion a year, accounting for around 15% of the island's GDP. Offshore oil has also recently been discovered meaning Cyprus now has the potential to establish strong export links with Lebanon and Egypt.

The island already has a good infrastructure, communication network and medical facilities. Wary of overdevelopment, the authorities have put strict building restrictions in place banning high-rise, high-density properties and outside the big resorts, many untouched areas can still be found. In the mountains, strong traditions are maintained, whilst the coast allows for a beach life with 340 days of sunshine a year. The climate is in fact one of Cyprus' main appeals coupled with its low cost of living, low levels of income tax, low local rates and low bills. With annual rental returns of 4–6% achievable the market has significant potential for buy-to-let investors.

Conversely, the market potential for capital growth is strongest over the medium term rather than the immediate short term. This means that for those looking for a quick sell, Cyprus may not be the best place to invest. Although house prices are expected to rise at encouraging levels, investors who bought into the Cyprus market a couple of years ago are finding it more difficult than expected to sell. With no clear exit strategy in place capital gains are at present inaccessible. It is also worth noting that non-EU property owners cannot rent out property meaning their buy-to-let potential is immediately extinguished.

As a mid to long term investment choice or for those looking for a lifestyle home in a beautiful country, Cyprus is a sensible option. It also feeds a two pronged market, catering both for the hedonistic, party-seeking youth as well as retirees and families seeking tranquillity.

Price History

Whilst property prices are up to 30% lower than in more popular European countries, they have been rising considerably for the past few years but are still perceived to be good value for money. With capital growth reaching an annual average of 20% and experts predicting that this level of growth will continue in the foreseeable future, it is no wonder that investors are flocking to the country. There are many and varied properties for sale, both new-build and resale, coastal and rural. EU membership and the resulting increase in Cyprus' accessibility is one of the main factors for the rise in prices, especially on the coast, and since the introduction of the Cyprus home price index 3 years ago, prices are reputed to have risen by 16.65%. The average price for a property in Cyprus now stands at around £112,300 ($226,500), although properties inland tend to offer better value for money.

Which Type of Property Should You Go For?

Non-Cypriots are entitled to buy an apartment, house or land, although any land, with or without property, must not exceed 4,014 square metres (a limitation due to be reviewed by the end of 2007).

The market is currently geared towards off-plan and new-build purchases, for which prices are rising rapidly but there is very little demand for re-sales (even off-plan). Indeed, the resale market is virtually non-existent. Cyprus is therefore much better suited to those seeking a second or holiday home, a retirement property, or rental income, rather than a short term investment property.

A recent survey by the holiday home website holiday-rentals.co.uk showed the average rental period was 18 weeks per year providing a 6.3% return on your investment based on average purchase price of £134,000 and average rental rate of £470 per week.

Hotspots

There are a number of places in Cyprus that could be described as hotspots, mainly concentrated around the tourist centres. In **Paphos**, for example, the mild climate and beautiful countryside have attracted visitors throughout history, and the town is now the tourist capital of the country. As a result, prices here are among the most expensive on the island, but the area is also one of the most unspoilt, with strict planning regulations. Prices range from £37,000 ($74,600) for a studio apartment ten minutes from the town centre to £1.6 million ($3.2 million) for a large 6 bed villa. Yields here range from 4.5% to 5.49%. Further west, near Polis, **Latchi** is also proving popular amongst those looking for an unspoilt location, with many charming fishing villages around the town. Prices here are also high, ranging from £49,000 ($98,900) for a one-bedroom flat to £190,000 for a 3 bed villa ($383,300).

Limassol, Cyprus' second-largest city, is the heart of the winemaking industry and the main passenger ferry port on the island, so is popular with tourists year-round. The city boasts ten miles of coastline, a large marina, a number of golf courses and excellent shopping facilities, offering a balance between practicality and the chance to escape from the banalities of daily life.

INSIDER TIP

Half an hour's drive inland from Limassol are the foothills of the Troodos Mountains, where quiet villages offer a gentle alternative to the bustle of the city. Property prices in Limassol range from a studio apartment outside the city for around £25,000 ($50,400), a one-bed apartment closer to the centre for £56,400 ($113,800) right up to £1,739,108 ($3,508,600) for a five-bedroom luxury villa in the prestigious Limassol Marina Bay. Yields on properties in this district range from 4.3% to 5.5%.

Larnaca, in the south-east of the island, is one of the oldest cities in the world, but also has a modern tourist centre with good shopping and is a popular holiday destination. The potential reunification of Cyprus could make this a good place to invest, as the city is relatively close to the northern sector. A small two-bed apartment here can be bought for around £46,000 ($93,000), rising to £141,900 ($286,200) for a three-bedroom apartment, and £147,300 ($297,000) for a four-bedroom detached house with private swimming pool and landscaped gardens. Yields in this region range from 3.8% to 4.79%.

Nicosia is the capital of Cyprus, and, like the island itself, is divided by the green line. As the administrative centre and the seat of government, the city has experienced impressive growth in recent years. A one-bed flat can be bought here for £58,800 ($118,500), while a three-bed flat costs £147,600 ($200,000) and a four-bed house is available for £370,000 ($745,700). In a bid to encourage investment, the Cypriot government have offered tax free rental income and the abolition of transfer fees for those buying properties in the old town in need of renovation.

Famagusta also offers good potential for capital growth and enjoys some of the best beaches and strongest indigenous demand. One-bedroom apartments can be found from as little as £10,400 and three-bedroom flats from as little as £65,000.

The Purchase Process

One of the great appeals of this country aside from its beautiful terrain and balmy climes is the simplicity of its purchase process. With a legal system that echoes that of the UK, the buying process is straightforward. Investors in Cyprus should employ a licensed estate agent who can offer impartial advice on any property they are interested in. When finding an agent or developer, ensure that they are members of CREAA, the Cyprus Real Estate Agents' Association or AIPP (Association of International Property Professionals) so as to guarantee their integrity.

Once a suitable property has been decided on and an offer is made and accepted, it is normal to give a nominal deposit – around CYP£1,000 to CYP£2,000 – to reserve the property, take it off the open market, bind the owner and secure the price. At this point the buyer's solicitor begins title and land searches and draws up the purchase contract. As there tends to be only one contract in Cyprus the buyer should ensure that all checks on the property have been concluded to both party's satisfaction before signing. The contract will be drawn up in the buyer's native language, and should be checked to ensure that all details and conditions are correct, including: details and identity verification of both parties, a full description of the property, the total area of the property and land, the purchase price, payment details and the inclusion of any fixtures and fittings. Depending on the nature of the property (i.e. off-plan or resell) either a stage payment or final monies are due when the contract has been signed. When it comes to contract closure, both the vendor and buyer will sign the document which will be notarised and once this has occurred, it should be deposited at the Land Registry Office within two months to prevent the vendor from re-selling the property. The buyer's solicitor will then apply to the Council of Ministers for the buyer's right to own the property. Once permission to own a property is granted the title deeds are transferred to the property investor's name and the transfer tax is due.

Generally the buyer has a month to make all taxation and fee payments. Taxes and fees are due as follows:

- VAT of 15% on new build properties which does not apply to homes where planning permission was applied for before 1 May 2004
- Property transfer tax of 3%–8%
- Stamp duty of 0.15% on properties of less than £100,000 and 0.2% on properties of over £100,000
- Annual property tax is charged on properties worth more than CYP£100,000 and is calculated depending on the value of the property
- Legal fees of 1%–2%
- Agents' fees of 3%–6%
- Local authority taxes of CYP£50–£150 per year
- Rental income tax of 25%
- Capital gains tax is payable at 20%, although the first CYP£10,000 is tax exempt or the first CYP£20,000 if property is jointly owned by a couple

Cyprus currently has double taxation agreements with over 26 countries and plans are underway to facilitate the purchase process yet further with plans in place to allow for unencumbered property acquisition by 2011.

As far as purchasing in the North of Cyprus is concerned, only 12% of land is owned by Turkish Cypriots, the remaining 88% of which is the property of Greek Cypriot refugees forced out of their homes by the Turkish invasion of '74. This therefore makes buying property here somewhat risky. If investors are even remotely interested in assessing the investment opportunities in the north, it is absolutely essential that they enlist the help of a reputable solicitor who will be able to ensure that title deeds are accurately searched and permission for the investor to buy in Northern Cyprus is correctly sought from the Council of Ministers. Care needs to be taken when properties in Northern Cyprus do not have international or government backed title deeds and are considered to have Greek Cypriot pre-1974 title. Such properties should be avoided even if they appear to offer great value for money as land disputes can easily ensue and can be incredibly difficult to resolve. It is also worth noting that escrow account structures are not recognised in Northern Cyprus meaning all payments go directly to the vendor or developer. This said, providing that an investor understands the different types of title deed available for properties and land parcels, they should be able to navigate the property buying process with relative ease.

Mortgages

Whilst a Cypriot national can often arrange a 90% mortgage, EU residents are not entitled to such high borrowing levels. For non-resident foreigners, it is possible to arrange a mortgage for the purchase of investment real estate for up to 70%–80% of the final purchase price and both interest only and repayment mortgages are available. Non-status mortgages are typically the easiest to arrange but the majority of good international mortgage brokers can advise further on this matter. Expect to pay a mortgage arrangement fee in the region of 1% of the amount being borrowed.

Key Risks and Opportunities

Cyprus is essentially a second home, holiday rental and retirement market not the most appropriate market for those looking for investment and capital growth, despite what many specialists say. The whole market here is based on new-build properties, and new developments are constantly being built. Consequently, once you have bought a property, you will find that the price of an identical property in an off-plan development will have risen by perhaps 40% in two years, however the apartment bought new-build two years earlier will not even have a resale value equal to that at which it was purchased. The vendor will be competing against brand new properties sold by developers, and will therefore have real problems selling.

Nevertheless, for a second home, holiday home or a retirement scheme, The Republic of Cyprus has a lot to offer. The climate, traditions and lifestyle will suit many buyers, the low cost of living will mean that a pension stretches much further than at home, and the infrastructure and health services here are excellent. There are, however, a couple of points to bear in mind. Although EEA nationals won't require a visa before moving to Cyprus they will need to apply for a Temporary Residence Employment permit Category F. In addition, those looking to retire to Cyprus must have a secure income of a minimum CYP£6,000 per person (around £7,000) and will not be allowed to work once their application has been approved. It is also wise to draw up a Cypriot will, as inheritance laws otherwise default all property to the spouse or children of the deceased as beneficiaries.

Opportunity Rating

The southern side of the island presents good opportunities in the rental market as demand grows ever higher for holiday lets, however the resale market here has proved to be soft, making it difficult to realise capital appreciation. Northern Cyprus may begin to present good opportunities for growth as political and land title issues are resolved.

Rating: $ $ $

Risk Rating

It can be very difficult to sell on finished property due to over supply and the attractions of off-plan developments. Both of these factors could seriously affect property prices moving forward. In the north the issues associated with land title are far from resolved and will continue for many years to come.

Rating – South: △ △ △
Rating – North: △ △ △ △ △

Denmark

CURRENCY
Kroner

EXCHANGE RATES
100 Kroner = £9.06
£1 = 11.04 DKK
100 Kroner = US$18.60
US$1 = 5.38 DKK

COPENHAGEN

Introduction

Boasting one of the highest standards of living in the world, with one of the best social welfare systems, and the highest gross national product per capita, Denmark is often seen as a model state. Though the majority of land is used for agricultural purposes, Denmark's main areas of employment are based in services, manufacturing and industry. The country is a long-standing EU member and has strong trade and business links within Europe, in particular with Germany.

Popular among Europeans as a short-break destination, Copenhagen is seen as a city with a laid-back, highly cultured population. The country itself is regarded as being friendly and relaxed, with a good arts and social scene, an attractive outdoor lifestyle and boasting an ecologically aware and socially progressive attitude.

However, recent attempts to curb immigration were the first sign that the country's relaxed, open-door ethos was changing. Plans to clear and redevelop the famous Christiana commune demonstrated how valuable land in Copenhagen now is, and was seen as a move towards a more economically focused society. So far the commune has managed to hold on and is in discussions about how development can move forward in a way that is compatible with both parties.

Like all Scandinavian countries, Denmark has a highly educated and skilled population that is generally fluent in English and is business orientated. It also has a flexible and efficient workforce. The Danish telecommunications system is one of the most advanced in the world and the level of computer literacy is excellent.

Taxation is extensive in all areas, leading to a higher cost of living compared to other European nations, however Denmark provides enviable public services, healthcare, education and infrastructure.

Is This a Good Place to Buy?

Denmark is one of the world's thriving business hubs and was ranked top of the 2006 Economist Intelligence Unit's Global Business Environment rankings as the world's best place to do business in the next four years. Geographically it is also well placed to conduct business with both established and emerging European markets and many of the world's biggest companies have their Nordic headquarters in the Copenhagen region. The Danish infrastructure and transport links are also of the highest standard with four airports offering good international connections with the UK, northern and eastern Europe, and the Baltic states.

'The Danish economy could not be more stable or its future more secure. This is no longer a market where high profits via fast capital appreciation should be expected, though steady, sustainable growth can be anticipated'

With free trade and movement between all Scandinavian countries there is a great deal of mobility amongst the populations in this corner of Europe which leads to a healthy demand for high quality properties to let. Given the high property prices in and around Copenhagen (which attracts the lion's share of migration) this is a potentially prosperous buy-to-let market.

Price History

A 2006 report by the Organisation for Economic Co-operation and Development said that the Danish government needed to work harder to reduce the amount of housing subsidies it paid and to relax the regulations that were holding back some areas of the rental market. In addition, it pointed out that zoning regulations in municipalities surrounding the capital were restricting development and needed to be addressed.

This may partly explain why house prices have been rising steadily at around 8% since 1995, though a property boom (some say bubble) has been in evidence for the past three years with prices rising by around 33% since 2006. This surge was as a result of low interest rates, rising salaries, and new, innovative mortgages. These together created conditions in which average prices of standard apartments in Copenhagen rose to around €596,000. Many analysts correctly predicted the market was overheated and in early 2007 prices slowed with expectations of an increase of only 5% over the year.

Which Type of Property Should You Go For?

The booming market in Copenhagen has seen a lot of very standard new-build apartment buildings and, as the market slows, it is these projects that are reportedly suffering slower sales. Quality projects in restored historic or iconic buildings that appeal to the city's professional classes should continue to be a good investment, particularly those within the centre or easily accessible suburbs.

However, in Copenhagen and other cities with a large student population and a young workforce more standard, lower-priced properties intended as buy-to-let investments should possibly be considered.

Denmark often has good summer weather and a large proportion of the local population traditionally enjoys taking holidays or weekends along the country's North Sea coast. The area is also becoming increasingly attractive to overseas tourists who are looking for alternatives to Mediterranean destinations. Therefore, cottages in coastal locations can offer both an attractive second-home option and viable buy-to-let purchases.

Hotspots

Copenhagen

Because it is such a small country, investment tends to be centred around the capital city. Copenhagen has seen increasing investment over the past few years by the government as well as from commercial sectors. This includes an airport that is considered one of the best in the world, a new metro system, and the Øresund Bridge, which opened in 2000 to link Copenhagen to the prosperous city of Malmo in Sweden. Increased immigration to the city from employees of multinational companies, as well as Danes, coupled with a limited amount of building land has significantly improved property prices and indicates that demand may outstrip supply. Recent gains of up to 175% in 5 years has proved unsustainable, but though growth has slowed the market was still up by 15.4% in 2006.

Aarhus

Aarhus is Denmark's second largest city and the main employment hub outside the capital. The town has around 300,000 inhabitants, a large number of resident companies and good regional transport connections. Aarhus is also a university city, creating a well-educated workforce. There has been much harbour–front regeneration in recent years and, as a result, property is as sought- after as Copenhagen. In 2006 average prices were €268,500 for a standard family home.

Other areas

Of the more provincial towns, key locations are **Skejby**, which is rapidly attracting a large number of biotech and IT firms, and **Viby**, also popular with smaller companies. **Aarlborg**, once the bastion of heavy industry and manufacturing, is attracting new industries, such as communications, IT and financial services. It has a ready workforce, thanks to the expansion of the university. **Odense**, is also a university city undergoing renovation of its old harbour. A large number of service sector industries, including banking, accountancy and insurance have settled here and it is in a good location for connections to other areas of northern Europe.

Holiday cottages are popular with the local market as places to spend the long summers or for weekending and can also be rented to overseas tourists. Popular locations include the long coast of Jutland, including Skagen, and the islands of Falster and Lolland. Prices have risen quite dramatically in the past five years and you should expect to pay from around €500,000. Rental returns can be between €400 and €1,500 per week depending on property and season.

The Purchase Process

There are no restrictions on buying property for EU nationals, but those wanting to live in Denmark need to confirm in writing that the residence will be used year-round. Non-EU nationals must have permission from the Ministry of Justice to purchase property, and must confirm that it will be for full-time residence. It helps if you can show ties to Denmark such as family connections or previous residency.

Before putting in an offer on a property you should get a property report, usually compiled by the vendor and containing all structural information, ownership and financial details. If a report is not provided the seller becomes liable for defects for 20 years after the sale. A transfer deed, paid for jointly by both parties, can be arranged which insures the seller against unforeseen defects and offers the buyer protection.

You should also instruct a surveyor to examine the property on your behalf. If satisfactory, the estate agent will draw up a purchase agreement and start negotiations with your lawyer as to the final purchase price. On signing the agreement, a deposit of 5% will be expected and there is a cooling off period of six days. Your legal advisor should also check the sale agreement and title deeds, run all searches, and issue an owner's certificate before completion.

Legal fees are around 2% of the purchase price with stamp duty levied on a sliding scale of 0.6–1.5%, plus property tax of 1%, local tax based on the land value of 0.5–2.5%, depending on location. There is also an additional county tax of 1%.

Any proceeds from the sale of property are exempt from capital gains tax as long as it has been owned for at least three years.

Mortgages

There are no restrictions on non-nationals buying via a local financial institution and they can borrow up to 80% of the purchase price.

Key Risks and Opportunities

Denmark is a thriving, business orientated nation with probably the best welfare state system in the world and a high standard of living.

Opportunity Rating

All indications are that Denmark and particularly its capital, Copenhagen, will continue to thrive with property prices continuing to climb at a sustainable rate. Buy-to-let opportunities are good in the major cities, although property prices are high.

Rating: $$$

Risk Rating

The Danish economy could not be more stable or its future more secure. This is no longer a market where high profits via fast capital appreciation should be expected, though steady, sustainable growth can be anticipated.

Rating: ⚠

France

CURRENCY
Euro

EXCHANGE RATES
100 Euro = £67.33
£1 = 1.49 Euro
100 Euro = US $134.62
US $1 = 0.74 Euro

Introduction

France is famed for its delectable cuisine and elite wines, its sunflowers and its lavender. Home to some of the world's most sought after vineyards, most famous artists and most pungent perfumeries, it is a country brimming with culture and timeless appeal. Thanks to its extensive and varied interior, France caters for a range of tastes and interests. To the east stand the Alps, offering some of the highest peaks and the best skiing in Europe whilst to the southwest, are the Pyrenees, equal in stature and appeal. Some of the world's finest cities and regions are also found within French borders. Paris, the city of love, is also the centre of French tourism, art, music and architecture and is eternally popular with tourists the world over. Similarly, the medieval Alsace, 18th century Bordeaux, the sun-drenched vineyards of Provence, as well as the stunning beaches and busy seaside resorts along the Mediterranean coast, all exert an unyielding appeal over visitors. With at least 75 million foreign tourists arrivals per year, France is the most visited country in the world, maintains the third largest income in the world generated through tourism and is second only to Spain as a holiday home destination for Brits. Nearly 50% of all foreign-owned homes in France are owned by Britons who have already succumbed to the allure of the relaxed pace of life and the great food and wine. Property prices here, while high, are still cheaper than in the UK, especially in rural areas.

Economically, France is in the middle of a transition from a modern economy featuring extensive government intervention and ownership to one that relies more on market mechanisms. The government has lowered income taxes and introduced measures to reduce unemployment and reform the pension system. Despite this, the tax burden remains one of the highest in Europe while unemployment hovers near 9%. The country then is suffering from a lingering economic slowdown, with GDP growth at just 2.1%.

Is This a Good Place to Buy?

Lifestyle and investment purchases are two very different procedures which take into account differing criteria. While good investment potential is judged on rental returns or long-term capital gains, a lifestyle purchaser will make their buying decision based on other features such as the quality of appliances and amenities and other aesthetic aspects. As far as France is concerned then, those looking for low costs and fast, high returns, may find that this country is not as suited to investment perhaps as it is to second home and lifestyle purchases.

Having said that, opportunities for investment can be found. French capital growth currently stands at around 10% per annum and although this figure is lower than in many of the riskier new emerging markets, French property does offer stable growth and a safe, tried and tested marketplace in which to invest.

'As far as France is concerned then, those look-ing for low costs and fast, high returns, may find that this country is not as suited to investment perhaps as it is to second home and lifestyle purchases'

Prices in France are generally much higher than they were 10, or even five, years ago, although there are many areas of the country that are still affordable. The cost of living in France is also fairly reasonable in comparison to that of the UK, especially in rural areas. Much of France's appeal remains untouched, and many are still drawn to the relaxed Mediterranean lifestyle and laid-back approach to life. Food and wine connoisseurs will be in their element, while the country's size means that there is a great variety of property available.

Rental investment potential is achievable in the cities, and a number of savvy buyers appear keen to take advantage of this. The country also still has great potential as a tourist destination, with both summer and ski resorts, an absorb-ing culture and a mostly temperate climate. Importantly it enjoys good connections and easy access from the rest of Europe.

Price History

For years now, France has been one of the countries with the most vibrant housing market in the EU and substantial house price increases have been occurring for the last ten years. Prices of new-build properties have risen by an average of 10% a year over the last decade, while in more popular areas such as the Côte d'Azur and Paris, this has been as much as 20%.

However, there is evidence to suggest that this hefty rise in property prices is slowing down. Growth of 15.5% was registered in 2004, and slowed to 10.4% in 2005 before falling yet further to 7.1% in 2006, reflecting a substantial slowdown.

Average property prices are currently around £142,000 ($286,400) for a one-bedroom apartment and approximately £253,000 ($510,300) for a three-bedroom villa although property prices vary considerably according to the region and its popularity.

Which Type of Property Should You Go For?

The type of property to purchase obviously depends on the requirements of the buyer. The French housing market offers plenty of choice in location, style and price. You can buy beach homes, city apartments, suburban family homes, farmhouses and even vineyards or a chateaux. A popular choice is to buy a farmhouse or another large property in an area popular with tourists and convert it into a *gite* or guesthouse, thereby gaining an income as well as being able to make the most of the country lifestyle. However, the popularity of this trend means that in many areas the number of *gites* has outstripped demand and they are far harder to rent out.

For those planning retirement or wanting to buy a second home, new-builds and off-plan properties are often the preferred choice. These types of property offer the ultimate in terms of comfort and guarantees, and also constitute a hassle-free, low maintenance package that appeals to many. It is also useful to note, if you are planning to relocate to France, that the health and education systems in the country are classed among the best in the world.

INSIDER TIP Due to the French inheritance system, where children take precedence as heirs, many young French people rent for many years before inheriting either a property or capital with which to buy a property. This means there is a substantial market for long-term rentals, especially in the larger cities and in the south of France near tourist locations. The current rental market attracts yields of around 7%–10% in sought after areas.

The French government is trying to improve the quality and quantity of holiday property in the country, and has therefore introduced a leaseback scheme.

Through this, buyers accept limitations on the amount of weeks per year they are allowed to spend in their property in exchange for a number of benefits. These benefits include: a guaranteed annual return of up to 4.5% for a fixed period (usually nine to eleven years – and the rental is usually index-linked, so as prices rise, so do returns); all expenses incurred in running the property are paid; and the government will return the VAT on the property, which on new developments is 19.6%.

Hotspots

When looking for a second home, the key to buying in France is to find a region that suits you and to rent a gite there for at least two weeks to give yourselves time to look around.

Choice is likely to come down to personal preference, although areas that have been popular with Brits in the past are the Dordogne, Cote D'Azur, Alsace, Charentes and the Loire Valley. However, this popularity is reflected in the prices in these areas as well as the high number of English tourists and expatriates.

For investment purposes, less popular regions within France are often preferable. Prices throughout the country will start high, but it is still possible to see good capital growth if you buy in the right area. Figures from the French National Estate Agents Federation indicate that from September 2005 to September 2006 both Lyon and Toulouse outperformed the national average, with prices appreciating by over 10%. If you can afford the entry prices in these areas then, they still constitute good investment opportunities.

Better prices and more potential for growth are available in other areas. **Languedoc-Roussillon** with its 42 beaches, for example, still has a long way to go before its potential is exhausted. Property is available here for all budgets, from £26,000 ($52,434) to over £660,000 ($1,331,174). The **Limousin** region has also been making its mark in recent years, especially now that budget airlines are flying to Limoges, in fact this is currently the most popular region with British buyers. Here, buyers with as little as £88,000 ($177,500) to spend can choose from a good selection of three-bedroom houses with good-sized gardens. Other up-and-coming areas include the **Auvergne, Burgundy, the Pyrenees, Lorraine**, and the **Champagne-Ardennes** region.

Beach and golf resorts are a good bet for rentals. New golf resorts are springing up all over France, and a new-build property on one of these can cost as little as £50,000 ($100,800).

In June 2006 the new TGV East service cut travel times between Paris and Strasbourg by nearly half. This greater accessibility will increase property prices in **Strasbourg** itself and also at other stops such as **Reims** and **Colmar**. Planned improvements to the service in Brittany, the south-west and the south should also raise house prices in places such as **Lorient, Narbonne and Angoulême**.

For those wanting shorter term and seasonal returns, the **Alps, the south of France** and **Paris** probably represent the best opportunities for rentals.

'France is not a place for speculative investment, as the French property market is tightly regulated, and fees and taxes are high'

France has two main ski areas; the **Rhone-Alpes and the Midi-Pyrenees**. The most expensive of these is the Alpes where studios will set you back anything from £61,000 ($123,000) and a two-bedroom apartment from £101,000 ($203,700). In contrast at Haute Pyrenees, a five-bedroom character village home is available for around £195,000 ($393,300) and a three-bedroom apartment for £101,000 ($203,700).

A recent survey by PricewaterhouseCoopers shows that **Paris** is Europe's top city for property investment, predicted to offer the best returns and lowest risk over the next two years. Regeneration around La Défense and house prices rising at an average of 11% are both contributing to Paris' success. Despite rising prices and capital gains, homes are still affordable; 60% cheaper than in central London. Moreover, there is a severe shortage of rented accommodation, and the city is never short of prospective tenants. The gross rental yield is currently running between 4.5% and 8% per year. When buying in Paris it is a good idea to choose a popular area. Central locations appeal to local professionals, while tourists tend to opt for areas such as the Latin Quarter, or Montmartre. A one- or two-bedroom apartment here will typically cost upward of £254,000 ($512,200) although properties in need of refurbishment and furnishings can be bought for around £120,000 ($242,000). There is now a good rental market for suburban houses, perhaps facilitated by the sheer pressures of living in small Paris apartments. Capital gains in these areas can reach as much as 13%.

The Purchase Process

All property sales in France are handled by a notary, or a *notaire*. The notaire is responsible for checking paperwork and ensuring that the correct procedures are followed, but will not protect or act in the interests of a buyer, so it is always a good idea to hire an independent notaire or solicitor. The services of a tax advisor will also prove invaluable, as the tax system is extremely complex and the rules change frequently.

Other than this, buying in France is relatively straightforward. Before seeing the notaire, it is necessary to have copies of all essential documents, such as birth and marriage certificates, translated into French. Once a price is agreed an initial sales contract, or *compromis de vente*, is signed and a ten percent deposit is paid (this is held by the notaire in a 'blocked' account until completion). A seven day cooling-off period follows, after which the contract becomes binding and neither party can pull out of the transaction. Completion typically takes place three months later, after your solicitor has completed all the necessary checks on the property. This involves the payment of the balance and the signing of the final deed – the *acte de vente* or *acte authentique*. After buying it is also a good idea to draw up a French will and check that it does not revoke your existing will. If you are married or have a long term partner, seek local, competent advice on the *regime matrimonial*. This governs how your assets are owned throughout the course of your relationship and dictates who gets what in the event of death or divorce.

Buying costs in France are among the highest in Europe. Amounts to be paid depend on the age of the property and those under five years old are subject to lower costs. Expect the following costs:

- For legal fees and registration taxes expect to pay between 4–10% of the purchase price.
- Estate agents' fees are around 2%–5%, which may be paid by the vendor, the buyer or be shared, although it is normally included in the purchase price.
- TVA (VAT) of 19.6% on a new property is applicable for 20 years under French law. Should the owner sell before this period expires, the balance will be repayable at a rate of one-twentieth per civil year. It is possible to avoid paying this tax under the leaseback scheme.
- Capital gains tax stands at 16% for non-resident EU citizens (33% for non-EU citizens) for up to 15 years after purchase. After the first five years there is a yearly discount of 10%, meaning CGT will disappear after 15 years.

As the owner of a French property you will also be liable for *tax fonciere*, or property tax and taxe d'habitation, or local taxes. These taxes are calculated on the theoretical rental value of the property and are payable by the owner of the property (although owners of new build properties are exempt from this tax for a period of two years from 1 January following the completion date).

Some sources say that certain French property laws regarding inheritance, insurance and renovation are being reviewed at the moment. Potential investors should therefore keep a close eye on any changes before buying property in France.

Mortgages

Financing is fairly easy in France. Mortgages can be arranged either through a UK bank or building society, or a French bank. If a mortgage is required, this must be declared at the time of the *compromis de vente*, and a clause must be added protecting the buyer's interest in case of the loan being refused. The house must also be valued by an expert.

French mortgages are now looking increasingly advantageous for the international property investor. Until now, in a traditionally strict system for overseas purchasers, the maximum loan-to-value (LTV) ratio typically offered by French lenders ranged between 80% and 85%. However, lenders will now offer up to 90% LTV to UK and Irish buyers on holiday homes, seasonal rental and lease-back properties in France, requiring a deposit of just 10%. This increased lending could provide a significant advantage for UK and Irish investors, with lower deposits resulting in higher gearing and magnifying real returns on cash invested.

Mortgages are calculated on the basis that the monthly repayment does not exceed one third of the buyer's income. Repayment periods also tend to be shorter than in the UK or USA and the repayments higher, so it pays to compare interest rates, terms and fees both at home and abroad. Mortgages in France are generally payable over a 25 year term at 4% interest rates.

Key Risks and Opportunities

In France, as in Spain and Italy, the property market is considered to be mature, and therefore entry prices are high. In remote and hidden corners of the country it is still possible to find properties for under £30,000 ($52,000), but they tend to be priced this low for a reason. They are likely to be miles from any amenities, have no facilities, electricity, mains water, sewerage or gas, and are generally uninhabitable. If you intend to buy a property to renovate, be aware that planning permission is required for any major, and sometimes minor, changes, especially to external parts of a building. It is also difficult to generate year-round income through a gite in an area which does not have access to winter sports, while in smaller villages everything closes early, especially out of season. It is therefore worth spending more to get a desirable property in a good area. If you have a low budget or are in the market for a serious investment with low entry costs, consider buying elsewhere. If you intend to live in France, it is also a good idea to conduct careful research into visa requirements – infringements are taken extremely seriously.

The main opportunities in France are therefore suited to those looking for a place to settle, or to rent and own a holiday home. The leaseback scheme offers substantial savings through the VAT concession, but it is worth noting that you are only eligible to claim this concession if the property remains in your possession and under the scheme for twenty years – otherwise a proportionate amount of the discount received on purchase will have to be paid. Higher returns and easier exit possibilities may be achievable by buying independently and hiring a letting agent yourself, though these are not guaranteed and offer greater risk.

France is not a place for speculative investment. The French property market is tightly regulated, and fees and taxes are high. To achieve a sensible return it is necessary, if possible, to hold on to an investment for 15 to 20 years. This will ensure that there will be no capital gains tax to pay, and if the property is bought on the leaseback scheme the purchase will be VAT exempt.

Opportunity Rating

France presents good opportunities as far as rental returns in the cities and some selected holiday areas. However entry prices are high and price growth in many areas appears to be slowing.

Rating: $ $ $

Risk Rating

Capital return possibilities here are substantially lower than in other European countries. The market is also closely tied to the UK holiday market, meaning that a UK change of focus to the more emergent markets could have an impact here.

Rating: ⚠ ⚠

Germany

CURRENCY
Euro

EXCHANGE RATES
100 Euro = £67.64
£1 = 1.47 Euro
100 Euro = US $136.3
US $1 = 0.73 Euro

Introduction

Germany is an investment market that has been braced for success for a number of years now. Dubbed the next big thing in real estate for several years, it is yet to realise its potential and some are beginning to wonder if it ever will. In contrast to the rest of Europe, house prices have actually fallen over the last decade, purchase fees and taxes are expensive and the Germans have one of the lowest recorded rates of home ownership. Indeed Germany is predominantly a rental market with only 42% of Germans owning their own home compared to 69% in the UK and US. What's more, GDP growth was an unremarkable 2.7% in 2006 whilst nominal economic growth of only 1.8% was expected for 2007. It seems then that perhaps Germany is struggling to shake its label as the 'sick man of Europe'.

However, despite the apparent risk associated with this market, some professional and institutional investors are looking to Germany and spending enormous amounts of money on residential purchases. These investors see German property as a bargain asset which just might perform in the long-term. This is because Germany is now considered one of the world's most undervalued property markets. Investors are therefore taking the opportunity to invest while the market has reached an all time low predicting a gradual turn around which should result in significant re-growth.

Germany is well known for its beautiful countryside and unpolluted coastlines but not so much for its tourism. Few people are known to buy holiday homes here and it is most definitely not one of Europe's key tourist traps. As a result, there are some question marks surrounding an investor's exit strategy – who they would sell their property on to? Considering locals' great reluctance to buy and the country's lack of regular tourist supply, it remains to be seen who exactly will be looking to buy German real estate.

Is This a Good Place to Buy?

Germany is a strong European market that could have the potential to offer investors high returns on investments in commercial and buy-to-let property, particularly in popular urban locations such as Berlin and Munich. Large scale investors in German property however are gambling with the possibility of being successful on a buy-to-sell basis due to the speculation as to whether the property will in fact re-sell. On top of this difficulty, any investor who re-sells will have to pay 15% speculation tax if the property has been owned for less than 10 years, and an estate agent fee of up to 10% of the purchase price, as well as a 1% notary fee when the property is first purchased.

'Dubbed the next big thing in real estate for several years, Germany is yet to realise its potential and some are beginning to wonder if it ever will'

Germany is therefore not somewhere to invest for short term returns although experts predict that the potential for long term investments is steadily increasing. Germany is Europe's largest country, most populous nation and Europe's largest residential market. With marginal house price growth of only 1.2% in 2006, property is 10 times cheaper here than London. Prices in Germany are depressed by a number of factors. In the past 15 years the number of German households in debt has almost tripled and people are beginning to declare insolvency meaning that the number of people able to afford to buy a property is limited. In addition, a sluggish economy, high levels of unemployment and low wages mean locals are reluctant to commit to mortgages. Also, because rental costs are fairly reasonable and the law provides strong protection for tenants, few are inclined to go through the hassle of the buying process.

Economic woes are compounded by demographic figures showing that Germany has a shrinking population which is expected to decrease a further 16% by 2050.

The problem of depopulation also has a regional impact. Although the German government has paid out a considerable amount of money to bring eastern productivity and wages up to western standards much of eastern Germany remains depopulated, unable to offer the employment and higher wages of the west. As a result there is now oversupply of property in the east with up to one million surplus residential units. Another problem, which will affect property sales in the future, is the aging problem in Germany. There is a fear that by 2030 the number of retired people relying on their pensions will peak, meaning fewer people will be looking for somewhere to buy.

'GDP growth was unremarkable in 2007. Germany is struggling to shake its label as the "sick man of Europe"'

Despite this negativity, Germany has attracted significant investment from some large institutional investors since 2004. UK based company, Alpha Real Estate investments, the central European property specialist, is initiating a variety of profitable opportunities for big Irish and UK investors who want to invest in Germany's capital with rental yields from 5.5%. Add to this Germany's good legal system, secure property rights and high quality judicial system and some chinks of opportunity become apparent. With a relatively undeveloped property market which has not yet reached its peak, Germany has good potential for capital appreciation over the long term. With so few German home owners, more people will be looking to buy or rent property at some point in the future. Moreover, there is a 10%–20% total growth in value predicted over the next five to six years.

Put all of this together and it is possible to see why intelligent investors are thinking seriously about placing money in Germany. The entry threshold is low and should home-ownership rise, capital appreciation will follow. Indeed some property companies such as propertysecrets.net and knightfrank.com strongly believe that Germany has potential for growth in the property market and that within the next two years residential property prices will improve significantly.

Perhaps then Germany is an opportunist's market, as long as one is prepared to take the risk.

Price History

Property prices fell 7% between 2000 and 2006 and were expected to continue to fall or at best stagnate during 2007. The rental market has suffered a similar slump and rents today are 13% lower than their 1994 peak. The fall in rentals however is smaller than the decline in property prices which explains why this sector is favoured by investors. It is known that Germans themselves prefer to rent accommodation than to buy and with an unemployment problem still evident it is unlikely that many will be able to afford to buy in the near future.

Real estate prices in prosperous cities such as Frankfurt are higher and as the market here is under-supplied, rents are going up.

Although the majority of Germans rent, it is claimed that this will only prove to be a marginally cheaper option in the long run. The German government is therefore trying to encourage German residents to buy property instead of renting to take advantage of the low property prices. It is also suggesting that buying as opposed to renting could lead to income tax breaks under a private pension programme known as the *riester-rente*.

Which Type of Property Should You Go For?

Centrally located city apartments are likely to be in the highest demand. In general, Germans move much less often than other European groups and, comfortable with renting, will look for years to find the right home. Higher quality buildings will therefore be highly valued and perform better in a market where over-supply continues to be a problem.

At least 75% of properties in Germany have been built after the Second World War meaning traditional homes are hard to come by and, as a result, are very expensive. Return on investment on these properties is therefore likely to be slim.

Whilst buy-to-let investments may offer the best potential, it should be mentioned that yields can become compressed because of high vacancy rates. The total housing stock in Germany is 39 million units and the vacancy rate is around 7% (fluctuating between cities and rural areas). However if Germans continue to favour renting the way that they do now, then it has been suggested that yields in the cities could reach 8%–10% in the future.

An established trend is for developers to buy whole apartment blocks for renovation and this is one of the grounds on which tenants may be given notice. Six to eight storey apartment buildings can be bought in Berlin for €200,000 – €300,000 and a renovated block in a reasonable area will then rent out for greatly increased prices.

Hotspots

Compounding demographic trends which see people moving from east to west and into larger cities, municipalities to the west and southern parts of Germany offer some of the better investment opportunities. **Frankfurt, Dusseldorf, Cologne** and **Stuttgart** are cities which will attract shrewd investors. In Frankfurt, a one-bedroom apartment costs from €120,000 and a two-bedroom apartment costs from €135,000 (£91,000/$189,000). A five-bedroom detached house can cost from €430,000 (£291,000/$592,000).

Prices in **Berlin** are exceptionally low, but with only 11% of the population owning property and a vacancy rate of 150,000 units in March 2007, the capital is best seen as a market for long-term investment.

Hamburg benefits from EU enlargement and is home to a number of key industries including chemical, IT and logistics. A good bet could be retirement properties with a guaranteed rental return, which have been known to offer 8% gross. **Leipzig** benefits from relocations within the automotive industry including BMW and Porche.

In rural Germany apartments can cost from as little as €20,000 (£14,000/$25,000) and houses start from €80,000.

The Purchase Process

Once the sale price is agreed, contracts are drawn up and translated. Among other details, the contract must include property details, agreed prices, payment conditions and clauses specifying what will happen should either party fail to complete the contract.

The next step is to choose a notary who acts as impartial liaison between buyer and seller. The notary has responsibility for checking the status of the property in the land registry and for witnesses' signatures. Both parties need to be present as the contract is read aloud. The notary is supposed to check that the buyer understands the commitment that they are entering into. You therefore need to be very confident with the contract or pay for a translator to be present.

Before signing the contract, the buyer should check the property to ensure that there are no obvious faults. The notary is not responsible for this and the seller is only required to point out any hidden faults with the property. The entire purchase process of a German property should take an average of 41 days to complete. After the contracts are signed the notary lists the change of ownership at the property registry and the transaction is complete.

Fees are comparatively high and are likely to total 6%–7% of the purchase cost. Stamp duty is 3.5%, the notary may charge up to 1.5% and land tax of 1% may be added. Non-residents may face an additional wealth tax of 0.5%. Capital gains tax is also levied at high rates, although property held for more than ten years will be exempt.

Mortgages

Mortgages are widely available with interest rates as low as 4.5%. A 70% to 30% balance between debt and equity is conventional and fixed rate mortgages are common. Having said this, the German mortgage/lending system is comparatively restrictive and it is very difficult for foreign non-residents to obtain a housing loan, NPL (non-performing loan).

Key Risks and Opportunities

Given the unique focus on renting, property bought in Germany may well take longer to sell than in other countries and immediate profits are unlikely. This is not the best market for people who may need to access capital quickly and anyone entering this market should be looking towards a long-term investment strategy, ranging from five to 15 years. It is also important to assess the strength of the local rental market wherever you choose to buy. High fees and initial outlays mean that costs are hard to recoup if the balance between supply and demand is unfavourable. Nevertheless, the current signs of recovery in Germany although cautious and gradual, are still positive, meaning the country is not considered an overly unstable or inherently risky market.

Opportunity Rating

Prices remain very low, yields can be high in the right location and it is often claimed that German property represents one of the most undervalued assets available. Government reforms and the country's emergence from a long recession should see prices rise significantly.

Rating: $ $ $

Risk Rating

The primary risks in Germany are first that economic recovery is very fresh and somewhat fragile, and second, the government has a lot to do in order to change the population from a rental culture into an ownership culture and as such provide more solid exit strategies for investors. If this is successful, price inflation and capital gains should follow. Commissions and taxes are still high and in the case of Berlin, the land tax is higher than the rest of Germany. However, all indicators suggest that Germany is capable of overcoming these risks.

Rating: ⚠ ⚠

Greece

ATHENS

Introduction

Greece is one of the world's great centres of history, civilisation and culture and its wide variety of historic sites and areas associated with legend and mythology attract tourists from around the world. There are 15,000 kilometres of mainland coastline bordered by the Aegean and Ionian sections of the Mediterranean. Much of the coast offers long sand or pebble beaches with safe swimming together with a plethora of rocky coves and natural harbours, making it good for both sailors and sunbathers. Scattered across these seas are 2,000 islands of which only 160 are inhabited. Inland areas vary from dry hillsides covered with herbs where goats graze, to pine-covered mountains. This countryside is highly attractive to walkers and outdoor enthusiasts. The land is fertile and lends itself to a wide range of agricultural uses from salad crops to olives, while the sea has created communities dependent on fishing.

With its rich history and culture and dramatic coastline, Greece has been a popular tourist destination since the mid 1950s. The country's economy benefited enormously with the explosion in package tours in the 1960s and 70s. Today tourism accounts for approximately 18% of the Greek gross national product. Record numbers of tourists visited in 2006 and this growth was expected to increase by 4% in 2007 according to the World Travel and Tourism Council.

Several of the world's best-known business names hail from Greece including legendary shipping magnate Aristotle Onassis and easyJet founder Stelios Haji-Ioannou. However, apart from agriculture, shipping and construction, tourism is the main lifeblood of the Greek economy, which has grown at a steady rate since the country joined the eurozone in the mid-1990s, mainly due to lower interest rates.

This growth was consolidated when Greece hosted the 2004 Olympic Games, which led to a cleaning up of Athens, the creation of a better infrastructure and an increase in tourist numbers. Nevertheless investment from overseas businesses has been somewhat hampered by the government's extraordinary levels of bureaucracy and red tape.

After pressure from the business community there is currently a move to reform the procedures by which companies can invest in the country. This, it is hoped, will encourage investment and boost tourism further.

Is This a Good Place to Buy?

Though winters in many parts of Greece can be cool and wet, the holiday season is considered quite long, and generally lasts from early June to the end of September, though some tourist activity is in evidence in mid-May and late October. Temperatures range from the low 20s into the mid 30s in high season.

Athens has become increasingly hip since it hosted the Olympics, with many new boutique hotels and restaurants. It is also easily accessible to the coast, with several upmarket resorts within a 45-minute drive or ferry ride. Athens is also the main transport hub for the region with numerous direct flights and shipping channels to other countries and the Greek islands.

In terms of home ownership, there are a range of options, with each island or mainland area having distinctive characteristics. There has been little of the rampant overdevelopment seen in comparable holiday destinations and building laws limit both where and how much one can build in sensitive locations. Official permission from the local authority is required to build outside a designated urban zone. Greek property is still considered highly affordable in comparison to other holiday destinations such as Spain or southern France and interest has increased from overseas buyers, which, in turn, has led to a fast rise in prices.

INSIDER TIP

One difficulty facing property owners wishing to access their second home is the lack of transport options to many locations during the winter months. Direct flights to all but the largest islands reduce or cease operation from October to early May and transport is then by ferry or connecting flights via Athens. However the recent increase in low cost flights during peak season should have a positive affect on both the tourist industry and property sales. For example from summer 2007 GB airlines increased their weekly flights to the Greek islands by 550% to five times a week to Crete, four to Corfu, two to Rhodes and two to Mykonos.

Price History

Since 1999 prices in Greece have risen steadily. Increases of between 12% and 15% were recorded in 2006 with the popular island areas seeing the highest returns. In Corfu and Crete, for example, rises of 40% for sought after coastal property were not uncommon.

Detached property with direct views of the sea cost from €400,000 up to over €1m. Apartments with sea views start from around €120,000 and standard new-build villas from around €250,000. Smaller restored stone cottages can be found for similar prices, however, places in need of work or inaccessible locations can be as little as €45,000 in some areas.

Coastal land tends to be more expensive than rural areas, with sea views commanding anything from €100,000 upwards for 4,000 sqm. The price you pay will depend on several things, including views, location and accessibility, availability of utilities and permission for building.

Athens has also seen good growth with rises of 12% per year on average. Apartments in the city start at around €80,000 for something measuring around 50 sqm but large properties in more central locations will cost around €250,000. Popular suburbs can be bought into from around €120,000 rising to around €400,000 for attractive villas in good areas.

Which Type of Property Should You Go For?

Those seeking rural or coastal locations have the option of buying land for building, traditional stone houses (many in need of restoration), or newly built villas or apartments. In many locations a car is often necessary as public transport is limited. In addition, Greece's package tourism industry has created a large number of busy and well-developed resorts with clubs, bars and retail outlets appealing to mass tourism.

The property market is considered to be under developed in comparison to other southern European countries, given the many attractions and benefits Greece offers. However, as interest has increased the market has started to move on from being very locally based, with sales centring around individual land plots or homes for restoration, to larger-scale, new-build developments in popular locations such as Crete, Rhodes and Corfu.

'Greek property is still considered highly affordable in comparison to other holiday destinations and interest has increased from overseas buyers, which, in turn, has led to a fast rise in prices'

Buying village properties is still possible in many locations and may suit those who are willing to integrate with the local population, particularly those willing to attempt to learn the local language and show respect for customs. Such residents are generally welcomed into the local community. The winter months in many rural locations, especially inland and in the mountains, may be cold and wet or even see heavy snow and buyers may wish to consider when they will want to use their property. When restoring rural property, it is often the case that you must do so in a way that is in keeping with local character – using local materials and techniques, for example, and avoiding incongruous extensions or more than two storeys.

Property in busy resorts will offer access to tourists for rental purposes but many towns that are heavily dependent on mass tourism close for the winter season and may not be suitable for those wanting a year-round lifestyle option.

Hotspots

Most buyers are attracted to the main islands of Greece, such as Crete, Corfu and Rhodes. The mainland is less well known to property buyers but areas such as the Peloponnese offer both coastal and village property and prices can be lower here and winter access easier.

Athens

Vibrant, lively and now considered very desirable, Athens is too busy and polluted for some but since the 2004 Olympics the capital has cleaned up its act. The infrastructure is far better than previously and there are lots of upmarket shops, hotels and restaurants. Standard apartments, even in central locations, can be remarkably cheap, while prestigious suburbs such as Ekali or the nearby island of Aegina can command very high prices.

Peloponnese

A large land mass joined to the Greek southern coast, the area is a mix of developed coastal resorts, a wealth of historic sites, peaceful mountain villages and rural areas. The area is also attractive to Athenians, who come to escape the city. Property ranges from standard apartments and new-build developments in popular tourist locations to small cottages in undisturbed villages or coastal towns.

Crete

Crete is the largest of the Greek islands and is very popular with both Dutch and UK buyers. Two airports mean both halves of Crete have their fair share of tourists. To the western side of the island are the busy towns of Chania and Rethymnon, while the east has the major towns of Heraklion and Malia, a sprawling resort. There are many pretty small villages both inland, among the mountains, and along the coast that offer a mix of traditional stone houses, renovated property and ruins ripe for restoration. There has been an increase in new-build villas and apartments and several developers have now moved into key coastal locations. As a result of the increased interest, prices have risen significantly in the past few years.

Corfu
A very green island, Corfu offers pine forests and a mix of long sandy beaches and small shingle coves. Property tends to be divided into high-end villas, often in small fishing villages on the north-east coast, cheap apartments in large-scale resorts and village properties. Much of the island is very well developed due to the long history of tourism and this offers scope for a longer season.

Rhodes
Rhodes is one of the largest and sunniest islands in Greece, offering a combination of cultural and historic sites, good beaches and lively resorts. There are restrictions on development to protect the coast and rural areas and there is a large ex-pat population of all nationalities. The northern part of the island is less developed by tourism and is popular with property buyers. Popular towns such as Lindo and Tsambika are particularly expensive.

Other islands
There are many islands in Greece to choose from depending on the lifestyle and type of property you prefer. Smaller, less developed places such as Thassos and Skopelos will appeal to those wanting more secluded and peaceful islands but travel services and property options may be more limited. Prices will not necessarily be any cheaper in these locations. Larger, more developed islands such as Kefalonia and Zakynthos often offer the best of all worlds: a good tourist season, good infrastructure and local services, and a mix of properties in all categories and prices.

The Purchase Process

Property ownership by non-nationals has only been possible since 1991 when the country relaxed its laws for overseas investors. Now anyone can own freehold in the country. However, a non-EU citizen must have the permission of the local prefecture in certain border locations, including northern Greece, Crete and Rhodes, to buy. This process isn't usually particularly time consuming.

Funds used to buy property in Greece can legally come only from an account held at a Greek bank. So any prospective purchaser has to open a local account. You will also have to obtain what is commonly called a pink slip, which documents all money transfers from overseas bank accounts. This is your proof that the money was legally brought into the country and should be kept safe.

Before purchasing, a prospective buyer must also obtain a tax number, called an AFM, from the local tax office. EU citizens need to show some form of photo-ID, such as driving licence or passport, to obtain an AFM.

Once the property has been found an offer is made to the vendor. If accepted a preliminary contract is drawn up detailing the terms of the offer and payment schedule of the sale. A non-refundable deposit of 10% is usually required to secure the property. If the buyer pulls out of the sale they forfeit this money and if the seller withdraws from the sale he must also forfeit the 10% and pay the buyer a further sum of 10%. The deposit will be refunded should any problems arise during the search or survey that cause the seller to pull out.

The seller must provide all documentation pertaining to the property, including evidence of ownership or clean title. The buyer's lawyer needs to check that ownership of property and land is clearly defined (a difficult process in Greece, where so many families have dispersed over the years). It is not unknown for missing family members to turn up during a sale and claim full or part ownership of the property. Buyers should always instruct their legal representative to thoroughly check all title deeds and ownership claims to property or land being bought and to obtain signed permission to sell from anyone who may have a claim against the property. A topographical report should also be done to establish legal boundaries.

When building a property it is important to note that permission to build can be given on plot of minimum size of 4,000 m^2, providing it is not within the town boundary and if there are no forestry or archaeology restrictions. Certificates clearing land by both forestry and archaeological departments should be obtained. If the land is within an urban planning zone or fronts a municipal road, permission can be given to build on plots of land measuring 2,000 m^2 or less. Obtaining planning permission to build can take up to 10 months. Don't assume that plots located outside urban zones (which in Greece also means villages) will have access to utilities such as water and electricity. These may have to be run to your property at a considerable cost.

Off-plan property should be approached with the same legal caution as resale. The developer's history, experience and the legality of the build should be checked before proceeding with purchase. All new property has to be earthquake proof by law. Planning permission is not usually required if the building is already in place and is being restored within its original footprint. All boundaries, rights of way and encumbrance should also be clearly documented.

Once all searches and surveys have been completed the final contract is drawn up and signed by both parties. The new title is registered with the land registry office and the buyer then becomes the official owner of the property. The process usually takes six to eight weeks and is overseen by an independent public notary and the real estate agent involved in the sale. It is also important to ensure that all documentation is translated from Greek into your first language. Never sign anything you don't fully understand.

When buying property in Greece you should also budget for:

- The notary's payment of 1%–3% of the property's price
- Legal fees of 1%–2%
- Land registration fees of 0.3 to 0.45%
- Transfer tax of 1%
- Property purchase tax of 9%–11%. Urban property in cities also attracts a further 2%.
- Post purchase you will have to pay annual property taxes of 0.25% of the property's value if the perceived value is more than €243,000.
- VAT is now payable on sales of new buildings and property built after 2006 now attracts capital gains tax of 10% to 25% based on the property's current value and number of years of ownership.

Mortgages

To apply for a Greek mortgage you will need to supply the lender your passport and proof of income for the last two years (this can include a P60 or similar, or tax returns). You will also need to pay all closing costs on the sale before the bank will release any funds. Mortgages are usually available as interest only or repayment products with 25-year terms and lenders will generally loan up to a maximum of 80% of the property value or purchase price, depending on which is lowest.

Key Risks and Opportunities

Greece has been a highly popular tourist destination for some time but the benefits and ease of property ownership there have only recently been discovered. The lifting of restrictions on non-Greek ownership is only now beginning to be fully explored and prices of both property and land in many areas are still reasonable. On popular islands, where the market is more developed there may be less chance to gain from capital appreciation and this will also affect rental yields for those buying now.

Opportunity Rating

Despite its continued popularity with visitors, the Greek market is still considered to be undeveloped with regard to both property and tourism and has the potential to grow by some considerable amount in the next decade.

Rating: $ $ $

Risk Rating

There are no major economic or political risks with buying in Greece, but buyers should be aware of the need to ensure that solid title is associated with properties to be purchased.

Rating: ⚠

Italy

CURRENCY
Euro

EXCHANGE RATES
100 Euro = £67.00
£1 = 1.5 Euro
100 Euro = US $138
US $1 = 0.73 Euro

ROME

Introduction

The birthplace of opera, Dante and da Vinci, Italy epitomises artistic elegance and cultural prowess. Home to magnificent beaches, unspoilt countryside, ancient cities, an enviable climate and a vibrant history, Italy is one of the world's favourite holiday destinations. Over 37 million tourists visit the country each year making it the fifth major tourist destination in the world. The cost of living is comparatively low, the health service and transport infrastructure are excellent, and the pace of life is refreshingly easy-going. Also, due to more stringent planning regulations than in Spain and other countries, Italy has kept its charm, remained largely unspoilt and is home to the greatest number of UNESCO World Heritage sights in the world. For lovers of the outdoors there is climbing, skiing and snowboarding in the mountains, while the more gentle hilly areas of Tuscany and Umbria are ideal for hiking and mountain biking. Numerous beach resorts dotted along Italy's coastline also provide excellent opportunities for watersports including sailing, windsurfing and scuba diving.

Economically, Italy is currently moving fairly slowly although it still boasts a GDP that is among the world's highest. Over the last decade the government has pursued a tight fiscal policy in order to meet the requirements of the Economic and Monetary Unions, and has benefited from lower interest and inflation rates. Numerous short-term reforms have been implemented, aimed at improving competitiveness and long-term growth, but other improvements, such as lightening the high tax burden and overhauling the rigid labour market, have not yet been put into practice. This is partly due to the economic constraints placed on the leadership by the budget deficit, which has breached

'Continued high levels of demand have pushed prices up, and Italy's property market now stands among the highest-priced in Europe'

the EU ceiling. Having said that, the economy performed better in 2006, with a 1.96% GDP growth rate, higher than the 2001–2006 average of 0.7%. The rate of unemployment also declined from 7.8% in 2005 to 6.9% in 2006, whilst inflation remains close to the average euro rate at 2.1%.

The property market in Italy is well established and attracts large numbers of investors keen to enjoy a slice of the beauty and passion that the country has become so famous for. Continued high levels of demand have pushed prices up, and Italy's property market now stands among the highest-priced in Europe. A marked economic imbalance however divides the country into two distinct areas. The North has traditionally been the main area of interest for foreign investors, and the market here is well and truly emerged. The south of the country on the other hand is somewhat less developed and offers a range of more affordable properties. It is these parts of southern Italy then that have the greatest potential for capital growth.

Is This a Good Place to Buy?

Italy guarantees a great quality of life, a secure investment and a fascinating cultural experience. It also has the advantage of no inheritance tax and, unlike France or Spain, there is no capital gains tax if you sell after five years.

If you are buying to rent, you will be committed to a four year contract with your tenant in compliance with the 1998 Rental law and as such will be restricted to fixed rental rates. As the law is strongly pro-tenant, renting can seem fairly unattractive. On the plus side, it does mean that you will have guaranteed rental for four years. While house prices throughout Italy have been growing at an average rate of 8.1% since 1999, rent grew by an average of only 2.7%, indicating the fragility of the rental market.

Price History

Following the recession of the 1990's, Italy's housing market has been engaged in a consistent and substantial recovery and from 1998–2006, has seen house price appreciation of a colossal 90%. Having said that, the annual rate of growth appears to be slowing. A 10.6% increase in 2003 dropped to 8.7% in 2004 and again to 7.1% in 2005 and was 6.3% in 2006. Explanations for this recent downturn can largely be attributed to the increase in mortgage rates. With 87% of mortgage loans floating or fixed for only a year or less, borrowers are very sensitive to rate changes. The mortgage interest rate for one year fixed loans rose from 3.47% in 2005 to 4.93% in 2007 and as such has impaired the rate of price growth.

Traditional *trullos* (stone dwellings with a conical roof found only in Puglia) in need of restoration are available for under £20,000 ($40,000), whilst three bedroom family homes are available for £170,000 ($345,000). The cost of a large luxurious villa rises to over £1million ($2million) although this will vary greatly depending on the popularity of the region.

Which Type of Property Should You Go For?

Whether you're looking for a *trullo*, an apartment or a large luxurious villa, Italy has a property to suit every budget. At the lower end of the property scale, renovation is often a must. However, the charm of traditional stone-built homes occupying amazing plots with tremendous views does make this process worthwhile.

For those interested in rental returns it is probably advisable to purchase an apartment in one of the more important Italian cities such as Rome, Milan or Florence where demand will be consistent and high. However, as a result of the emphatically pro-tenant rental laws, the rental market has dwindled in recent years. While rental dwellings accounted for 25% of all property in 1993, statistics a decade later saw this number fall to 16%.

While wealthier second-home buyers are likely to buy in popular areas, investors looking for capital growth are advised to look to less developed areas such as Puglia, in the south, poised to become Italy's hotspots of the future.

Hotspots

At the top end of the market are areas such as the **Italian Lakes**, or the larger cities. The Alpine region around the lakes is a playground for many wealthy Italian second-home owners thanks to its proximity to Milan. This part of Italy boasts the romantic lakes of Como, Maggiore, Garda and Lugano, but also has a huge range of property available, from period villas to brand new apartments. The area attracts people of all ages, and there are a variety of year-round activities including water-sports, fishing, and skiing in the winter. Lakeside properties regularly sell for well over £700,000 ($1.4 million), and a more modest family home away from the water will cost upwards of £250,000 ($500,000). If investors are prepared to commit to renovation projects however, properties can still be found from around £50,000 ($100,000).

Investors seeking rental potential should look to the larger cities, such as **Rome, Florence, Venice** or **Milan**. These areas symbolise Italy both in their historic and spectacular architecture and in their fashionable shopping districts, which are considered to be some of the best in the world. It is possible to find a two-bedroom apartment in St Peter's Square in Rome for £550,000 ($1,100,000), while a four-bedroom 19th Century luxury apartment in the historic centre with a two-car garage is available for £1.4 million. Yields here range from 3.7% to 5.3%. In Milan, apartments (studio to three-bed) can be bought for between £88,000 ($178,000) and £155,000 ($314,000) and can enjoy yields of between 4%–5.2%. In Florence meanwhile, a one-bedroom apartment in the heart of the city is available for £403,600 ($827,000) and should yield between 4.8%– 5.8%, while an eight-bedroom country house just outside the city will cost £870,000. Finally, in Venice, a two-bedroom fully-furnished apartment, which is estimated to yield £675 ($1,200) a week in rent, can be bought for £210,000 ($426,000).

'Italy has the advantage of no inheritance tax and, unlike France or Spain, there is no capital gains tax if you sell after five years'

Italy's best-known region is probably **Tuscany**, with the areas around Pisa, Siena and Florence being the first place many UK residents think of when look- ing for second homes. The blankets of countryside and quaint hilltop towns and villages throughout the region show what life was like in ages past – this area is truly the heart of Italy. However, high demand, fuelled by the availability of cheap flights to Pisa, means that Tuscany is now every bit as expensive as it is lovely, with prices having risen by more than 40% since 2000. Two-bedroom town- houses and apartments start at around £50,000, while a basic four-bedroom farmhouse here costs around £400,000 with the same needed to be spent on renovation. However, the north of the region is considerably more affordable as it is often overlooked due to its mountainous setting.

Neighbouring **Umbria**, a sleepy, verdant region dotted with medieval towns and castles, is easily accessible and is often cited as a cheaper alternative, although prices here have also shot up in recent years. Property tends to be most expen- sive in the two main tourist towns, **Orvieto** and **Assisi**, and also in the south of the region, but prices are more reasonable around Lake Trasimeno and further north around Citta Di Castello and Umbertide. A two-bedroom apart- ment here will cost around £120,000 ($240,000), while £250,000 ($500,000) buys a three-bedroom house with a swimming pool and a substantial garden. Both Tuscany and Umbria are extremely popular with those looking for a prop- erty to renovate or for a buy-to-let purchase. The holiday rental market here is also generally good, though competitive, and a large, high-quality farmhouse can earn as much as £4,000 a week.

> Those with an eye for a bargain should consider **Sicily** and the increasingly fashionable **Sardinia**, both of which offer perfect climates, great beaches and their own cultural idiosyncrasies. Property is generally cheaper than on the mainland – a good-sized family home can be bought for less than £200,000 ($400,000).

More affordable regions include **Le Marche** and **Puglia**. Le Marche was, until recently, unknown by tourists, but due to the efforts of the regional tourist board and press coverage in the UK, it has become increasingly popular. The region boasts the elegant towns of Urbino and Macerata, with Urbino recently being hailed as 'The ideal city of the Renaissance' and 'The Siena of Le Marche'. In Le Marche, it is possible to buy an enormous fifteen bedroom farmhouse in need of extensive restoration for £300,000 ($610,000), while family-sized farmhouses in need of restoration go for around £50,000 ($100,700). Puglia's stock is also rising rapidly, with house prices seeing a 20% rise in recent years. The attractions of Puglia are year-round sunshine, a good variety of beaches, affordable house prices and a less tourist-orientated atmosphere. Low-cost flights allow for easy access through Bari and Brindisi airports, and an old ruin in need of renovation can still be bought for about £80,000 ($160,000), while a four-bedroom house can be found for under £270,000 ($550,000). Traditional Trulli can be bought in this area for around £20,000 ($40,000) and two bedroom houses can be found for under £11,000 ($22,000). For even lower prices, the more adventurous buyer might consider **Basilicata**, although this is well and truly off the tourist map. It is worth noting that the south of the country in general is considerably less affluent than the north; the service infrastructure is less reliable and local government corruption can be a problem. Unemployment is relatively high here too.

The Purchase Process

A foreign citizen wishing to purchase in Italy must obtain a *codice fiscale*, a tax identification number. The first step in a purchase is for the buyer to make a verbal offer to the vendor, usually using an estate agent as an intermediary. The offer is then placed in writing and becomes legally binding on the buyer's part. Once the seller accepts the offer, the parties have a binding contract, which is formalised with the execution of a *compromesso*, a formal agreement under which the parties agree to buy and sell the property and agree on the terms and conditions of the sale. These terms and conditions include full details of the property, details of the vendor and buyer, the purchase price, any financing, the closing date and any other details or conditions that must be met before completion. On signing the *compromesso*, the buyer pays a 5–10% deposit of the purchase price (30% on a new-build property). Unless otherwise indicated, in the event that either party withdraws from the sale the other party has a right to force the sale and/or collect damages and/or retain the deposit (if the seller is the breaching party the penalty can be twice the deposit amount). Completion is achieved on signing the final deed (the *rogito*), which is drawn up by a notary, usually six to eight weeks after signing the preliminary contract. When the necessary documents have been returned, the balance is paid, along with fees and taxes.

Fees will vary depending on whether you buy old or new and whether you are buying through an agent or privately. Fees associated with buying in Italy include:

- Registration tax or stamp duty of around 10%
- Purchase tax of 3–10%
- Land registry tax of between 1% and €129.11
- VAT, currently 20%
- Notary fees: usually about 4% of the declared price
- Mortgage fees: usually around 2.2% with a mortgage tax of €129.11 for resident first-home buyers on top of this
- Legal fees: 1%–2%
- Estate agent's fees (both the buyer and seller pay estate agency fees of between 3–8%, but the buyer is often expected to pay all of the agent's fees).

Italy is one of the highest-taxed countries in the EU, and you are advised to seek the services of a good accountant. Property tax is levied at between 0.4% and 0.7%. Capital gains are taxed as income at around 30% during the first five years of ownership, and disappear after this period.

Mortgages

Mortgages are only available on completed buildings at 80% LTV with interest rates starting from around 5%.

Key Risks and Opportunities

When buying a property in Italy, it is advisable to make a separate Italian will and to nominate a fiscal representative residing in the country, especially if you don't plan to live there on a permanent basis. This representative can be a friend, neighbour, lawyer or tax advisor. Your UK lawyer can advise you on this. You should also appoint separate legal representation. Appointing a *commercialista*, an accountant or business advisor, is also vital to assist in dealings with the Italian bureaucracy (Italy has more laws, rules and regulations than any other country in Europe).

If you are looking for a renovation project, it is a good idea to conduct thorough research and establish a budget before committing to anything. Get a full survey carried out before you buy, and employ a surveyor that you can trust. Renovation costs can easily rise astronomically, and access roads can cost from £30 per square metre. However, if you buy a castle in Italy you may receive a contribution of up to 50% towards the cost of the renovation from the state as well as a contribution of 25% of the taxes of the purchase. Furthermore, you do not have to pay mortgage interests or ICI (annual tax when owning property in Italy).

Italy offers most to the wealthier buyer wanting to purchase a second home in a country renowned for its lifestyle, its cuisine and its people. The more fashionable regions offer extremely desirable properties at exorbitant prices; however it is still possible to find lower prices. Better chances for profit are found by looking outside the already-established markets to up-and-coming areas, so investors looking for rental returns and capital growth are also catered for.

Opportunity Rating

Italy is at the high end of the market, with high prices and several bureaucratic obstacles which hinder and prolong the buying process. The north of the country is more suitable for lifestyle purchasers although there are still good opportunities for profit in the southern regions.

Rating: $ $ $

Risk Rating

The aforementioned bureaucratic obstacles constitute the major risks here, with regards to planning permissions and the buying process. However risks in general in Italy are extremely low.

Rating: ⚠

Montenegro

CURRENCY
Euro

EXCHANGE RATES
100 Euro = £67.33
£1 = 1.49 Euro
100 Euro = US $134.62
US $1 = 0.74 Euro

Introduction

Recently propelled into the public eye via the medium of film, Montenegro triggers images of stunning lakes, captivating coastlines and a 'Bond-esque' gracefulness and style. It is one of those property markets that still offers exceptionally good value for money. It may be one of the smallest countries in Europe, but it has mountains, lakes, pine forests, fjords, walled cities, world heritage sights; and, most of all, mile after mile of beach.

In the 1960s and 70s Montenegro's upmarket Sveti Stefan Resort exerted a magnetic attraction over the rich and famous. Elizabeth Taylor and Richard Burton are said to have disturbed other guests with their arguing, whilst Sofia Loren gave the chef lessons in how to cook pasta. This happy state of affairs persisted until the war in the former Yugoslavia. Although Montenegro itself never saw fighting, visitor numbers plummeted and the tourism industry suffered. Only in the last few years has tourism in Montenegro returned to anything like its pre-war supremacy. Since its split with Serbia in 2006, the country has once again begun to attract the well-heeled visitors that frequented its shores during the 1960s and 1970s and is now being dubbed as 'the next Monaco'.

The nature of the market also seems to be changing. Traditionally a favourite with Italians, Germans and Russians, the Brits and Americans are now falling for Montenegro's charm and arriving in droves. English is widely spoken, and the beach resorts are being redesigned to attract wealthy higher-end tourism comparable to that in Croatia and Italy.

The World Travel and Tourism Council now tips Montenegro as the number one country for tourism growth over the next ten years and visitor numbers are expected to rise by an average of 9.9% every year between 2007 and 2015.

> *'Since 2006 the value of real estate has soared making Montenegro not only one of the most attractive destinations in Europe, but in the world.'*

Montenegro is therefore becoming a regular fixture on holiday programmes and in travel supplements and many industry professionals privately consider this to be one of the best opportunities around.

Is This a Good Place to Buy?

Montenegro's direct competitors are probably Turkey, Bulgaria, Croatia, Italy and the Mediterranean Islands. Cheaper than other Adriatic states, but with more old world charm, better year round weather, and a more sensitive attitude to development than the Black Sea states, Montenegro has all the best ingredients of the European sun and sea destinations.

Hailed as the 'fastest growing travel and tourism economy in the world' infrastructure improvements are underway to cater for the predicted rise in visitor numbers. The amount of construction underway is dramatic as numerous private and public investors have poured millions into improving local amenities. In total, more than €500 million has been channelled into new developments and rebuilds. This level of investment will clearly pave the way for similar projects, helping Montenegro transform its tourism product from that of a low-yield, mass-market destination to one offering the highest quality for customers and the strongest yields for investors. Alongside infrastructure improvements building projects include the reconstruction of Montenegro's tired Soviet era hotels whilst the rather decrepit, but beautifully set island resort of Sveti Stefan has been bought out by luxury hotel group Aman Resorts and is due to open in 2008 or 2009. Despite this redevelopment, careful planning has, so far, helped Montenegro to avoid building the type of concrete jungle risked by other Black Sea states.

Montenegro has other advantages: the overspill of buyers from Croatia means that the property market is rising steadily. At present prices are rising fastest in the north of the principality, but with only 290 kilometres of coastline the balance of supply and demand should favour early buyers and keep prices high.

Based on the results of the 2006 referendum, Montenegro declared independence on June 3 2006. It became the 192nd member state of the United Nations, and in May 2007, the 47th member state of the Council of Europe. Independent from industrial Serbia, the principality will be able to concentrate on development as a tourism hotspot and is officially recognised as a potential candidate for the EU, boosting the country's profile.

Montenegro is also steadily getting richer. The country leads the way on returns from PDI and is one of Europe's top three countries for GDP per capita. EU funding is being used for new roads and infrastructure and since 2006, the value of real estate has soared making Montenegro not only one of the most attractive destinations in Europe, but in the world.

Price History

Property prices have reportedly risen by 85% since 2004 and, with a backdrop of strong economic growth and a booming tourist industry, it is believed that the values of coastal property will soar by more than 50% in 2007.

Average prices range from around £63,700 ($128,400) for a one-bedroom apartment, £83,000 ($167,400) for a two-bedroom apartment and £150,500 ($303,500) for a three-bedroom house. Houses needing a significant degree of reconstruction cost from £20,000 ($40,000) to £30,000 ($52,000) getting more expensive moving closer to the coast. New-build apartments start from a higher base, costing upwards of £40,000 ($80,600).

Which Type of Property Should You Go For?

Montenegro has all the qualities required to make it a top holiday and second home destination and for those with renovation or project management skills there are many opportunities. The country has a high number of good quality stone buildings which have been either abandoned or allowed to fall into disrepair and although requiring a lot of work, are often very good value (see picture 14 in the colour section).

For most buyers however, it makes sense to invest in one of the new apartment or villa developments being built along the coast which offer increasing opportunities for buy-to-let investment. Montenegro is aiming to remain an upmarket destination and new build trends should reflect this, making off-plan investment both viable and attractive. With foreign and domestic investors given parity of treatment, rising tourism and a stock of attractive good-sized buildings, Montenegro is also a good location for people hoping to set up bars, cafes or seasonal lets.

Hotspots

A new wave of buyers is exploring Montenegro after crossing the border from Croatia. Interest is therefore focused predominantly towards the north of the country and particularly towards Kotor Bay.

Kotor is a Unesco World Heritage Site and a medieval fortress city, which makes it more than just the usual beachfront resort. The area has already seen substantial investment and prices in this area are generally well above the national average, and are comparable to the most expensive areas in Croatia. A one-bedroom apartment here can sell for around £100,000 ($201,600), while a three-bedroom house costs around £210,000 ($423,400). Although the market remains popular, it has more appeal among those looking for holiday homes than among dedicated property investors.

> *'Montenegro has more secure property title than many of the surrounding countries as property here was never expropriated'*

In coastal areas south of Kotor, property prices are considerably lower and **Herceg-Novi**, **Budva** and **Bar** are emerging as popular resorts and investment hubs. **Budva** is a walled town placed just outside Sveti Stefan surrounded by 24 miles of beach and thanks to its pale stone town walls, is frequently compared to Dubrovnik. This area around Budva and Sveti Stefan is one of the most intense areas for development throughout Montenegro and a three-bedroom house in the historic town of Budva costs an average of £86,600 ($174,600).

Tivat is also tipped as a hotspot and property prices are set to rise here significantly. The local airport makes Tivat very accessible and it is also the site of a huge marina and resort project led by the tycoon Peter Munk.

INSIDER TIP   **Cetinje** is the traditional capital and cultural centre of Montenegro. Now a university town, property can be picked up cheaply and rented to students.

In general, opportunities for capital appreciation are now better in the south or inland at mountain and lake resorts although any properties near beaches like Buljarica or Becici are also likely to see a healthy price rise. Another good bet is **Ulcinj**, which has 8 miles of beach and prices which remain at good value. There are increasing numbers of projects available in other regions of Montenegro, including the capital **Podgorica**, and the area around **Skadar Lake**. Prices are starting to go up, but you can still find a stone house on Skadar Lake for upwards of £20,500. Most importantly, given the minimal investment to date, the mountain regions are now hotspots for investment and the government, donor agencies and NGOs are now promoting these heavily.

The Purchase Process

As with most European countries, the purchase process is in two parts; signing the contract and taking legal possession of the property, and then making sure that the process is duly recorded at the land registry. The process is remarkably straightforward. Montenegro uses the euro, and except for public lands such as parks and roads there are no limits on the property in which foreigners can invest. Like close neighbours Slovenia and Slovakia, Montenegro has computerised the registration process and from beginning to end, registration is unlikely to take more than a couple of days.

The buying process is as follows: after agreeing a purchase price with the seller, a 10% deposit is standard. Should the buyer fail to hand over the balance of the purchase price by a set date the deposit is forfeited, but if the seller fails to complete the deposit is returned plus an additional 10% penalty fee. After the contract is drawn up it must be signed by both parties or by representatives with valid powers of attorney. The signatures must also be attested, purchase tax of around 2% of the property value is paid and the change of ownership registered with the land office.

There are no restrictions on foreigners buying in Montenegro and non-resident investors are given tax-breaks, whilst assets from sale of property or other investments can be freely transferred out of the country. Currently non-residents pay tax on capital gains at the rate of 15%, through withholding. Residents pay tax on capital gains annually. However, an individual who sells real property is exempt from tax on the condition that he/she has used that property for personal housing purposes for at least three years prior to its sale. The top level of income tax is 24%, property purchase tax is 2% and legal fees equal around 1%.

Mortgages

Montenegro is quite an undeveloped market in terms of foreigners obtaining mortgages however, this is changing quite quickly. In July 2007, 50% mortgages at a rate of approximately 9% were available. It is expected that in a very short space of time, mortgages of 70% LTV will be offered with interest rates below 8%.

Lenders will only lend on completed buildings meaning anybody looking to purchase off-plan properties will not be able to obtain a mortgage until the property is completed.

Europe

MONTENEGRO

Key Risks and Opportunities

Montenegro has more secure property title than many of the surrounding countries as property here was never expropriated. As development intensifies, some of the more popular resorts may risk the kind of over-building seen in Bulgaria and Turkey. At present the authorities are taking a more thoughtful approach to planning and encouraging the rejuvenation of older buildings. Long may this continue.

Opportunity Rating

Before the early 1990s, Montenegro was one of the most desirable holiday locations on the Mediterranean. The government is now attempting to rekindle this reputation and should be able to do so now that the country's affiliation with Serbia has ended. Prices remain low; but they are climbing fast as tourism increases along with the necessary infrastructure for international investment which will equate to increased capital gains.

Rating: $ $ $ $

Risk Rating

Specific risks lie in the clarity of title and buyers should ensure that a good local solicitor is employed. Investors may also be thwarted by the poor quality of local infrastructure and difficulty in obtaining finance.

Rating: ⚠ ⚠ ⚠

Poland

CURRENCY
Zloty

EXCHANGE RATES
100 Zloty = £17.78
£1 = 5.63 Zloty
100 Zloty = US $35.32
US $1 = 2.17 Zloty

WARSAW

Introduction

Nestled in the centre of Europe, Poland occupies a pivotal geographic position and is a stepping stone between the east and west of the continent. Thanks to its situation, it is rapidly becoming one of Europe's key business regions and is receiving consistently high levels of FDI. In fact, Poland remains the largest recipient of foreign investment among Eastern European emerging countries and enjoyed FDI inflows of over $10billion in 2006.

Alongside its prevalent commercial strengths, the country is also blessed with a rich culture. Home to both contemporary and medieval towns, the land maintains the essence of its ancient traditions whilst keeping abreast with modernity. Peppered with a mix of towering mountains, gushing streams, and the oldest primeval forest in Europe, Poland is home to the last of the European bison and the coveted amber gem stone.

Since joining the EU in 2004, Poland's economy has gone from strength to strength and has been engaged in a cyclical recovery. With close links to neighbouring Germany, Europe's largest economy, Poland is being successfully integrated into the EU and, due to its size and economic clout, has been one of the most high profile 2004 entrants. Contrary to previous decades, Poland now enjoys a combination of strong balanced growth, low inflation, rising employment and a small current account deficit. GDP grew by 5.3% in 2006, was expected to grow a further 4.5% in 2007 and should rise by over 50% by 2010. Poland is expected to join **the eurozone** in 2009.

As Poland's economy burgeons, so too does the appeal of its property market. Property prices increased by 33% in 2006, although much higher increases were experienced in certain cities such as Krakow. In the past, Poland has arguably attracted more pure investment buyers from Ireland, the UK and Germany than any other country and it is likely that this interest will continue for the foreseeable future.

As local wealth increases, Polish families are demanding better quality residential property and the level of home ownership is rising steadily. Currently there are on average only 310 housing units per 1,000 inhabitants, compared with 450 in Western Europe. As a result demand for new off-plan apartments is outstripping supply by 40% with the need for nearly 40,000 new houses per year. New units are sold almost instantly and the demand for two bedroom apartments has overtaken the demand for luxury penthouses. Demand should further increase as unattractive grey Soviet apartment blocks which still make up much of the housing stock, are replaced with newer more appealing buildings. New developments are springing up fast and Poland's major cities are becoming characterised by suburbs of inexpensive housing catering to young professionals and Poland's growing middle classes.

For foreign investors, Poland is ripe with opportunities and considered to be one of the safest countries to buy in Central and Eastern Europe. Just three hours from London, BMI, easyJet, Ryanair, Wizz Air and British Airways now fly direct to Poland, at relatively low prices making access quick and affordable. Add to this steady capital appreciation of 10%–12% per annum, a competitive mortgage market, a stable economic and political situation, low cost entry and relatively low buying fees and Poland's investment appeal becomes evident.

Locals too are latching on to their country's potential. Encouraged by the fact that several large blue-chip companies are relocating to their cities and aware of the increase in tourist visits over the last few years, locals have been influenced to buy and first time mortgages have been rising over the last four to five years. It is estimated that since Poland joined the EU in 2004, more than 500,000 Poles have emigrated to the UK and are using the money they are earning abroad to invest back home in the Polish property market.

Is This a Good Place to Buy?

The 2006 study of potential capital appreciation over the next ten years conducted on behalf of Channel Four's *A Place in the Sun*, concluded that Polish real estate could offer returns of 393% and was ranked second after Romania. Although Poland does present a good investment opportunity, it is unlikely that this level of growth is attainable. However, according to the *Emerging Trends in Real Estate Europe Report* released jointly by the Urban Land Institute and PriceWaterhouseCooper in 2006, Poland should show the largest increase in residential sales across Europe. Property prices in Poland have increased faster than any other country in the world and experts predicted that prices would continue to rise throughout 2007 by 10%–15%.

There is no doubt that Poland is taken very seriously by educated investors and with residential yields in cities of up to 6.06%, it is easy to understand why. Indeed, whether Poland can still be classed as *emerging* is debatable.

'There is no doubt that Poland is taken very seriously by educated investors and with residential yields in cities of up to 6.06%, it is easy to understand why'

A construction boom, which started in Warsaw and Krakow has now spread to regional centres such as Gdansk and Poznan and thanks to EU funds, the country as a whole will benefit from an improved infrastructure. Poland will have 27.8 billion euros to spend between 2007 and 2013 on the Infrastructure and Natural Environment program which accounts for more than 40% of all EU subsidies. It is expected that the programme will bring Polish infrastructure closer to EU standards. As well as being used to build new roads, funds will also be poured into modernising airports and the air control system, repairing railway lines and constructing a high-speed railway project.

A recent increase in the availability of credit facilities is also indicative of the strength of Poland's real estate market. It is estimated that lending is now a part of around a quarter of transactions and interest rates have fallen, making borrowing more affordable. The mortgage boom is characterised by borrowing in foreign currencies as opposed to zlotys as this can be more expensive. The interest rate on a loan in Swiss francs can be as low as 5%, rising slightly to 6% for loans taken in euros.

House prices should also benefit from Poland's joint hosting (with Ukraine) of the UEFA 2012 soccer tournament.

Price History

Prices in Poland have been rising steadily over the last decade. According to the Royal Institute of Chartered Surveyors' (RICS) European Housing Review, capital appreciation was close to 20% in 2002 and 2003 whilst prices rose by 10% in 2004. In 2005 growth hit 27% and topped 33% in 2006. Following the RICS survey of 26 European countries and their rates of house price growth, Poland was the best performing country. Krakow is a city performing particularly well and was named Europe's number one property hot spot in early 2007 after its property prices had risen by 58% in the preceding year.

Luxury apartments in historic buildings in the very centre of Warsaw can now cost zl.10,000 – zl.20,000 per square metre whilst studio flats designed for young professionals can be found from as little as €60,000 (£42,000/$73,000). Three bedroom houses in the suburbs cost about €145,000 rising to €300,000 for sizeable properties in very good locations. A price spike was predicted towards the later end of 2007 when investors rushed to buy before the imposition of an increased VAT rate levied on new-builds not deemed to be low-cost housing in nature from January 2008. Currently only 7%, the tax will soon jump to 22%. At the time of writing the Legislature had not declared whether this would be retrospective in application and had not clearly defined 'low–cost'.

Which Type of Property Should You Go For?

The rule in Poland is either to buy new or old and avoid anything in between. Large scale building programmes in the 1970s and 1980s contributed to a massive increase in residential stock however the quality of build was not high and as a result, over 60% of the housing stock is now in need of repair.

Instead of investing in these unreliable properties, local analysts instead suggest buying new build apartments or small houses in the suburbs of major cities. These properties are suitable for renting to Poland's growing local middle classes and expatriate communities and can return a reliable rental yield of 6%–7%.

Older properties are also a good buy especially turn of the century apartments with high ceilings as these can command high prices. Developers are also turning their attention to renovating townhouses before sub-dividing them into apartments.

Hotspots

In 2006 Poland's three best performing areas were Warsaw, Krakow and Wroclaw each enjoying 20% capital appreciation. As a result these destinations have become increasingly popular with investors.

Warsaw

Warsaw is not just the titular capital of Poland but also its economic centre. The number of professionals relocating to Warsaw is expected to double by 2010. GDP in the city is increasing at a rate up to four times faster than throughout the rest of the country, boasting GDP per capita more than 75% of the European average. There are indications that prices in the city centre may have topped out, but interest in the suburbs is still strong. Rental yields here stand at approximately 6%. Warsaw still reigns supreme when it comes to market standards and offers some of the best investment opportunities combining the lowest risks with good returns.

Krakow

Krakow attracts interest because of its place on the Unesco World Heritage list and status as a favourite weekend break and inter-rail destination. However, although tipped as the property hotspot for 2007, Krakow is actually the hardest city in Poland to get building permission and the returns are not as strong as in Warsaw.

Gdansk

Alongside Poland's large commercial cities, smaller municipalities are beginning to materialise as important investment destinations enjoying fairly stable growth of around 15% per annum. **Gdansk** (German Danzig) set on the Baltic Coast and surrounded by good beaches was the best performer in 2005 (see picture 3 in the colour section). A historical port and industrial centre, Gdansk functions as a crossroads for trade routes from Germany to the East. It also has a charming old town, painstakingly reconstructed after the Second World War which helps boost the city's tourist appeal. Cheap flights are now available from London to Gdansk international airport and tourism here has been growing by an average of 20% per year.

Prices here are some of the cheapest in Poland, a third of prices in Lodz, Wroclaw and Krakow and half of prices in Warsaw. One-bed apartments are available from £50,000 including VAT, and rental yields are currently very high ranging from 8%–11%. With large government and municipal expenditure developing the Tri-City rail and road networks, the Special Economic Zone of Sopot to attract business, and the very high level of education, Gdansk should continue to attract multi-national companies and pose as a strong investment hub in the future.

The student population in Gdansk is especially large meaning rental demand is high and there is a growing buy-to-let market here. Low property prices and demand for tourist accommodation mean strong yields are achievable, making Gdansk an attractive place to invest.

Zakopane

Located in southern Poland against the Tatras Mountains, Zakopane is Poland's premier ski resort attracting 2.5 million visitors a year. With good access to Poprad airport across the Slovakian border and the proposal for a new motorway intersection linking Zakopane and Krakow airport, transfer times should soon be reduced to only one hour. Budget flights now fly into both Poprad and Krakow Airports from the UK meaning flight costs are pleasingly low.

Thanks to the area's varied leisure activities, Zakopane caters for both the summer and winter tourist seasons giving a rental window of around eight months each year. Holiday homes in Zakopane are currently most popular amongst the Polish meaning the value of property has remained steady and affordable. One-bedroom apartments in the Zakopane resort are available from £45,000 plus VAT (7% of property value). Outside the resort, new developments are being sold for £77,000 including VAT with estimated rental yields of 5%, whilst yields in the resort are 7%–9%. Euro mortgages are available locally, although foreign investors need a permit to buy here.

Lodz

Set against the stunning Sulejowskie and Jeziorsko lakes, Lodz is the fastest growing second tier city in Poland experiencing 4.1% growth per month. With good transport links and a growing economy, the city is a regenerating manufacturing base offering attractive property investments. Capital appreciation was forecast for 25%–50% in 2007 and GDP predicted at 6%.

During the first four months of 2007 property prices in Lodz rose by 16%. Property prices are still relatively low compared to cities such as Warsaw and Krakow with one-bedroom apartments available on average from between £10,000 to £15,000 less than Warsaw prices. Loft style apartments in renovated warehouses have been popular amongst foreign investors costing approximately £35,000 for a one-bedroom flat in a good area. Commutes to Warsaw take only 45 minutes thanks to a new high speed train link and direct flights from budget airline Ryanair now fly into Lodz airport from the UK. Rental yields of between 8%–9% are reportedly achievable.

Wroclaw

Perched on the Odra River, Wroclaw is situated between Prague, Warsaw and Berlin close to both Germany and the Czech Republic. Thanks to the construction of a new multi-million pound airport aimed for completion in 2009, the city's prominence and investment potential should steadily develop. With a GDP per capita more than 45% above the national average and capital appreciation reaching 20% in 2006, Wroclaw is one to watch.

The Purchase Process

Foreigners can freely buy condominium units in Poland. Land for commercial purposes can be bought by citizens of the European Economic Area (EEA). Those EEA citizens wishing to buy land for housing and recreation not intended to be the foreigner's place of permanent residence however, require a Ministry of Internal Affairs and Administration (MIA) permit.

Once a property has been decided upon and a price agreed, a preliminary contract will be composed, committing both parties to the sale and setting a date for the final contract signing. A deposit of between 10% and 20% is usually due at this stage. The role of a notary is to then check the property title for undisclosed charges, and also to ensure that the seller has the right to sell.

The final contract is then signed by both parties before the notary who then logs the change of title at the property registry. This is a slower process than in many of the new European member-states and registration can take up to three months. The purchase price is transferred after the final contract is signed.

Agent's fees are charged to both buyer and seller, with the buyer paying 3% of the property value. Notary and property taxes are charged at 2%–2.5% of the sale price, and are somewhat less for apartment buildings. Capital Gains is treated as ordinary income and is charged on real estate held for less than five years at the standard 19% corporate income tax. 7% VAT is levied on new-build properties until Jan 2008 and it is expected to rise to 22% for luxury builds.

Mortgages

Mortgages are available through international lenders and local banks. Terms are some of the most attractive offered on an overseas property purchase – reflecting the comparative maturity of the overseas investment market here. Typical loan to value is 85% with interest rates starting from 5%. Self certification is available but with less desirable rates. Banks will include foreign income in their assessments and there is even a specific buy to let mortgage which takes account of expected rental returns. Mortgages are available over a thirty year term.

INSIDER TIP **Buyers can borrow in different currencies and tend to avoid the zloty. The value of the Polish currency has risen more than 15% since foreigners were given the right to buy in 2004 which adds a corresponding 15% to the value of the mortgage. Loans in Swiss Francs tend to have the lowest interest rates.**

Europe

POLAND

Key Risks and Opportunities

Poland has experienced some difficulties in the past with unscrupulous developers, who have either taken deposits and run, or delivered something that differs radically from the original plans. The problem is concentrated in areas where development is something new. In Warsaw and Krakow, developers can often recommend previously successful projects and contacts. In emerging hotspots such as the TriCity area on the northern coast, a more cautious approach is important in order to verify a developer or agent's integrity.

For buyers interested in off-plan property, local experts also recommend visiting the site in person, as surroundings can vary widely and may be situated in large run down environs.

Opportunity Rating

Poland was a high profile EU entrant and shows many fundamental strengths indicative of a good investment location. There is however, already evidence of over-supply in certain areas as well as extensive emigration of young Poles seeking higher paid employment in other parts of the EU. However, there are some great buy-to-let opportunities in Poland, particularly in cities on the inter-rail circuit. Good properties in reasonable areas should experience healthy long term growth. Thanks to the growing middle classes, reliable demand for property over the medium term at least, is likely.

Rating: $ $ $

Risk Rating

Poland still has a long way to go to prevent its currency from over appreciating. It also needs to concentrate on further reducing unemployment levels and creating a fair taxation system that will prevent tax avoidance. Looking to the future however, the investment climate in Poland is healthy and holds lots of potential, making the country a good choice for real estate investors.

Rating: ⚠ ⚠ ⚠

Portugal

CURRENCY
Euro

EXCHANGE RATES
100 Euro = £67.20
£1 = 1.47 Euro
100 Euro = US $13.4
US $1 = .75 Euro

LISBON

Introduction

Portugal has been a very popular tourist destination for over 20 years and has many British ex-pats. It has beautiful countryside and coastlines, elegant cities and a Mediterranean ambience, despite being on the Atlantic Ocean. The Algarve, in particular, has seen an outstanding level of development, especially in relation to golf tourism, with new areas opening up towards both the western coast and the Spanish border to the east. Northern coastal regions are also very beautiful, though with less good weather than the south and have also proved a magnet for the golfing industry. The Duoro Valley and city of Porto are well known for wines with Port and Vinho Verde its best-known exports.

Once a strong colonial power with outposts in India, South America and the Far East, Portugal is one of the smaller EU states. After a period of revolution and major economic change in the mid-1970s, the country attempted to stabilise under a succession of new governments every two years and grew steadily through the following two decades. In recent years however, growth has slowed somewhat and Portugal showed the least growth of all EU countries in 2006, despite the government having imposed a series of drastic changes (including raising VAT, restricting pay rises for government workers, raising the retirement age and cutting public spending). There is huge disquiet among Portuguese residents at their country's low growth compared to neighbouring Spain.

The state of the country is mirrored in the fortunes of the capital, Lisbon, a beautiful and lively city that is only now recovering after a period of decline and neglect. Restoration work is taking place, with the help of EU funding. New infrastructure is being built, services are being improved and large numbers of buildings are being renovated. The current airport is undergoing expansion and a new, larger airport is also scheduled for a 2017 opening.

Is This a Good Place to Buy?

Though it has had a reasonable amount of political and economic upheaval in the past few years, Portugal is now seen very much as one of the more stable and established EU countries. Prices as a whole have been depressed for several years but the main holiday hotspots are seeing vast amounts of new investment and development.

In terms of second home ownership, coastal Portugal offers a secure long-term investment. It is a welcoming environment for overseas ex-pats and is also perennially popular with tourists. The country was one of the earliest investors in golf tourism and that has paid off handsomely with some of the finest mature courses in the world. The high season may not be as long as southern Spain but hot summers and mild winters are ideal for attracting a wide mix of golfers, beach lovers and those escaping northern European winters. Rental prospects are good for buy-to-let investors with Portuguese tourism bringing in around 12.8 million people per year. However, oversupply of property may again become a problem if too much development is allowed along the Algarve and Silver coasts.

Lisbon and smaller towns such as Sintra and Oporto may be good invest-ments for the long term, though they have less certain buy-to-let returns. Prices are still depressed, which may make it a good time to buy. All the cities in ques-tion are beautiful, historic and popular with weekenders, and are likely to see gains over several years, as buyers priced out of other locations, turn their atten-tion to northern Portugal.

Price History

There are two property economies in Portugal. The Algarve and the rest of the country. Most buyers are really only interested in the south coast, though further north (what has become known as the Silver Coast) is also starting to attract interest.

The Algarve has been the major area for both construction and sales for the second home and holiday rental market for at least 20 years and is the main location in which northern Europeans buy. Prices rose quite spectacularly in the period to 2003 when Lisbon saw peaks of around 18%, but then a slump set in. This was partly due to weak economic growth as well as oversupply and changes in the law that allowed buyers to own their property as part of an offshore company, thus avoiding stamp duty.

Europe

However, the market has since picked up again and prices rose by 5.9% in the Algarve in 2006. Other locations were not so fortunate with Lisbon only seeing rises of 1.3%–3%, depending on location, and the rural Alentejo area actually seeing a drop of 3.5%. Average prices in Lisbon are currently around €2,500 per square metre.

'Rental prospects are good for buy-to-let investors with Portuguese tourism bringing in around 12.8m people per year.'

PORTUGAL

Prices in the Algarve vary widely from small apartments within the busy and, some might say, overdeveloped resort areas costing less than €100,000, to palatial villas on exclusive golf developments priced in the multi-millions. Average prices on the coast are currently around €3,500 to €4,000 per square metre. Ironically, it is the high-end of the market that seems to be doing best in this area with properties on select estates selling well for extremely high prices.

Despite having negative growth in the past year, property in the rural Alentejo region is not cheap for the overseas market. Prices can start at under €100,000 for small village houses or country ruins but something large or in good condition can be advertised from €250,000 or more.

Price rises of Portuguese property from 2000 to 2006 were 16.9% overall but the Algarve's effect on that cannot easily be dismissed.

Which Type of Property Should You Go For?

The obvious choice in Portugal for both short-term rentals and capital appreciation would appear to be golf property either on the Algarve or Silver Coast, as this is where the majority of the country's successful tourist and golf industry is located. Villas with pools or apartments in attractive residential developments with facilities such as spas and tennis courts are now more popular with visitors than traditional stand-alone property.

This does not translate across the board, however. Low-cost property in the highly built-up areas has not been as in demand or seen the same gains as high-end property on expensive estates. This is maybe because Portugal, in general, attracts a more sophisticated market than other tourist hotspots.

In Lisbon, one or two-bedroom apartments in quality areas are the most likely to see better appreciation and rental prospects. The districts of Lapa and Chiado tend to attract locals and longer-term tenants, while Alfama and Barrio Alto are more popular with the tourist and a younger market.

Hotspots

Algarve

Central areas of the Algarve around Albufeira, Vilamoura and Faro have been heavily developed in terms of tourism and the property market for several decades. Property for sale here is a mix of apartments in standard high-rise blocks (which can be found on the market from upwards of around €100,000), family townhouses and small villas in purpose-built complexes (from around €300,000), and large, exclusive properties in high-end communities (from €650,000). The latter properties are usually to be found in the so-called 'Golden Triangle' of resorts such as Quinta do Lago and Vale do Lobo, most famous for attracting well-known footballers and golfers.

As a result of a recently completed motorway from Faro, the quieter, opposite ends of the Algarve are now also opening up. The west is slightly wilder than the eastern end, with fine sand beaches and areas of national park. Towns such as Lagos and Burgau still have a very Portuguese character, despite attracting many tourists in the summer months. Development has only recently started to happen on any kind of scale and is generally high end and low key. The prices here were once quite low by Algarve standards, but they are now beginning to rise sharply. To the east, on the border with Spain, much of the new-build is happening around the town of Tavira. A lot of development here is on a less sophisticated level than further west, with much of the property being aimed at the cheaper end of the market.

Lisbon

The capital is a beautiful and bustling city with a great deal of historical attractions, multi-cultural restaurants and bars and a fabulous river location. It has been allowed to become a little frayed round the edges but a programme of EU improvements has started to give it back its self respect. Prices here are showing only minimum rises at present but the feeling is that the time is ripe for its fortunes to improve. Small studios in nice central locations can still be found for less than €150,000, while apartments in converted palaces sell for around €350,000.

Silver Coast

The coast from Porto to Lisbon has become an alternative to the Algarve for those who want sun and sea. Though the weather is not as temperate as the southern coast, the region is popular with a mix of ex-pats and Lisbonites, who come to spend weekends and summer holidays here. Development has started to increase in this region and several large residential and golf complexes, such

1. Luxury villa in Bacolet Bay Resort and Spa, Grenada with the potential for net yields of between 6.5% and 15% pa

2. Sunset in Sabah, one of Malaysia's less developed and most beautiful regions with one of the highest tourism growth rates

3. Thanks to the recent increase in low cost flights, Gdansk is easily accessible making it increasingly attractive for investors

4. The Petronas Towers in Kuala Lumpur city centre where capital appreciation is just over double that of the rest of the country

5. The innovative design structure of The Cube in Dubai, a country welcoming 250,000 new residents a year and where 85% of the population is made up of expatriates. Property is generally in high demand

6. A beachfront villa at Nexus Residence, Malaysia comes fully furnished to a luxury modern spec, with broadband, private balcony, water features and a pool

7. The master bedroom of a Nexus pool villa. The interiors at Nexus Residence are of the highest quality

8. A pool villa in North East Brazil where cheap land and construction prices are creating an environment of rampant capital appreciation

9. Hampshire Residence, situated in a central location in the heart of Kuala Lumpur with modern luxury facilities. It is expected to achieve 8% yields

10. Grenada, occupying an early stage in the development cycle, offers excellent value by regional standards and relatively low cost entry into the Caribbean market

11. A lively souk in Marrakech where the current trend for property developers is to buy old houses, knock them down and build modern apartment blocks in their place creating a 'pied a terre' market for long weekenders from Europe

12. The unspoilt landscape of Mongolia whose current market positioning has been compared to Shanghai's before its enormous economic growth began

13. The Tatras mountain range bordering Slovakia and Poland enjoys both summer and winter seasons creating a prime investment destination

14. Montenegro has numerous vacant stone buildings which are perfect for renovation projects

WHERE TO BUY PROPERTY ABROAD

15. Penthouses at Royal Breeze in Ras Al Khaimah, UAE, where property prices are significantly cheaper than Dubai

16. South Africa, with its spectacular landscape, is also a promising investment destination, reputed to have the best deeds registration system in the world and property prices less than a tenth of prices in the south of England

17. Spectacular Shanghai, home to the powerful Shanghai Stock Exchange, one of the world's most important trade and finance centres and one of Asia's most exciting investment hotspots

18. Whilst all the major Turkish cities offer interesting investment opportunities, it is the historic areas of Istanbul, in desperate need of reconstruction and renovation, which offer some of the best investments

19. Whilst investors were primarily drawn to Bulgaria's coast, more recent interest has focused on the mountains as investors realise their potential as a year-round holiday hotspot of the future

as Praia d'el Rey and Bom Successo, have opened. Prices are now comparable in these upmarket resorts to areas of the Algarve.

> **INSIDER TIP**
>
> **Within 30 minutes of Lisbon are the coastal magnets of Cascais and Estoril, popular with those who live in Lisbon as a weekend retreat and with those who choose to live there and commute into the city. In general, these resorts have a sophisticated reputation and property (and its prices) reflects this. However it is possible to find cheap property in the less sought-after areas of Cascais for less than €100,000 as there are a lot of older apartment blocks in the town. Suburban apartments and villas with gardens here are popular with both buyer and rental markets.**

The Alentejo

People who want to live in Portugal but find the coast too expensive are moving out to this large rural area. Most of them are in search of village properties or rural farms to buy and renovate. Prices here have risen a lot in the past two years, even though there is little local demand. Many claim that the quiet villages in this region offer a chance to see the real Portugal.

Purchase Process

Non-nationals have the same rights when buying as locals and are offered the same protection. Even so, many experts advise hiring a local, English speaking lawyer as well as a UK lawyer who understands Portuguese law to ensure your best interests are looked after.

Before buying you will need a tax identification number known as an NIF (*Numero de Indentificacao*), which can be obtained from any local tax office. Once in possession of an NIF, you will be able to act more quickly when you see a property you want. When making an offer, it is possible to sign a reservation contract that holds the property for you while you have all of your searches and legal checks done. The fee for this is usually around €2,000–€3,000 and is refundable if it turns out that there is something wrong with the property.

Make sure you verify the vendor's right to sell the property. You should also investigate whether there are any boundary issues or disputes, whether there are any outstanding debts on the property or any other claims to ownership.

If everything is normal the buyer and seller sign a preliminary contract known as a *Contrato Promessa de Compro e Venda* in the presence of a notary. A deposit of 10% is usually paid at this stage. If either buyer or seller pulls out of the sale he loses the deposit and may have to pay a further 10% in compensation to the injured party.

The buyer's legal advisors have up to four weeks to finalise all their legal searches and checks on documentation before the final contract, the *Escritura de Compra e Venda*, is signed. The balance of the property purchase price is then paid and the property can be registered under the new owner's name at the land registry office.

Additional fees include a transfer tax (IMT), which is charged on a sliding scale up to 8%, legal fees of up to 2% notary fees and stamp duty which add on a further 1%.

Mortgages

Because Portugal is not seen as a risky market, mortgages are available to non-nationals via a number of overseas brokers some high street banks and large corporations such as Front Financial Service. Products are generally in euros and can be repayment or interest only. Mortgages are available up to 80% of the property value and can be from 5–30 year terms and with interest rates starting from 5%.

Key Risks and Opportunities

Buyers should be aware of 'black money', the practice of under-declaring the purchase price on the official sales contract. The remainder of the agreed price is then paid in cash, under the table, as it were, to the vendor so that he doesn't have to declare it to the tax authorities. This practice is illegal and could cause severe problems for the new owner later on or when he comes to sell.

It is also not uncommon for agents dealing with overseas investors to hike up the price of property compared to what a local would pay. Buyers are advised to shop around and get to know the market thoroughly before approaching agents.

Opportunity Rating

Portugal holds an important position within Europe. It is generally well regarded, has a growing tourism industry and, despite occasional downward blips, offers a relatively secure investment market. Capital appreciation is not as spectacular as other countries. Nevertheless, if its tourism and development sectors continue to grow and the government carries out financial reforms, there is no reason why it would not be an enjoyable and profitable place in which to own property.

Rating: $ $ $

Risk Rating

There are no major social, economic or political risks associated with buying in Portugal but, with such slow capital growth in some locations, buyers need to consider their own investment needs carefully.

Rating: ⚠

Europe

PORTUGAL

Romania

CURRENCY
Romania New Lei

EXCHANGE RATES
100 New Lei = £20.50
£1 = 4.86 New Lei
100 New Lei = US $41
US $1 = 2.44 New Lei

BUCHAREST

Introduction

With fairytale castles, majestic mountains, seaside resorts, traditional villages and cities full of architecture, Romania has been said to be where the Czech Republic was around a decade ago in terms of tourism status. Lying in south-eastern Europe, the country is bordered by Ukraine, Moldova, Bulgaria, Hungary, Serbia, Montenegro and the Black Sea and is therefore ideally placed for trading with its Eastern European neighbours. The Danube flows along the southern border and forms a beautiful delta. The Carpathian Mountains and Transylvanian Alps divide the country into Wallachia in the south and Transylvania, famous as the home of Vlad the Impaler (aka Count Dracula), in the north. Spring is pleasant, summers hot, autumns cool and winters regularly below freezing, when abundant snowfall provides ideal skiing conditions.

Despite concerns that Romania was not financially or socially ready to join the EU, it became a member in January 2007 having met a number of stringent targets for improvement. It is generally acknowledged that the country still has a long way to go, but it is hoped that improvements in infrastructure, increased commercial investment and growth of the tourism and property markets will help to bring greater stability to the country.

Romania's GDP grew from 5.1% in 2002 to 7.7% in 2006, and was expected to be around 6% in 2007. Romania's skilled and numerate young workforce has cornered the software industry, drawing in multinationals such as Microsoft, Alcatel and Hewlett-Packard, especially to towns in the north of the country. Many more traditional manufacturers have also moved into Romania, including Wrigleys, Nestlé and Renault, partly to take advantage of new markets and also to benefit from the large, well-educated and skilled workforce and their low wages.

Romania was named as the top place to invest by Price Waterhouse Cooper and Channel 4's *A Place in the Sun* programme in 2006, with their research material predicting gains in property of over 414% over the next ten years.

Is This a Good Place to Buy?

With a growing economy, high levels of inward investment and increased levels of investment from the EU for infrastructure improvements and public facilities, Romania's investment market is set to flourish. Funds are likely to be channelled into airport and major road improvements making the country increasingly accessible and easier to negotiate.

Property can still be found at significantly lower prices than in other European countries and with expected price gains of 30% in Bucharest in 2007 and possible rises of 15% to 25% elsewhere, the potential for capital gains in Romania is a strong one.

Low rates of personal and corporate tax and favourable taxation on new-build property are just some of the incentives enticing investors to buy in Romania.

Price History

Presently, property remains cheap by Western standards, but prices are rising rapidly and have been predicted to increase by 20%–30% in 2007 as many new apartment blocks are completed and released into the marketplace. In Bucharest, the capital, new studios start at around £40,000, rising to £300,000 or more. Elsewhere, prices for a new-build range from £45,000 to £150,000 whilst a modest, rural three-bedroom house can be bought for around £25,000.

Which Type of Property Should You Go For?

Romania has a very ownership-centred culture, making the property market more suited to capital growth investments rather than rentals. Foreign investment in Romania tends to concentrate on dwellings and business property as non-resident foreigners can only buy land by forming a Romanian registered company. This restriction however is due to be reviewed within the next five years now that Romania is part of the EU.

The biggest capital rise in 2003 was for block apartments built before 1989, which usually sell for below €30,000. Glossy new builds, conversely, can be about 40% more expensive than most property in Romania, but with development at an early stage, these properties may be a worthwhile investment.

> *'Romania was named as the top place to invest by Price Waterhouse Cooper and Channel 4's* **A Place in the Sun** *programme, with their research material predicting gains in property of over 414% over the next ten years'*

As tourism in the country increases and the holiday market establishes itself, Romania's buy-to-let potential should open up. Due to the short summer season however, investors must ensure that their property is in a location lending itself to both summer and winter months so as to guarantee year-round demand and secure profitable rental returns.

The true romantic may prefer to buy a *conac*, the Romanian name for a cottage owned by the aristocracy of the country at the turn of the 20th century. These homes are often in need of some repair work, but their charm and authenticity make renovations worthwhile. Another alternative might be a mountain home or getaway, for which prices start at around €20,000. A superb villa in a choice location would be about €100,000, and most homes in these areas come with spectacular mountain views and are surrounded by pine tree forests and meadows.

Hotspots

Bucharest

The capital of Romania, holds the nickname Little Paris, thanks to its wide, tree-lined streets and imposing architecture. However, the Communist era has left its mark in many areas, especially the central district, much of which was razed and rebuilt by former dictator Ceaucescu. The city is an interesting mix of French-style Belle Epoque buildings, traditional Romanian architecture, Communist-era Neo-classicism and faceless Soviet-style blocks.

Prices in the city have risen by 30% in the past year and show no signs of slowing down just yet. As such, the city is becoming comparable in terms of price with other areas of Europe though it still remains one of the cheapest capital cities.

By the end of 2006 old-style apartments were selling for an average of €500–€1,200 per square metre, depending on quality and location, however new-build property was selling at an almost comparable average of €1,000–€1,300 per square metre. This unusual state of affairs may reflect the lack of supply of quality accommodation for the market. High-end projects aimed at the wealthier buyer cost on average €1,500 to €2,300 per square metre. Some top locations are commanding prices of more than €3,000 per square metre and at this level rental yields begin to look less attractive. Average prices for apartments in the capital are around €75,000, with rental yields in older buildings around €1,000 to €1,500 per month. The market in new-build rentals is too young to have definite return figures as yet but many agents are predicting returns of 7–8%.

Those looking for cheaper property outside of the city centre may want to investigate the suburbs and outskirts of Bucharest which offer low cost entry with the potential for substantial long-term returns as the city expands and properties in these areas become more integrated.

Timisoara

Known as Little Venice, Timisoara is one of Romania's richest cities, on the western border with Serbia and surrounded by the lovely countryside of the Banat region. The city has attracted a lot of commercial investment with several large companies such as Procter & Gamble and Nestlé. Property here is thriving with many residents moving away from apartments and seeking new villas in the suburbs and surrounding countryside. Prices rose 25%–30% in 2006/2007 and predictions say they will continue to rise at the same rate for the next year or two. Rural homes can be bought from around €36,000 with apartments in city locations from around €60,000.

> **INSIDER TIP**
>
> **The city of Arad is hotly tipped as the next big investment location, Arad is a designated free trade zone (with only 5% taxation) and as a result is attracting much heavy industry and businesses. Situated on the proposed new Bucharest-Budapest route it is well placed for trade links. Prices start at around €75,000, though the market is undersupplied. New development is underway and yields of around €1,500 per month make it a good proposition for future rental and capital returns.**

Transylvania

The central region of Transylvania is forever associated with the myth of Count Dracula and pulls in substantial tourism as a result. It is also a rural paradise of forests, fairytale castles and the Carpathian mountains. Cities worth considering for investment include, **Cluj-Napoca,** a populous and thriving hub for many corporations. The city has good transport connections, including an airport scheduled for expansion and new motorway connections with Bucharest and the Black Sea. A large student population may make this a good buy-to-let option whilst the potential for capital appreciation is also strong with price rises of up to 20% in recent years.

Europe

ROMANIA

'Low rates of personal and corporate tax and favourable taxation on new-build property are just some of the incentives enticing investors to buy in Romania'

Brasov in southern Transylvania has good commercial links and a large university. Property here consists of new apartments in the slightly sprawling industrialised areas and contemporary and older-style family homes. Average prices here are upwards of around €70,000 with large farmhouses with land or new villas priced from around €240,000.

Other areas

Sibiu, a beautiful and historic town, is the 2007 European Capital of Culture and has had much interest from the media and tourism as a result. Substantial investment has gone into infrastructure and commercial investment. Property here is short in supply and therefore prices are higher than some areas with new apartments selling from around €37,000.

Poiana Brasov, **Predeal** and **Sinaia** are Romania's main ski resorts and as such offer investment as well as second home opportunities. With the potential for year-round rental, unlike on the coast, prices on average in the mountains range from around €36,000 for new-build apartments and from €75,000 for log cabins, with rentals pitched currently at around €300–€950 per week depending on season and quality of property.

The country's Black Sea Coast resorts are not as well known or developed as those of neighbouring Bulgaria and the short summer rental season of only four months each year has curtailed investment. Nevertheless, the towns of **Constanta**, **Costinesti** and **Mamaia** are busy with eastern European tourists all summer and prices have been rising by around 15% recently, with property costing from around €45,000 plus for apartments, and villas (which may be in need of updating) from €110,000.

The Purchase Process

As Romania is still a relatively new market for western investors, finding good, independent legal advice from a lawyer with local knowledge is always advised when buying. Once an offer has been made, a pre-contract is signed between buyer and vendor and a deposit of 10% is settled on the property. All legal documents, including title deeds and searches are carried out and, if satisfactory, an application to register the property is sent to the land registry office. On registration of the property in the name of the new owner, the remainder of the purchase price is paid.

Foreign freehold ownership of land in Romania is not currently permitted according to the country's constitution. However this is set to change in the next three or four years now that Romania is an EU member. Until then non-nationals will still need to set up a Romanian registered company in order to own land, a straightforward process which takes around four weeks and costs €300.

A flat tax rate of 16% is levied for both personal income and corporate profits and 19% VAT, though there is no VAT due on off-plan property. The 16% tax is also due on any rental income and capital gains. Agents' fees are usually 2%–3% and legal fees will vary from 2%–10%.

Mortgages

Romania's mortgage market has rapidly become more developed on a monthly basis. Interest rates start from as low as 6% and mortgages of up to 75% LTV are on offer. Some banks offer 0% interest rate periods to help clients find a tenant whilst others offer interest only periods for up to 3 years.

Key Risks and Opportunities

Despite the wave of economic optimism which flooded the country a few years ago, unemployment has now risen to 7.8% and many younger workers are now seeking to migrate to areas of Europe offering higher salaries and increased opportunities. As a result, some employers are already considering relocation from Romania to the Far East.

However, with an estimated €30 billion of foreign funds due to be invested in infrastructure, services and employment opportunities over the next 6 years, the country and its economy should pick up. Also, a cut in income tax to 16% has raised consumer confidence and given the local workforce increased spending power which should in turn bolster the property market. This, coupled with Romania's rising tourist levels, should soon provide a relatively stable market backdrop.

Europe

ROMANIA

Opportunity Rating

As a culture, Romania is much more orientated towards ownership than renting and so investors are advised to concentrate on capital growth rather than rental yields. However, if prices continue to stay high and local buyers are priced out of the property market, this situation could change. Romania is a country offering low cost entry into a property market ripe with the potential for high rewards and good long-term capital growth.

Rating: $$$$

Risk Rating

On the flip-side is the high risk associated with a country that is still finding its feet. This may make it too unpredictable an opportunity for the cautious investor. Therefore the most important thing to remember when investing in Romania is to proceed with vigilance and care. Legal, economic and political changes can occur extremely rapidly.

Rating: ⚠ ⚠ ⚠

Slovakia

CURRENCY
Koruna

EXCHANGE RATES
1,000 Koruna = £20.00
£1 = 49.00 Koruna
1,000 Koruna = US $41.00
US $1= 24.00 Koruna

BRATISLAVA

Introduction

Peppered with a mixture of fortresses and castles, gothic churches and 15th-century town squares, evidence of Slovakia's vibrant history is prominent. A previously understated tourism destination, the country has managed to stave off much of the rampant commercialism which has overtaken some of Western Europe. Peasant traditions and quaint farm practices are still prevalent in many rural villages and townships giving the country an authentic, original feel. With nine national parks and acres of untouched countryside as well as several castles, spas and picturesque lakes, Slovakia has a lot to offer as a tourist destination and is starting to experience growing popularity.

Nestled in the very centre of Europe the republic is bordered by Austria, the Czech Republic, Poland and Hungary and as such links the prosperous western countries with the new emerging markets and manufacturing wealth of Eastern Europe. Further, Slovakia has more natural beauty than most of the markets which provide direct competition and as advertising budgets become more generous; travel and tourism figures are increasing.

The availability of cheap flights to and from Western European cities such as London, Paris, Berlin and Dublin mean tourism is expected to rise 3.8% in 2007 and 5.3% per annum, between 2008 and 2017. Slovakia saw a whopping 38.6% increase in UK tourism between 2006 and 2007. It is also expected that Bratislava will establish itself as popular weekend getaway in the near future.

For those who prefer skiing or mountain walking to over-crowded beaches or concreted resorts, Slovakia is the ideal place for a second home although it also offers promising investment opportunities. Many of the purchasers who come here combine Slovakia's dual market strengths and often have a second home for personal use before looking for an apartment for investment.

Is This a Good Place to Buy?

The Slovak Republic enjoys rising prosperity and an ideal central European location and as such has great investment potential. Whilst joining the EU in 2004 did not necessarily help Slovakia to stabilise or ensure any returns on investment, it did guarantee EU legal rights to all investors. In addition, foreign nationals no longer need to establish a company to purchase a property here.

Slovakia has one of the fastest growing economies in Europe and has out-performed all of its neighbouring countries over the last two years. GDP growth reached around 8% in 2006 and a similar rate of growth was predicted for 2007.

'The national bank of Slovakia has recently cut the interest rate to 4.25% which should entice more people to invest. As a result, property prices should be bolstered'

In 2004 Slovakia introduced a flat tax system, which has since been adopted across Central Europe. The government hopes that the new flat tax of 19% will lure foreign investors and high-earning Europeans into the country with the temptation of new, low rates. The National bank of Slovakia has also recently cut the interest rate to 4.25% which will make the cost of borrowing cheaper and should entice more people to invest. As a result, property prices should be bolstered.

Although Slovakia has the second highest rate of unemployment in Europe after Poland, things are changing. Unemployment rates dropped 10.69% between 2005 to 2006 and a further 12.82% between 2006 to 2007 and this trend is expected to continue. What's more, thanks to the introduction of the government scheme 'Tourism Development Strategy' which will run until 2013, increased tourist visitor arrivals should be fostered.

With plans to adopt the euro in January 2009, mortgage borrowing should become even easier, and the property market in Slovakia given a boost against regional competition.

Price History

Like many of the new European member states Slovakia has a real estate market sharply divided between an expensive capital and much lower prices throughout the rest of the country. After the fall of communism, the Slovakian property market experienced a 10 year lull when all building ceased.

Construction firms are now responding to this intermission and have re-commenced building projects to satisfy increasing demand for new buildings. As a result of this growing demand property prices are growing steadily and increased by 15% in 2006.

'The demand for property in all areas of Slovakia is booming and the property market is improving. Investors who are looking to purchase now are buying into a prolonged period of growth while the economy improves'

In Bratislava prices are now comparable with any other European capital, with apartments selling from €44,000 (£30,000/$61,000) up to €200,000 (£135,700/$275,540). Prices however are still said to be 30% cheaper than more exclusive cities such as Prague. Prices in more rural areas remain less expensive and it is not uncommon to find a villa for as little as £30,000.

Which Type of Property Should You Go For?

The current shortage of properties and significant domestic demand will con-tinue to push property prices up, especially new flats built in popular residential areas. Strategically placed new build developments are therefore likely to offer the best investment opportunities and should avoid problems with title. The quality of build is also likely to be of a more reliable quality than older homes.

Within Bratislava, attractive older properties are likely to sell at a premium, but may also be subject to property title problems and planning permission issues for any alterations. Although an older home may exude greater aesthetic charm, renovation might not be worth the time and effort. Investors should also remember that winters in Slovakia can be severe, with temperatures dropping as low as −20°C meaning reliable heating systems in older properties although costly, will be essential.

Hotspots

Bratislava

Bratislava is one of the most popular places to invest in Slovakia and, as the country's capital, attracts a constant stream of tourists. Downtown Bratislava has been tipped as the best place to buy, thanks to local government efforts to install a beautification programme. When the new highway between Bratislava and Vienna is built, living in and around Bratislava will become even more popu-lar with locals as commutes between each city will be reduced to 45 minutes. Yields in central Bratislava are currently at around 10% and an apartment complex a short walk away from Bratislava centre has prices starting from £79,450 (€117,432/$161,862) for a one-bedroom apartment.

Elsewhere

Although a beautiful capital with extensive investment opportunities, Bratislava is not the only place to buy. The high **Tatras** are one of the most attractive high mountain ranges in Europe, offering the only truly alpine standard skiing in Eastern Europe. Offering both winter skiing and mountain summers, the Tatras provide year round appeal (see picture 13 in colour section). Investors however must be prepared to suffer slow transport links especially if their property is in the depths of the countryside.

 INSIDER TIP   With a significant portion of the Slovakian property market aimed at the younger generation, a good place to consider is Trnava. Far more affordable but just 20 minutes' drive from Bratislava, this university town has cheap property prices and rentals that are increasing by 15% a year.

Another good place to consider is **Poprad**, Slovakia's luxury holiday resort overlooked by the Tatras Mountains. With an international airport, good quality amenities and surrounded by stunning countryside, Poprad's property prices should rise in the near future.

Liptov is a final area worthy of consideration. A resort between the High and Low Tatras, the area has a reputation for being both beautiful and affordable.

The Purchase Process

As in most EU countries, the purchase process in Slovakia is straightforward. Once you have made your choice, a deposit of 10% secures the property. At the time of the deposit a pre-purchase agreement is signed. If the buyer changes their mind after the deposit is paid, the seller's expenses are deducted and the rest of the deposit returned. Should the seller back out, the deposit is returned in full.

After surveyors' reports are completed, the buyer's solicitor checks that the seller does indeed have the right to the property, and that there are no legal impediments. The Cadastral Register ("*kataster nehnutelnosti*") discloses the property owner, and indicates the extent to which the land is encumbered with mortgages and other forms of legal servitudes. Currently, all Slovak agencies require the seller to provide a *Kataster* paper that contains the legal state of the property before selling. The paper cannot be older than three months to safeguard the buyer from any legal disputes. It is advisable that the buyer requests a copy of this paper before paying the rest of the balance.

The solicitor then prepares the main contracts and should arrange for certified translations to be made. After contracts are signed, the *Kataster* (land registry) transfers ownership between the buyer and seller which could take up to four weeks. Once this is completed, the property is officially yours.

Buying property in Slovakia is also straightforward financially. Fees should be paid by the seller, but in reality are likely to be passed on to the buyer as part of the quoted buying price. There is no stamp duty or transfer tax in Slovakia and lawyer's fees will be around €500 (£338/$689). Capital gains tax is calculated at the flat 19%, but is waived for apartments owned for more than two years and on other properties owned for more than five years.

Mortgages

Mortgages for foreign nationals are widely available within Slovakia, both through local banks and international brokers and are dealt with on an individual basis. The interest rates vary depending on the amount of money borrowed and the length of the term but interest rates usually start at around 5%. LTV mortgages are available at 70% and fixed rate terms are available. Terms usually start from 20 years.

Key Risks and Opportunities

Although the Slovakian property market is renowned for providing high rewards with low risks, it is always worth taking fundamental precautions. Buyers should ask to see ownership papers, and check that the property is registered under this name at the land registry. Your solicitor should also make a search to determine whether there are any unpaid taxes or other charges. Older properties may have problems with title and it is important to confirm that the house is correctly zoned and that any alterations have planning permission.

As Slovakia is getting richer, there is some confusion about the 'right price' for property. Sellers may quote prices widely divergent from those that a house or apartment would fetch on the local market. A good way to check whether you are being quoted an unreal price is to visit internet ex-pat forums and ask people with local knowledge. There is a particularly good forum for Slovakia run by a local English language paper which can be found at www.slovakspectator.sk.

Europe

SLOVAKIA

Opportunity Rating

The Slovakian economy is growing fast and development in the ski areas should continue to attract local and international investors as well as ski enthusiasts. The demand for property in all areas of Slovakia is booming and the property market is improving so that the investors who are looking to purchase now are buying into a prolonged period of growth while the economy improves. As such, investors are more than likely to receive worthwhile rewards.

Rating: $ $ $

Risk Rating

The main risks in Slovakia relate to title and a lack of transparency in local property prices. Buyers should employ a good lawyer and ensure that they research the area well to make sure that they are paying a fair price.

Rating: ⚠ ⚠ ⚠

Slovenia

CURRENCY
Euro

EXCHANGE RATES
100 Euro = £68.00
£1 = 1.47 Euro
100 Euro = US $138
US $1 = 0.73 Euro

LJUBLJANA

Introduction

An Alpine coastal country in southern central Europe, Slovenia is renowned for its unspoilt countryside, beautiful lakes and snow-capped mountains that cover 30% of the country. In a country smaller than Wales, all these natural attractions are within easy reach of each other. Occupying an excellent location, bordered by the successful and established countries of Hungary, Italy, Austria and Croatia, Slovenia is in a position to flourish. For those who enjoy outdoor pursuits, Slovenia has a lot to offer; from hiking, skiing and snow boarding, to riding, climbing, golfing or simply strolling in the midst of awe-inspiring scenery. It also boasts 46 km of Adriatic coastline, bordering the popular Istrian peninsular that the country shares with Croatia.

Slovenia joined the EU in May 2004 and the Eurozone in January 2007 and is a popular investment location with UK, Irish and other northern Europeans. The country's economic growth may have been slower than other emerging markets but it has a GDP per capita substantially greater than the other transitioning economies of Central Europe, so that Slovenia is a model of economic success and stability for its neighbours from the former Yugoslavia. GDP growth was steady at a 5.2% growth rate in 2006, firmly up on 2005's 4% growth rate, while inflation was only 2.1% per annum in February 2007. GDP growth was estimated to be just under 5% in 2007. The workforce is generally well-educated and unemployment is currently lower than it has been in the past, at 8.7%. An educated and expanding workforce combined with higher wages should therefore broaden the market in the future.

The country also has excellent infrastructure and improving international connections including a new motorway link between Ljubljana and the Austrian border. Budget airlines such as easyJet and Whizz Air fly regularly from the UK into the capital Ljubljana and the flight time from London is just two hours. Tourism is Slovenia's fastest growing industry welcoming 1.2 million foreign tourists a year. Travel and tourism activity is expected to grow by 3.9% per annum between 2008 and 2017 which should provide increasing investment opportunities, especially in the property sector.

Is This a Good Place to Buy?

Slovenia, in investment terms, is seen predominantly as a country offering potential for further growth while still remaining unspoiled by mass tourism and development. With diverse scenery stretching from the snow-capped Julian Alps, to the beautiful Lake Bled and the sliver of Adriatic coastline, Slovenia also has a growing property market, driven by foreign investors and rising local employment and wage rates.

Reforms in taxes and the business sector have paved the way for increased overseas investment into the country, particularly from Western European buyers, however investment levels are still low in comparison to other European destinations. In 2006, foreigners bought 740 properties and leading the pack were Britons who purchased 360 properties. House prices have risen accordingly, by around 20% per year, since EU entry in 2004.

'Slovenia offers strong opportunities for investment in an emerging market with the best GDP per capita and economic growth of all of the other transitioning economies of central Europe'

Most Slovenian property purchases from overseas buyers are for second or holiday homes rather than for pure buy-to-let investment. However, investors should be aware that there are growing opportunities in the buy-to-let sector as tourism expands. Average rents in the popular areas of Kranjska Gora and Lake Bled are between £400 and £700 per week depending on the quality and size of the property and season. An increase in tourist numbers offers opportunities for buy-to-let and entices visitors who may wish to own after holidaying there.

The buying process is uncomplicated, relatively fast, and since EU accession, legislation allowing foreign property ownership has been introduced. However, although private purchase is legal, the government has created a loophole allowing it to restrict property sales to foreigners for up to seven years if deemed necessary.

Much of the industrial sector is still state-owned leaving a workforce that remains resistant to change and businesses that are uncompetitive in a global market place. The current government has pledged to work towards lower taxes and the privatisation of state-operated industries in order to get the economy moving much faster.

Price History

Property prices have escalated in recent years with rises of 10%–30% in some areas and are expected to continue rising into the future. For the year following the adoption of the euro in January 2007, experts predicted increases of 17.5%.

Much of the high-end accommodation is a similar price to other EU states, especially in the capital, Ljubljana, a small and beautiful town, which has seen unprecedented rises. However, bargains can still be found in Slovenia's rural, untouched countryside.

Which Type of Property Should You Go For?

Available property runs mainly to lodges in the mountains and farmhouses or cottages in the countryside where there are plenty of opportunities for renovation. Many of these properties however may be isolated or in poor condition. When considering purchasing renovation projects you will need to take into account the cost of any work that needs doing, labour is generally cheaper than in the UK.

Holiday homes and buy-to-let purchases can be found in ski resorts and major cities and with tourist numbers increasing, these are the types of property that could offer worthwhile investments. Popular tourist areas, where buy-to-let should be profitable, include the ski and summer resorts of Kranjska Gora, Bovec, Lake Bled and Lake Bohinj, where rental income can average between £400 and £700 a week. Cities such as the capital, Ljubljana, offer the potential to rent to students and young professionals, with yields of around 6%. On a more negative note, the rental income tax is high and owners will be forced to pay 25% tax on 75% of their rental income.

Europe

SLOVENIA

> In Slovenia's unspoiled countryside there are still excellent opportunities for investment. Rural property prices are low by European standards, meaning there is good opportunity for capital appreciation. Prices start from £30,000 for a renovation property, while picturesque mountain chalets start from £50,000 – a fraction of the prices in France. For £70,000 you can buy a pretty thatched house surrounded by vineyards and forest.

Hotspots

The Julian Alps

These mountains, in the north-west of the country, attract winter sports enthusiasts but also enjoy good summer trade from walkers and cyclists. Popular tourist haunts also include the Triglav National Park, an area of outstanding beauty dominated by Mount Triglav. **Kranjska Gora** and **Bovec** are the two best-known ski resorts in the region. Designed mainly in Alpine style, the resorts offer a range of skiing at all levels. At over 1,700 metres, Bovec has a long season marred only by the fact that it is in an earthquake zone. Average prices start at around £47,400 for small traditional stone houses with apartments. Larger chalets in the resort centres cost between £94,700 and £270,500 depending on location and the quality of the accommodation.

Lake Bled and Lake Bohinj

These lakes are also favourite spots with holidaymakers, golfers and second home owners. The island of Bled with its famous church is one of the country's most recognizable landmarks. As well as a location for waterside holidays the resort offers direct access via chairlift to the ski area of Straza. Property in traditional, family-sized chalets is pricey and averages between £169,100 and £228,700, with one and two-bedroom apartments costing around £135,300.

Maribor

Maribor is a key hotspot for investors. Slovenia's second city offers a gateway to the Prekmurje, the wine-growing region and the Mariborsko Pohorje mountain range. Ryanair started a service to Maribor in June 2007 opening up the region to further investment and tourism. The area includes famous thermal spas and the Goricko Regional Park and is undergoing a programme of development. A new motorway will increase access from Ljubljana. Property here is still relatively affordable with rustic cottages and new-build apartments available from around £27,100 to £101,500.

Piran

Lying on the beautiful and popular Istrian peninsular, Piran has Venetian roots, pretty beaches and an outdoor café culture. Nearby Koper and Potoroz are also of interest. Expect to pay around £40,600 to £54,100 for a traditional house inland, with larger and newer properties priced between £67,600 and £135,300.

Ljubljana

Slovenia's historic capital city has many beautiful baroque, art nouveau and contemporary buildings. It also boasts a young population and cosmopolitan atmosphere. Approximately 15% of the country's population live here and the university brings in a large student population. Young professionals and students offer good long-term rental prospects. The most sought-after properties are the attractive character apartments in the city centre and, as a result, they tend to be highly priced with current average costs of £1,700 per square metre. Prices over a million euros aren't unknown. More affordable new-build developments and small houses can be found in the outer suburbs, where one-bedroom apartments are available from £100,000.

The Purchase Process

No visa is needed for EU citizens to visit or reside in Slovenia but in order to purchase you must have an EMSO number (a type of identification number). Non-EU citizens residing in a country that offers reciprocal investment can invest but such purchases need to be accompanied by an application for the establishment of reciprocity to the Ministry of Justice.

Once you have found the appropriate property and had an offer accepted, a deposit of 10% will be necessary. All documents and contracts will need to be translated into English (for which you may need to pay additional translation costs) and should be examined in the presence of a lawyer. In Slovenia the same lawyer often acts for both vendor and purchaser but this is not necessarily recommended. Buyers should look into engaging their own legal advisor. If you cannot be present to sign contracts you will need to engage a public notary to oversee the procedure. The cost of this is often less than 1% of the purchase price.

The costs associated with property purchase in Slovenia are as follows:

- Property purchase taxes range from 8.5% (for new-build apartments for private use) up to 20% for commercial or buy-to-let property.

- Property transfer tax costs around 2%, with an agent commission of 4% plus VAT of 20%
- Stamp duty is 4% and can be split between the vendor and buyer
- Capital gains tax is charged at 20%, unless the property has been held for over 20 years, when there is no capital gains tax levied.

Mortgages

As a developing market, Slovenia has only recently opened up its mortgage market to foreign non residents. 70% LTV mortgages are now available with interest rates of approximately 8%.

Key Risks and Opportunities

Slovenia provides the great combination of a strong post-transitional economy and a new market with good potential. Entry prices are still quite low and tourist numbers and foreign investment are set to increase. As a result, a market has been created where investment in a holiday home or buy-to-let property is an attractive prospect especially as prices are currently rising.

Disadvantages include the high tax on rental income and the potential risk of the government restricting foreign purchase.

Currently FDI in Slovenia is one of the lowest in Europe on a per capita basis. However, there are hopes that this will improve in a spiral of investment as new opportunities emerge and new business and infrastructure projects are planned.

Opportunity Rating

Slovenia offers strong opportunities for investment in an emerging market with the best GDP per capita and economic growth of all of the other transitioning economies of central Europe.

As an emerging market, entry prices are still very low by European standards and outside the centre of Ljubljana good potential for investment in both second homes and buy-to-let purchases are available. Slovenia also currently has a strong pro-landlord rental market.

Rating: $ $ $

Risk Rating

The main risk lies in the loophole that enables the government to restrict foreign purchase for up to seven years if it so wishes.

Rating: ⚠ ⚠

Spain

CURRENCY
Euro

EXCHANGE RATES
100 Euro = £67.37
£1 = 1.48 Euro
100 Euro = US $137.84
US $1 = 0.725 Euro

Introduction

Spain, the land of matadors, flamenco dancing and Gaudi's modern architectural lines, occupies 85% of the Iberian Peninsula, and is Europe's third largest nation. As the second most mountainous country in Europe, flat land is limited and housing is mostly concentrated on the coastal strip alongside the Mediterranean. Without doubt the attractions of this vast and varied country are obvious: beautiful beaches, 320 days of sunshine a year, delicious food and wine, the mountains of Andalucía, and the magnificence of cities such as Madrid and Barcelona. Spain has one of the most fascinating cultures, with the bonus of an easy-going and laid-back lifestyle.

Spain is second behind France for Worldwide Tourism and the market is increasing at a steady 5% annually. At the start of 2006, Britons owned 90,000 residences in Spain, a 29% increase from the previous year. It is predicted that more than one million foreigners will buy on the Costas in the next six years rising to three million by 2025 whilst the Office of National Statistics found that Spain accounted for 27% of all second homes bought abroad in 2006.

The Spanish economy between 1986 and 1990 boomed, averaging 5% annual growth. This growth resumed at a lower level in 1994 after a Europe-wide recession, and stood at 2.5% in 2003, 2.6% in 2004, and 3.3% in 2005 – satisfactory given the background of a faltering European economy. In 2006 economic growth was on the rise at 6.1% although this dropped to 4% in the first quarter of 2007. Although a cloud of doom currently hangs over Spain's property market, growth of a steady 5%–7% is predicted over the next 10 years.

> ## 'Spain's market is somewhat false as, despite distinct price appreciation, capital gains cannot be easily released'

The socialist president, Rodriguez Zapatero, has initiated economic and social reforms, and the country is working towards reducing unemployment (which, although higher than other countries is decreasing and at the end of 2005 was 8.7%, the lowest end of year rate in 25 years) and to adjusting to the monetary and other economic policies of an integrated Europe.

Is This a Good Place to Buy?

Media coverage of Spain's property market has recently been muddied by reports of an imminent crash and end to the veritable boom the country has experienced over the last decade. Indeed, the Spanish property market has recently seen a slow down in its foreign investment sales; a 14% decline was seen in the first 9 months of 2006 and a total fall of 77.6% has been estimated from 2005–2007. Moreover, foreigners spent an estimated 13.2% less on property in 2006. Sensing this shift, the Spanish authorities have tightened control on off-plan buying, committed millions to new infrastructural projects and imposed stricter urban planning laws. It seems then, that the market in many areas is maturing, with interest shifting from serious investors to lifestyle buyers wanting a longer term, lower risk investment. Whilst there has been a definite slow down recently, this has been explained away as a correction in the market with prices falling to a soft landing, away from the previously high and rising annual figures. What cannot be explained is why by mid-2007 there were reportedly 4 million empty properties in Spain yet the government has given permission to build a further 3 million.

Whether Spain is teetering on the brink of a housing market collapse or merely resisting a re-evaluation of property prices remains to be seen, but one thing is for certain, with 18% of Spain's GDP invested in the housing market, the government are unlikely to let it slump without a fight.

Drawn by reliably hot summers, mild balmy winters, a laid back lifestyle and 2-hour flight from the UK, British investors have arrived in their droves and find Spain eternally appealing. In line with this interest, Spanish property has increased in value by 160% over the last 10 years and remains one of the most popular second home destinations.

The main problem investors come across is a distinct lack of a clear or reliable exit strategy. In this way, Spain's market is somewhat false as, despite distinct price appreciation, capital gains cannot be easily released. Tangible gains therefore are hard to acquire.

Price History

With the phenomenal price rises over the last decade, the Spanish market is very well established. More recently though, prices in many areas have begun to level out and overbuilding on some Costas has even pushed prices downward.

The first sign of a slow down in the property market was detected as long ago as 2004 and continued throughout 2005, although the OECD (Organisation For Economic Co-operation and Development) yearly report stated at the end of January 2006 that prices for dwellings in Spain were still 30% overvalued. From 2007, prices are forecasted to fall by approximately 20% and then flatten staying at the same level for some time.

Although such price drops are yet to become evident, there has been a decrease in sales. In response to this downturn, 100% financing was made available to Spanish locals with payment terms up to 50 years, but 15% increases in interest on mortgages in 2006 counteracted this move and halted the market again.

Properties are still selling in Spain but at the extreme ends of the market. Cheap properties below €120,000 are popular and luxury homes over €500,000 offering sea views are also selling. As sales have fallen, house price appreciation has slowed falling from 9.1% in 2006 to 7.2% in 2007.

Spain's real estate market future then remains uncertain. If the economy slips into a recession, house prices are likely to plummet. However if the country manages to stabilise and dissipate the current risk, then prices should merely stabilise rather than fall.

To give a general indication of Spain's average property prices, a one-bedroom apartment can be found from £117,000, a 2 bed apartment from £175,000, a three-bedroom bed villa from £280,000 and a 4 bed villa from £350,000. These prices however are averages based on popular tourist areas meaning if you head inland to less well known areas, property prices will start at a much lower rate.

Which Type of Property Should You Go For?

There are a number of options in Spain, each with its benefits and shortcomings. The type of property a buyer chooses will usually depend on personal preference, what their aims are, or on the location in which they intend to buy.

Apartments offer the cheapest prices and potentially high returns, but there could be a lack of privacy. Linked, terraced and townhouses on two levels with a third floor or roof terrace are comparatively cheap and easy to resell. Townhouses also give easy access to amenities, and have the additional benefits of modern surroundings. Corner properties or duplexes are also a cheap form of building and are frequently used as holiday homes, while detached properties often offer more privacy but cost more, and insurance companies may charge a premium for these. Traditional homes are common, and community properties, with a shared area, are always popular – the cost of maintaining the shared elements is split between the owners. Any of these accommodation types could be used as a holiday, second or retirement home, or as an investment for capital growth and rental returns.

INSIDER TIP Most new homes on the Costas are sold off-plan, however since the price dip it is not recommended to buy off-plan developments as many developers are starting new builds and having to halt construction half way through, sometimes never finishing because of extensive over supply. Shrewd investors should avoid big building projects with thousands of dwellings as well as property with unrealistic letting promises.

Serious investors wanting high returns would be best advised to overlook Spain and to go for newer emerging markets with lower initial costs and a higher level of return. The Spanish market is more suited to those who want to buy a holiday home or retirement base.

Those hoping to exploit the buy-to-let market should also take care. Many foreigners are unaware that under Spanish law a licence must be acquired before a property can be used for rental purposes and if this procedure is not honoured, owners could face fines of up to £20,000. These licences can also be hard to attain.

Hotspots

Almost every article written on Spain names a new property hotspot billing it as the 'next big thing' and it is true that there are a lot of areas offering potential for investment, if buyers are willing to head inland and leave the coast behind. Contrary to other reports, GE Money believes the Spanish market will rise strongly in 2008 because of the bargains available in less well-known towns and villages and claims that investing in Spain is still safer for long term investments than investing in new emerging markets.

Despite the trepidation surrounding the predicted Spanish property market crash, it seems that there are pockets of Spain which offer affordable properties with some potential for capital growth and rental income.

Although eternally popular with tourists, Barcelona enjoys minimal yields of between 2.6% and 3.75%. What is more, enormous price growth of 17.2% and prices 148% above the national average, make it a market only the most monied can invest in.

With good flight connections and prices 30% cheaper than the national average, **Seville** is becoming increasingly popular with foreign investors. Recommended property types for longer-term investments are either one-bed apartments with parking in the city centre or a 'finca' (family home) with a pool outside the city. With a huge student body in need of rental accommodation, Seville saw a 33% growth in property values from May 2005 to 2006, a trend which shows no signs of abating. There are also still property bargains to be had with average property prices being 41% below the national average at €144,000.

'If immediate returns are not your first priority then Spain can offer potential for capital gain over the long-term but this should not be relied upon'

One region tipped as a particularly good investment destination is the area around Valencia, made strong thanks to a massive programme of state and private investment in preparation for the 2007 Americas Cup. House prices were set to increase by 20% during the build up and the event is estimated to generate over 10,000 jobs and contribute to an overall economic impact of more than €1,500 million. Tourist numbers are also increasing with nearly five times the number of arrivals than in 1992. Infrastructure has also been dramatically improved including a new metro line, connecting the port with the airport and a new central station to accommodate the High Speed Train (AVE), which travels at speeds of 300km per hour and interconnects all the major cities in Spain. The traditionally Spanish coastal town of Castellon, north of Valencia, in particular saw a marked price increase of 35% from May 2005 to May 2006 from €167,000 to €225,000.

Whilst the sunny, sandy Spanish Costas are areas that have attracted the vast majority of foreign investment historically, high price and over-development mean they are no longer considered a canny investment hotspot.

Galera in northern Andalucía would suit people with a smaller budget wanting peace and quiet away from the coast. Renovated cave houses are common in this area and are available from as little as £13,500 un-restored. Restored cave houses are still relatively cheap, most costing under £80,000. Approximately £80,000 can also buy a range of properties in surrounding areas from farmhouses to village houses all in need of restoration but still cheap to attain.

Less-developed coasts such as the **Costa de la Luz**, the **Costa Almeria** and the **Costa Tropical** also offer lower prices with greater room for development. These areas attract people looking for a more authentic experience of Spain, and a landscape less ravaged by construction. Property prices on the

Costa Tropical are cheaper than on the Costa del Sol, and the area is proving popular with foreign buyers. The Costa de la Luz is Spain's largest coast, and property here still offers good value for money, having escaped the mass tourism that affects other areas of Spain. This area couldn't be more different from the Costa del Sol, though the two are neighbours. Its golden beaches are long, wide, wild, often deserted – and more likely to be backed by sand dunes or pine trees than high-rise apartment blocks. Because 30% of the region is a protected area, it has remained quiet and undeveloped.

Islantilla near Ayamonte or **Chiclana** near Cadiz offer first-time investors good value for money, with apartments available from around €100,000 (£68,000) and beautiful beaches, golf courses and unspoilt countryside on the doorstep.

The Costa Almeria is probably the area that will be expanding most in the near future. The province hosted the XV Mediterranean Games in 2005, and easyjet has begun operating cheap flights to Almeria airport. The 12-month period between May 2005 and May 2006 saw a steady 12% increase in property prices from €171,000 to €191,000 whilst enquiries for two and three bedroom properties in the area increased by 14% in the first half of 2006 compared to the same period in 2005.

Another area that is worth watching is **Fuerteventura**, the closest of the Canary Islands to Africa and the least developed of the four main islands. Fuerteventura has the warmest year-round temperatures of the islands, with winter highs of around 20°C recorded, making it a good bet for year-round holiday rentals and also giving it the potential for a 52-week rental income. Prices for houses here average at around €235,000 (£158,024), much lower than the other Canary Islands, Spain and Portugal.

The Purchase Process

If you are buying property in Spain, regardless of your residential status, you must apply for a fiscal number NIE (*Numero de Identificacion de Extranjeros*). Once you've found the property you like, it is necessary to reserve it with a holding fee that can reach up to £2,000. This fee ensures that the property is taken off the market while your lawyer checks that all the paperwork is in order, that the person offering the property for sale is its legal owner, and that there are no outstanding debts on the property. A '*nota simple*' tells you the specifics of the house; the vendor's name, the size of the property and if there are any debts currently against the property etc. In the meantime, you will also have a chance to arrange financing, for which banks will require a value assessment.

A private purchase contract is then signed stipulating the buying price, the deposit (usually 10%), the completion date and what is included in the price. The deposit is then paid. At this stage the contract becomes binding. If you withdraw from the purchase after signing the purchase contract, you lose the deposit – if the seller withdraws they are also liable for up to twice the deposit, depending on the wording of the contract. The solicitor will then prepare the public title deed (*Escritura de Compraventa*) to be signed by you (or your solicitor if they have power of attorney) and the seller before a Spanish notary. The balance is due at this point. On completion the notary will send details of the title deed to the local land registry to inform it of the identity of the new owner. Approximately three months later, the official Escritura will be returned to you after checking and registering.

When buying in Spain, you should allow 10% of the purchase price for fees. Transfer tax (IVA) on the declared value is 6% on a second-hand property and 7% on a new-build; stamp duty 1/2% (1% in Andalucía); legal fees 1%; notary and property registry fees between 300 – 600 Euros. Four main taxes are applicable to property purchases and ownership: wealth tax, income tax, capital gains tax and succession (inheritance and gift) tax. If and how much you have to pay depends on your residency status. If you choose to let your property, the tax rate is 25%–35% depending on whether you are a registered resident in Spain. From the 1st January 2006 non residents' capital gains tax, charged when selling a house, was changed to the same as Spanish residents, dropping from 35%–18%. Other taxes include: municipal taxes (*basura*), applicable on the increase in the value of the property since its last sale. It is called 'plus valia' and can vary from 10% to 40% of the annual increase, depending on the length of time between sales and the town in which the property is located. Local authority rates (IBI) are charged at 0.5% to 1% of the house's rateable value.

Buyers should be aware of a 'finca rustica'; agricultural farmland or land where building is not permitted. Plots are often sold to foreigners and it is only after purchase they find out that they are not able to build on them. You must therefore get written confirmation from the local town hall that building is permitted when buying a plot in an urbanisation. The vendor can guarantee building permission as part of the sale and will have to return your money if building is not allowed.

Mortgages

LTV mortgages of 80% are available over a 40 year term. Interest only mortgages are also available and interest rates start from 5%.

Europe

SPAIN

Key Risks and Opportunities

The most prominent threat to Spain's housing market has to be its current fragility. Sales are slowing, prices are dropping and average selling times are increasing. It now takes in the region of 24 months to sell an apartment on the Spanish coast compared to 11.5 months in 2004 and 6 months in 2005. As a result, sellers have had to reduce prices by an estimated €18,000 (£11,800) as initial offers of up to 10% below the asking price are becoming increasingly common. These trends reflect the beginnings of a softening market and if they continue, could spell disaster for potential investors. They also mean that previous investors have become somewhat trapped, unable to sell and release the capital locked up in their property.

Other risks are the LRAU or 'land-grab' law as it became known in the 1980s. Essentially, this law re-classified 'rustic' land as 'urban' land and if an owner was unlucky enough to have property in the re-classified areas, developers had the right to purchase the property or land surrounding it, in order to develop the area. Investors need to be extremely careful then, when buying rural property (especially as it is likely to be significantly cheaper and appear to offer great value for money) and should seek legal advice and ensure necessary searches are conducted prior to purchasing to ensure they are not going to fall prey to this re-posession.

There is also continuing widespread non-compliance with planning regulations across the country, and the government is taking steps (announced in 2004) to enforce planning laws – measures which may result in property being demolished. It is wise therefore to check everything very carefully before purchase, especially when planning to refurbish a property.

Further, relatively few estate agents in Spain speak English, and many are also unregistered and inexperienced which has led to mistakes in the purchase process and exploitation of foreign buyers. It is vital therefore to ensure that you employ a reputable agent (who can speak both English and Spanish) or solicitor to check all details of the property and to guide you through the buying process. Many estate agents will recommend a lawyer, but bear in mind that lawyers referred in this way may be acting in the agent's best interests rather than yours.

There is also a 'tradition' in Spain for purchasers to 'help' the vendor in reducing his capital gains tax liability. Generally speaking the vendor will ask for a greatly reduced purchase price to be stipulated in the purchase contract and for the buyer to make up the difference between the contract price and the actual price in cash. This is illegal, and could have unfortunate repercussions when it comes to your turn to sell – you will either have to persuade a buyer to go through the same process, or pay substantially more gains tax than you should have to.

To say that Spain has been consumed by greed and corruption is dramatic and also incorrect. Having said this, the country has lost much of its attraction; high prices don't allow for much value appreciation, inflation has driven investors to countries where property and life are still cheap and the constant construction program and cranes are not attractive to older people wanting to retire. However, Spain still offers potential for those who can afford to spend the money to invest here, or for those who want a lower risk investment than is offered by newer markets.

Opportunity Rating

In less well known areas of Spain, as you start to head inland, village houses can be picked up with a relatively low cash outlay. The Spanish property market offers the greatest opportunity to lifestyle buyers looking for a laid-back lifestyle in a beautiful country. If immediate returns are not your first priority then it can offer the potential for capital gain over the long-term but this should not be relied upon.

Rating: $

Risk Rating

The biggest risk in Spain is oversupply and slow price growth, especially on new build property. Property developers are losing touch with reality and starting projects that cannot be finished. As mentioned before, a lack of viable exit strategy also poses a marked risk for investors.

With high entry prices in the property market and with the emergence of destinations such as Croatia and Morocco, Spain is facing fierce competition, leading to a drop in demand and therefore in prices. The country is also not exempt from the issues of domestic terrorism, crime and security of ownership.

The last word then, should probably be one of warning. Investors are advised to err on the side of caution and think strongly before considering Spain as a safe investment destination.

Rating: ⚠ ⚠ ⚠ ⚠ ⚠

Turkey

CURRENCY
New Lira

EXCHANGE RATES
100 New Lira = £38.60
£1 = 2.59 New Lira
100 New Lira = US $77.76
US $1 = 1.29 New Lira

Introduction

From the Trojan War through to the Roman, Byzantine then Ottoman empires Turkey and its former capital Constantinople (renamed Istanbul in 1453) has created evocative images of bloody crusading wars juxtaposed with exotic spice traders and teaming souks. However modern Turkey is far removed from these ancient images and has evolved into a major tourist destination for Western Europeans attracted by the beautiful coastline and low costs. Turkey attracted 25 million tourists in 2005 although this fell in 2006 as a result of wide spread terrorism threats. As long as political calm can be maintained, all indications suggest that demand will recommence its growth at a steady rate. The World Travel and Tourism Council predict 4.5% annual increases in real terms between 2008 and 2017 and Conde Nast named Istanbul as their top tourist destination for 2006.

As tourism has grown Turkey has simultaneously developed into one of the fastest growing emerging property markets in Europe. Offering affordability and high capital appreciation Turkey is drawing some of the highest concentrations of UK buyers outside Spain and France. Although it is the far sighted investors who plunged in early that seem to be having the last laugh, there is still potential for buyers wanting to invest in Turkey's dynamic housing market.

A few years ago Turkey's property market was far from thriving. With non Turkish nationals facing impediments to freehold ownership; it was in effect a closed shop with regards to investment opportunities. This all changed in 2003 though, when the decade old legislation regulating foreign ownership was amended in order to spur on foreign investment. Since then interest in Turkey has flourished with Britons, Irish, German, Dutch and Danes buying property here.

This interest was further enhanced when a new law was passed in January 2006, confirming the right of foreigners to buy property under 2.5 hectares in size for personal use or business. (This threshold may be increased to a maximum of 30 hectares, upon application to the Council of Ministers, on condition that this figure does not exceed a total of 0.5% of the land area of the province in question.) Plus, since the introduction of the new mortgage laws foreign investors are now able to obtain local mortgages.

Is This a Good Place to Buy?

If this book was merely about choosing a nice place to build a second home, Turkey would be high on the list. The climate, Mediterranean life-style, wonderful food, beaches and hospitality combine to make Turkey very appealing to second home buyers. However, this book is also about investment and choosing a property which might increase in value. Does Turkey therefore belong on this second list?

The answer is yes, and for reasons that have more to do with hard-headed finance than with sun and sand. The housing market in Turkey has lagged behind Europe and the previous difficulty in obtaining mortgages has meant that prices have stayed artificially low. But with the opening up of the mortgage market this is about to change. It is not just the mortgage situation which will have long term effects on the market – Turkey is getting richer and house prices should grow alongside the wealth of the country. The Turkish economy grew by 9.9% in 2004 alone, the highest recorded growth that year within an OECD (Organisation for Economic Co-operation and Development) country. Growth in 2005 was still high at 7.4% and to the third quarter of 2006 GDP was 5.9%.

Turkey first started to appeal to Europe in 1963 although things moved slowly until 1999 when Turkey was recognised as an EU candidate. Negotiations were pushed further when Tayyipp Erdogan was elected prime minister, a man with strong European ambitions. Erdogan believes Turkey could join the EU by 2012 but realistically negotiations are set to continue, and could take in total fifteen years, meaning Turkey will not join until 2019. Fifteen years is a long time in property investments and has dampened some of the wilder optimism of local property agents. Although the required legal and financial services reforms will help to place the market on a sounder footing some feel that the market is now so dynamic that entry itself will not be the catalyst it might once have been.

'Whilst all the major Turkish cities offer interesting investment opportunities, it is the historic areas of Istanbul, in desperate need of reconstruction and renovation, which offer some of the best investments.'

The best results for the real estate sector lie in better mortgage provision. The government is committed to strengthening the mortgage market, an important step because in the past short loan terms (only 60 months for loans in lira) and high interest rates (up to 22.5%) have meant that only a small percentage of housing finance in Turkey currently stems from bank mortgage credits. Currently 5% stems from credits, and although low, has increased by 2% since the introduction of new mortgages. Where domestic housing loans accounted for 2% of GDP in 2004, by the end of 2006 they accounted for 14.4% of total GDP.

More than 60% of real estate purchases are funded through inheritance or savings which sets a limit on how far prices can rise before they simply become unaffordable and the market stultifies. Lower interest rates will make mortgages more affordable and cause house prices to head upwards.

This fiscal optimism is also supported by demographics. According to an article in FDI Magazine ('Housing Ambition' Metin Demirsar) the maths are as follows: Turkey's population stands at 72 million, with 59% of the population aged less than 29 years old. 55% of the available housing stock is in shanty towns, and at least 40% is ready to be renewed. This adds up to huge domestic demand for housing, quite apart from the market for holiday homes.

Price History

Price increases vary across the country and the government does not release authoritative statistics, but Agents Knight Frank predict property prices will increase by 12.5% in 2007, placing Turkey in its top 10 best markets for this year. 2006 saw real estate purchases by foreign investors exceed US $2.5 million, having doubled since 2004 and increased five times since 2002.

Mass tourism hotspots such as Antalya or Alanya offer low budget apartments from £15,000 ($30,234) where as luxury apartments on the Bodrum Peninsula, appealing to the more affluent buyer, can cost anything from £68,000 – £300,000 ($138,530 – $604,805).

Which Type of Property Should You Go For?

With such a young population there has been enormous growth in urban areas and apartments in city centres are proving the most popular.

Whilst all the major Turkish cities offer interesting investment opportunities, it is the historic areas of Istanbul, in desperate need of reconstruction and renovation, which offer some of the best investments.

Apartments are also popular on the coast, but as the majority of second homes are bought new or off-plan it is difficult to quantify whether prices are rising more quickly for villas or apartment property.

Hotspots

Alanya, Bodrum, Dalaman, Didim, Fethiye and **Kusadasi** are all tipped to be good holiday investment hotspots. These coastline towns are not necessarily anymore attractive than others but offer a better infrastructure and are established tourist destinations with an existing expat community and regular international flights. Bodrum, for example, already has over 3,000 British families based there.

Rental yields are also high on the coast averaging 13–16% during the summer season.

Whilst the coast offers numerous attractions for the second home owner the real investment opportunities lie closer to the capital, **Ankara** and the historic city of **Istanbul** (see picture 18 in the colour section). Rental yields in both Ankara and Istanbul can be as high as 10% with houses in the suburbs of Ankara even achieving yields of around 12%. Unsurprisingly, residential property in Turkish cities was identified as an outstanding opportunity in the 'Emerging Trends in Real Estate: Europe 2006' report produced by the Urban Land Institute.

INSIDER TIP

Turkey is one of the world's top 20 most populated countries – growing at a rate of 2% per year – well above the world average. Rapid urbanisation of a predominantly young population is creating a severe housing shortage in Turkey with recent studies highlighting a need for more than 5 million new houses by 2010. This combination of demand and limited supply will continue to push prices up in the major cities and towns in the foreseeable future.

Property funds based in Europe and the Gulf are also pouring money into the country. Dubai is a particularly heavy investor, regarding Turkey as an attractive destination for the real estate boom in the United Arab Emirates. A flagship project is the twin towers (a pair of twisted skyscrapers) being constructed by Dubai Holdings in Istanbul at a cost of $500 million. The city also boasts a new IKEA and Harvey Nichols stores and budget airline easyjet has daily flights to Istanbul from the UK with prices starting at just £30.

The Purchase Process

After purchase terms have been agreed, the next step is to request a copy of the TAPU or title deeds. A number of checks are recommended including:

- Whether the current TAPU is in the vendor's name and if any other names are on the TAPU they have given permission to sell. The address must also match exactly and a visit is recommended to confirm this.
- Whether 'Permission to Build' has been granted, if the property is a new build ask to see the Insaat Rahsati (document verifying completion to specification).
- Whether the TAPU states 'Permission to live'.
- There are no taxes or liens outstanding on the property. Arrange for any outstanding debts against the property to be paid on exchanging of monies.

Other checks are recommended relating to garbage taxes and billing for water and electricity. It is also important to ascertain whether there are any current rental agreements in place. If buying a villa check the agreements on 'combined road use' near your property.

The next step is to arrange for preliminary contracts to be drawn up; the contracts should include full property details, details of the deposit which should be around 10% and details of the price. If the seller suggests recording a low sale price in order to reduce stamp duty be wary, as this leaves you at risk of legal action and may rebound on you when you come to sell the property on.

Some unscrupulous sellers may specify that you are to pay their share of taxes and dues as well as your own. A good translator is a worthwhile investment. The Turkish embassy also suggests that you should list the fees being paid to professionals in order to clear yourself from any tax evasion perpetrated by them.

Finally, the contract should specify under what conditions the sale may be cancelled, how matters will be resolved in the event of a dispute and the national identity and numbers of everyone involved in the sale. Another useful clause is to disclaim responsibility for any overdue taxes or charges, as these will otherwise be transferred into your name with the property. As with any transaction in a foreign language, either arrange for a bilingual contract or pay for a certified copy rather than rely on a verbal translation. In order to make the transaction absolutely watertight, you can sign both copies before a notary public.

Having signed the contracts, the next stage is to apply to the land registry or TAPU office to transfer the title. Turkey has some areas, military and protected lands, where foreigners are not allowed to buy. The TAPU Office should give you the formal confirmation that your house is not listed in one of these areas. After clearance has been granted, you will be given deeds of ownership.

The final step is to contact the Municipality within the first year of ownership. After filling out a simple form the tax liabilities on your property will be explained to you. Overall costs should be as follows:

- *Solicitor's fees* – approximately £450 ($914.41). *Public notary's fees* – £90 ($182.89).
- *Initial purchase tax* – 1.5% of the (declared) purchase price.
- *Annual purchase tax* – approximately 0.5% of the (declared) purchase price.

Capital gains tax in Turkey varies from 15–40% but if you hold onto the property for 4 years or more after the date of purchase there are no capital gains taxes at all.

The cost of earthquake insurance varies depending on property type and location, but is compulsory in many areas. Properties sharing communal facilities will be subject to a maintenance charge which varies from approximately £100–£500 annually.

In Turkey, a group of people are allowed to build an apartment complex together under the name of a Co-operative. It is illegal for a foreign person to be involved in a Co-operative and it is also illegal to sell any part of the Co-operative to a foreign buyer if in any way unfinished. After completion a foreign buyer is free to purchase any part of the Co-operative although fees may be charged.

Mortgages

In January 2008 a new mortgage law is due to come into force which will open up the market to new types of investor as it allows mortgages with tenor of up to 30 years. British buyers can currently obtain loans of up to 75% with interest rates at around 7%.

Europe

TURKEY

Key Risks and Opportunities

There is a risk in some coastal areas of over-building and so a personal inspection trip is advised. There have also been reports of difficulties with unscrupulous vendors and as much as 60% of existing properties in Turkey are believed to have some irregularity with property title or planning consent – 600,000 in Istanbul alone. A reliable lawyer is therefore essential.

Opportunity Rating

Turkey has many of the ingredients of an excellent investment location. Prices are low and there are good fundamentals making the country popular as a tourism destination and a place for holiday home buyers. Mass urbanisation will continue to create a strong market in the major cities and for pure investment potential our recommendation would be to buy in Istanbul.

Rating: $ $ $ $

Risk Rating

Turkey presents a range of risks. Terrorism has been a problem of late and the political situation is not as stable as in more developed markets. Turkey's accession into the EU is by no means a certainty although negotiations are progressing and relations remain strong.

Rating: ⚠ ⚠ ⚠ ⚠

China

CURRENCY
Chinese Yuan Renminbi (CNY)

EXCHANGE RATES
1,000 CNY = GBP 65
GBP 1 = 15.34 CNY
1,000 CNY= US$132
US$1 = 7.56 CNY

BEIJING

Introduction

One of the world's oldest civilisations, with cultures dating back more than six millennia, China is steeped in fascinating history. The source of some of the world's great inventions and home to the world's longest written language system, the culture is unique and engaging. As the world's most populous and fastest growing country, and with the fourth largest economy on the planet, China is an economic powerhouse and one of the world's most important markets in almost all industry sectors.

Since the start of the Chinese Economic Reform in the late 1970s, China's extraordinary economic growth has been widely acknowledged by the international community and with GDP growth averaging between 8% and 9% for the past quarter of a century it is not hard to understand why. In 2006, China's GDP was US$2.79 trillion at the current exchange rate, an increase of 11.1% over the previous year. For four years in a row, China's economic growth has reached or slightly exceeded 10% without significant inflation. According to a 2007 Ernst and Young survey China was positioned the number one country in the world in terms of attractiveness for foreign investors.

According to the Global Competitiveness Report 2006–2007 published by the World Economic Forum, 'China's buoyant growth rates coupled with low inflation, one of the highest savings rates in the world and manageable levels of public debt have boosted China's ranking on the macroeconomy pillar of the GCI to 6th place'.

Is This a Good Place to Buy?

China has showed openness to progress and development by its accession to the World Trade Organisation (WTO) in 2001 and, in a bid to encourage more FDI and non-FDI inflow, China also has dual taxation agreements with 78 countries, including the UK (further details of these agreements can be found at www.chinatax.gov.cn/ssxd.jsp).

A key element of China's new-found economic freedom was the introduction of property rights in 2004 which guaranteed that 'legally obtained private property of the citizens shall not be violated'. The constitution further states that 'the state may, for the necessity of public interest, requisition or expropriate citizens' private property and pay compensation in accordance with law'.

The most recent adoption of China's Property Rights Law (PRL, passed by China's National People's Congress in March 2007, and to be implemented from October 2007) is a milestone in China's legal system and goes further in defining and systematically regulating general property rights. The PRL, for the first time in China's history emphasises that private, collective and public property are equally important and enjoy the same level of protection. The PRL primarily deals with the rights to both immovable and moveable property and covers ownership, rights and obligations and property rights protection. As a result, potential investors should be confident that their investment in China is a secure one.

Price History

2007 was the tenth year since China allowed urban real properties to be purchased and owned privately (Chinese Property Reform). As the world's most populous country, it is not surprising to see that since the property reform in China, the average property price in major cities has been growing at around 22%. Such a booming market has not only attracted many multi-national property developers, such as Capitaland and Hutchison Whampoa, but also a large number of institutional and individual property investors. For example, Morgan Stanley, has bought US$1.5 billion worth of Chinese property for the past few years and in March 2006 the world's biggest security firm announced plans to triple its investment in the Chinese property market. JPMorgan has also been actively involved in China's property sector and has now ranked number one in China real estate equity and equity-linked offerings since 2004. The Goodman Group, the world's second largest industrial property firm announced in 2007 that it had plans to invest some US$2–3 billion in the next three to five years in China's real estate sector.

To ensure that the healthy growth and sustainability of the real estate sector is preserved, the Chinese government has taken various measures in a bid to control development. Taxes, interest rates and deposit requirements have been raised whilst restrictions on certain types of sales have been imposed.

'Demand for property is growing enormously and the country has possibly the strongest fundamental reasons for property price growth of any country in the world'

Such tightening however has not impinged on property price increases. In May 2006, prices in 70 large and medium-sized Chinese cities rose by 6.4% year-on-year. Five cities saw double-digit growth in prices for new homes with Shenzhen leading with a 12.3% rise. Beijing prices rose by 10.3%. According to China's Economic Review in 2006, a total of $8.23 billion of foreign investment was injected into China's property market, up 51.9% year-on-year. Further, a report by China's National Bureau of Statistics (NBS) shows investment in the country's property sector reached $94.7bn during the first 5 months of 2007, an increase of 27.5% on the same period in 2006. Such growth perhaps is due to two very different reasons, on the one hand, investors see the property sector as more transparent and regulated, making long term investment less risky; on the other hand, some institutional investors are speculating on the revaluation of the Chinese currency by purchasing large volume of Chinese properties. Either way, China offers great investment opportunities.

Which Type of Property Should You Go For?

All property in China is under a "land use right" system, similar to the western leasehold concept. There are three types of lease on land: residential, which is run on a 70-year lease (the Property Rights Law became effective in October 2007 which allowed such leases to be renewed), and commercial and industrial land which are on 40 to 50-year leases.

Although the Chinese economy has grown rapidly for the past quarter of a century, its per capita GDP in 2006 was approx. US$2,000 (US$7,600 with PPP), still low by world standards. To ensure that the majority of the Chinese people will be able to afford homes into the future, the Chinese government has introduced new measures to restrict foreign purchases. Foreign individuals can acquire one home having been a resident in China for over a year (they will

Asia

CHINA

need to have obtained a residence visa for over a year). Alternatively, properties can be purchased by foreigners through a local vehicle, either by setting up a fully owned foreign enterprise (WOFE) or a joint venture company (JV). Registering such companies however, can be time-consuming as well as costly.

These measurements are likely to be relaxed in the near future once the central government can see that the real estate sector has maintained a good period of sturdy growth.

Hotspots

There are a number of different regions attracting investment in China each with differing legal requirements and investment opportunities. The major cities or first tier cities remain Shanghai, Beijing, Guangzhou, Shenzhen, Macau and Hong Kong. The secondary cities or second tier cities have increasingly become excellent locations to investment due to the recent domestic economic growth and inflow of capital. These cities include Chongqing, Chengdu, Tianjin, Qingdao, Suzhou, Nanjing and Dalina. Due to rapidly rising local wealth, domestic tourism is also taking off in China meaning it may well be profitable to invest in either ski or beach resorts.

For the purposes of this book and due to shortage of space, Shanghai, Beijing, Chongqing and Macau will be considered in detail.

Shanghai

Home to the powerful Shanghai Stock Exchange, Shanghai rubs proverbial shoulders with New York, Tokyo and London and is one of the world's most important trade and finance centres (see picture 17 in the colour section). Its GDP growth exceeded one trillion yuan in 2006 rewarding its economy with double-digit growth for the 15th consecutive year.

INSIDER TIP Having won its bid to host the World Expo in 2010, Shanghai is enjoying US$2.3 billion dedicated to new urban infrastructure. The resulting influx of people has caused demand for property to far outstrip supply and stands the market in very good stead.
Considering the city's current status, the price of property remains attractive – you can purchase here at a fraction of the cost of other world financial centres, and at half or even a third of the prices in Hong Kong or Taipei. This means that the potential for capital growth is substantial, and prices are likely to rise sturdily over coming years.

In Shanghai's residential market, government rules regulating foreigners buying property began to show their effects in the fourth quarter. The price of the luxury residential properties dropped slightly, whilst the rental yield increased by approximately 2.5% year-on-year. In 2007, luxury residential property prices were expected to remain steady whilst the numbers of property transactions were expected to decline further. According to Colliers International report, the rental yield for luxury residential properties will be 6.6% for 2007.

Overall, and supported by strong economic conditions, the Shanghai real estate market performed well in 2006 and with a positive outlook continuing into 2007, its future looks solid.

Beijing

Beijing is the capital, main political and cultural centre of China and enjoyed 10.7% growth year-on-year in the first nine months of 2006. Due to host the 2008 Olympics, the city will without doubt become a property investment hotspot and already has received a total of US$705 million through property investment transactions.

As China's tourism centre, serviced apartments and hotels in the city represent a good buy and are set to benefit greatly from the increased levels of Olympic tourism. In addition, excellent infrastructure should ensure that the city maintains its position as a key investment destination long after the Olympics have finished.

In the luxury residential property sector, prices are averaging US$3,000 per square metre, whilst rental is about US$20 per square meter per annum. Although rental yields for luxury properties (predicated at 8.1% for 2007) are better than many of the world's other metropolitans, the vacancy rate is alarmingly high, currently standing at 19%.

Chongqing

The yield compression in first tier cities are diverting some institutional investors' attention to second tier cities. Among the second tier cities, Chongqing becomes the most obvious hotspot.

Chongqing is located in Central China at the confluence of the Yangzte and Jiangling Rivers and following Chinese government policies aimed to further develop western China, Chongqing has become a 'Gateway to the West'. Chinese central government has committed US$2 billion annually to improve Chongqing's infrastructure; support that is predicted to continue for at least a decade. In 2005, the nominal GDP rose 11.5% year-on-year, and is predicted to remain at 10% per year for the next 10 years.

Asia

CHINA

Central government's 'go west' plan is providing an enormous boost to the city and the 3 Gorges Dam project (impacting tourism and the relocation of residents) and increasing FDI will result in increased demand for commercial space and accommodation.

Property prices are about five or six years behind the Shanghai cycle and about a quarter of the price. The property market is a healthy one with prices growing slower than incomes. As a secondary city, Chongqing is beginning to be recognised as an upcoming market with enormous potential for high rental yields and capital appreciation.

Macau

Dubbed the Las Vegas of the Far East, Macau is one of the world's most famous off-shore banking centres and tax havens. Only 70km southwest of Hong Kong, property prices in this small territory (only 23km^2) are about a third lower.

The revenue from its gaming industry was greater than Las Vegas in 2005 (about US$6 billion). After the completion of Sands Macau, the world's biggest casino in 2004 and Wynn Macau in 2006, 15 new casinos will become operational by the end of 2009 along with a number of new hotels and should draw higher levels of tourists. Macau already receives 25 million tourists annually, so its future is very positive.

'With its robust economic performance and continual wealth enhancement, Macau's property market is attracting more and more sophisticated investors and prices have already increased by over 100%'

GDP growth has been averaging 10% per year since 2001, and in 2006, Macau's GDP grew by 17.7% year-on-year. It is even rumoured that Macau's GDP may soon outstrip Hong Kong's. Meanwhile, unemployment stands at a low 3.8%.

With its robust economic performance, continual wealth enhancement, booming gaming and gaming related tourism industries, Macau's property market is attracting more and more sophisticated property investors and property prices have already increased by over 100%. The supply of new dwellings is very limited and the property vacancy rate is low, making Macau a prime market with great potential. Rental yields for residential properties are about

6% but are expected to grow quickly as large numbers of foreign expatriates and highly educated staff move to Macau to take advantage of the burgeoning gaming and tourism industries.

The Purchase Process

To many, investment in China may seem like a difficult prospect. Apart from language and cultural differences, concerns range from opaque laws and regulations, to complicated bureaucracy.

Most importantly, investors first of all need to check whether they are even in a position to purchase a property in China – i.e. a foreign resident in China for over a year or one who has registered a WOFE or JV.

Before purchasing a property, certain checks must be made on both the seller and the property. During the purchase process itself, a number of legal documents must be signed and require legalising by the Chinese Embassy or Consulate. Some of this documentation must be completed in China, but this can be done through an agent and a power of attorney arrangement.

Once you have decided to buy, it is necessary to open a local bank account and to register it with the appropriate authorities. This bank account will be the base for any transactions, such as rent payments, to be made with regard to the property. A bank with internet and telephone banking is recommended for this process, as buyers are thereby able to keep track of transactions and funds.

To reserve a property, it is necessary to pay a small deposit. The buyer and seller will then enter into an 'official sales contract', which must be notarised if the purchaser is foreign. If property is off-plan, payments are often made in stages, which vary depending on the seller. Once the property is completed and the full payment is made, application will then be made to the government Deed and Title Office for the deed transfer from the seller to the buyer, on payment of the relevant taxes and fees (which will typically amount to around 5% of the purchase price). Before this transfer can be made, the seller must have paid off any existing mortgage on the property. This payment schedule also varies depending on the developer.

Mortgages

Up to 70% LTV mortgages are available with interest rates starting from around 6% depending on the **tenor** which can be up to 20 years for non resident foreigners.

Asia

CHINA

Key Risks and Opportunities

The implementation of the Property Rights Law should provide more security on private property rights and give domestic and foreign investors more comfort when investing in China's property market. The property markets in China's secondary cities and areas like Macau have not yet been targeted by too many foreign opportunity funds or speculative investors, making now an ideal time to invest.

Property prices and supply in certain districts in China's major cities are no longer sustainable meaning investors have to be cautious when choosing the location of their investment. Furthermore, China's legal system as well as its tax system are still not very transparent, making it essential to procure reliable legal and tax advice before and whilst investing.

Opportunity Rating

China is set to become the world's biggest economy by 2020. Demand for property is growing enormously both locally and internationally, and the country has possibly the strongest underlying fundamental reasons for property price growth of any country in the world.

Rating: $ $ $ $ $

Risk Rating

There are many perceived risks in China, predominantly related to politics and the protection of private property. However, private property rights are now protected in the Chinese constitution and the Property Rights Law and China's recent accession to the WTO should continue to ensure that the government maintains an investor-friendly approach. In some cities, prices have increased rapidly in recent years, creating fears of a bubble, however while in the short term there may be some price deflation, these locations still present good medium to long term opportunities.

Rating: ⚠ ⚠

India

NEW DELHI

Introduction

India is home to the most populated city, most prolific film industry and one of the most favoured cuisines in the world and as such, has a lot to offer. From northern Mumbai, home to both the Indian Stock Exchange and Bollywood, to the south characterised by paddy fields and coconut plantations, India is a land of colourful diversity. With a plethora of languages, customs, religions and arts, the country has consistently been a popular tourist destination.

India is undoubtedly an emerging market and has very good potential for capital appreciation. On top of this it is a market where transactions take place in English, finance and banking is straightforward, and a growing middle class ensures a healthy rental market. The rocketing population creates a constant demand for property, meaning that India unarguably presents an interesting and very real prospect for investors.

There is, however, a catch. The opportunity to buy is largely restricted to people with strong personal links to India, defined as either non-resident Indians (NRI) or persons of Indian origin (PIO). This means either Indian citizens living abroad or people who have held an Indian passport at some time, have a parent or grandparent with Indian citizenship or are married to an Indian citizen.

Technically foreign citizens of Indian origin also need agreement from the Reserve Bank, but a general permission to buy immovable property has been granted.

If the buyer has status as an NRI or PIO the rule is as follows:

An Indian citizen residing outside India (NRI) can acquire by way of purchase, any immovable property in India other than agricultural, plantation or farm house.

> ## *'India's stability, lack of a communist government, and the right to freehold property makes the real estate market here in many ways preferable to that in China'*

He is allowed to transfer such kind of immovable property to a person resident outside India who is a citizen of India or to a person of Indian origin resident outside India or a person resident in India.

A useful website to consult may be the Reserve Bank of India *(www.rbi.org.in)* which has up-to-date information on the legal regulations for property purchase.

Is This a Good Place to Buy?

If you are entitled to buy in this emerging market, then there are many options open to you. The economy posted an average growth rate of more than 7% in the decade since 1996. With a GDP growth rate of 9.4% in 2006–07, the Indian economy is among the fastest growing in the world and is still growing at a rate double that achieved by the West during the Industrial Revolution.

India's stability, lack of a communist government, and the right to freehold property makes the real estate market here in many ways preferable to that in China. Eligible emerging market investors then, who might otherwise turn to China, may prefer the greater degree of stability and ease of investment in India. There is also ample room for the real estate industry to develop.

Residential growth drivers include rapid urbanisation of 2.5% a year and changing attitudes to home ownership. The average age of a new homeowner is now 32, compared to 45 a decade ago. A growing middle class with disposable income is also a crucial factor in raising the demand for housing. Indeed, the growth of India's middle classes is one of the big demographic stories of the past ten years. It is now growing by 15 – 20 million people every year and by 2025 half of the population will be categorised as middle class. This creates a new class of young, relatively wealthy consumers who are moving into homes of their own.

Net income in India has grown 100% over the last ten years and population growth is expected to help India take China's place as the most populous country by 2030. Twenty million houses will be needed in the next five years if supply is to keep up with demand meaning investors couldn't ask for a better set of market fundamentals.

There are over twenty million non-resident Indians and they retain close links to the country. Remittances by overseas Indians are higher than for any other country in the world. They totalled US $24.6. billion from 2005 to 2006; ahead of India's two closest followers, China and Mexico. Overseas and non-resident Indians often like to maintain a base in the country and their wealth provides a constant boost to a property market which has been one of the strongest internationally over the past few years.

Price History

The property market in India first boomed and then crashed in the mid 1990s as over-optimistic developers released too much residential and commercial supply onto the market. Prices declined until an expansion of the mortgage market allowed them to appreciate again and prices have largely been rising ever since.

There is still huge potential for investors if you choose your region carefully. It must be noted though, that India's property market is still immature and in certain areas prices have recently fallen after their rapid rise. The Reserve Bank of India raised its interest rates five times between 2006 and 2007 to a five year high of 7.75%, while some mortgage rates are as high as 12%. Rising interest rates and concerns over mortgage defaults have caused residential property prices in India's largest cities, Mumbai and New Delhi, to drop by an average of 15% in the first 6 months of 2007, after rising 60% in the two years previous to this. However, in the medium to long term, the economic growth in India, through its rapidly expanding BPO & IT sectors, combined with government expenditure on health and education, will lead to significant state improvements, such as extreme salary growth and real estate appreciation.

What Sort of Property Should You Go For?

Local property consultants tip high quality apartments and villas in central locations as the best stock to invest in. Whereas property prices in the countryside or suburbs of different cities may remain static, prime property in most major cities should continue on an upwards trajectory.

Hotspots

Those looking for a pure investment buy will probably be tempted by cities such as Mumbai, Delhi, Bangalore and Chennai which have all undergone radical growth in the last few years. By 2015 India's 'Mega-Cities' of Mumbai and Delhi will be the world's second and third largest cities.

Mumbai is generally regarded as expensive. Identified as the commercial and financial capital of India and with a fantastic public transport network, no area is out of reach and property is in high demand. Apartments in South

Asia

INDIA

Mumbai cost around £4,457 to £5,100 per square metre, prices comparable to many of the world's leading cities. However, a one-bedroom apartment can still be found from upwards of £13,500 and an apartment with three bedrooms from £27,000.

A degree of caution needs to be exercised when investing in Delhi or Mumbai as severe price drops in residential property prices occurred during 2007. That said, providing you choose your development and area carefully, you can still make a profit.

Buyers would do best to invest in other rapidly developing cities such as **Bangalore** in India's 'Silicon Valley' (Karnataka) or **Jaipur** (Rajastan). Bangalore is firmly established as a technology hub and its economy is rising rapidly. Total demand for apartments here is estimated at 24,000 units each year, with an expected annual growth rate of 20% over the next several years. Average prices in Bangalore range from £217–£326 per square metre.

Jaipur forms part of the 'Golden Triangle' of Delhi-Agra-Jaipur. Popular with tourists, it is universally famous as the 'Pink city' with stunning lakes, forts and palaces. It is also the site for substantial IT and industrial development. Here a 3 bedroom apartment can be found from upwards of £10,000.

Other fast moving cities include **Chennai** (Tamil Nadu), **Hyderabad** (Andrhra Pradesh) and Pune (Maharastra) which are proving to be highly attractive business locations, thus attracting residential demand. Massive infrastructure improvements are being planned for new international airports at Bangalore, Hyderbad and Pune while 'The Quadrilateral' project to provide an interstate road link between Delhi, Mumbai, Kolkata and Chennai, is nearly complete. The current thirst for infrastructure improvements is likely to have a favourable stimulus on the Indian economy, real estate and tourism markets.

INSIDER TIP **IT and retail are key drivers of the real estate in Pune. Its transformation into a vibrant corporate city with close proximity to Mumbai has made Pune a hot destination for the real estate investor. Here average city prices are around £323 per square metre, with the up-market Boat Club Road seeing prices of over £560 per square metre.**

For buyers looking to pick up a second home for holiday use or for the holiday market, the best letting opportunities are in **Goa** and **Kerala** in southern India. With 100km of stunning beaches, over 400,000 tourist arrivals

a year and prices that have risen over 25% in the last 3 years, Goa is a hot destination for investors. The Goan government is cracking down on rogue agents
and sales to non-indians have to be reported to the government to ensure
they are legally conducted. Often nicknamed 'India for Beginners' it is a delight-
ful blend of east and west that has already attracted some 5,000 foreign investors,
3,000 of which are British. It is also rated as one of India's best states to live in
and one of the safest Indian regions, becoming increasingly popular with retirees
from the west. Kerala, also known as the 'Queen of the Arabian sea', is a collection of islands and narrow peninsulas with a warm tropical climate. The area has
become increasingly popular with tourists over the past few years. In both Goa
and Kerala, an apartment in a gated compound can be a good buy. Remember
that a sub-tropical climate can have a harsh effect on buildings so buying into a
serviced apartment block means less can go wrong in your absence. Apartments
in Goa are advertised from £5,000 ($10,100), with three bedroom villas from
£28,600 ($56,400).

Wherever you choose to buy, you will find India well supplied with research
resources. Indiaproperties.com for example, has a regional market section
which gives up to date information on costs in different areas of major cities.

The Purchase Process

It is important to choose your developer carefully and ensure that you hire a
reputable agent. Check also that the property you are interested in and its
land-title have been certified by independent solicitors. It is also wise to verify
that there are no ownership or boundary disputes (this is a common problem
in India).

After agreeing the purchase price, contracts are signed in the presence of a
notary, who then registers the change of ownership. It is possible to buy using a
power of attorney and funds should be paid out of a rupee account.

Stamp duty is set at state level and ranges from around 4–10%. A registration fee of approximately 1–2% of market value is also required. Legal fees are
around £100 using local lawyers which you will find through a good agent.

Mortgages

Mortgages from Indian banks are available to PIO or NRI buyers. Interest
rates tend to be fairly high and can be as much as 12%. Terms tend to last for 10
years with buyers needing a minimum of 15% deposit if buying off-plan, or 20%
for a resale property.

Key Risks and Opportunities

Prices have risen so fast in some urban areas that local experts are warning of a potential bubble. In 2007 some prices in Delhi and Mumbai suburbs began to fall after their rapid rise. Information on the state of a particular local market can be found in the property section of the local English-language newspaper.

Repatriation of funds can be a problem. According to PriceWaterhouseCoopers NRIs/PIOs are permitted repatriation of sale proceeds up to $1 million per financial year for a maximum of two houses. However, the property must have been paid for from a rupee account and repatriation of funds is only permitted up to the amount originally invested. Unless investment laws are further liberalised, this suggests that returns have to be made from rental income rather than capital appreciation. Non-resident Indians are allowed to rent out property and to repatriate the income earned through the banker/authorised dealer.

Opportunity Rating

The burgeoning Indian economy and a rapidly growing middle class make India an outstanding investment opportunity, albeit for a restricted market. The internationalisation of the economy and India's emergence as an economic force should all add up to excellent long-term performance in the real estate market.

Rating: $ $ $ $ $

Risk Rating

India is not without its problems and corruption can still be an issue. However, the biggest risk for foreign investors is access to their profits. However, liberalisation is making this easier.

Rating: ⚠ ⚠ ⚠ ⚠

Japan

Introduction

Japan has always held an intense fascination for outsiders. Having developed for centuries in almost total isolation the country has a rich history and culture that is unlike any other. Japanese society is both highly structured and ritualised, it clings fiercely to its past yet it is also innovative and open to change. From the country's historic temples to the glitz and glamour of Tokyo's Rappongi district, Japan is a maze of contradictions. Visitors come to see cherry blossom and Geisha girls but they also stay in some of the world's most modern hotels and ride the futuristic bullet train.

In business, Japan is renowned for being stiflingly formal, while its gaming parlours and karaoke bars thrive by offering respite. Many people know little of Japan outside Tokyo, though it has several large and important cities, such as Osaka, Kyoto and Okinawa. There are 3,000 islands and 30,000 kilometres of coastline, thermal springs and, of course, symbolic Mount Fuji. In the Hokkaido region the mountains provide some of the best and most reliable skiing in the world and, as you move further south the climate changes from temperate to sub-tropical.

During the middle of the 20th century, Japan successfully rebuilt its economy after the devastation of the Second World War, developing new, key technologies and creating a well-educated workforce. During this period the country achieved one of the world's highest economic growth rates leading to a softening of economic policy and increased lending. Through the 1980s Japan was the world leader in technology and business, exporting not only its products but its ideas, culture and style to the rest of the world. However, by the start

---

'European investors who want easy-to-manage, buy-to-let options that are accessible may not see Japan as a worthwhile investment'

---

of the following decade the country was headed for deep recession. This was partly caused by changes to the laws, reducing speculation in the property market, and increasing interest rates.

In the past five years, and despite a few false dawns, there has been a definite move towards growth. The country is predicted to continue in this way for at least the next year with GDP growth hovering around the 2.5% mark. The yen was also predicted to gain in strength by the start of 2008, after a weak performance through 2007, and this was expected to be accompanied by a rise in interest rates. The country is the fourth largest global economy and has one of the world's biggest home markets with a population of 130 million, however this may not be enough to help it face its challenges. The culture of the country and stringent regulations makes it difficult for overseas businesses to invest. In addition, there is an aging workforce and the government still has to reverse the precarious financial position it created for itself by attempting to stimulate the economy in the mid-1990s. Around seven million tourists arrive each year from all over the globe with the majority being from Korea and Australia.

Is This a Good Place to Buy?

Japan's changing fortunes may well make it worth considering for the long-term or buy-to-let investor but there are a number of issues to consider. Despite large price drops over the past 15 years, property in the major employment hubs isn't cheap by the standards of many other countries and prices are not growing as fast either. Any price rises likely to be slow for the foreseeable future.

That said, there are no restrictions on ownership so the market is open to overseas investors. The law favours landlords with tax breaks and rent negotiation, plus there is an increasing demand for rental property, with prices currently low enough to offer respectable yields. In the past few years there has also been a distinct pattern of migration of young people from the smaller towns and more rural locations to cities. Women are marrying at a later age and young couples are choosing to remain childless for longer, leading to a sector of the population with more disposable income.

These people prefer to buy or rent more upmarket properties with higher-quality fittings than their parents did but there is a lack of supply in this market, all of which may offer good rental prospects for landlords who buy in the right locations. The Global Property Guide index shows landlords can expect to achieve yields of between 4.7 and 7.2% in Tokyo, depending on location and style of property.

Because of the issue of distance and cultural differences, European buy-to-let investors may find it easier to engage a management company. This shouldn't be an issue as there are many rental agents in the cities but costs of their services will need to be factored into any profits.

Price History

The real estate market in Japan has seen out a long, hard recession over the past 15 years, which saw real estate prices dropping by around 50% in some areas. The country appears to be well on the way to recovery now though, with prices up by 4% in 2006 and further increases of 7.75% in the first part of 2007.

On average, apartments outside central Tokyo currently cost from around 32m yen. In the most sought-after central districts of Chiyoda, Minato, Chuo, Shibuya and Shinjuku apartments cost from around 120m yen up to 500m yen. Houses in the outer suburbs cost around 80m yen.

Other cities have pretty much shared Tokyo's fate with stalled prices that start at around 30m yen for a small apartment. In rural locations prices have declined markedly due to the recession and migration of the workforce and such homes are unlikely to offer good investment returns. Ski property is one area that is seeing large overseas investment and appreciation in popular resorts has been as much as 40% in some areas, with prices currently starting from around 25m yen.

Which Type of Property Should You Go For?

Due to overcrowding in the cities, properties in Japan tend to be small, with an average new-build home measuring just 94 square metres (a gain over older properties, which measured around 60 square metres). Central apartments of reasonable size are by far the most sought-after properties and the changing demographic of the country has led to new condominium projects targeting younger, wealthier residents by including leisure facilities and more luxurious 'western-style' fittings. These are sought after by young professionals with higher levels of disposable income than has been seen in previous generations.

Asia

JAPAN

INSIDER TIP **Ski resorts are currently one of the lowest priced property options, yet offer a busy tourist season due to their reliable snow. There is a lot of interest in mountain resorts and a great deal of new development. A large proportion of tourists come from Japan's home market but resorts also attract huge numbers of skiers from areas such as Southeast Asia and Australia.**

Family homes in suburban city locations can be lucrative if you target the expat community. Properties in areas near good international schools offer the best opportunity for long-term, buy-to-let returns and can generate between 250,000 and 650,000 yen per month or more in rental income.

Always bear in mind that Japan is a typhoon and earthquake zone, and properties must be built to last. The likelihood of an earthquake or typhoon could be an influencing factor as to whether to buy. Land is seen as much the safest option and prices are starting to rise again after a 16-year slump. Commercial land outside city centres saw rises of 2% last year with prices in sought-after areas of Tokyo rising by as much as 40%, though prices remain lower than those seen during the 1980s boom.

Hotspots

Unless you speak Japanese well or can visit in person it may be difficult to buy property anywhere in the country. Most agents outside Tokyo only list in Japanese and only a few overseas developers are operating in Tokyo and some tourist areas, such as the ski resorts.

Tokyo

Buzzing with life and commercial activity, Tokyo is one of the world's great cities offering an urban environment that many find simultaneously exciting and alienating. However, among the high-rise, neon-clad commercial and residential properties, the city still has pockets where Japan's traditions are celebrated – temples, tea houses and gardens still play a large role in Japanese culture. For many years Tokyo was the most expensive city in which to own property and it still remains near the top of the rankings, despite having seen such a long recession. Those without at least 40m yen to spend may find little to attract them in Tokyo.

The city is broken down into nine districts, each encompassing several distinct areas. The Shinjuku district is popular for its excellent transport links, large public gardens and areas that offer a more traditional feel. On the border of the Shinjuku and Chiyoda districts are Yotsuya, Ichigaya, Iidabashi, all locations that Western residents aim for, due to the foreign language schools. Prices here range from around 50m yen to 200m yen or more depending on building, apartment size and location. Other areas with overseas schools include residential Meguru and Minato, one of the most expensive and sought-after central areas to own property. Prices here start at 75m yen to over 200m for apartments measuring between 50 and 120 square metres but larger, more contemporary property can cost as much as 500m yen. Minato is home to a cosmopolitan mix of shops, businesses and leisure facilities, many of the latter in the notorious Rappongi district where hotels and bars jostle for space with new apartment developments aimed at a young population.

Within the Meguru district are the fashionable suburbs of Daikanyama, Ebisu and Nakameguro, places that appear to be attracting a hip, young population. The more established suburbs of Shinagawa and Osaki may offer good prospects for those seeking more affordable property with good transport connections and amenities such as parks, schools and low-key shopping areas that appeal to families. Prices tend to start at around 35m yen for small apartments, with larger, three-bedroom apartments and small houses costing from around 80m yen. Similarly, the district of Western Setagaya is also somewhere families seek out for access to larger properties with easy access to the city. Expect to pay around 85m yen for an apartment with two bedrooms.

Osaka

The second largest city in Japan, Osaka is a busy commercial and industrial hub. It has a population of 2.6m, of which just over 200,000 are overseas nationals. The surrounding Osaka region has around 8.8m people. The city was recently listed as the eighth most expensive in which to live and is currently regarded by the Urban Land Institute in Washington as offering some of the top prospects for investment and development. According to their report, all commercial sectors in Osaka, including retail and industrial property, offer potential, while residential property offers a good investment in the long-term.

This is partly due to a huge decrease (79%)in the price of commercial land during the crash. Prices have not yet climbed back to their former level and overseas investment institutions have moved in, buying up large areas and sparking a boom in development. The city is host to the 2007 World Athletics Championships and Kansai airport is soon to open another runway. Osaka's main station and surrounding area is currently being redeveloped into upmarket retail and commercial space, while established businesses are also revamping themselves and mass regeneration of public areas is being undertaken.

Falling prices have attracted people back to the city in search of more affordable accommodation. A relaxation in building restrictions on residential property has also increased the amount of apartments now available. Average apartment

Asia

JAPAN

prices in outer areas start at around 20m yen and go up to over 400m yen with rental returns of around 80,000 to 100,000 yen per month.

Ski resorts

Japan has 650 ski resorts with a long snow season lasting from November until early May. Snow is reliable and often deep and attracts tourists from a large catchment area including China, Taiwan, South Korea and Australia. The best known area is **Hokkaido** where a number of resorts are undergoing regeneration and there are plans for two brand new resorts. Property in this region is a mix of old chalets in need of restoration and new-build property, mainly apartments.

In the popular **Hakuba** resort, apartments cost from around 25m yen, while log cabins and older resales can still be found from around 20m yen with average rental returns of 3% to 5% net through the peak December to March period. Property in **Niseko** has also become highly sought after with prices rising between 20% and 40% over the past six years. Visitor numbers in 2006 were 1.51m, with 480,000 staying in resorts. As a result, higher-end property is coming into the region as more development companies take note of the area's appeal and prices are likely to go up in the short term. Older property currently sells from around 30m yen and new apartments go for upwards of 40m.

The Purchase Process

Price setting of property in Japan is often done by the seller, who tells the agent how much he wants. This may bear little relation to the actual market value and buyers are advised to look at comparable properties in the area to get an idea of what an apartment may be worth. Before you can start the purchase process you need to obtain a purchasing application from the authorities.

The background searches on a property, such as its legal and building history and title deeds are usually undertaken by a licensee – often a third-party estate agent. You will also need a lawyer to draw up the contract and once this has been done, the buyer signs and pays a deposit of 10% of the purchase price. The contract and title deeds need to be forwarded to the bank if any loan is being raised for the property and, along with regular insurance, you'll be expected to take out earthquake insurance. On completion, about four to five weeks later, the outstanding balance is paid and transfer of ownership of the property is required to be registered by a legal representative.

Buyers, rather than sellers, pay the estate agent's fees in Japan. This can work out at around 3% to 4% of the property purchase price plus the government levies an additional 63,000 yen. Other costs include:

- Legal fees of 100,000 yen for every 1m yen of the property price
- Stamp duty, levied at around 6% to 8% of the purchase price
- After purchase the value of the property is appraised, based on 50 to 70% of the construction costs, and the owner pays 3% of this figure in acquisition tax.
- Annual city tax varies depending on the local planning department but is around 0.3%, any tax due after purchase for that year is traditionally paid to the seller who settles up the whole bill, including his own payment, at the end of the year

Mortgages

Japanese banks are unwilling to loan to borrowers who are not Japanese citizens or do not live in the country. Without a visa and proof of permanent employment it is difficult for an overseas investor to get any form of financial help with purchase. Those who qualify may be lent up to 98% of the value of the property, depending on which bank they go to. Financial consultancies aimed at foreign nationals also offer mortgages with qualification depending on credit status. Interest rates are currently around 2% and fixed-rate mortgages are available over five years.

Key Risks and Opportunities

European investors who want easy-to-manage, buy-to-let options that are accessible may not see Japan as a worthwhile investment. Large banks and real estate corporations are buying into Japanese cities on a big scale and that does show confidence in the market but for the smaller, less-experienced investor prices may be too high, even at entry level. And although the market is recovering, any large gains will still take a few years to happen.

Ski resort property may be attractive to small-scale investors. Prices are still reasonable and returns in the winter season are dependable. However, the services of a rental management company will probably be essential to maintain the property and market it out to the available local and eastern-based markets.

Those who buy in Japan could see solid yields as property becomes more highly priced and the local market is forced to rent, however, in terms of capital gains, investors must take a long-term view. Japan is highly likely to recover its former status as an economy to be reckoned with during the next decade but there are still hurdles to jump and the prospect of new elections and rising interest rates could negatively impact on the market.

Asia

JAPAN

Asia

JAPAN

Opportunity Rating

Japan offers a secure, stable environment both politically and economically at present. There may be small peaks and troughs on the way to full-scale recovery and currently growth is slow. However, commercial activity in the country and confidence from overseas companies appears to show that it is moving in the right direction. In addition, unemployment is dropping and consumer confidence appears to have had a small boost, which is good news for the economy.

Rating: $ $

Risk Rating

Though economic recovery appears to be happening it is still slow. This may indicate a strong, steady climb back to its former position as a global powerhouse or it may be a sign that the market is likely to stall once more. Interest rate rises from the Bank of Japan are also forecast and may hit property buyers and homeowners, leading to a downturn in the vulnerable property market and a slackening off once more in consumer spending. Those prepared to wait for returns must purchase for the long-term and be prepared to hold for at least five to ten years.

Rating: ⚠ ⚠

Malaysia

KUALA LUMPUR

Introduction

Malaysia is spread across the South China Sea, occupying a peninsula bordering Thailand and a third of the Island of Borneo. The area is one of the most beautiful corners of the world, famous for palm fringed white beaches, gentle seas and rainforest and a key point for shipping and trade in South-East Asia.

Geographically it has beautiful coastal areas, including the popular resorts of Penang and Langkawi, and a tropical interior. Several mountain ranges run through the country, with forests of native sandalwood, teak and ebony. Malaysia also has abundant mineral resources, oil and gas, and a large agricultural base.

Early introduction of rubber trees was highly successful and became a main export for over a century. A former British colony, the country's political structure is based on the UK's. Independent since 1963, Malaysia is now one of the main dragon economies that saw huge growth in the mid-1990s but suffered economic downturn in 1997. Economic reforms instigated in the early part of this decade have proved fruitful and stability appears to have been achieved. Now highly developed economically and commercially, the government has instigated an ongoing programme of encouraging inward investment from overseas corporations and individuals.

Malaysia takes the education of its workforce seriously. Literacy rates are high at 94 per cent of the population, and Malaysian workers tend to be highly motivated and service orientated. Labour laws in the country are relatively well-formulated to offer employment security. Science, technology and finance are favoured subjects in further education and universities and colleges receive substantial government funding. In addition, local companies often have privately funded colleges and training schemes and cross-cultural institutions are in evidence.

These days, the country's main exports are electronic goods and electrical machinery, with much of the domestic production based on manufacturing and export of goods and services. Malaysia's GDP in 2006 was 5.9%, which has seen a drop from 7.4% in 2004, and is expected to be only 5.5% in 2007 (as opposed to government predictions it will be 6%). It has nevertheless continued to grow steadily despite setbacks such as political unrest in areas along the Thai border and health scares such as SARS. The country is moving forward with a policy of creating a strong knowledge base in the fields of technology, research and development. Free Trade Zones and high-spec technology parks have also been set up across the country to aid businesses and research companies.

'The best long term opportunities lie in the buy-to-let market of Kuala Lumpur, particularly with high end or serviced apartments'

The country's infrastructure is well developed. Major new road schemes link all commercial hubs, including the seven international shipping ports (95% of Malaysia's trade is via the sea). In addition a well-run rail freight service has begun operations between Kuala Lumpur and Bangkok and will eventually form the Trans-Asia Rail Link connecting all the countries in the region. The country also has five international airports with the largest, Kuala Lumpur International, being highly regarded and able to take up to 25 million passengers per year.

There is speculation about the longevity of the present government, which may call an early general election, otherwise not scheduled until 2009. But otherwise the situation both politically and economically is safe and stable. In 2007, the central bank was expected to refrain from announcing an interest rate rise.

Many non-nationals are drawn to Malaysia by the quality of life, which offers lower property prices and everyday costs than western countries, a sunny, tropical climate, safe environment, good healthcare and education services. Coastal areas tend to be most popular, with Penang drawing a large number of residents.

To this cultural and geographical vibrancy, Malaysia adds flourishing financial and high-tech industries based in Kuala Lumpur. Popularly known as KL, Malaysia's capital has a modern cityscape dominated by the Petronas Twin Towers, at present the second tallest building in the world (see picture 4 in the colour section). It has become more heavily developed as demand for property has intensified over the past few years. Many non-nationals choose to live in gated communities in the suburbs, while young professionals are moving to high-end contemporary developments within the city or at its fringes. With an annual population growth of 1.8% Kuala Lumpur is growing fast. Ex-pats make up 7% of the capital's population, a testament to the economic strength of the city.

The investment opportunities in KL mean that most property buyers look here first, often beginning in the prestigious 'KLCC,' the popular acronym for Kuala Lumpur City Centre. Investment opportunities also exist in Sepang, Port Dickson, Penang, Langkawi and Sarawak and Sabah. Prices are highest in Kuala Lumpur with rental yields between 7.4% and 8.7%, but rental yields generally average 7.36% in most locations.

Is This a Good Place to Buy?

Overseas investment in the property market concentrates on Kuala Lumpur with a secondary market in the resorts and islands.

The Malaysian government recently scrapped capital gains tax on property and relaxed its laws on foreign ownership. In addition it is promoting investment and relocation via the Malaysia My Second Home scheme (MM2H) (see www. malaysia-my-second-home.com), aimed at allowing individuals with a certain level of income long-term residency. The policy has encouraged a mix of over-seas buyers and it is hoped that the removal of capital gains will increase demand and capital appreciation, which has remained at around 6 % in recent years. At the start of 2007 it was evident that a large number of cash-rich buyers from India had began to invest heavily in Malaysia.

> *'The Malay economy is now important enough, especially in regards to trade with China, to survive all but the most damaging economic shock'*

Demand has also been promoted by a flourishing tourist industry. 2005 saw the highest ever number of arrivals (16.43 million visitors), with demand more than 10% higher than in 2004. 2006 saw this number increase again to 17.55 million and visitor numbers are predicted to be 20 million in 2007. The proposed introduction of budget flights by AirAsiaX from London to KL by August 2008 is also likely to enhance tourist numbers to all the key coastal holiday destinations.

Two trends are discernable: firstly, there is a concentration of affordable luxury properties with the numbers of gated housing projects and non-landed luxury units increasing. Secondly, there is growing demand for serviced apartments,

Asia

MALAYSIA

particularly in central locations. The demand is attributable to the large numbers of professionals who relocate to the city every year. Relocation can be permanent, but more commonly people will be relocated for between three and six months, making serviced apartments the ideal solution for their companies.

Price History

During the 1990s Malaysia was one of the leading **Asian Economic Tigers**, with a booming economy and a real estate market to match. Prices in KL rose rapidly, and new commercial and residential real estate projects sprang up across the city.

In 1997, the Malaysian economy, along with the rest of South East Asia crashed due to the Asian Economic Crisis which ignited as speculators caused regional currencies to fall through the floor. Every aspect of the Malay economy was affected, including the real estate market. The buoyancy of the market in previous years had led to many developers undertaking vast, ambitious projects. As the economy cooled, many developers went bankrupt leaving half completed buildings. Large amounts of completed stock also helped maintain a glut through oversupply.

In the years since 1997, Malaysia has recovered, faring better than many of its neighbours. By the early noughties demand for real estate in KL had begun to catch up with supply and prices have been rising steadily ever since. By 2005 house prices in Kuala Lumpur were increasing at 7.2%. These remarkable increases continued in 2006 with prices up 6.9% (Global Property Guide).

Despite the increases, Malaysian property has a proven track record at higher prices. Today the economy is more stable and more open, meaning that higher prices are likely to be far more sustainable than in the 1990s. All this suggests that property in Malaysia represents a good bet.

Which Type of Property Should You Go For?

The best long term opportunities lie in the buy-to-let market of KL, particularly with high end or serviced apartments. The rise of Malaysia as a tourist destination has also awoken the resort markets in Langkawi and Penang. In these locations, luxury property can seem very cheap and the year round climate means that annual rental yields from short-term holiday lets can be very attractive.

Hotspots

Kuala Lumpur

Fast developing into a highly cosmopolitan, high-tech city, Kuala Lumpur is attracting increasing levels of investment from commercial sectors and is seeing larger numbers of immigrants. New residents are drawn from both overseas and local markets and tend to be young professionals seeking better employment prospects in a growing city. Property is mainly in tower blocks, with many developers offering luxury, serviced apartments, often with guaranteed rentals of between 6% and 8% for those wanting a buy-to-let investment (for example, see picture 9 in the colour section).

In 2006 warnings were issued, as there was a definite slowing of sales, attributed by many to a glut of similar property coming onto the market. In addition average rental yields were predicted to be lower than the 8% previously achieved. Due to a new band of cash-rich investors however, this was not the case in early 2007. Capital appreciation in Kuala Lumpur Central is just over double that of the rest of the country at around 13% and average prices are now in the region of €170–€215 per square foot, with high-end developments such as the iconic Twin Towers and One KLCC, fetching nearer to €430.

Suburban locations are also popular and many new developments are targeting high-income families with new communities offering on-site facilities such as golf courses, pools, shops and services. The Klang Valley and Monte Kiara in particular is attracting high levels of investors and developers, and prices have risen to around €64 per square foot with upmarket homes costing between €64,800 and €108,000. Appreciation is in the region of 15% currently with rental yields averaging a healthy 8–10%.

Sepang Gold Coast

This 22km stretch of coastline on the western coast, around 25 minutes from Kuala Lumpur airport, is already the location for the Formula One Grand Prix circuit and is earmarked for further development. A great coastal project is planned featuring hotels, retail outlets, leisure parks and a whole new residential town. The first development is the vast Golden Palm, which will be built offshore. Prices for properties in the first phase start at €105,000 and, in the long-term, the resort is likely to attract a lot of interest from buy-to-let investors.

Port Dickson

Port Dickson is a popular coastal resort, around an hour's drive from Kuala Lumpur, that is proving attractive to the weekend and second-home market. There has been an increase in development of this area over the past three years with large numbers of condominiums and water chalets appearing. Prices start at around €65,700 for a standard one-bedroom waterfront apartment or chalet. Larger properties sell for between €124,120 and €146,000. Much buy-to-let property is in evidence here with lots of developers offering guaranteed rental returns of around 8%. Though the resort has attractive beaches to the

Asia

MALAYSIA

south, there are also petrochemical plants further north and this may deter some buyers.

Situated on the island of Borneo, Sarawak is the largest state in Malaysia and is a heavily forested region that the government is actively targeting for growth. Tax incentives and protection of foreign investment are two of the steps it has taken to encourage investment in the region. Tourism is a major activity, as is palm oil production. The main centre for commercial activity is Kuching, which has a thriving centre and a wealth of new apartment developments priced from around €80,000. Many of the new residential developments aimed at overseas investors are in the Sabah area, which is less developed and has a beautiful coastline (see an example residence in picture 6 and 7 of the colour section). Property tends to be villas in resort-style developments aimed at second home and buy-to-let market, with prices at around €100,000.

Penang

Penang is a heavily developed tourist island with a growing resident population. Many believe it is now overdeveloped, with a large number of new complexes and condominium buildings. Most of the development is on the west coast with prices for average apartments starting at around €43,200 for 900 square feet. Larger properties of over 2,500 square feet in waterfront locations will go for upwards of €302,550. Penang is subject to different laws with regard to property purchase with prospective residents needing to pay application fees of €215 for individuals within 30 days upon receiving approval to buy from the local authorities.

Langkawi

Actually a cluster of 99 islands on the Straits of Malacca, Langkawi is around an hour's flight from Kuala Lumpur. Most people holiday and buy on the main island of the same name. Measuring around 25 kilometres, the island is known for its long, white sand beaches, traditional stilted fishing villages and upmarket resort complexes. Much of the land here is jungle and designated as reserve land, which means it cannot be sold to non-nationals. The property market here is not as developed as in Penang and private sales are common. Prices range from around €40,000 for a standard-size townhouse or apartment in a new development. The whole of the island of Langkawi is a Duty Free haven.

The Purchase Process

The purchase process in Malaysia will be relatively familiar to UK buyers as much of the legal system is based upon UK law. Non-residents have the right to own property and even apartments are sold on a form of freehold known as strata title.

From January 2007, FIC approval is no longer required for the purchase of residential property above MYR250,000. There is also no restriction on the use of the property or the number of units purchased. However, the approval of the State Authority pursuant to section 433B of the National Land Code, 1965 is still required.

Non-nationals don't need to join the MM2H scheme (see above) in order to purchase, but there are some tax and mortgaging advantages. To qualify for a renewable 10-year residency visa under the MM2H scheme applicants under 50 years old must hold at least €64,840 in a deposit account, but can use this money to buy a property, and keep a minimum balance of €13,000 for subsequent years resident in the country. Applicants aged 50 or above need a deposit account of €32,400 and to keep a minimum balance of €13,000 while living in Malaysia. They must also show proof of medical insurance cover.

Upon completion of a new build project and obtaining the Certificate of Fitness (CFO) for the buildings, the developer is required by law to put in the application for strata title for each of the units. Upon issuance of the strata title, the title will be transferred and registered under the purchaser's name as the registered owner of the property. This document of title is the evidence of ownership and will be the instrument for any subsequent and further dealings.

Purchase costs will vary from 2%–4% of the property price. Specifically, the costs are as follows:

- Legal Fees on signing of a sales and purchase agreement and Deed of Covenants
- 1% on the first MYR150,000 (subject to a minimum fee of MYR300)
- 0.7% on the next MYR850,000
- 0.6% on the next MYR2,000,000
- 0.5% on the next MYR2,000,000
- 0.4% on the next MYR2,500,000
- (in some cases, if buyer is happy to use developer/seller's lawyer to assist with property buying process, minimum legal fee is required)
- Legal Fees for application of State Consent: RM200.
- Stamp duty on Transfer of Title

- - 1% on the first MYR100,000
- - 2% on the next RM400,000
- - 3% on the remainder

In April 2007, the Real Property Gains Tax was abolished. Anyone entering under the MM2H scheme may import one car, which will be exempt from import taxes and any sales tax. Income tax for foreign non-residents is a flat 28% (mortgage interest payments and certain other property maintenance costs can offset the income tax).

Repatriation of funds is not a problem; but buyers do need to disclose the source of the funds (from the sale of the property). Details on repatriation of funds by foreign non-resident individuals are stated on Malaysia Central Bank's website.

Mortgages

Finance is readily available to non-residents in Malaysia at up to 85% loan to value.

Mortgages often involve a standard legal fee, which is levied as follows:

- 1% on the first MYR150,000 (subject to a minimum fee of MYR300)
- 0.7% on the next MYR850,000
- 0.6% on the next MYR2,000,000
- 0.5% on the next MYR2,000,000
- 0.4% on the next MYR2,500,000

Key Risks and Opportunities

The previous risks in the Malay economy have now been overcome and significant advances have been made in making the market more transparent. As always, Malaysia remains open to regional shocks as seen by the impact of bird flu and SARS in other parts of the region. However, the Malay economy is now important enough, especially in regards to trade with China, to survive all but the most damaging economic shock.

Properties in this part of the tropics can degrade quickly so it is important to employ a good property management company or to buy in a complex where these issues are taken care of.

Opportunity Rating

Prices in Malaysia remain significantly below their peak in the late 1990s and there is every reason to expect that with the current level of economic performance they should once again achieve these heights. Malaysia's emerging position in the world of tourism should fuel demand, especially in the island and coastal resorts such as Langkawi, Penang and Sabah.

Rating: $ $ $ $ $

Risk Rating

There are no major political or social risks in Malaysia, although price growth is very dependent upon economic performance, which remains closely tied to trade with China.

Rating: ⚠ ⚠

Asia

MALAYSIA

Mongolia

CURRENCY
Mongolia Tugriks (MNT)

EXCHANGE RATES
100 Tugriks = £434.30
£1 = 2,302.7 MNT
100 Tugriks = $859.66
$1 = 1,163.25 MNT

Introduction

Mention Mongolia and it evokes romantic visions of another era. Far removed from the 21st century, one imagines a sprawling empire where natives traverse the land on horseback, clad in animal skins. Mongolia is, after all, probably best known by its great grandfather, the famous adventurer and warrior Genghis Khan and the thought of buying property there evokes amazement, even disbelief.

Located between two of the global economic superpowers of the future, Russia and China, Mongolia is the second largest landlocked and least densely populated independent country in the world. Home to a striking terrain of mountains, lakes, deserts and grasslands (see picture 12 in the colour section), the country also enjoys a vibrant capital city. It is a commodity rich country abundant in natural resources, minerals and ores including coal, molybdenum, tin tungsten and gold as well as the largest copper deposit in Asia. In recent years therefore, Mongolia has seen many high profile mining companies such as BHP, Ivanhoe and Rio Tinto, relocate operations to its capital in order to take advantage of the untapped resources.

Today then, Mongolia is a country full of excitement, hope and energy whose economy is buzzing and whose tourism industry is going from strength to strength. What's more, the country offers an astonishing opportunity to savvy real estate investors with an eye for the unusual.

Is This a Good Place to Buy?

Over the past 15 years, the Mongolian economy has undergone major structural changes. The old centrally planned economic system has been abolished and measures have been taken towards privatisation, price and trade liberalisation, banking reform, and a general opening up of the economy.

As a result, Mongolia is currently experiencing an economic boom and a rapidly developing tourism industry. With high levels of FDI, GDP growth averaging over 6.6% per annum for the last five years, minimal purchase costs, low taxes and positioned between two future global financial superpowers (Russia and China), both Mongolia's economic future and investment potential look set to explode.

'Mongolia is currently experiencing an economic boom and a rapidly developing tourism industry. Both Mongolia's economic future and investment potential look set to explode'

Inflation in Mongolia is low and stable, predicted at 4.2% for the 2007 (Bank of Mongolia). With such high levels of FDI (the US government are committed to providing $250m for general development), an open and forward thinking government, high standards of education and various schemes and incentives for entrepreneurialism, unemployment is attractively low at just 3.3% in 2005 (CIA world factbook).

Mongolia now enjoys a parliamentary democracy and won the award for the Best New Democracy in 2006. It joined The World Trade Organisation in 1997 and is also a full member of the Multilateral Investment Guarantee Agency of the World Bank Group. In July 2006 Mongolia was accepted as an EBRD (European Bank for Reconstruction and Development) country of operations, helping to foster market economies and democracies. This admission allowed the EBRD to start financing projects in the country by October 2006. Mongolia has also prepared a complete set of measures for the stabilisation of the banking sector, which should result in an increase in public confidence.

Mongolia's tourism sector is also ameliorating rapidly with the tourism dynamic changing from back-packers to more high net worth individuals. The recent emergence of well known hotels such as the Hilton and Shangri-La in Ulaan Baatar are indicative of the capital's prevalence as a developing tourist destination welcoming 500,000 visitors each summer – a figure which, according to the Mongolia National Statistical Office is expected to double between now and 2009 and will increase the already limited demand for accommodation.

Price History

Almost a century ago, just after the revolution in 1921, only 9% of the total population lived in urban areas and there was almost no civil infrastructure,

Asia

MONGOLIA

except the telecommunications department, newspapers and publishers. Aside from dirt cattle tracks there were no roads at all in the country. From the mid-1940s, the capital city, Ulaan Baatar, began to thrive and from the beginning of the 1960s, the cities of Darkhan and Erdenet were founded.

The socialist system which embraced Mongolia from 1921 until 1990 meant that the majority of land and property were owned by the state and no real estate market existed. It was not until the dissolution of this structure that the concept of private property, the consideration of the rights of the owner, and the protection of private property became apparent. In 1996 the "*Law on Housing Privatisation*" was established and from 1997 up to 2004 nearly the entire housing stock was privatised. This was the first step to creating private immovable property. It was succeeded by the implementation of two new land laws in 2002.

'Rapidly appreciating land values and increasing salaries have pushed up rents meaning yields currently sit at around 20%.'

The current situation in Mongolia sees 52% of the population living in traditional nomadic ger settlements and is analogous to what Hong Kong was experiencing in the 1950s and 1960s when a large percentage of residents actually lived on junk boats without any permanent housing. As the economy in Hong Kong then grew, interest rates came down and mortgage products entered the market place, allowing for the migration of local inhabitants from the junks into apartments. Many predict that this pattern will be echoed in Ulaan Baatar (as locals move from gers to apartments) meaning demand for housing which is already high, will be sustained in the foreseeable future.

Recent price trends reflect the unyielding nature of this progression. Prices for Grade A apartments have risen from about $450per sqm in 2003 to around $900 per sqm in 2006. This is fairly normal price appreciation for an economy that is growing at 10% and is trying to supply housing for 500,000 wishing to migrate from their hillside tent houses to city apartments.

Which Type of Property Should You Go For?

As mentioned above, the demand for medium grade apartments to supplement traditional ger accommodation is rocketing. With around 50% of the capital's population still to house in immovable property, it can be assumed that such accommodation is likely to remain in high demand over the coming years and should not only benefit from substantial capital appreciation but regular and sustainable rent.

However, mid-range accommodation does not necessarily present the most promising investment opportunity. With vast numbers of expatriates and executives relocating to the capital to take advantage of the mining opportunities, there will also be substantial demand for properties at the very top end of the market.

With many MNC executives' budgets reaching up to $6,000pcm, averaging $2,700pcm for a 150 sqm apartment, managers are finding it practically impossible to attain the kind of high quality property that their budgets afford. There is therefore a severe supply shortage unable to feed the demand emerging from all international ambassadors, consulates and executives from BHP, Rio Tinto, Ivanhoe etc.

With land prices and construction costs still relatively low, final purchase values can be very attractive, as low as $900/sqm for high-grade city centre apartments. Taking into account this high demand, high-end rentals can command anything from between $13/sqm/cm – $17/sqm/cm, delivering annual yields of 22%.

With the recent influx of mining executives and the migration of locals from traditional ger settlements into medium grade apartments, the capital Ulaan Baatar currently offers the best investment opportunities in Mongolia. Ulaan Baatar was described by British press in 2007 as 'the new hot destination for foreign-property buyers'. Rapidly appreciating land values and increasing salaries have pushed up rents meaning yields currently sit at around 20%. What's more, falling interest rates as the economy explodes mean real estate growth currently stands at 30%+ per annum. Land and construction costs throughout the country are still low making purchase prices incredibly attractive.

The Purchase Process

There are no restrictions on foreigners owning apartments in Mongolia. Upon approval by the government, landlords are issued an ownership certificate (which can be used as collateral in banks) and gain full ownership rights to the apartment. It is important to note that it is virtually impossible to own land in Mongolia. The majority of land in the city has a renewable long term lease. Once an immovable structure, (i.e. a building) is constructed on the land, it becomes an immovable property (ownership of which is freehold) the land can be returned to the government at the end of the lease. For foreigners the lease can be between 15 to 60 years.

Asia

MONGOLIA

'Falling interest rates as the economy explodes mean real estate growth currently stands at 30% or more per annum'

The Mongolian legal system provides appropriate guarantees concerning investment dispute settlement procedures and ensures free access for foreign or domestic investors to international commercial arbitration unless otherwise provided by the contracting parties.

Stamp duty which is the equivalent to transaction tax is 2% and is not required for off-plan purchases. Title acquisition fees are payable upon the issue of the title on the property issued by the immovable property office. From January 2007, personal income has been taxed at a 10% flat rate. The Government has also lowered its value-added tax from 15% to a flat 10% and reduced the corporate income tax from two brackets of 15% and 30% to 10% and 25% respectively. There is currently no capital gains tax in Mongolia and the government does not impose withholding tax. Funds can be repatriated through any major banks in Mongolia and developers will sometimes help with this process.

Mortgages

Residential mortgages are available. However, the concept of a 'mortgage' in Mongolia is envisaged only over a very short period of time – an average of 3–5 years, 10 at the absolute maximum. Also, interest rates are currently very high so for non-resident foreigners it is both difficult and expensive to obtain end-user mortgages.

Nevertheless, banking confidence is rapidly increasing across the country and developer finance is now offered from various sources including local and international banks. With large numbers of international banks now willing to invest in the Mongolian economy, it will only be a matter of time before mortgages are more easily attainable and interest rates lower.

Presently 16 banks are operating in the banking system, six of which have state shares in their equity funds and six more of which are fully owned by the private sector. Mongolia has also prepared a complete set of measures for the stabilisation of the banking sector, set to result in an increase in public confidence.

Key Risks and Opportunities

You should be aware that the pace of construction is inhibited by the country's harsh winters, when temperatures plummet to around -40°c. The emerging building industry is further restricted by insufficient funding and limited production capacity.

Mongolia does however offer investors the chance to invest in a country whose fiscal future looks set to flourish. Experts have likened Mongolia's current market positioning as one reminiscent of Shanghai before its enormous economic growth started.

Opportunity Rating

Bordered by two of the economic superpowers and with an extensive supply of natural resources, Mongolia's economy should have every chance to prosper over the coming years. Demand for property is huge and unlikely to be fully satisfied by supply for some years making for some very promising investment opportunities.

Rating: $ $ $ $

Risk Rating

Price growth is very dependent upon economic performance, which remains closely tied to trade with China.

Rating: ⚠ ⚠

Asia

MONGOLIA

The Philippines

CURRENCY
Philippine Pesos

EXCHANGE RATES
1000 Php = £10.75
£1 = 92.96 Php
45,830 Php = US $1000
US $1 = 45.83 Php

MANILA

Introduction

The Philippines is a collection of 7,107 islands situated just north of Malaysia in the South China Sea. The islands are grouped under three regional heads: Luzon is the largest and most northerly island and the location of the capital, Manila and Quezon City. The second is Mindanao and the third group is the Visayas Islands, of which Cebu is the central island and a prominent tourist destination.

The Philippines has a diverse natural environment, with a warm and humid tropical climate. There are vast areas of jungle and forest, beautiful beaches, fertile farmlands and volcanoes of which several are still classed as active. With so many islands there are also numerous beaches offering white sands and great diving, plus some beautiful inland areas, such as Lake Sebu in Mindanao, a vast lake surrounded by forested hills.

Tourist numbers in recent years have been growing and now account for just over a million visitors per annum. Cebu saw a majority of those numbers with 500,000, an increase of 24% on the previous year. Unfortunately, the Philippines suffer repeated typhoons, which mainly strike during the wet season in June to November, and earthquakes are also a regular occurrence.

The country has a reputation for being warm and friendly and the cost of living is low. The Philippines are seen by many as having the potential to be as successful in business and tourism as other countries of Southeast Asia, such as Thailand and Malaysia. However, there are accusations from business sectors of problems with corruption and bribery that have put some corporations off investing here. In addition, there have been reports of kidnappings in Manila of members of the business community. Several terrorist attacks also happened in Manila and Mindanao province a few years ago and, though these have not reoccurred recently, there are areas of the country where religious tensions exist.

Domestic growth has been well managed in recent years and has increased by 6%, with predictions that the Philippines will continue to grow by around 5.6% next year. Part of this has been achieved by privatisation and revision of the tax system in the country. However, this is still an emerging economy and issues of poverty, reform of education, health and general welfare in many areas need to be addressed.

Is This a Good Place to Buy?

The Philippines is attempting to move towards being a main player in the global economy and is tipped by analysts to achieve that goal soon if it continues on its current course. The government is more stable than it has been in many years, and more inward investment and tourism is coming into the country. The amount of money and investment brought in by Filipino ex-pats is an additional boost for the economy.

Overseas investors will need to consider the restrictions on ownership if they wish to buy here, as non-nationals cannot own property outright, apart from in certain circumstances. Though there are ways of circumventing the law it may not suit all types of investor.

'The Philippines is attempting to become a main player in the global economy and is tipped by analysts to achieve that goal soon if it continues on its current course'

For those who do decide to invest, prices are extremely low by European standards, the Philippines offer good opportunities in both city and beach locations. The distance may make it too far as a holiday-home destination for European investors without a base or links to the region and so the main attraction would undoubtedly be as a buy-to-let investment with a focus on long-term capital growth. Overseas investors will, however, need to consider the costs of owning and renting here. All income, including rental returns, earned by non-residents is charged 25% tax. Value added tax of 12% is also added onto the overall costs if rent exceeds 10,000 Php per month and there will be the outlay of a management firm to organise rentals.

Price History

The Philippines suffered a big price drop during the 1997 economic downturn in Southeast Asia but prices have climbed overall in the past five years by just under 27%. In 2006 there was around 4% average increase in the Philippines market with Manila seeing luxury apartments rising by around 9.5%. Nevertheless, prices in all areas of the Philippines are substantially cheaper than in more developed markets. Square metre prices average around 68,600Php and apartments start at under 2million Php but much of the cheaper property will be in areas that are not necessarily attractive to the better-off tenant or future buyers. Decent property in rentable locations starts at around 4 million Php (for a one-bedroom apartment in a complex with facilities such as a gym, a swimming pool and 24-hour security). High-end, three- or four-bedroom apartments in swanky Fort Bonifacio or the Greenbelt area sell for around 20–30million Php. The government is considering relaxing restrictions on foreign ownership, if this happens prices will probably climb at a faster rate.

Which Type of Property Should You Go For?

Because of the restrictions on foreign ownership it is easier for overseas investors to buy into apartment blocks than houses with land. This makes commercial sense at the moment too as rental yields are high.

Beachfront property is an attractive option if one wants a holiday home in an exotic location with good opportunities for capital appreciation and rental returns. However, non-nationals will have to buy through a company or own on a leasehold basis, which is a popular way of owning in areas such as Boracay but may not suit all investors.

In recent years the most sought after property in the Metro Manila area has been small apartments, which bring in average returns of around 13% to 15%, while larger apartments earn less, typically around 10% to 13%. This may reflect the needs of a younger workforce who don't need the extra space.

Hotspots

Though the Philippines has a large number of coastal locations and rural areas, most investment gains will be in a small proportion of the country. Namely, around Manila and the larger Metro Manila region and on the nearby coastal areas of Batangas.

Metro Manila

The country's capital, **Manila**, is a city of high-rises and high expectations. There is also a historic area, Intramuros, founded by Spanish settlers in the 16th century and a large number of open squares, parks and public gardens. Manila is on Manila Bay and is part of a wider area called Metro Manila situated on the island of Luzon. Metro Manila is divided into 17 cities and municipalities, including former capital **Quezon City** and bustling **Makati**, both desirable residential locations. Property in central areas and more upmarket districts costs from 2.5 million Php for a studio in a standard block or an apart-hotel type complex up to over 100 million Php for a substantial house on a large plot. The majority of property costs around 5million to 10 million Php for large apartments or family homes in a good location. The population of Manila is one of the densest on the planet with 10 million people living and working here.

Batangas

Around two-hours' drive from central Manila is this coastal area offering attractive beaches, decent diving, historic colonial architecture and laid-back but growing tourist resorts. The region in general has been identified as a growth area and Batanga City has seen a programme of development over the past ten years along with the local port, which is one of the most important trading hubs in the country. It will not be possible to buy land unless you have Filipino citizenship but you may be able to lease it for up to 75 years. Land costs from around 6,000 Php per square metre upwards, depending on area and whether it is in a residential resort. Apartments sell from around 2.7 million Php. Homes with sea views go for 10 million Php and inland property sells for around 700,000 Php.

Cebu

An island in the middle of the main Philippine archipelago, Cebu attracts divers, tourists and anyone doing business in thriving **Cebu City**. Property isn't cheap as the region attracts a lot of ex-pats. Mountain locations are just as sought after, if not more so, than beach locations. Properties tend to be in gated communities though there are more apartment buildings being sold off-plan than in previous years. Prices start at around the 1–2 million Php mark for very small houses. Beachfront land can still be found at around the 3 million Php mark. Apartments in good locations sell from around 10 million Php and rent for between 30,000 Php and 60,000 Php per month.

Boracay

Boracay Island in the Western Visayan group is one of the most popular coastal destinations in the Philippines. Development into a resort with a large number of bars and restaurants has reportedly begun to damage its famous 14 kilometre-long powder-white sand beach and clean seas but the area still attracts large numbers of visitors. Land costs from around 3,000Php to 7,000Php for plots on or near the beach, depending on size and location. Prices for nice, coastal property average around 4mPhp–9mPhp, with some properties from as low as 2mPhp and large villas with pools from 55mPhp.

The Purchase Process

Non-citizens cannot hold property or land in their own name, only in the name of a Filipino spouse or via a company. If using the company method, at least 60% of the capital must be owned by Philippine nationals and by at least five shareholders. You will own the remaining 40%. In this case the property must be secured by a bank account, the funds of which can be under the sole jurisdiction of one named owner of the company.

This is only necessary when buying land or individual residential properties. When buying an apartment in a resort complex, non-nationals are allowed to own freely, providing not more than 40% of the development is owned by non-Philippine nationals. Alternative methods of ownership include land leasing agreements of up to 75 years in renewable 25-year stages. In such cases the property built on the land is owned outright by the leaseholder.

Non-residents of Filipino descent may be able to buy land if they can prove citizenship but are restricted on residential property to 1,000 square meters within an urban development or one hectare in rural areas.

Providing the title is legal and clean, the purchase of property should be relatively straightforward. Once the buyer and seller have agreed a price, an Absolute Deed of Sale is drawn up via a lawyer and signed in the presence of a public notary along with a contract. The contract should include a surveyor's explanation of the property's size, style and condition and needs to be signed on every page by the buyer and seller. A land tax declaration is then issued by the tax authorities and any real estate and transfer taxes need to be paid by the buyer before the sale can continue. The property title is then transferred and registered under the new owner's name.

Prior to the signing of the contract the buyer should ask his legal representative to check the title lodged with the local Registry of Deeds. Properties may have issues relating to ownership, boundaries, debts or conditions and these should be thoroughly examined. In some rural areas property is not titled and should be avoided.

In addition, large tracts of land in mountain regions may not be sold to private individuals or developed. Again, legal checks on the ownership and rights of the land should uncover any issues.

Buyers should expect to pay a value added tax of 12% of the purchase price, plus 1.5% in stamp duty and a 0.5% transfer fee. Annual property tax is levied at 1–2% of the building's perceived value, depending on the location.

Mortgages

The mortgage market has gained ground in the Philippines in recent years and banks will lend up to 70% of the purchase price with interest rates between 9% and 10%. However, with prices still so low compared to US, Asian and European markets, many buyers opt to pay cash.

Key Risks and Opportunities

There is no doubt that the Philippines has the potential to increase both its commercial and tourism potential over the next five to ten years. Businesses are seeking low-cost environments from which to run operations and tourists are looking for more exotic and off-the-beaten track locations. The potential to capture a large share of both markets in Southeast Asia is huge, particularly when you also factor in the size of European and US markets (showing increasing interest in the region), and the increasing number of Chinese and Asian investors.

What may hold the Philippines back is a lack of belief in the government, which, despite being re-elected recently, remains under suspicion and offers little confidence in its promises and reforms. Corruption in business, tangled bureaucracy and the threat of terrorism and crime, though not daily worries, are issues that investors should be aware of.

One of the fundamental changes that would open the property market up in the country is the relaxation of ownership laws and more clarity in the purchase process and ownership regulations.

Opportunity Rating

The country does not yet offer a market or economy as strong as some other Southeast Asian countries but there is potential to improve both. Economic growth is slow but steady and evidence shows the country is moving in the right direction, especially with an annual nominal house price change of 9.63% between 2005 and 2006.

Rating: $ $ $

Risk Rating

If the Philippines does not work harder to improve aspects of government, social and welfare reform it may be left behind by its more dynamic neighbours. Overseas investors may need better incentives to move into a country that has a poor reputation for efficiency, safety and fair trading, however low those actual risks might be. Poverty is an issue, as is welfare and education.

Rating: ⚠ ⚠

Asia

THE PHILIPPINES

Cape Verde

CURRENCY
Cape Verde Escudo

EXCHANGE RATES
10,000 Escudo = £61.00
£1 = 164 Escudo
10,000 Escudo = US $121.00
US $1 = 82.5 Escudo

PRAIA

Introduction

Lying just off the coast of Africa, 16 degrees North and 24 degrees West, a thread of tropical islands pepper the deep blue waters of the North Atlantic Ocean. The Cape Verde Islands lie in a delicate cluster and are graced with some of the most unspoilt beaches and beautiful scenery in the world today. Already dubbed as the African Caribbean and expected to rival, if not supersede the success of the Canary Islands, these treasured islands are beginning to enjoy a surge in popularity and prosperity.

In 1975, the islands separated from Portugal, and have since been an independent republic. Their interiors are wild and volcanic offering a captivating backdrop to the array of beautiful beaches and all enjoy a consistently temperate climate never varying much from an average 25°C.

The full extent of their charm was illuminated in 2006 when property expert Amanda Lamb named the collection of 10 islands and 8 islets the number one destination for overseas buyers. A host of other acclaims then followed, including *A Place in the Sun* ranking it 12th in the top 20 best places to buy abroad and Expedia, one of the largest internet-based holiday companies, predicting that it will be the number one destination for jet-setting Brits in 2007. As a result, after Europe, Cape Verde is now the most popular location for British looking for a holiday home.

Statistical data goes yet further in confirming the Islands' promise and growing popularity. Real economic growth in the country has averaged 6% over the past few years and GDP growth was estimated to be 5.8% for 2006, expected to rise to 7% in 2008. Through the third quarter of 2006, tourism exports almost doubled and FDI increased by roughly 60% compared to the same period of 2005. Significantly, the largest quota of FDI has been injected into the tourism industry which represented a 54% share.

That more development is needed on the islands is certain: the lack of schools and roads mean that this is not yet the place to look for a second home. These islands are not renowned for their practicality, however their antiquity is, to a certain extent, part of their charm. Cape Verde has retained a sense of peace and tranquillity that more developed islands and Eastern Europe have now lost.

Encouragingly, the government sees tourism and the second home market as the best way in which to guarantee prosperity for Cape Verde meaning infra-structure and amenities are likely to see continual improvement over the coming years.

Is This a Good Place to Buy?

Cape Verde's accessibility has improved dramatically in the last few years with direct flights from the UK now available through Astraeus from both London and Manchester to Sal's Amilcar Cabral International Airport. Thompson also flies direct to Sal. As of July 2007, Astraeus launched weekly flights from the UK to Boa Vista costing around £377 return including taxes and extra charges. It is worth noting that airlines usually sell cheap flight seats to early bookers with direct flights on Thursdays being the cheapest from as little as £369 from Gat-wick and £394 from Manchester. Connections to the US have been in existence for some time with weekly flights from Boston's Logan Airport to Sal. There are also flights from Belfast, Dublin, Edinburgh, Glasgow and the Channel Islands as well as direct flights from Italy, Portugal, Germany, Denmark, Holland, Senegal and Brazil. Currently there are only international airports on two of the islands, Sal and Santiago however local airports exist on five other islands. Two of these local airports are currently under conversion to accept long-haul aircraft on Boa Vista and Sao Vicente with completion anticipated in 2007 and 2008 respectively.

Inconvenient and time-consuming travel connections are therefore no longer a deterrent and with increasingly positive media coverage, Cape Verde is expected to attract growing numbers of tourists over the next few years. Prop-erty experts fully expect that the now emerging real estate industry will grow simultaneously with the tourism market and believe it has the potential to pro-vide profitable returns. Buying into an off-plan development that is due to complete in the next two years should put investors in a good position to reap the benefits of the burgeoning tourist industry. In a couple of years they will be able to sell on their property to tourists looking for finished second homes.

Africa & Middle East

CAPE VERDE

'With the climate, beauty and low crime rates of the Caribbean yet resting safely outside the hurricane belt and only 5.5 hours' flight from Europe, these charming islands could mature into a lucrative property market'

On average, tourist arrivals to Cape Verde are said to be growing at a rate of 22% per annum. It is predicted that the islands will be receiving over 1 million tourists annually by 2015. According to data from the National Statistics Institute, over 125,000 hotel stays were recorded in the first 6 months of 2006 – an increase of 33% over the same period in 2005. 92.6% of all hotel check ins were from international visitors, a figure that confirms the fact that tourism on these islands is beginning to take off. Tourism now contributes 10% of Cape Verde's GDP. Aiming to do all they can to facilitate the growth of the tourist and investment markets, Cape Verde authorities approved of investment projects totalling US$300 million in 2006 alone.

Investors should also be encouraged by the stability of the country's political and economic positioning. The American CIA sees Cape Verde as a country that 'continues to exhibit one of Africa's most stable democratic governments' while the British foreign and commonwealth office believes Cape Verde to have 'an efficient and generally uncorrupt bureaucracy'. What is more, investors need not worry about severe exchange rate risks as the Cape Verde Escudo has been pegged to the € at a rate of CVE 110.3 per €1 since January 1999.

In a bid to foster all the foreign investment that it can, the Cape Verde government has constructed several incentives for foreign investors. For the initial 5 years, buyers enjoy a tax holiday as well as an exemption on import duties for building materials. Private investors who invest more than £23,673 or employ in excess of 13 nationals are entitled to residency. The government also gives foreign investors important guarantees such as privately managed foreign currency accounts that can be credited only in foreign currency from abroad or from other foreign accounts in Cape Verde. It also allows unrestricted repatriation of dividends, profits and capital from foreign investment operations.

In short then, Cape Verde appears to offer a very promising investment market. Paralleling the climes, beauty and low crime rates of the Caribbean yet resting safely outside the hurricane belt and only 5.5 hours flight from Europe, these charming islands could mature into a lucrative property market. Importantly, authorities are keen to avert Spain's over-development so environment-sensitive developments are favoured and very much encouraged. Due to the islands' relative underdevelopment, the build quality of off-plan developments is hard to measure and is something that potential investors should look into thoroughly.

Price History

Cape Verde is still a very new market, meaning prices are not easily understood or easily generalised. They often vary significantly from island to island. Apartments on Maio can be found from £27,000 whilst similar studio accommodation on Sal starts at £45,000. Two and three-bed villas on Sao Vicente are available from £65,000 and £77,000 respectively. What is at present then, a somewhat turbulent market is likely to stabilise and become more logical in the future. In the meantime it is worth comparing properties and prices carefully so as to avoid fraudulent developers who have been known to take advantage of foreign buyers' lack of local knowledge. Ideally you should work with a reputable agent that has the capability to identify the best opportunities. Another aspect attracting tourists and investors alike is the cost of living which, in comparison to most of Europe, is relatively cheap. Pizzas are available from £3.80, small beers from 70p to £1 and a half litre jug of wine is about £3.

Which Type of Property Should You Go For?

The lack of infrastructure means that it can be difficult to refurbish and furnish an older property to your satisfaction. A furnished off-plan apartment or villa will therefore be the easiest and most popular option for investors. It is also likely to be easier to access a new build as development on the islands is beginning to take off with lots of new accommodation planned.

Hotspots

Development has so far been concentrated on the islands of **Sal** and **Santiago** as these two islands offer the most developed infrastructure, including international airports. Sal, offering the best night life, water sports and most advanced development registers 66.8% of all hotel check-ins in 2006 and is generally the easiest of the islands to access.

Macau businessman, David Chow, is planning to invest over US$130m by 2009 in building a tourist complex on the islet of Santa Maria, off the coast of the Cape Verdean capital. It is rumoured to include a hotel, marina, restaurants and swimming pools. Chow has also said that he plans to invest over £194,047 (US $390m) in Cape Verde, particularly in the capital over the next decade. This huge inward investment is likely to stimulate property price rises in the area.

Africa & Middle East

CAPE VERDE

Santiago is an island that investors should take a close look at. The largest of the Cape Verde Islands, it combines bustling nightlife in the capital Praia with calm landscape offering tranquil escapism. The island also has more varied terrain than most of Cape Verde and even boasts mountain ranges.

San Vicente also offers interesting investment opportunities. It has long been the island of culture and history but is now formulating plans which should transform it into an elite holiday destination and thriving business centre. The west side will become the island's business hub while the completion of the grand marina will mean the island has the capacity to welcome a host of flotilla and light craft. Development of a new golf resort should also augment the island's tourist appeal. An extension to the airport's main runway near San Pedro will allow smaller international charter flights to access San Vicente and should help encourage and cater for the growing visitor arrivals. The island has also signed an agreement with Spain's Canary Islands and the Portuguese archipelago of Madeira to promote and operate cruises in the mid-Atlantic which should again deliver an increased number of tourists to San Vicente's shores. Units in a new development on the west coast will be available from £80,000.

The Purchase Process

The legal system in Cape Verde is similar to that in Portugal and is therefore relatively straightforward. The first step is to obtain a Personal Fiscal Number from the tax office and your solicitor or agent will be able to advise you on how best to go about doing this. A personal fiscal number is also usually assigned if you open a local bank account, which may prove to be a shrewd decision as it makes payments and general property management easier as all taxes have to be paid in the local currency. The contracts will be agreed in two stages: first the Promissory Contract (*Contrato de Promessa de Compra e Venda*) and then the final contract (*Escritura*).

Once your offer has been accepted or a purchase price has been agreed, the Promissory Contract is signed and a deposit of 10–30% is handed over, as well as the 3% transfer tax.

The deposit is non-refundable but secures the property. Before signing the contract, your solicitor should conduct checks at the land registry to ensure that the vendor has the right to sell and that it is free of unpaid taxes. A number of documents will also be needed to complete the transaction. From the land registry you have to obtain a registration certificate which describes the legal history of the property, and from the local tax office a document enumerating the yearly taxes which must be paid on the property. If the development is new, a temporary certificate will be issued. Finally your solicitor will help you to obtain a licence of use confirming that the property is for residential use (for example).

After the promissory contract the next step is to sign the final contract, known as the Escritura. At this time the balance of the purchase price has to be paid, along with final taxes and notary fees. Added together, the fees may amount to 13% of the property price, including solicitor's fees, estate agent's fees, sales tax, conveyance tax, registration fees etc.

The Escritura has to be signed in the presence of the local notary and is then registered with the Land Registry and the Tax Office. After the change of ownership is registered with the Land Office the property is yours to keep.

As far as taxes are concerned, CGT is levied at a flat rate of 3% if the sale value exceeds a 30% increase from the original purchase price; inheritance tax is 3%.

Mortgages

Cape Verde banks are now offering euro rate mortgages to foreign buyers investing in off-plan properties. While previously mortgages were only offered on completion, those buying off-plan can now borrow up to 70% of the total property value. The current interest rate is 7%. However, some buyers choose to pay instalments as their off-plan property is completed and then take out a mortgage on the finished house to release the capital already invested.

Key Risks and Opportunities

The prices in Cape Verde may be lower than in the Balearics, but equally they may not always represent a genuine bargain. Some developers may be placing their pricing at the highest level they think will be found acceptable by the market rather than genuine cost. Some villas are now on the market for £470,000 ($938,300) – a price that has more to do with optimism than the realities of the market.

Opportunity Rating

Cape Verde offers good long term opportunities as the islands develop into a mainstream tourist destination. The country's emergence as a leading holiday spot may take some years but there is every reason to expect that it will one day achieve a status similar to that of the Canary Islands.

Rating: $ $ $

Risk Rating

Development of the property market is dependent upon government schemes to attract tourism. Should any of these infrastructure projects fail or the government alter its focus, then the tourists may not arrive, leaving investors with empty properties. There are no obvious political or macroeconomic risks. Buyers should however be mindful of build quality and watch out for inflated prices.

Rating: ⚠ ⚠ ⚠

Africa & Middle East

CAPE VERDE

Dubai

CURRENCY
UAE Dirham

EXCHANGE RATES
100 Dirham= £13.66
£1 = 7.32 Dirham
100 Dirham = US $27.22
US $1 = 3.67 Dirham

Introduction

Dubai is one of the seven United Arab Emirates, which sit on the Arabian Penin-sula facing the Arabian Gulf. Fuelled by business, soaring tourism and hedonism, Dubai is the best known of the emirates and the newest playground for the rich and famous. These days the country doesn't require much introduction as a result of the numerous television programmes and press articles on what has become the biggest construction phenomenon of modern times. Dubai has also become a major tourist destination with the number of visitors expected to rise to 15 million by 2010.

Where once lay a sleepy pearl fishing village, a city vision is rising from the desert sands. Dubai is a project on a grand scale. Rather than a city as we know it, it is a piece of master planned architecture where record breaking projects such as the Palm increasingly seem to be no more than ornamental details on Sheikh Mohammed bin Rashid Al Maktoum's creation. His vision was for a mod-ern metropolis unrivalled in its luxury, that is both the Florida and Singapore of the Middle East; only bigger and better.

Dubai itself is a project that is still far from completion. The scale of ongoing and planned development is almost inconceivable. Most countries in the world struggle with one mega-project, but in Dubai there are currently more than 26 such projects in various stages of completion. From Dubai Land which offers 2 billion square feet of leisure development to the Dubai International Finance City, Hydropolis, the world's first underwater hotel, and the Burj Dubai – set to be the world's tallest building when it completes at the end of 2008. It is virtually impossible to move in Dubai without bumping into a record-breaking structure from the world's largest shopping mall to the biggest man-made canal. Dubai can even boast the world's longest indoor ski slope. With 20% of the world's construction cranes based in Dubai, numerous high profile sporting tournaments and the relocation of the QE2 as a permanently moored floating hotel, there seems no let-up in the determination of Sheik Mohammed.

The vision for Dubai is to transform it from a small regional trading hub and oil dependent economy into the leading business and leisure destination of the region. To build their vision, the government of Dubai created three major development companies, Emaar, Nakheel and Dubai Holding. These organisations were charged with the task of creating the master planned developments and ensuring that the vision of Dubai becomes reality.

'Failure to moderate demand by reducing development expansion or accommodate it through improved infrastructure could lead to Dubai's downfall'

In 2002, to support this process, Sheik Mohammed declared that freehold property rights would be given to non-UAE nationals within these master planned developments. This was the start of the Dubai property rush. In March 2007 this policy was ratified within the Dubai Property Law when Sheik Mohammed confirmed that foreigners may own property within designated zones, accounting for around 30% of the land in Dubai.

Within the freehold zones, the master planners have conceived extraordinary residential and commercial projects which are often themed. Well known master developments include The Palms (Jumeirah, Jebil Ali and Deira), The World, Jumeirah Beach Residences, Dubai Marina, Jumeirah Lake Towers, Dubai Land, Discovery Gardens, International City, Dubai International Finance City, Business Bay, Sports City... the list goes on.

In many cases the actual development of individual buildings is undertaken by private development companies that buy sub plots from the master developers. This has led to a wide array of different building types and styles being constructed (see picture 5 in the colour section). It also means that the experience of developers varies greatly, but the master planning system ensures that a good level of quality management is imposed by the likes of Nakheel.

So far Sheik Mohammed's plans seem inspired. A combination of clever marketing, which has raised the profile of the country, and the creativity and ingenuity of the developments, has attracted investors, expatriates and second home buyers from around the world. Additionally, numerous businesses are moving into the country, attracted by the free trade zones, zero taxation and modern infrastructure. Expats make up 85% of Dubai's population and around 250,000 people are moving to Dubai each year. According to the British Embassy in Dubai, by April 2007 there were 100,000 British nationals living in Dubai.

Is This a Good Place to Buy?

Whether the growth in Dubai property prices is sustainable comes down to one question: can Sheik Mohammed complete the vision? If Dubai fails to become the leisure and business hub that is expected, current price levels could be unsustainable. Sheik Mohammed is fully aware of the risk of oversupply and has recently stopped 200 projects he saw as excessive. He has also placed caps on rental rises to try and stem the effect that high rentals have had up on the number of people moving to Dubai. Nevertheless, there are still plans to build 700,000 new homes over the next five years and some worry that there are not enough commercial buildings to balance this. According to a report by EFG Hermes property prices will fall by 25-30% by 2010 (www. efg-hermes.com).

Price History

Other than residents of the UAE and the Gulf states, the most active buyers in the market are British and Irish, who have been drawn to the region by the impressive rises in real estate values. Villas on The Palm Jumeirah (the man-made palm-shaped island where numerous members of the England football team have bought houses) were initially sold at £90 per square metre but now sell for as much as £4,207 per square metre. Villas on the development will have changed hands ten times before the development is completed in May 2008 and now are worth around £2.8 million each.

Which Type of Property Should You Go For?

There is a tremendous amount of property to choose from in Dubai. 90% of properties are still off-plan. Combined with rising prices, this creates ideal conditions for an investment market. However, the same conditions could potentially create a bubble. So far, this doesn't seem to be happening as so much of the supply is still under construction that the relationship between supply and demand is not quite the same as anywhere else. The sheer amount of off-plan property available means that prices are rising fastest for completed properties and for villas rather than for apartments.

Africa & Middle East

DUBAI

> **INSIDER TIP**
>
> **Rental yields are high in Dubai (6–15% dependent on location) as demand continues to outstrip supply. Rents are largely paid in advance, sometimes up to one year in advance, which is surely a motivating factor for those considering a buy-to-let property in Dubai. On the downside, service charges on new development can be anything up to £4,000 per annum and may be requested by the developer up front. Also, the whole rental market may be due for a shake up when mass supply hits the market in 2008 on release of numerous finished projects.**

Hotspots

Recommending hotspots usually means picking out the towns or regions where growth is expected to impress. For reasons of geography, this doesn't apply to Dubai in quite the same way. The size of the emirate means that in the eyes of international buyers, Dubai and Dubai City are interchangeable concepts. Already, the built up areas extend almost from the border with Abu Dhabi to the border of Sharjah.

Unlike other countries, hotspots in Dubai are based on individual developments rather than cities or areas. Luckily the emirate has a very internet-conscious society. Google the name of any project and you'll find ten honest opinions within a minute.

The Purchase Process

The buying process in Dubai is very straightforward. In most cases buyers need to pay a holding deposit of around £1,500 ($2,500) which holds the property open for them for a certain period; often only 48 hours. Within that period buyers then need to transfer the remainder of the deposit which is typically 30% of the purchase price, but can vary 5–30%. Once the payment is processed by the developer they issue a purchase contract. Contracts in Dubai are always very similar as each one has to be approved by the master developer. This ensures a certain amount of protection for buyers, as the master planners are at least partially government owned.

If you keep the property until completion you may need to pay a property registration fee to the Lands Department of 1.5% of the purchase price. If you re-sell the property prior to completion, the developer will charge an administration fee, which is usually around 2% but can be more. As there are no searches to be conducted or issues with title, it is not technically essential to have a solicitor, however it is always recommended. There are a number of UK based firms offering legal advice on Dubai. One of the best is The International Law Partnership LLP.

On completion of the property, buyers receive a residency visa which covers the buyer, their husband or wife and any children under 18. There are no restrictions on renting your property and management fees are usually between 5% and 15% of rental income. There is no tax department in Dubai so neither rental earnings nor capital gains are subject to any taxation, although there may be implications for your UK tax bill depending on your status.

Mortgages

Mortgages are available in Dubai but can be difficult to arrange and on prohibitive terms. Some developments do offer finance schemes backed by banks such as Tamweel or HSBC, but these have to be prearranged by the developer. Many such schemes are also only available to locals or have greater restrictions for non-UAE nationals. At the moment, if the developer hasn't pre-arranged finance it is almost impossible to arrange finance privately until the building is completed. In addition, foreign buyers will only usually be advanced 70% of the value of the property and repayments should normally be completed before your 60th birthday.

The paperwork on Dubai mortgages can be prohibitive and you will normally be expected to provide evidence of income over the last five years and proof of employment. Lenders will not take into account expected rental income as a contribution towards the mortgage. Arranging mortgages on off-plan property is extremely difficult, with developers preferring staged payments rather than a mortgage.

All of this adds up to an undeveloped mortgage market. Buyers with spare cash or with equity to release may find the Dubai market an easier investment than others.

Key Risks and Opportunities

Limited space on the coast means that property close to the beach is likely to rise and rise in value. The appeal of the coast means that it may also be worth looking to other emirates such as Abu Dhabi. Neighbouring Sharjah is cheaper than Dubai, however the emirate has a strict attitude towards alcohol, which puts off many buyers. Close to Sharjah, **Ras al-Khaimah** is only forty minutes' drive from Dubai on the new Emirates Highway and is developing a reputation for a gentler, more luxurious resort lifestyle (see picture 15 in the colour section).

Location is everything but extensive research is never more vital than when buying in Dubai. Planning permission is given easily so there are many cases of apartments being sold with promises of views of Marinas and the sea – then prior to completion all views are obliterated by newer towers being built around the original site.

Africa & Middle East

DUBAI

The property market may be developing at a phenomenal rate, but it is also worth keeping an eye on infrastructure development. Already Dubai's main highway, Sheikh Zayed Road, is a congested bottleneck as it is the only major route in and out of the city. This is likely to be made worse by the hundreds of thousands leaving Dubai's Palms [tourists, residents, maintenance workers, hotel staff etc]. The road structure could easily reach gridlock. Failure to moderate demand by reducing development expansion or accommodate it through improved infrastructure could lead to Dubai's downfall.

Opportunity Rating

The question of whether the Dubai market is a bubble is often asked. If Dubai's leadership manages to create the financial and leisure hub that it hopes, prices and rental demand will continue to rise. Some consider that by 2018 the Dubai property market will be at its peak – Dubailand, set to be the World's biggest amusement park, will see completion of its first phase in 2008 and final completion in 2018, creating thousands of jobs.

While Dubai remains an alcohol accepting state, tourism is set to continue to grow – all good news for the holiday buy-to-let market.

Rating: $ $ $

Risk Rating

The big risk for Dubai is oversupply, with property analysts predicting falling rentals from the end of 2007 as a massive supply of finished property arrives on the market. However the reality of the situation is hard to judge and is dependent upon Dubai's leadership and its success in building Dubai into an international centre. Dubai has every chance of succeeding but there is a chance that it will fail, only time will tell.

Other risks are limited as the Dubai government realises the importance non-residents have played in developing the property market and the economy as a whole.

Rating: ⚠ ⚠ ⚠ ⚠

Africa & Middle East

DUBAI

Morocco

CURRENCY
Dirham

EXCHANGE RATES
1,000 Dirham = £60.5
£1 = 16.5 Dirham
1,000 Dirham = US $119.3
US $1 = 8.4 Dirham

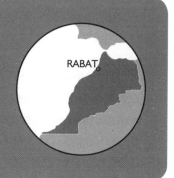

RABAT

Introduction

Morocco, teetering on the brink of North West Africa, is a country brimming with the enticing allure of a foreign land. Oozing colour, charm and a deep rooted culture, the country boasts an enthralling history and a varied and beautiful landscape. Sun-drenched terracotta buildings, a sultry fragrant air and deep blue skies are home to a rich and fascinating race. The buzzing souks and an aromatic cuisine, considered one of the best in the world, together with year round high temperatures tempt visitors to return time and again.

With snow capped mountain peaks, miles of white beaches, undulating hills and old towns bustling with life, Morocco has an enduring appeal which has attracted people from all walks of life. Winston Churchill, Jean Paul Gaultier and the Rolling Stones as well as Kate Moss and P Diddy, have all succumbed to Morocco's charm and fallen for the country's timeless appeal.

Recent figures confirm the country's growing popularity. Tourism in the first quarter of 2007 rose by 7% compared to the same period in 2006, while the number of British holidaymakers staying in classified hotels in the first half of 2006 grew by over 40%. Experts predict that travel and tourism will continue to grow by 4% per annum in real terms between 2008 and 2017.

As Europe's 'Gateway to Africa', Morocco enjoys long-established trade links with the UK, and commerce between the two countries has increased three-fold in the last decade alone, with the UK being one of Morocco's top six investors. FDI in Morocco rose from £811million in 2005 to £1bn in the first nine months of 2006 and is indicative of the increasing global interest in the country's tourism and investment markets.

Indeed, the tourist industry currently contributes a significant amount to Morocco's GDP and is considered to be a key sector in the national economy. The UNWTO World Tourism Barometer says that North Africa was one of the world's fastest growing tourist destinations in 2006. It is expected that the travel and tourism economy will contribute 10% of Morocco's GDP in 2007 and will represent 1,658,000 jobs – one in every 6.5 jobs.

'Following the introduction of an open skies agreement last year, Morocco has become increasingly accessible and should plans for a proposed tunnel under the Gibraltar Strait go ahead, Morocco could be within an hour and a half's train ride from European shores'

These healthy figures look set to increase year on year under the government's Vision 2010 plan, through which infrastructure and resources are being improved. In a development programme entitled Plan Azur, 80,000 hotel rooms are being constructed (creating 600,000 jobs), and visitor figures are set to reach 10 million before Morocco's acceptance into the Euro-Med free trade zone in 2010. £2.2bn is being injected into infrastructure and in conjunction, the EU plans to invest €650m over the next 3 years to help support economic and social reforms. These plans aim to increase tourism contribution to GDP by 8.5% annually so as to reach 20% by 2010. Six new coastal resorts are also under construction, with facilities including 5-star hotels, golf courses, apartments, villas and spas. Importantly, the largest property development company in the world, Emaar Properties has committed billions of dollars to the further expansion of the Moroccan property market suggesting a boom in international investment is imminent.

The last five years have seen a considerable rise in the number of foreigners buying houses in Morocco which is partly due to the fact that King Mohammed VI is actively encouraging foreign investment and, in 2001, changed the law to allow foreign investors to take proceeds of property sales out of the country. 100% repatriation of funds is therefore achievable and a very appealing factor for non-resident foreign investors. The government has also created the Investment Promotion Unit in order to attract further foreign investment and does not legally differentiate between foreign and domestic investors. Following the introduction of an open skies agreement last year, Morocco has become increasingly accessible and should plans for a proposed twin track tunnel under the Gibralter Strait go ahead, Morocco could be within an hour and a half's train ride from European shores.

Africa & Middle East

MOROCCO

Is This a Good Place to Buy?

Currently nine miles and an hour's ferry ride from southern Europe, Morocco has been dubbed 'the new Spain' and is seen to share the attractions of the Costa del Sol without its high cost of living, overdevelopment or crime rate. The Moroccan cities of Marrakech, Casablanca, Fez and Tangiers evoke images of the hippy trail, and the population, a mixture of Africans, Berbers and Arabs, are unrivalled in their hospitality. House prices are much lower than they are in Europe and represent extremely good value for money, comparable to the market in Spain twenty years ago. Property in Morocco is currently almost five times cheaper than in Spain. On top of this, the country enjoys 300 days of sunshine per year, allowing for a year-round tourist market with excellent rental opportunities.

In economic terms, Morocco provides an appealing investment climate. The Moroccan currency is relatively stable, with a foreign exchange rate anchor, a well-managed monetary policy, and inflation rates that have been held to the levels of industrialised countries for the last decade. According to World Bank and IMF reports, the dirham has appreciated by 18% in real terms since 1990 whilst GDP real growth in 2006 was estimated at 9.3% and unemployment stood at a rate of 7.7%.

Along with the year-round rental potential mentioned above other attractions include:

- No restrictions for foreign purchasers
- Familiar conveyancing laws based on the French system
- The possibility of buying architecturally unique property
- Availability of finance and capital growth currently between 15%–30% per annum.

Price History

Morocco offers properties for all budgets starting at anything from £10,000 to £1 million. Prices for luxury properties have been rising for the past thirty years, reflecting increasing European interest in the property market coupled with consistent demand and low vacancies in holiday lets.

Although prices have been rising at around 15% per annum they barely compare to those of nearby Spain where prices for a three-bedroom villa in the exclusive Marbella, Golden Mile vicinity can often exceed the £1m mark. It is currently still possible to buy a large villa for around £123,500 however outside the popular Tangiers area.

Africa & Middle East

MOROCCO

Which Type of Property Should You Go For?

The current trend for British buyers is either to purchase off-plan apartments and villas in the coastal developments, or to purchase traditional Moroccan houses for renovation. For renovation projects, the most popular properties are the traditional *riads* or *dars*, which can be found inside the medina (old town enclosed in ramparts accessed through imposing gates, with maze-like streets). A riad is a house built around a central garden with a fountain, while dars are similar but don't have the garden. Most of the traditional houses in the medina need restoring, and are drawing British buyers seeking a creative outlet. Restoration gives buyers the licence to inject their personality into a property and personally monitor progress. Remember that houses a short walk into the medina will usually be cheaper than those by the gates (cars are not allowed in the medinas). Potential investors are advised that renovation can cost anything from between 50% to 100% of the original cost of the property.

INSIDER TIP
If you intend to buy a number of properties it may be worth setting up a Moroccan Private Limited Company (set up time is about three weeks). The minimum equity capital is 100,000 dirhams (around £6,000). This is a good mechanism for unifying your Moroccan property investment activities and will make managing your various profit streams for repatriation considerably easier.

The supply of homes and villas for reconstruction is, however, shrinking, which makes new builds a good-value buy. Also, with new builds, there will be no issues with title, a problem the more traditional properties often incur. The construction plans for Vision 2010 are also opening up an interesting market with a lot of potential for off-plan property investment, so it may be worth looking away from the traditional homes and taking advantage of the newer markets.

Land in Morocco is less easy to purchase than property. In fact foreigners cannot buy land outside the urban perimeter. However in a bid to attract investors, the Moroccan State can authorise the change of the legal nature of the land from agricultural to residential. To avoid the sometimes arduous process of obtaining permission, you can buy direct from a developer who has already bought the land and therefore completed the process. Many developers in the main coastal resorts are willing to sell portions of land for sub-developments, so this is an option for people with the money and expertise.

Hotspots

The most popular places for property sales in Morocco are Marrakech, Fez and Essaouira, although the new resort developments along the coast offer exceptional opportunities.

Marrakech and the Surrounding Area

Marrakech is known as the 'entertainment capital' of the country, and has long been the most popular tourist destination due to its year-round desert heat, its rose-red medina and its boutiques (see picture 11 in the colour section). It also has the most developed property market. A fabulous mix of traditional and modern, the city is within easy reach of ski slopes and also boasts three fantastic golf courses, with seven more planned in the coming years.

Marrakech has attracted stars such as Jean-Paul Gaultier and Yves Saint-Laurent, and until recently was the most accessible Moroccan destination from the UK. This made it the most sought-after place to buy property, and prices reflect this. The current trend for property developers is to buy old houses in the commercial district of Gueliz, knock them down and build modern apartment blocks in their place, creating a 'pied a terre' market for long weekenders from Europe.

Whilst Marrakech still presents good opportunities for investment and is an exciting destination, prices here may be prohibitive. An alternative option is to buy land in the countryside around Marrakech and to build on it: the **Route d'Ourika**, the **Route d'Ouarzazate** and the **Route de Fez** are three areas which are gaining in popularity, the first due to the stunning views and the second two due to their proximity to facilities such as the American School, large supermarkets and Club Amelkis, a new 18-hole golf course.

Tangier

A less popular destination but one set to dominate the Moroccan property market in coming years, is Tangier. Located on the northern tip of Morocco this bustling port enjoys lively markets, a superb bay and delectable beaches. What's more, if the proposed tunnel link with Europe goes ahead it will welcome a constant stream of pleasure-seeking tourists each year. Prospects for short-term letting options are encouraging. Experts are finding that there is also growing demand for long-term rental property making it ideal for an investor seeking stable investment options.

Fez

Fez is a kind of Moroccan Florence, and prides itself on having the most elegant and highly-decorated houses in the country. It is also considered to have the

Africa & Middle East

MOROCCO

best preserved medieval medina in the world. Although it is somewhat quieter than other Moroccan hotspots, it is the ideal place to go to get your hands on a traditional home at a bargain price. Indeed, property can be 50% cheaper than Marrakech with the potential for between 20%–30% capital appreciation every six months.

The city, once the nation's capital has a significant number of run-down properties left vacant or poorly maintained when inhabitants fled to the new capital Rabat and new commercial hub Casablanca in 1912. All these properties are apparently for sale and offer great opportunities for developers wanting to build stylish hotels, or individuals lured by the challenge of a restoration project. Traditional un-renovated dars here are available from anything between £6,800 to £40,580 whilst riads generally cost between £24,870 and £74,609. The fact that riads are so sought after is reflected in their elevated prices, meaning it is often better to opt for a dar which are more easily attainable and therefore cheaper.

It is unlikely that Fez's property market will mirror the success story that is now Marrakech within the short term. However, for those willing to invest in a long term market, Fez may well be the ideal location. Those interested in taking advantage of the growing tourist industry should be cheered by the fact that the Moroccan Tourist Ministry have made it easy for foreigners to obtain licenses to operate bed and breakfasts in Fez.

Essaouira

Two and a half hours from Marrakech on the Atlantic coast is Essaouira, a picturesque fishing town popular among travellers and the second most popular destination for homebuyers after Marrakech. Tourists are attracted to the town by its art scene, Gnaoua culture and music and excellent windsurfing conditions. The city was once the port for Timbuctou, and as a result has a wide mix of cultures.

The area has proved popular with film-makers, and was the location for Oliver Stone's *Alexander* and Ridley Scott's *Kingdom of Heaven*. The new mayor has, however, placed restrictions on the construction of guest houses after a surge in the numbers being built provided too much competition for the larger hotels. The market here is mainly for second homes, and property tends to be cheaper than in both Marrakech and Fez.

Saidia

An example of an area benefiting from Plan Azur investment and emerging as a promising investment hub, is Saidia. This large master planned resort development is three hours by air from the UK, has a perfect Mediterranean climate and is being built by one of the largest developers in Spain. It is also the only

Plan Azur area situated on the Mediterranean coast and has a variety of villas, apartments and penthouses for sale. The €1.6 billion development of Mediterrania Saidia is due to complete in 2009 and is poised to create a region blessed with world-class amenities which in turn will lead to a series of resorts that have already been billed as 'Europe's new holiday centre'.

The increase in tourism is likely to create a situation where demand significantly outstrips supply, and at least over the next five years, capital appreciation should be very good. One bedroom apartments at Mediterrania Saidia are available from £52,600 and appreciation on these properties is expected to be strong.

The Purchase Process

The buying process in Morocco is straightforward (once issues of title and price are settled) and can be completed within 10 to 15 days. Purchase takes place in four stages: agreement, sale, registration of sale and final confirmation. Payment must be in dirhams (which cannot be exported) meaning the usual procedure is for buyers to open a bank account with a finance company in Morocco. To help the process flow as flawlessly as possible it is imperative to use a recommended estate agent or simsaar and ensure that every legal document is translated into English from either French or Arabic.

When the price is agreed, you will need to pay a deposit of between 10% and 50% and agree a completion date. Investors should avoid paying this deposit until their solicitor can verify that all title deeds are in order otherwise it is very difficult to determine exactly who owns the property/land. A *notaire* (notary) is the only person who can make title searches and obtain the necessary legal documents to make the transaction possible. The notaire will then establish that the deeds are in order, those with a claim to the property have agreed to the sale, and that all outstanding bills are settled.

Crucially, banks are more willing to grant a loan if the title process has begun and been paid for so it is worth setting this process in motion as soon as possible. Once the two parties have come to an agreement, a preliminary contract, a *'Compromis de Vente'* is drawn up containing all the clauses and conditions precedent to the sale. It then usually takes one to three months before the parties are gathered together for the signing of the final title deed *'Acte de Vente'*. Completion occurs when the final deed of sale is signed and legal ownership is transferred to the buyer.

Morocco has a dual tax agreement with the UK to ensure that purchasers don't end up paying capital gains tax in both countries. Taxes include:

- Property Registration Fees of 2%
- Property Rental Tax. If investors do not live in the property at all, a tax of 13.5% of the rental value is levied

Africa & Middle East

MOROCCO

- Tax on Rental Income. The first three years can be exempt of tax, but afterwards investors must pay tax on 60% of their generated income at levels between 22% and 44%
- Property Tax. The first five years are exempt and then after this tax is due based on the annual rental value of the property
- Rubbish Collection Tax. The owner of a property is exempt for the first five years and then taxed at 10% of the property's annual rental value
- Capital Gains Tax. If a property is sold within five years, capital gains is then charged at 20% of profit with a minimum of 3% of the sale price. A property sold between six and ten years of ownership will pay 10% capital gains tax and 0% thereafter
- Inheritance Tax is 0% for family members providing a legal Moroccan will and professional tax advice has been sought
- Buyers are advised to budget for 2.5% agency fees.

Mortgages

Mortgages can be found in Morocco, for a maximum of 70% of the purchase price or valuation. The usual maximum mortgage period is 15 years, and cannot extend beyond retirement age. Interest is negotiable, with a typical rate of 5.8%, and proof of income is required.

Key Risks and Opportunities

One of the main problems with buying property in Morocco is issues which arise with regard to title. Some properties do not have title deeds, and if anything, have a scroll written by an *adoul*, an official scribe, documenting ownership which sometimes goes back hundreds of years. As inheritance laws state that everybody with a claim to the property must agree to a sale (this can be a sizeable group of people), it is a good idea to employ a lawyer well-versed in the intricacies of Moroccan property to trace the title holders and to arrange the purchase. If possible, it is better to buy from one or two owners, and the longer they have had the house the better. It is possible to get an official title by paying 1% after buying a house, and some people do this via a notary during the buying process. Houses with title are more likely to bring a higher price in the future.

Potential issues with title mean it is often easier to buy direct from a developer. This doesn't have to exclude purchases of older style properties though, as many developers are buying up areas of traditional properties and renovating them into clusters of well appointed homes with shared facilities. In these developments, the developer should have secured all title issues before they begin selling.

Finally, it is worth remembering that government procedures here are not always transparent, efficient, or quick, and routine permits can be difficult to obtain. However, since coming to power in 1998, the government of Prime Minister Youssouffi has made strengthening transparency and the rule of law a high priority. In this regard, Morocco has begun cooperation with Moroccan civil society and business organisations as well as with the World Bank on measures to combat corruption more effectively. Such problems are, therefore, being reduced, and the Investment Promotion Unit should carry this work forward substantially.

Opportunity Rating

Morocco presents a good opportunity, as increasing numbers of people realise how close and accessible the country is. The infrastructure is improving, tourism is on the increase and the government is making moves to develop and attract investment from abroad.

Rating: $ $ $ $

Risk Rating

As with any Muslim country, there is always a potential risk of antagonism and terrorism directed towards foreign properties and investors, although the risk in Morocco is less than in many other areas.

Rating: ⚠ ⚠

Africa & Middle East

MOROCCO

South Africa

CURRENCY
Rand

EXCHANGE RATES
1000 Rand = £70.82
£1 = 14.12 Rand
1000 Rand = US $142.82
US $1 = 7.00 Rand

PRETORIA

Introduction

South Africa is a country with a breathtaking natural landscape and opportunities for adventure, through safari, mountain walking, city or beach life. The natural terrain varies from savannah to snow-covered mountains, forests to swamps, endless beaches and peaceful rivers to bustling towns and cities. Unsurprisingly, there is plenty to explore: vibrant Cape Town, Robben Island where Nelson Mandela was imprisoned, the Cradle of Humankind near Johannesburg, the Kruger National Park, Table Mountain and the Garden Route which comprises of 600km of coastline between Cape Town and the Tsitsikamma Forest. The country has gone through impressive changes over the last ten years and its tourism market has opened up significantly.

South Africa is considered to be an emerging market with an abundant supply of natural resources (see picture 16 in the colour section). The financial, legal, communications, energy and transport sectors are well-developed, and the country has a modern infrastructure. However, growth has not been strong enough to substantially lower South Africa's high unemployment rate (which was at 25.5% in 2006), and the economic problems from the apartheid era remain serious, especially regarding poverty and a lack of economic empowerment among disadvantaged groups.

Economic policy is currently focusing on targeting inflation, liberalising trade, improving job growth and household income. GDP growth in 2006 was 5%, up from 4.5% in 2005, while inflation in 2006 stood at 5%. This improvement is steady, and the country is showing good potential for the future. The Economist Intelligence Unit anticipates that real GDP will accelerate again, to 5.2% in 2008.

On the back of this growth and new-found prosperity, the demand for property has also increased, particularly among a new black middle class and overseas buyers lured by the warmer climate.

Is This a Good Place to Buy?

South Africa is a country of great variety, offering something for everyone. There are beautiful beaches, unspoiled countryside with an abundance of wildlife, mountains, bustling cities with a vibrant night scene (including Cape Town, one of the most popular cities in the world), impressive relics from the dawn of humanity, fine wines and a range of cuisines. South Africa is especially popular with Brits seeking winter sunshine, and has the advantage of being in the same time zone as the UK whilst boasting a considerably cheaper cost of living. House prices here are much lower than in the UK or USA and in some areas, prices are less than a tenth of prices in the South of England. Standard family homes are available from around £65,000 ($132,000) and two-bedroom apartments start from about £42,000 ($85,300) – though prices vary depending on location, style of property and local amenities.

As a second home, holiday or retirement destination, therefore, the country is an attractive proposition. This is compounded by the fact that, as long as they are in the country legally at all times, owners of property in South Africa are permitted to reside there for as long as they wish. From a legal point of view, then South Africa is one of the safer countries in which to buy a home. Non-residents who own in the country have all the normal rights of ownership, including the right to recover rental income.

> *'Because South Africa has a stable economy, a good amount of security, possibilities for good rental potential and capital growth, demand is likely to stay high, and investing here offers relatively safe prospects.'*

South Africa is reputed to have the best deeds registration system in the world, with an exceptional degree of accuracy and tenure guaranteed as long as the proper precautions are taken regarding contracts, deposits and obtaining proper title. Property can be owned individually, jointly in undivided shares or by an entity such as a company, a close corporation or trust or a similar entity registered outside the country. There are, however, procedures and requirements which must be complied with in certain circumstances. If a foreign entity purchases property in South Africa, it needs to be registered locally. In the case

Africa & Middle East

SOUTH AFRICA

where the shares of a local company are owned by a non-resident, a South African resident public officer will need to be appointed for accounting purposes. In the event of a non-resident purchasing property in the country with the intention of residing for longer periods, permanent residency will have to be applied for in accordance with the given requirements and procedures of South African law.

South Africa has proven especially popular among those looking for holiday or retirement homes. However, because it also has a stable economy, a good amount of security, possibilities for good rental potential and capital growth, it will continue to attract more serious investors looking for returns on their investment. These factors mean that demand is likely to stay high, and that investing here offers relatively safe prospects.

Price History

The majority of the price rises in South Africa occurred during the first five years of the 21st century, as the economy began to grow at a noticeable rate after the lull at the end of apartheid. *The Economist* put South Africa's property market growth from 1997 to 2005 at 271% and an average annual growth of 23% was registered in 2005, following an impressive 32% rise in 2004.

All segments of the property market experienced a slowdown in 2006 compared to the previous two years. In 2006 house prices decelerated in growth to between 12% and 15% annually and indications suggest that this slowdown will continue throughout 2007. It is therefore a good idea to conduct careful research into growth potential before putting money down.

However, despite this slowdown, property prices are still rising and there remains plenty of room for investment. The capital is unlikely to maintain the very high growth rates achieved during the 2004/5 periods, but, according to the ABSA (one of the largest mortgage lending banks in South Africa), growth is predicted to maintain a steady rate of 12% to 13% per annum.

Average property prices are approximately £96,000 ($195,000) for a one-bedroom apartment and £287,000 ($583,100) for a four-bedroom villa, but of course vary from area to area.

Which Type of Property Should You Go For?

There is no shortage of properties in South Africa, so whatever type you are looking for, there is likely to be plenty to choose from. Most properties for sale tend to be apartments, villas and duplexes in new-build developments, or older properties such as farmhouses and cottages, though it is also possible to buy a plot of land and build on it. Provided the title deeds have been endorsed '*non-resident*', any funds put into a property and any income received, including profit from sales, can be repatriated easily.

INSIDER TIP Cluster homes, which are part of security complexes, are convenient and popular with overseas buyers as 'lock up and leave' properties. Although new properties may lack the charm and character of older buildings, they have advantages in that there are no costs associated with modernisation or renovation, while heating and maintenance are generally cheaper. The standard of modern development in the country is strictly regulated and is producing higher quality properties than were constructed previously (check that the developer is reputable, though, and have all aspects of the building checked before signing). Delayed payment options add to this appeal.

More modern properties also have good resale potential and are considered a good investment by South African buyers, although they are usually smaller than older properties and rarely come with a large amount of land.

There are advantages in buying a resale property. Such properties are likely to be in a more developed area with good local facilities and services. They are also more likely to have an individual design and style and avoid the usual teething problems associated with a new property. There will also be no need to install water, communications or electricity meters and buyers are likely to get more for their money, in the form of a larger plot of land, an established garden, and extras such as furniture included in the price.

The previously strong buy-to-let sector has recently diminished with the growth in rental yields lessening. This is the result of an influx of investors and rising yields unable to keep abreast of price rises. However, for those who can afford to buy cash, the buy-to-let sector still represents a good investment. As mortgage interest rates remain high, the rental market is still a cheap option and more and more local South Africans are finding that renting is more cost effective than buying on finance. Although yields are dropping then, demand for rental accommodation is still high. Yields remain highest in the luxury segments whilst inner city rentals can also be a good investment. Johannesburg's luxury segment offers yields of between 8% and 10%, because of its slower house price growth rate. The luxury market of Cape Town has lower yields at 3.4% to 5.3%, while middle segment properties yield around 4.7% to 6.6%. Properties in Durban have lower yields again. For those who are looking for

Africa & Middle East

SOUTH AFRICA

rental returns and can pay up front then, apartments generally offer the best value, and will have year-round rental potential in good locations. Despite the recent slowdown, rental rates in 2007 were still predicted to rise by 12–15%, according to South African property experts.

Hotspots

The most popular area for overseas buyers is the **Cape Peninsula**, one of the most desirable places in the world. White sandy beaches, proximity to the Garden Route and Cape Town's cosmopolitan urban centre have all combined to raise the profile of the property market. **Cape Town** has been heralded as the 'Saint Tropez of Africa', and the dynamic city is home to a wealth of cafes, bars, museums, shops and restaurants. With a highly desirable location and easy access from UK, it receives 1.6 million foreign tourists a year. More than £1.07 billion has been invested in the city since 2000 and the fact that it is due to host the 2010 FIFA World Cup is bolstering the city's investment popularity. Indeed, studies conducted following the World Cup '98 in France reported that property prices rose by 60% in the year prior to the competition and it is predicted that the tournament will have a similarly beneficial effect on house prices in Cape Town and the surrounding area.

Properties are still available in central Cape Town for under £80,000 ($140,000), but demand is strong, so this will not be the case for long. Cape Town's southern suburbs perhaps represent one of the most desirable areas of the city – safe and family friendly, but close to amenities. A two- bedroom apartment on a secure complex in the popular **Hout Bay** area costs from £41,000 ($86,300). In **Malmesbury**, north of Cape Town, you can buy a large four bedroom house with a fibreglass pool and indoor barbeque area for £43,000 ($87,400). Further north in the town of **Langebaan**, nestling beside the scenic Langebaan Lagoon, a spacious three-bedroom house with indoor barbecue area and an open-plan living area can be bought for around £80,000 ($162,500).

Most properties bought by Brits are in the **Western Cape**, which stretches from St Helena Bay in the west to Durban in the east. The Garden Route, the coastline of the Western Cape, has long been a popular holiday spot for South Africans from inland areas as well as foreign investors. Prices along the Garden Route now rival those in Spain. For example a 3 bedroom villa near Mossel Bay costs around £150,000 ($304,800). Although you get more for your money and prices are still low, it is no longer quite the price haven it used to be.

Over the Christmas holidays, **Plettenburg Bay** is transformed from a sleepy coastal town to a bustling holiday resort. There is much that appeals here, and **Knysna**'s arty lagoon community and Plettenburg Bay's beaches have begun to attract outside interest, pushing prices up and creating good rental potential. Two-bedroom apartments are available from around £64,000 ($130,100).

The hottest new name is **Durban**. The south coast around Durban has long been popular with locals who have been visiting the area's seaside resort towns for years. There are stunning beaches and a number of golf resorts, another factor which makes the area a popular one. Moreover, Durban will be one of the hubs for the football world cup in 2010. It is upgrading its airport and direct flights from the UK will follow. As a result many recent developments are starting to focus on this area. For example the Blythedale Development built along an untouched stretch of coast NE of Durban has prices from £54,000 ($109,800) for a three-bedroom townhouse overlooking the golf course. The development includes three resorts centred around forest, beach and golf and will contain 4,500 homes.

Gauteng, formerly **Johannesburg**'s environs, is the main commercial hub of the country. Demand for property from the local market is therefore strong, and as prices here are lower than in Cape Town, this is tipped as a good investment area. **Pretoria** is also reputed to represent a good investment opportunity where owners are seeing the best increases in rental returns. Over the past ten years, rents for flats grew by an average of 12% per annum in Pretoria, compared with 9% in Cape Town and Port Elizabeth.

When it comes to favoured locations, the above areas are the ones attracting most overseas investors. However, increasing interest is also being seen in **Kwa-Zulu Natal**, where prices since 2004 have risen by as much as 36% in areas such as Balito and Umhlanga. In Pietermaritzburg, Kwa-Zulu Natal, a three bedroom family home with a swimming pool can be found for £90,000 ($182,900).

The Purchase Process

All contracts to acquire land in South Africa must be in writing, contain certain prescribed information and be signed by both buyer and seller to be valid and legally binding.

"*Voetstoots*" is a standard inclusion in all deeds of sale and implies that the property is bought 'as is.' 'As is' means in the exact condition in which the property is found. However, all patent and latent defects present in the property within the seller's knowledge must be brought to the attention of the purchaser. It is not standard in South Africa to conduct property surveys but these can be arranged with the assistance of the estate agent or an attorney and should be included as a *condition of the purchase*.

It is advisable to seek advice from a reputable law firm.

Africa & Middle East

SOUTH AFRICA

A deposit is not mandatory but serves as a gesture of good faith on the part of the purchaser and an indication of financial ability. This amount will be invested by the estate agent/conveyancer under cover of the requisite Fidelity Fund. Provision will be made in the Agreement for a guarantee in respect of the balance of the purchase price.

The registration of a property transaction is handled by a specially qualified attorney known as a conveyancer. It is customary for the seller to appoint the conveyancer to attend to the registration of transfer of a property sold, whilst the costs attendant to same are for the account of the purchaser, unless contractually agreed otherwise. The purchase price, legal costs and all statutory charges are secured by the conveyancer prior to lodgement in the Deeds Office.

Brokerage is payable where an estate agent is responsible for concluding a sale of property. Brokerage is customarily payable by the seller who mandates the estate agent to procure a purchaser for the property. The seller is also responsible for the cost of procuring a 'beetle free' certificate in areas that require it and a mandatory electrical compliance certificate. On the subject of estate agents, ensure that your agent has a current fidelity fund certificate – this means that the agent is registered with the government-established Estate Agency Affairs Board, under which they are required to conform to a code of conduct. The commission charged by estate agents varies, with an average cost of around 7.5% excluding VAT.

The purchaser is responsible for the payment of transfer costs and the costs of registering any new mortgage bond over the property purchased. Transfer costs will depend on whether or not you buy from a developer or a private individual. If purchasing from a developer, the transaction will be subject to VAT at 14% inclusive, whereas when dealing with a private individual, transfer duty is applicable detailed as follows.

Transfer Duty is always payable by the Purchaser in accordance with the following: (1) If the Purchaser is a company, a close corporation or a trust, the transfer duty is calculated at approximately 8% of the gross selling price or the reasonable value of the property, whichever is higher. (2) If the Purchaser is a natural person, the transfer duty is calculated at a fixed rate based upon the Purchase Price or portion thereof.

The transfer costs relate to the transferring attorney. They are calculated on a sliding scale regulated by a tariff and amount to between 1–2% of the purchase price.

Mortgage costs of 1–1.5% of the purchase price are the costs incurred for raising mortgage finance. These fees include initiation and valuation fees. Mortgage registration fees are charged according to a prescribed tariff and are payable to the registering attorney.

Stamp duty was abolished in the 2004 budget. Capital gains tax stands at 25% for individuals and 50% for companies on any profit made from a sale. It is paid by adding the applicable percentage of profit to the owner's income for that year and taxing it at the individual's income tax rate (non-resident owners will therefore have to register and submit a tax return in the year that they sell). Any rental income will also be subject to income tax, and it is the owner's responsibility to register with the tax authorities.

Documentation prepared by the conveyancer pertaining to the registration of transfer of the property and any mortgage bond to be registered over the property is required to be signed in black ink and must be authenticated if signed outside South Africa. This is sometimes inconvenient and it is possible, and often advisable, to leave a General Power of Attorney in favour of an entrusted person within South Africa to assist in this regard. Where the purchaser is married, which marriage is governed by the laws of a foreign country and a mortgage bond has been applied for, please note that the spouse of the purchaser will be required to assist the purchaser in signing the mortgage bond documentation. Marriages according to the laws of England and Scotland are exceptions to the aforegoing rule.

A purchase is usually completed within three to four months of making an offer.

Mortgages

Mortgages are available to borrowers between the ages of 18–70, for terms of up to 20 years and can be of the fixed interest or repayment types. Current prime mortgage interest rates of 11%–12.5% may be high by international standards, but are historically very low. LTV mortgages of up to 80% are available.

Africa & Middle East

SOUTH AFRICA

Key Risks and Opportunities

There are a number of risks associated with buying property in South Africa, so it is advisable to employ a lawyer before signing any contracts or paying any money. Buyers should be aware that there is potential for some properties to be seized and redistributed to original African owners who can prove a claim to the land, (all municipalities have lists of lands with claims on them which are free to view, so either request that your lawyer checks them or do so yourself). Since 2006 the government has been considering introducing a moratorium on the buying and selling of property by foreign investors, to control escalating property prices. This moratorium would allow the government to conduct a 'land audit' and establish the extent of foreign ownership, and could be followed by new laws banning foreigners from buying freehold property and restricting the length of their leaseholds. However this moratorium is yet to come into effect.

If you plan to live in South Africa, remember to invest in private healthcare as the public health service is underfunded and overloaded.

Opportunity Rating

Despite significant price rises over the last few years, entry prices are still reasonable in many parts of the country, meaning there is the potential to achieve good capital appreciation. Values are still on the way up despite a recent slowdown in price growth. Good rental opportunities are available for those in a position to make cash purchases or to raise finance in lower interest environments than South Africa.

Rating: $ $ $

Risk Rating

Aside from the ever-present security risks which do not seem to be having much of an effect on foreign interest in the country, the main risks here are based around the possibility of a government-imposed moratorium on foreign property transactions, which would dampen the market. This will only be a temporary measure, however, so in the long term, the market should not be greatly affected.

Rating: ⚠ ⚠

Brazil

Introduction

The fifth-largest country in the world, Brazil borders every country in South America except for Ecuador and Chile and straddles four time zones. Thirty-five times the size of the United Kingdom, the country boasts a huge variety of landscapes, from the dense jungle of the Amazon rainforest, to the beautiful white beaches of the 7,250 km coastline, to the mountains, valleys and waterfalls of its interior. Such diversity, along with the climate, the rich cultural life and the hospitality and passion of the Brazilian people, has made Brazil one of the biggest tourist destinations in the world, with something for everyone.

Historically Brazil's economic fortunes have been mixed. However, it is now keen to assure the world that it is a country on the way up. In 2002, whilst the USA was focusing on security and on a potential war against Iraq, Brazil became part of the BRIC alliance, signing a trade and cooperation agreement with Russia, India and China and securing an agreement to supply these countries with raw materials and natural resources. Following this, the country's GDP grew by 5.3%, its fastest rate since 1996.

Since 2003, President Lula's administration has steadied exchange rates and aided social stability, and today Brazil ranks as the 13th largest economy on the planet. Moreover Goldman Sachs has predicted that it will become the fifth largest by 2035, making it one of the most compelling equity investment cases among the world's large countries.

Is This a Good Place to Buy?

Brazil is classified as a developing country, a description that more often than not means poor, with inadequate infrastructure and sometimes corruption.

It can however also signify an untapped country rich with natural resources, a definition which fits Brazil perfectly. Property and land prices, though rising, are still undervalued and have a lot of potential.

Aside from the tropical climate, spectacular and varied scenery, the culture of enjoyment and the year-round sunshine (giving an annual potential occupancy rate of around 30 weeks), there are a number of practical reasons to buy property here. Brazil is considered low risk in terms of war, terrorism and natural disasters, and the economy is relatively stable. Infrastructure improvements are being put in place throughout the country, especially in the North-East, which is the area seeing the greatest development both generally and where the property market is concerned. Along with these improvements, there has been a sharp rise in the development of high-standard hotels and resorts.

'Ensure that your property is relatively close to the necessary amenities – there is always higher demand for properties within easy reach of an international airport and the beach'

The low property prices in the country leave a lot of room for growth, which in some areas has been as high as 20% in recent years. There is also impressive rental potential for well-placed properties, close to amenities, towns and beaches. There are frequent flights from London to Salvador, Bahia that can be found for as little as £180 return.

Property can be purchased on a 100% freehold basis, and both property rights and title are secure while taxes remain low (property taxes stand at around 0.2% to 2% of the assessed value). The cost of living in Brazil is some 20% lower than in the UK and the currency exchange rate is favourable.

Retirees are entitled to instant residency from the age of 50, otherwise multiple-entry visas are available.

Investors in rental properties can expect returns of approximately 6–7% per annum, based on an average of 60% occupancy, and property prices are increasing by over 15% a year. Also, the selling process is easy.

All of the above means that demand for property in Brazil is on the increase, especially in the north. Rio de Janeiro and Sao Paolo are still attractive areas, however the markets here are much more developed and therefore entry prices tend to be higher and percentage returns lower. Wherever you buy in Brazil, ensure that your property is relatively close to the necessary amenities – there is always higher demand for properties within easy reach of an international airport and the beach.

The Americas

BRAZIL

Price History

Prices in Brazil have been relatively unstable over the past few years. In 1999 Brazil experienced a decrease in property prices following the devaluation of its currency. In the four years leading up to 2005, property that had previously been sold for R$150,000 (£38,000/$65,000) went down to less than R$100,000 (£25,000/$42,000). Prices are therefore still relatively cheap but with the economy now stable there is a strong basis for them to climb again. Detached villas start at around £15,000, although a significant premium will be added to property close to Rio. Prices are also higher in the popular regions of North-East Brazil (see picture 8 in the colour section).

Another factor behind these predictions is the recent success of the tourism sector. The World Travel and Tourism Council report for Brazil in 2007 stated that Brazil is a 'very large ... and fast-growing Travel and Tourism economy'. *Someplace Else* magazine reported that tourism arrivals rose by 30% in 2006, and in the first quarter of 2007 tourism arrivals were up by 9.6% on the same period in 2006. The modernisation of main airports and construction of high-standard hotels and resorts (many of them operated by international groups) have boosted tourism in the northeast, and the government is committed to fostering this market.

Daily flights are available from a large number of European cities, and a week's holiday from the UK including flights and accommodation can currently be found for as little as £299. Capital appreciation in Ceará in the North, where the number of foreign tourists has increased by 26% since 2000, reached 20% a few years ago, a figure matched in a number of towns in Brazil.

Which Type of Property Should You Go For?

In urban areas, the best option is probably to invest in a serviced apartment in a reputable and secure area. Building a home has proven popular for those planning to invest inland. Many investors have also found that building a pousada, or guest house, in a small village in one of the chapadas (valleys) makes for a profitable investment as well as a relaxed lifestyle.

In beach and coastal areas, where two thirds of Brazil's population live, an increasing number of luxury resort developments are coming onto the market. When looking at these choose properties which have good access to the beach, nearby cities and an international airport, and have a good range of facilities. A nearby golf course would also be a draw when considering rentability and occupancy rates as a holiday destination.

The Americas

BRAZIL

As in any market, ensure that the chosen property stands out from others in terms of quality and amenities.

Hotspots

As the largest and most famous cities in Brazil, **Rio de Janeiro** and **São Paolo** are the safest opportunities for investment, although prices are likely to be high in the desirable areas and percentage returns will diminish proportionately.

Sao Paolo is the centre of government and finance in the country, and is therefore likely to be popular with those looking for commercial and office properties, whilst Rio, the *cidade maravilhosa* (beautiful city), has a reputation for Carnival and the arts. Sandwiched between mountains and the sea, Rio has 45 miles of white-sand seafront, including the famous Copacabana and Ipanema beaches. Rio is likely to be popular with those who want to take advantage of high tourist numbers and the city's reputation as one of the great romantic destinations.

Whilst these cities are undoubtedly popular destinations, higher returns and greater potential for growth are more likely in the north of Brazil. The area is attracting interest from investors as it is relatively underdeveloped and has a wealth of natural beauty. With rainforest sweeping down to some of the finest beaches in the world, the north combines a fresh, unexplored feel with properties designed to a luxury standard.

INSIDER TIP

The most attractive areas for property ownership are currently in the coastal north-east of the country, notably Natal, Joao Pessoa, Ceara, and throughout Bahia. Here prices are still very affordable, but in areas where infrastructure is improving, they are rising extremely quickly.

Confidence in this area is sufficiently high for some agents to offer guaranteed returns of up to 6% on selected waterfront properties. Supportive infrastructure is under development. In **Rio Grande do Norte**, the Mayor's office is planning an investment of about R$400 million in hotel construction in the next four years. The state is reported to have the cleanest air and the purest water in the whole of South America (second in the world behind the Antartic), and in a recent survey the city of **Natal** was found to have the lowest crime rate and one of the highest quality of life rankings in the country. It should be noted that many other less developed areas along the coast have security issues.

Aside from Rio Grande do Norte, other states which are proving popular in the north include **Ceará**, a major tourist hub which has already reported significant returns on property; **Pernambuco; Alagoas; Sergipe; Paraíba**; and **Piauí**. An ambitious investment project has significantly improved infrastructure in these areas, road improvements between the cities being one of the measures taken. Bahia is also tipped for increased growth, although the tourist industry is already somewhat more developed here than in the above-mentioned areas.

The Purchase Process

The purchase process in Brazil is relatively simple. To buy a property it is necessary to obtain a CPF (*Cadastro das Pessoas Físicas*) number, a personal ID number which allows utilities and bank accounts to be registered. There is a nominal fee for this, and most developers should be able to process the application for you. This registration also provides details of capital brought into the country and allows for full repatriation of funds. The Brazilian government advises overseas buyers to appoint an imobiliárias who is a member of CRECI (*Conselho Regional de Corretore Imobiliários* – the Regional Council of Property Managers).

All properties built or administered after 31 December 1973 have a document called a Matrícula. This contains a detailed description and historical records of all legal, judicial and financial transactions pertaining to the property, as well as a description of the property itself, its precise address and location, past and present owner information and outstanding mortgages.

As in any foreign market, it is advisable to employ an agent, translator or lawyer who is well-versed in the legalities of the local property market to guide you through the purchase process, even though much of it is managed through a cartório (notary office). All contracts are in Portuguese and English, with a written and binding guarantee of full title.

Deposits usually stand at 10%, but can range from 5% to 20% depending on the property. Payment can thereafter be made in instalments or in a lump sum on delivery. Funds for purchase must be wired into the seller's bank account but need to be registered by the central bank. Be sure that your lawyer registers any transfer of funds through the correct channels as otherwise neither the transfer or the sale will be legally recorded. Bear in mind though that interest rates are high and there may be a currency risk: if the value of the Real drops your property value will do the same.

Legal Costs & Implications
- Stamp duty (5%)
- Agents' fees (typically 4–10%)
- Legal and sundry fees £200–£500
- Foreigners seeking permanent visas must show that they have investment funds of at least $50,000 – although this figure can

The Americas

BRAZIL

be reduced if you can show that you plan to employ Brazilian staff. Retirement visas are granted to people who are over 50 years of age and have a minimum pension of $2,000

Taxation

- Income is taxed at 15% from around £3,000 to £6,000. For income levels above this the rate goes up to 27.5% – these rates are also applicable to capital gains
- Purchase tax (2%–7%)
- 1% import tax on funds brought from abroad
- Property taxes (between 0.2% and 2% of the assessed value of the property per year)
- Resale property carries a capital gains tax of 15%, but if the profits from a sale are put into another purchase the tax does not apply.

Mortgages

The mortgage market is underdeveloped in Brazil and foreigners usually find the money through methods such as re-mortgages at home or equity release mechanisms. Nevertheless, developer finance is available on a few developments although clients will pay a premium for this luxury.

Key Risks and Opportunities

There are a few key factors to bear in mind when considering buying in Brazil. As with every rapidly evolving market, dubious 'due diligence' and heavily-inflated prices have led to one or two horror stories. Comparing properties agent by agent is laborious, but does reveal discrepancies in pricing, exposing those who have added 25% to their prices. Analysis also reveals the truth behind situations where agents and developers are offering 15% guaranteed rentals – they may just be giving the buyer's money back to them. As they say in Brazil, Brazilians *sabe jogar* (know how to play). It is important, therefore, to be careful, to check rental agreements carefully before purchasing and to use a reputable agent. Asking expats who have already bought in Brazil to recommend a reputable agent is a very good idea.

Trading practices differ considerably from those in the UK. Some Brazilian developers also have an unusual pricing structure that allows for increments once a development is finished (although this practice is diminishing now that the economy has stabilised). Selling, on the other hand, is relatively straightforward – find a buyer, transfer the deeds and the transaction is complete.

The general price history in Brazil may also be cause for caution; it is by no means certain that prices are going to continue to rise. Brazil is not a country that tailors its financial policy to foreign investor interests, and it is far from certain that the next financial cycle will copy the last one with relatively high inflation and stable exchange rates. Investors should bear in mind that the value of a property that costs £30,000 today could fall as well as rise.

Opportunity Rating

With rising tourism, a growing economy and high levels of infrastructure improvements, Brazil's property market looks to have a fairly solid future and substantial gains can be made from carefully chosen investments.

Rating: $$$$

Risk Rating

Brazil is still too insecure a market to invest your total worldly wealth and portfolio diversification is advisable. Unscrupulous agents and developers probably pose the biggest threat to foreign investors although sufficient due diligence should alleviate the severity of this risk. The lack of available finance may also deter some investors.

Rating: ⚠ ⚠ ⚠

The Americas

BRAZIL

Canada

Introduction

Canada is the second largest country in the world and the 21st richest. Generally it is well regarded for being easy-going, tolerant and stable. It has one of the fastest growing populations among industrialised nations, currently standing at 31.6 million. Last year's national census revealed that increasing immigration and movement of the population from rural to urban areas was significantly altering the country's demographic profile. Much of the economic and political power base showed a westward trend, towards cities such as cosmopolitan Vancouver and Calgary in the oil-rich province of Alberta. Almost half the citizens of Canada live in or around Montreal, Vancouver and Toronto.

Canada's economic fortunes are strongly linked to its US neighbour and account for 80% of its export income. GDP growth in the country is predicted by the Economist Intelligence Unit to be at only around 2.1% in 2007, due to effects generated by the slowing of the US economy and housing market. Should the US economy pick up, however, things may also look better for Canada.

Part of the British Commonwealth, Canada has two official languages: English and French. The country is regarded as a clean, safe and green place to live and work, and its main cities regularly rank highly in terms of quality of life. In the 2007 Mercer Human Resource Consulting survey of worldwide cities and their quality of life all of Canada's major cities were in the top 25. Politically, Canada is very stable.

In addition to Canada's main industries of oil, gas, logging and agriculture, the service sector and tourism play an important role in the economy. The Canadian Tourism Commission claims there were approximately 18 million overnight international visitors in 2006, which were worth approximately $67 billion in spending power. Areas of central and eastern Canada report that tourism plays an increasingly important role in their development.

As well as attractive and historic cities, which have grown as centres of industry, commerce and business, Canada is blessed with vast areas of beautiful and environmentally critical open spaces, including The Rockies, the Labrador Coast and the grasslands of Saskatchewen. Much of the countryside has been given over to protected national parks, though there are also large areas of land that contain reserves of natural resources and minerals that may possibly be developed in future years.

Is This a Good Place to Buy?

Non-nationals have only recently started to buy for investment in Canada. Until around four years ago, the majority of people would only consider buying if they took a lot of holidays there, had family in the country or planned to relocate. However, Canada is well placed to take advantage of visitors from all areas of the world and the advent of reliable, cheap air transport, low property prices and growing investment in tourism has altered people's perception of the country. Now buyers from both Europe and the Pacific Rim, are targeting Canadian cities and holiday areas in increasing numbers.

It is the ski resorts that have seen some of the biggest levels of overseas investment and buy-to-let purchases. These areas are receiving a large amount of investment into their infrastructure and services. Resorts such as **Banff, Whistler** and **Mont Tremblant** rival many American and European areas in terms of numbers of visitors and popularity. By European standards, prices in Canadian resorts and cities remain low or, at least, offer better value than in many other developed countries.

In holiday areas, it also appears there is room to grow. Canada has one of the longest ski seasons, lasting from November until early June. In addition, with warmer winters predicted to affect snow reliability in Europe and in lower lying regions, the higher areas of Canada's mountain ranges, in particular areas of the Rockies, are expected to offer one of the few reliable ski seasons in years to come. Canada's mountains and forests also lend themselves well to outdoor tourism, such as boating, white water rafting, climbing and hiking, all of which are becoming increasingly popular. Golf is another industry that the Canadian developers are turning to in order to increase the year-round viability of tourist resorts.

Politically stable and with an affiliation to both Britain and France, Canada is a country in which many European buyers feel safe and welcome. In addition, crime is generally low and services, transport systems and amenities in cities

The Americas

CANADA

'Politically stable and with an affiliation to both Britain and France, Canada is a country in which many European buyers feel safe and welcome'

---

are first class. Rising levels of immigration may offer increasing buy-to-let opportunities in urban locations for investors who understand the market. For the lower level investor, an apartment or chalet in a developing holiday location, which can be used by the owner as well as rented out, may prove an enjoyable option.

Canada is one of the major countries that appeals to those looking to relocate from Europe and the UK. The fact that it is both English and French-speaking plays an obvious part. The legal and parliamentary systems are based on Britain's and the quality of education, healthcare and social services are considered high in most areas.

Price History

Canada's property market is very mature. Although there has been increasing development in tourist areas, this is still a relatively new occurrence. Canada is such a large country with varying regions, ranging from wealthy cities to rural and often quite deprived communities, that there can be large differences between areas in terms of price and desirability. Compared to many European countries, Canada's property has traditionally been considered lower priced, however mid-summer figures in 2007 saw rises of 9.5% and average property now costs $303,000.

Rises have been steady rather than flamboyant with gains of 5–10% over the past three years, depending on location. **Alberta**, however, saw increases of up to 50% in 2006, due to rising immigration to the area in search of employment. In the cities of **Edmonton** and **Calgary**, depleted property stock caused prices to rise by record figures of 30–80%. This has prompted some analysts to start murmuring about a bubble market, though more property was released to the market in Calgary in 2007 and prices have started to slow somewhat.

Despite seeing lower appreciation than in previous years, proposed changes to the cost of land transfer tax are believed to have fuelled sales in **Toronto**. The record sales figures in 2007 led to many buyers being priced out of the more affluent areas and prices in prime locations shot up above the $1m mark. Apartments are averaging around $270,000 while standard family homes are around $385,000 to $500,000. Even the traditionally expensive city of Vancouver has also seen record rises recently, with increases on 2006 figures of 10–14%. Standard apartments cost from around $250,000, on average, and family homes between $400,000 and $800,000 depending on style and location. In other cities such as Ottawa, Halifax and Montreal, property prices tend to be lower with averages of between $130,000 and $240,000. If the Bank of Canada raises interest rates then this may slow the market.

Which Type of Property Should You Go For?

Property aimed at the tourist market can be a good long-term investment that also capitalises on short-term rental potential. Tourism in Canada is growing markedly, and mountain and waterfront property in particular is becoming more sought-after in terms of holiday lets and for long-term or retirement homes. Potential rental markets and resale markets exist in both the local and overseas sectors, giving a wide pool of opportunity. Holiday apartments in a complex designed for year-round living or individual homes in resort areas (especially those offering summer as well as winter activities) that have easy access to amenities are worth investigating.

If you are aiming at the local rental market, one or two-bedroom apartments in the main cities and areas of industrial growth are always likely to show good, steady appreciation. Avoid markets where prices are already high if you want good returns, however. In Vancouver, for example, yields are only just above 3% on average, while in Toronto, Ottawa and Montreal average yields pan out between 5.5% and 6.5%.

Hotspots

Alberta

The province of Alberta has large oil reserves and the strongest economy in Canada. As a result, it has been pulling in vast numbers of migrant workers. **Calgary** saw rises in the number of sales of 18% per month at the end of 2006, however agents are predicted a slow-down in 2007 due to a rise in the number of properties coming to market, increasing interest rates and a lack of affordability. Even so, average price increases at the start of the year were still high at 30–40%. **Edmonton** is another area with fast growth and price rises of 45–80%. Prices in both cities start at around $200,000 for a standard apartment. Family homes start at around $300,000. Interest from buy-to-let investors hoping to cash in may also be fuelling price rises.

The Americas

CANADA

Toronto

The revitalisation over the past five years of what was already an important industrial and commercial hub has increased interest in Toronto. Property sales figures in the city reached record levels in 2005 with prices rising by 6–10% across the centre and suburbs. However, by 2006 this dropped to around 5.4% and early 2007 saw lower gains of 4–6%. Nevertheless, May and June 2007 saw record sales figures and, with increasing migration from rural to urban centres across the country, the city is still somewhere investors should consider.

The average price of Toronto property is $372,000. Standard apartments start at around $150,000 and rise to over $1m for property in the revitalised waterfront district. Houses also range widely, depending on location from around $250,000 in less sought-after suburbs up to $2.5m for executive homes in Midtown Toronto.

Quebec province

Certain areas of Quebec have become hotspots over recent years. Though not experiencing the gains of other major cities, at the start of 2007 Montreal and its suburbs saw rises across the board in almost all areas with wide fluctuations in prices, depending on location. Apartments range from $150,000 to around $270,000 with standard single storey homes costing from around $250,000 and large family homes costing from around $450,000 to well over $1m in sought-after areas.

The Laurentian Mountains are around an hour-and-a-half from Montreal and are becoming popular for weekend homes. Mont Tremblant is a ski resort that has drawn a huge amount of investment recently and recent purchases by celebrities have increased its cachet. Prices for studios or one-bedroom apartments start at around $120,000, while larger apartments in popular developments sell for between $230,000 and $400,000 on average. Property in more rural, water-side or non-resort locations sells for a wide variety of prices depending on size, location and outlook. Wood and shingle cabins, sometimes with lake frontage, can still be found for less than $200,000, with more upscale properties retailing from upwards of around $300,000. There is a big population of wealthy investors moving to the area, which is sending prices for large properties on several acres of land into the $5million bracket.

Whistler and Vancouver

The city of Vancouver has long been popular for its vibrant culture, fast-paced business environment and beautiful surroundings. As a result it also has some of the costliest real estate in Canada. Prices range from $390,000 for a standard townhouse and from $255,000 for standard apartments. The apartment market saw rises of more than 10% in early 2007, while housing saw gains of 8–19%. Vancouver was voted the joint third best city in the world to live in, according to the 2007 Quality of Living Survey by Mercer Consultings.

Though some agents have reported flat sales for the past few years in Whistler, the resort is reputedly becoming more sought after again, thanks to the 2010 Winter Olympics. Appreciation may have slowed but there is little available for under $200,000. Houses cost from around $300,000 for something small in a less-desirable area, going up to several million dollars for larger properties in sought after mountain or lakefront locations.

The Purchase Process

Regulations for non-Canadian buyers vary from province to province. In most areas non-nationals have the same rights when buying freehold property as Canadian citizens, however, there are restrictions on rights of residency in the country and non-nationals are allowed only to reside in Canada for a maximum of six months per year without full residency status.

Once the purchase price is agreed, both parties sign a preliminary contract called an 'Offer to Purchase' or 'Agreement of Purchase and Sale'. A negotiable deposit is required when signing the contract and a date of completion is agreed.

At this stage an offer can be firm or conditional, depending on whether the buyer can secure the necessary financing to buy but also on the outcome of surveys and searches. If there are no conditions, a firm contract can be signed but if for any reason the buyer breaks this contract they forfeit their deposit. If the vendor breaks the contract he may also be financially penalised.

On completion, if all contract conditions have been met and all legal searches and surveys are satisfactory, the remainder of the purchase price is paid along with all fees relating to the purchase. Both buyer and seller sign a final contract. In Quebec Province things are slightly different. The sale completion is managed by a notary who is responsible for the conveyancing and represents the buyer and seller. The notary should not take the place of your own legal representation.

Fees will add around 15% to the purchase price and include legal and survey fees of approximately $4,000. There will also be provincial fees of approximately $100 and land transfer taxes, which are generally calculated on a percentage of the purchase price depending on the region in which you are buying. If the services of a notary are used you'll need to pay up to $1,000 and purchase tax is also levied at 0.5%–2%.

To buy in Canada, a 35% deposit is usually required on the property.

The Americas

CANADA

Mortgages

Several major institutions in Canada are happy to lend to non-national buyers. The majority of Canadian mortgages are full-status loans based on a complete check of the borrower's credit history and income. 75% LTV mortgages are available at interest rates of 5.5% over a 25 year term.

Key Risks and Opportunities

On a practical level there are no major risks in buying within Canada, the only issue for overseas nationals is the restrictions for residency that prohibit visits of more than six months per year without full residency status being granted by the government. In terms of investment risks, there are worries that certain areas currently experiencing a property boom may suffer a downturn, however the western and central industrialised Canadian provinces have historically always shown higher prices than the east. Increases are linked to the good employment prospects in these areas and confidence in their markets.

Tourism offers good buy-to-let opportunities, especially with Canada's long ski season. Golf is currently one of the fastest growing sports in North America and buying into a ski area that also has access to golf courses may be a good move.

An aging population is also boosting demand for leisure/retirement property such as waterfront cottages. Properties of this type saw gains of around 13% on average over 2006/2007. However, the country's fortunes are very much linked economically to those of the United States and what will happen if the US economic downturn continues is still a subject of speculation.

Opportunity Rating

There are currently a lot of opportunities to buy wisely in Canada. Prices, on average, are still below similar property in the UK and certain areas of Europe. Both the tourist regions, which are currently developing in step with demand, and the industrial hotspots offer potential for investment returns with regard to long-term capital appreciation and short-term rental gains. However, prices are starting to rise. Some areas are now being discussed in terms of overheated or 'bubble' markets, namely Vancouver in British Columbia and Calgary and Edmonton in Alberta, where rises have been jumping up quickly for the past couple of years.

Rating: $ $ $

Risk Rating

There are no major political, social or economic risks with buying in Canada. The property market is stable and only subject to the usual fluctuation in market conditions seen in any western economy.

Rating: ⚠

The Americas

CANADA

Honduras

Introduction

Honduras is the second-largest Central American country and is bordered by Guatemala, Nicaragua and El Salvador. It has Caribbean and Pacific coastlines and includes several islands, with Utila and Roatan being popular holiday and diving destinations. The country is tropical, mountainous and subject to heavy rains. The swampy eastern coastline is famously known as the Mosquito Coast.

Honduras is one of the world's poorest nations and is highly dependent on overseas aid. This is mainly provided by the United States, which also owns most of the large companies operating in the country and has an active trading relationship with it. Honduras has little industry and relies on agricultural production, despite having only 15% of cultivable land. Many of its natural resources, including timber and minerals such as silver, copper, zinc and lead, have been depleted over the years. Its main exports include crops such as bananas, coffee, corn and rice and seafood. There is a flourishing textile industry, known as maquila, which is mainly run by Asian companies set up in free-trade zones. During the 1900s Honduras was colonised by US companies, which set up plantations and held influence over the country's politics.

The country is naturally beautiful with forested mountains and long, white-sand beaches, in addition to several historically important sites, such as the Mayan ruins at Copán and the fort of Omoa. It has had a tumultuous history, including a war with neighbouring El Salvador, several highly destructive hurricanes and mass migration from Nicaragua of the Contra Rebels. Politically Honduras swayed between liberal and military leadership for many decades and the 1970s and 1980s were periods of serious political upheaval that resulted in US intervention calling for free elections. The past ten years have seen the country experience a period of stability with many reforms introduced to improve welfare and tackle corruption and inequality, though not all have been hugely successful.

More recently there have been attempts to lessen the crimes and drug trafficking problems, although the effect will take some time to show. Economically the Honduran government needs to continuously work to control inflation (at around 6% at the moment) and unemployment (currently at an estimated 28%). Despite this, economic growth in 2007 was predicted to be around 4.7%.

'There are restrictions on non-national owner-ship in some coastal regions and legal advice is necessary to ensure clean purchase'

Improvements in infrastructure and market conditions are currently on the cards due to an agreement with the United States that will see over $200 million invested in the country, in addition to the $37 million in aid it has also lent this year. Tourism to Honduras has grown by 13% every year for the last four years and the country has been selected to be developed into Central America's leading tourism destination. Significant funding has been provided by the World Bank and the Central American Bank For Economic Integration. Around 800,000 tourists visited Honduras in 2006 spending around $500m.

Is This a Good Place to Buy?

Despite current Honduran stability and attempts to increase tourism, investing in property is still to be approached with some caution. There are often issues over land title. In addition, there are restrictions on non-national ownership in some coastal regions and legal advice is necessary to ensure clean purchase. However, the way to secure the property purchase is to use an experienced law firm to carry out a thorough due diligence check on the seller as well as the property before putting down an offer. With the assistance of a good law firm, the conveyancing procedure can also be done fairly efficiently.

That said, the country is beautiful and blessed with fabulous beaches and thriving marine sites. Many investors run successful rental businesses in the mainland resorts and on the islands of Roatan and Utila. Beach tourism, diving and sailing are the main draws and the government is both increasing and encouraging investment into resort areas. Property prices here are higher as a result.

Price History

Because the market is still relatively new to overseas investment, prices are generally below those of developed countries, though possibly not as low as you might expect. Mainland coastal areas and the islands have seen the most interest from investors and it is here that prices are starting to rise. Property in coastal resorts starts at around $120,000 for an apartment to around $250,000 for a nice, new-build villa, possibly with beachfront access or ocean views. However, basic property costing less than $100,000 can be found away from the main centres. Land prices vary depending on size of plot, location and views but around $500,000 will buy a parcel of approximately four to five acres of beachfront land on the Caribbean coastline, with smaller beach plots costing from around $100,000 and inland plots from around $40,000 for a quarter of an acre. Away from main resort areas reasonable size plots of beachfront land can be found for less than $50,000.

The main bay islands of Utila and Roatan have attracted huge interest mainly from US investors and in the past two years prices have more than doubled. Beachfront chalets on Roatan, which would sell three years ago for around $120,000 now cost from $300,000 upwards. Beachfront plots that in 2005 cost around $35,000 now cost from around $200,000 with inland plots starting at around $50,000. Property prices start at around $150,000 for an apartment and the amount of highly priced property has increased, with many homes costing over $1,000,000. Recent conversion to a free-trade zone and the impending new development of two cruise ship harbours, alongside the cachet brought by celebrity residents has also driven prices up.

Which Type of Property Should You Go For?

Land in Honduras has always been at the heart of controversy with the government, large landowners and the indigenous population fighting for ownership. Large-scale overseas investment in holiday homes and buy-to-lets is a relatively recent concept. Many investors are currently buying land and building properties at a cost of around $50 per square foot. Property in the capital, Tegucigalpa, and the second city, San Pedro De Sula, is really only of interest to those with connections to the area or sophisticated investors who really understand the market. For those who do buy here, average rental yields of around 4%–6% can be expected. And larger properties in more affluent suburbs gain returns of around 8%.

For the individual or small-scale buyer, coastal property is probably the best option and the one in which you will get the best returns if the market remains

The Americas

HONDURAS

buoyant and stable. There are good opportunities to buy beachfront land and build substantial property at the moment both on the mainland and islands, however, in order to curb speculation owners will need to build on their land within three years.

There is currently a variety of villa and apartment projects under construction or completed in many resort areas that could offer an easy route into the market. Returns on such coastal property are high, ranging from 12% to 35%, based on occupancy of nine months per year.

Hotspots

Honduran property is experiencing a surge of interest but only in certain areas. The cities are largely being ignored by investors who prefer to buy in and around beachfront resorts. Property advertised privately is often cheaper than property offered by larger, overseas-focussed agents or developers, but there are legal complexities and this type of purchase should be undertaken with caution.

Tegucigalpa

The capital was originally a silver mining camp and is situated on a high plateau surrounded by mountains, which gives it a fresher climate. There is a charming old town area with a Baroque cathedral, some handsome buildings and attractive public parks and gardens but the city is, in general, a badly planned urban sprawl. Around a million people live in the city, which has a reputation for being cosmopolitan but also a bit chaotic and unpredictable, with large areas of deprivation. Vast numbers of people here do not own property and values placed on these unsubstantiated single-storey dwellings are less than $20,000. City centre property costs on average around $1,000 per square metre, though wealthier residents tend to live in the suburbs in gated communities that can cost less than $200,000 for a three-bedroom house.

San Pedro de Sula

Honduras' second city, San Pedro de Sula is highly industrial and has good air and rail connections. The city was founded in the 1500s but much of it is relatively new and well planned. There are some historic buildings but it mainly draws people seeking employment in the many industries that the town supports. Properties range in price from as little as $50,000 for a small family home in the suburbs to around $250,000 for something larger in a better neighbour-hood. Rental income can vary between around $1,000 to $3,000 per month.

Tela

An increasingly popular resort town on the Caribbean coast with beautiful white sand beaches, Tela is part of the government's plans to increase tourism in Honduras by creating a large area for development of villas, amenities, golf courses and hotels. As a result, the town already has a growing property market with the emphasis on new, gated communities. Prices start at around $50,000 in such developments with completed homes from around $100,000 including land. Private sales could net you small villas from around $50,000 or land plots from $25,000. Tela also serves as a starting point for those wanting to explore the area's other small towns and national reserves, such as Lake Yojoa, the world famous Mayan Ruins at Copán and Punta Sal.

Trujillo

The former colonial capital, Trujillo still has many pretty, Spanish-style, period buildings. It also has some lovely beaches and, as a result, it is currently being developed into a tourist resort. The government is putting effort into restoring the town and its historic monuments such as the Fortress of Santa Barbara. The nearby airstrip may well offer possibilities for tourist traffic as visitor numbers grow. New-build villas with pools are popular and cost from around $225,000.

La Ceiba

The main focus of tourism on this stretch of coastline, La Ceiba was once a thriving commercial hub thanks to the fruit packing companies who based themselves here. As a result it has good road and rail connections as well as an international airport, taking flights from within central and north America. In addition to excellent beaches, the town is the central point for access to the surrounding mountains where hiking and kayaking are popular. This coast also offers some of the best dive sites in the world. Property starts at around $150,000 (for an apartment in a new development) to around $245,000 for a family-sized home in a good location. Inland building plots can be found for less than $60,000 with beachfront costing from $100,000 upwards depending on location and size.

Bay Islands

There are six Caribbean islands 50km off the coast of Honduras but only two, **Roatan** and **Utila**, are major tourist destinations. These islands have been attracting visitors, mainly among the diving community, for some time due as they offer some of the most pristine reefs in the world. Direct flights are available to Roatan from Miami, Atlanta, Milan, Newark and Houston by TACA (the official airline of Central America). There are also charter flights from Canada. Domestic flights from San Pedro Pula on the mainland to Roatan are provided by TACA, American Airlines, Continental, Iberia Airlines and Cayman Airways. Flights from the UK go via the US and cost from about £800 return.

Over the past five years there has been increasingly more development on the islands attracting beach tourists and investors looking for affordable property. In addition, cruiseships have discovered the area, bringing in around a million passengers a year. Prices on both Roatan and neighbouring Utila have increased significantly in the past three to five years and are still expected to grow further. Properties here are still much cheaper than properties on other Caribbean Islands. At the moment you should expect to pay from around $300,000 for beachfront property.

Yields also remain high on the islands. Rental yields start at $600 per week, depending on quality and style of property, with a year-round market. The other islands may also now find themselves coming into the spotlight as development and interest in the region picks up. **Guanaja** is already emerging as an area for property speculation with prices now comparable to Utila and Roatan, even though access and infrastructure is much poorer. **Morat, Barbarata**, **Helene** plus the **Cayos Cochinos** are significantly less developed but are unlikely to remain so for long.

The Purchase Process

The standard 30 day visa for tourists can be extended to 180 days if required but those planning to stay longer will need to apply for residency. Those with a minimum of $50,000 to invest in a business can apply as an investor. Those of retirement age can also apply, as long as they have proof of income. Non-nationals are not permitted to buy more than 3,000 square meters of land and they are required to build on the plot within three years of purchase or face a financial penalty. It is possible to get around these restrictions by forming a Honduran company, which conveys the full rights of citizens on the owner, including the ability to own larger tracts of land without building timescales. This costs around $1,500 and the services of a lawyer.

Any offer on a property will be made in writing via the estate agent. A 10% deposit will also be required at this stage with the balance paid on completion, which usually takes two months. Prior to completion a survey should be carried out in order to confirm the state of the property and its legal boundary.

The Americas

HONDURAS

Your legal representative should speak Spanish as well as your first language and should be well educated in Honduran law. Your lawyer will need to thoroughly check all title deeds and, on completion, will need to register the buyer as the new owner of the property. This is done using a transfer document known as an *Escritura Publica* or *Dominio Pleno*. It then takes several weeks for the new title deeds to be released. On completion the buyer either signs the papers in person or names a representative (usually the public notary or lawyer) to sign on their behalf.

Costs of buying add about 6% to 8% on to the purchase price, including legal fees, government land transfer taxes, stamp duty and registration duty. There is an annual property tax of between 0.1% and 5%, which is set in accordance with the property's declared value and varies depending on the area.

Mortgages

In general, mortgages are available for American and possibly for European citizens. However, mortgage products in Honduras are complex to obtain and vary according to the circumstances of the sale. Foreign investors may therefore find it easier to buy in cash through financing in their home market. Interest rates are currently around 10% though developers may offer terms on off-plan projects over the period of the build. You should take independent legal advice on any financial contracts.

Key Risks and Opportunities

Honduras is a beautiful country with a fascinating culture and history that holds lots of appeal for visitors and there is no doubt that the Honduran government is aiming to attract more tourism into the coastal areas. However, it is still a developing nation with high incidences of unemployment, poverty and corruption and any investment here should be made under guidance. The low prices may make it a sound future investment if the intention is to buy and hold, but prices in some areas are already rising past a level where some investors may feel comfortable or confident of making a good return.

Honduras has experienced a period of political stablility although there is still some way to go before it can be viewed as offering the same level of investment security as other, more developed countries in the region. Large sectors of the population are uneducated, industrial action is common and the government relies heavily on overseas aid. These factors do not bode especially well for strong or immediate economic development

The Americas

HONDURAS

Land ownership has always been a troublesome issue, especially in rural areas and much of the land is untitled, leading to possible future disputes. The legal system is not as watertight as it is in most developed countries and buyers should be aware of the risk of prolonged legal action with the possibility of unresolved disputes. It is therefore important to hire an experienced law firm to carry out a thorough due diligence check on the vendor prior to purchasing any property. With the assistance of a good law firm, the conveyancing procedure can be done fairly efficiently.

Opportunity Rating

For investors prepared to take a risk, Honduras may provide good future returns. However, prices are currently rising fast in many popular areas and so this may not be the case for long. Investors need to be prepared to wait at least five to ten years to see a return on their investment.

Rating: $ $ $

Risk Rating

Though Honduras has committed funds to generate revenue from the tourism sector, this is currently only a small proportion of the country's income. Honduras relies heavily on exports that are subject to market variations, such as fruit and coffee, and diminishing natural resources. The government has attempted to increase the pace at which reforms are carried out but has not tackled poverty, welfare issues or crime and corruption as well as was hoped.

Rating: ⚠ ⚠ ⚠ ⚠

The Americas

HONDURAS

The Caribbean

Antigua – East Caribbean
Dollar (XCD)
£1 = 5.4 XCD
£100 = 540.3 XCD
1 XCD = £0.19

Barbados – Barbadian Dollar
(BBD) £1 = 4.0 BBD
£100 = 403.8
1 BBD = 0.25

Dominica – East Caribbean
Dollar – see above
Guadeloupe – Euro €- £1 = €1.5
£100 = €148.3
€1 = £0.67

St. Vincent and Grenadines –
East Caribbean Dollar – see
above

St. Lucia – East Caribbean
Dollar – see above

Trinidad and Tobago –
Trinidad and Tobago Dollar
(TTD) - £1 = 12.7 TTD
£100 = 1,274.5 TTD
1TTD = £0.09

THE CARIBBEAN

Introduction

Mention the Caribbean and it evokes idyllic visions of soft white beaches, brilliant turquoise seas and a luxurious pampered lifestyle. One of the most popular regions for romantic rendezvous and sun kissed weddings, the dazzling Caribbean also appears regularly as the backdrop for various films including James Bond and the Pirates of the Caribbean. The living is laid back and easy, the locals are some of the most friendly on the planet and the climate is coveted by tourists the world over. It is no wonder then that the Caribbean is the destination of choice for wealthy holiday makers, celebrities and affluent investors, with islands such as Barbados and the Bahamas constantly in the headlines. But it is the less developed islands that are currently in the limelight, not only for their unspoilt beauty and lifestyle, but for the exceptional investment opportunities they offer.

Recent developments in infrastructure, plus a diversification in the kind of property on offer means that the Caribbean has blossomed into a thriving investment market with high rental returns based on the region's year round season. English is widely spoken throughout and accessibility to the most frequented islands is relatively straightforward. Mortgages of up to 70% loan to value are available and there are low property and capital gains taxes on most of the islands. As a result Caribbean property prices are rising at up to 10% a year.

'Although traditionally associated with the rich and famous, the Caribbean does offer fantastic opportunities for anyone wishing to own a holiday or retirement home or to invest in a tropical paradise'

Is This a Good Place to Buy?

There are plenty of investment opportunities to be found in the Caribbean with more than 100 islands or regions to choose from and a selection of reasonable properties for sale on many. Buyers will be able to take advantage of the massive tourist economy with good holiday rental options, while those looking to relocate or to buy a holiday home will gain access to year-round crystal-clear seas, balmy temperatures, an extremely rich cultural heritage, incredible cuisine and a lifestyle that is second to none. Property taxes are low on most islands, as is the cost of living, and properties can cost as little as £24,000 in some areas.

Price History

As is the case with any emerging market, the price history of the Caribbean tends to follow a relatively similar pattern which is dependent on the popularity of the island. Across the Caribbean as a whole therefore, prices vary immensely. The area has a reputation for being an exclusive, pricey holiday destination, and in the past has been most popular with the wealthier investor. Areas such as St. Lucia, Barbados, St. Kitts, Antigua and Nevis reflect this, with prices that would generally be beyond the budget of all but the most wealthy, but other areas offer alternatives which are much easier on the pocket.

Grenada for instance, offers entry into the real estate market at costs which echo those experienced by Barbados and St. Lucia in their infancy and as such, offers great investment potential. Thanks to the fact that the island already has better infrastructure and accessibility than many other islands spectators predict annual price rises of 10% or more over the medium term.

Which Type of Property Should You Go For?

Property types range from plots of land, to studio apartments, to eight bedroom villas each with their own benefits and selling points. The cost of building is low in most parts of the Caribbean, although it is a good idea to check what local regulations and requirements are in place. Apartments, houses and villas in tour-

The Americas

THE CARIBBEAN

ist areas have good rental and capital growth potential while those looking for second home or retirement properties will also be inundated with choice. Some islands have more favourable residency allowances and regulations, so personal research is always worthwhile.

> **INSIDER TIP**
>
> **Due to the fact that the Caribbean is such a thriving tourist destination, highest demand for property focuses largely on the holiday rentals sector. High-quality villa and hotel accommodation are most likely to offer the best returns in the coming years, not least because there is a distinct shortage of these properties on some of the less developed islands. Hotels and resorts are able to attain much higher incomes than standard holiday lets because accommodation is let on a nightly basis and they are able to offer comprehensive facilities and services. Equally, resort properties have a much higher occupancy level than private rentals ensuring consistent yields are secured.**

The Caribbean has something for all those wishing to invest or to own property in a sun-lover's paradise. Accommodation is available to suit all budgets, although more serious investors would be advised to stick to the popular tourist destinations on the islands. Whilst this will often mean that investors wanting to own a piece of the Caribbean will require a fairly high sum of money to enter the market, exceptions do exist on those less developed islands where prices can be up to 27% lower. Those wanting to live or to have a second home in the Caribbean will be able to find something cheaper as their purchase choice will not be affected to such a high extent by the availability of amenities, potential rentability and infrastructure.

Travel costs for any buyer are likely to be their biggest outlay so it is a good idea to check how accessible an area is before settling there.

Hotspots

With the sheer number of islands in the Caribbean, it is difficult to select 'hot' areas without having to include a huge number of destinations. The following, then, is a small selection of what is on offer with potential for investment purposes.

Antigua

Antigua has experienced a recent property boom thanks to improved flights and extensive investment around Jolly Harbour. The outstanding golf and

The Americas

THE CARIBBEAN

yachting facilities on the west coast add to the allure of the island as does the legend that there is a beach for every day of the year. A low crime rate, laid-back lifestyle and rural feel combine to make the island very popular. Buying here is also financially advantageous, as it is one of the few countries in the world that does not levy personal income tax, capital gains tax, inheritance or wealth tax on its residents. Antigua's laws are based on English legislation, a fact which also makes it accessible for UK buyers. A plot of land here costs between £30,000 and £70,000 ($120,000), depending on location and views. In other locations, such as Jolly Harbour on the west coast, 2 bed properties can be bought from £112,000.

Barbados

Barbados too, is a popular choice for real estate as its renowned Gold Coast offers the delights of some of the region's most famous beaches. Indeed it is one of the most popular Caribbean islands amongst British investors thanks to its reputation as a 'traditional' holiday location. A vibrant party scene dominates the island and mixes calypso rhythms with reggae in a setting of stunning natural beauty. Barbados was one of the first Caribbean islands to employ tourism as a major economic tool, and is therefore one of the most well-established and economically prosperous. However, as a result of its popularity, Barbados has become somewhat over-developed in recent years and property prices have risen to extortionate levels with villas on the west coast often selling for millions of dollars.

Dominica

Known as the 'Nature Island of the Caribbean', Dominica is covered by lush rainforests and has a mountainous terrain fringed with waterfalls, lakes and rivers. The island is the only one where the Caribs, the original Caribbean inhabitants, have survived, and the island is fast becoming one of the world's best eco-tourism destinations. There is no capital gains tax here, and property taxes are negligible. In general terms it is fair to say that the majority of the island's real estate is available for not much money. Top end properties cost around £400,000, although there are also a number of two or three-bedroom properties around the £55,000 to £150,000 ($260,000) mark.

Guadeloupe

The volcanic island of Guadeloupe is characterised by rolling hills, tropical forests and banana plantations. The island is a 'department' of France, uses the euro and is governed by French law, giving a real taste of France in the Tropics and making the island a low-risk option. Property here is comparable in price to buying in the south-west of France, and while there are expensive properties here, it is possible to find studio apartments in Guadeloupe's premier resort for as little as £24,000.

St. Vincent and the Grenadines
This collection of 32 islands and cays were recently made famous by the success of the Pirates of the Caribbean, and give a feel of the real essence of the Caribbean. Several are privately owned, including Mustique, where villa prices start at around £3 million. The best deals are likely to be found on other islands such as Bequia, an increasingly popular tourist destination in the area. Property prices here are rising, but it is still possible to find a bargain. With a wide range of property available and a thriving tourism industry that has created a rental pool that should maintain a property on a year-round basis, the island offers great investment opportunities. Studio apartments in Buccament Bay St. Vincent are available from £110,000.

St. Lucia
Voted the world's most beautiful island, with 19 acres of rainforest and an array of outstanding beaches, St. Lucia rivals the more established Caribbean destinations. Thanks to the 2007 Cricket World Cup, it has received £11 million investment in infrastructure making it one of the most modern and efficient islands. Stable government and exchange rates, excellent health facilities and direct flights from the UK, means St. Lucia has a lot to offer both tourists and investors alike. More importantly, its property prices are around 27% below those on neighbouring Barbados meaning properties there have excellent potential for capital appreciation. 3 bedroom villas are available from £160,000.

Trinidad & Tobago
Trinidad and Tobago is a tiny twin island republic of 1.3 million ethnically diverse people. It has an ecological and geographical diversity that is truly unmatched in the Caribbean. Located just off the tip of Venezuela, Trinidad, the larger and livelier of the two islands, is the energetic heart of the republic; a thriving and highly developed island boasting exciting nightlife and a robust industrial sector. Tobago, in contrast, is the islands' serene escape with its palm-lined white beaches, lush rainforest and some of the richest coral reefs in the Caribbean, home to over 600 species of fish. Being at the most southerly point in the Caribbean, Trinidad and Tobago are the only islands where yacht insurance against hurricanes is available.

The Americas

THE CARIBBEAN

Trinidad and Tobago offers exciting investment opportunities. The GDP is amongst the highest in the region with a GDP real growth rate of 11.9% in 2006. It is becoming a popular holiday spot, while also fostering a strong eco-tourism policy. Total demand for travel and tourism in Trinidad and Tobago is expected to grow by 15.5% in 2007 and 4% per annum between 2008 and 2017.

'Grenada offers entry into the real estate market at costs which echo those experienced by Barbados and St. Lucia in their infancy and as such, offers great investment potential'

With Barbados now pricing itself out of the reach of many Brits, Tobago is one of the islands to step into the breach. Prices are rising with the average price for coastal properties being £1,282 per square metre. This is cheaper than most other islands, as little as half of the prices in St Lucia and one fifth of many prices in Barbados. This creates the potential for excellent capital appreciation. Prices in Tobago range from £132,800 for a three bedroom bungalow with private swimming pool near to the beach, to villas costing upwards of £2.2 million. In Trinidad a three-bedroom house with a shared pool in a gated community costs around £132,760.

Moreover the buy-to-let market offers other opportunities as Trinidad and Tobago's rental market is buoyant, driven by foreign industrial investment as well as tourism. High yields can be reached, especially in Tobago. Yields are approximately 9.5%–11.3% in Tobago, while they are currently lower in Trinidad at 4–6%.

There is no capital gains tax on the island and outsiders can buy up to one acre for residential purposes without a licence. However, there are some disadvantages, namely high rental income taxes and relatively high buying costs, though not as high as on many of the nearby islands.

Grenada

Arguably the most exciting investment market is Grenada. Renowned for its picturesque interior of rainforests and waterfalls and its coastline of protected bays and secluded beaches, Grenada is the last undiscovered jewel of the Caribbean but one whose popularity is rising rapidly (see picture 10 in the colour section). Visitor numbers between 2005 and 2006 increased by 60.5% and the total inflow of FDI into the tourism sector for the same period rose by 73%. The number of visitors from the UK between January and September 2006 grew by 68% representing a market share of 20.10% and intimating the country's thriving tourist industry.

The Americas

THE CARIBBEAN

Occupying an early stage in the development cycle, the island offers excellent value by regional standards. The over-saturation of development land on more established neighbouring islands has caused shrewd local investors to focus on islands such as Grenada and take advantage of their lower property prices.

Concerted government efforts to increase the number of high quality hotel rooms by 1000, to keep up with current demand, means that the island is very investment friendly. High demand also means that prices and yields on resort properties are constantly being pushed up.

Benefits such as tax exemptions and customs concessions for tourism market investors are being implemented and substantial infrastructure improvements are taking place. Accessibility is also improving with direct flights from the UK, USA and Continental Europe. There are also two cruise ship terminals.

There are already a handful of new high-class developments under construction including Prickly Bay Waterside development at Lance aux Epines, the proposed Four Seasons project on Mount Hartman Bay and Hog Island, Bacolet Bay in St. David's (see picture 1 in the colour section) whilst in the capital Port Louis Trading Company is to develop a 400 berth international yacht club and marina in association with the Ritz Carlton. In line with the emergence of these high end resorts, it is expected that there will be annual price rises of 10% or more over the medium term. As such land prices have started to reflect the growth in property development going up from $15 per square foot five years ago to $30 per square foot now.

The Rest

Other locations offer different benefits: in the **Cayman Islands**, a two-bed condominium can be bought for £250,000 with no taxes other than stamp duty at rates up to 9% on transfers of real estate. Cayman also has no sales tax, no income tax, no capital gains tax, no property tax and no inheritance tax and the purchasing process is relatively easy. Local laws simply stipulate that the prospective buyers present personal documents, including certificates of identification and confirmation of the source of funds, to their real estate agent.

In the **Bahamas**, prior government approval is not required for non-Bahamians to purchase residential properties of less than five acres. Such acquisitions are, however, required to be registered with the Investments Board and the Central Bank. There are no taxes levied on capital gains, corporate earnings, personal income, sales, inheritance or dividends. Residents are also free from succession, inheritance, gift, or estate taxes. The only indirect taxation is a real property tax, ranging from 0.75% to 1% for owner-occupied property, 1% for unimproved property and 1%–2% on all other property.

The Americas

THE CARIBBEAN

The Purchase Process

The best way to find out about the purchase process for the island on which you hope to buy is to find a reputable lawyer or agent who can advise you on the particular rules which will apply. These vary so much between islands that it is impossible to give a general overview (note that googling property in the Caribbean will get you nowhere – internet searches must be specific). In Antigua, for example, there are no restrictions on buying for UK citizens, though you will have to apply for a foreign landholder's licence, which will cost around 5% of the value of the land to be purchased. This document may take four months to issue. Buyers of freehold property must also pay a 2.5% purchase tax, 1–2% in legal fees and the 1% closing fee.

In Dominica land ownership by foreigners is governed by the Aliens Holding Regulation Act, and those wishing to buy land over a certain size (over three acres in Dominica) will need to apply for an Alien Land Holding Licence from the government before making a purchase, usually costing US$150. If the land is for a development project, details of any plans must be supplied, plus details of estimated costs. A lawyer will be able to make the necessary applications for this. The same is true in St. Vincent and the Grenadines where an Alien Land Holding License is required before any property can be purchased. As you can see by these few examples, each region has its own specific legal regime, making it essential to conduct in-depth individual research.

Key Risks and Opportunities

It can be expensive and difficult to enter the Caribbean property market, particularly if you do not conduct sufficient research. This research is a vital part of the purchase process as no two parts of the Caribbean will have the same policy regarding non-nationals buying property. Each region will also have its own tax and transfer costs, and rules vary according to whether you plan to build or to buy a completed property. Each area will also have a different degree of accessibility, something which will affect anyone with business or family interests elsewhere. These are all things to check before taking any action, and the local tourist board or a local real estate agent should be able to advise you of all the different costs and laws. Once the financial and legal details are established, living in your chosen location for a while before purchasing is a good idea, to confirm that it is the right one for you.

Although traditionally associated with the rich and famous, the Caribbean does offer fantastic opportunities for anyone wishing to own a holiday or retirement home or to invest in a tropical paradise. There is such variety here that there should be something for everyone, as long as the necessary research is conducted and precautions are taken.

Opportunity Rating

The Caribbean is one of the most desirable areas on the planet, and as links with the rest of the world improve, so too does interest in the region. There are still a number of areas in the Caribbean where property can be purchased at a reasonable price and evidence suggests that these markets will grow to a level mirroring that of their more expensive neighbours in the future.

Rating: $ $ $ $ $

Risk Rating

For much of the Caribbean, the only major risk is from hurricanes. This risk is relatively easily mitigated with insurance, and buyers should also take comfort in the fact that even the worst-affected areas tend to recover relatively quickly. Remember the further south you go the less likely the island is to be hit by bad weather.

Rating: ⚠ ⚠

The Americas

THE CARIBBEAN

Panama

PANAMA

Introduction

Panama is the entire isthmus connecting Central and South America. It is bordered by Columbia and Costa Rica and has two long coastlines, on the Pacific and Caribbean. It enjoys a mountainous interior and has a large number of protected national parks mostly made up of dense, tropical rainforest with a rich variety of flora and fauna. In addition, on both coasts there are long stretches of fine, sand beaches with upmarket tourist resorts that are now starting to develop more fully. The Pacific coast offers good conditions for sports such as surfing and as a result tends to attract a younger, sporty set. Meanwhile the Caribbean coast offers coral reefs, island archipelagos still inhabited by the local Cuna Indian population, and quieter waters that are good for bathers and divers.

The country languished under Columbian rule until 1903 when, backed by America, there was a revolution that secured independence. America was granted land rights and allowed a military presence in Panama, during which time it announced it had plans to build the now-famous shipping canal between the Pacific and Carribbean. In 1914 the canal opened and Panama became one of the most important global shipping destinations. The business brought by the canal was a crucial addition to the country's economy but the US retained the rights to own both the canal and all adjoining lands until 1999.

Unlike many other Central and South American countries, Panama does not tend to base its income around export of goods but in providing trade and service industries. The country is seeing a huge boom as a result. Economic growth is expected to be around 11% in 2007 with rates continuing at 9% over the next two years, a higher rate than any other country in the region. Overseas investment is responsible for 16% of GDP as foreign companies move in, attracted by the central location of Panama's main urban zones, its tax incentives and low-cost workforce.

The government is actively pursuing overseas investment by offering free-trade agreements alongside tax breaks for businesses, investors and individuals and easy-to-obtain visas for foreign residents. The recent decision to expand the canal and levy higher charges to pay for the amount of work involved is also likely to bring substantial economic benefits and long-term investment from overseas institutions.

'Economically, Panama does not offer a risky market for purchasers. The government is stable and actively encouraging inward investment'

Panama has a close relationship with the United States and is only a three-hour flight from Miami and two hours from Dallas. Though the local currency is the Balboa most transactions are in dollars, which are worth the same. Residents do not have to pay tax on any income earned overseas, which has encouraged large numbers of US and European citizens to take residency here.

Panama is politically stable and is increasing the welfare of its population via investment and economic growth. Medical facilities are first class and education is improving, though an estimated 40% of the population still live in poverty. Unemployment, though falling, currently stands at 8.6%. Corruption has proved a stumbling block for several international companies working here and crime and drugs can be an issue in many areas, including some poorer districts of Panama City. Although there are large numbers of glittering new-builds, there are still areas of slum dwellings in the cities. There are also fears that tourists may be a target for crime or guerrilla activity in some out-of-the-way areas, such as the Darién Province near the Colombian border. However, the majority of the national park areas are generally safe, and visitors travelling with a guide should feel secure.

Amid some rumours that Panama is seeing an unsustainable economic bubble, tourism is also growing by 15–20% per year, bringing in $1.4bn annually. However, there is evidence to suggest that, as yet, Panama has not explored its full potential and the government is working on a 20-year plan to exploit the country's attractions and increase the number of cruise ships and flights coming into the country.

The Americas

PANAMA

Is This a Good Place to Buy?

Panama is undoubtedly experiencing an exciting period of growth and investment but any small-scale investor buying here has probably missed out on any great gains or rental yields as prices have already risen dramatically and the market is already well developed in all sectors.

There are still regions where prices are substantially lower than in the main cities or resorts but these locations may not be secure or may not offer infrastructure or utilities. There are tax breaks on new-build property and these are attracting buyers and pushing up prices very quickly. Buyers have a five to 20-year amnesty before having to pay any property taxes, depending on when construction permits on the property were awarded.

Price History

Due to the canal and foreign business interests in the country, Panama has always been a bit of an anomaly in South America. Prices here have not been low, by European standards, for some time and have risen by 25% per annum over the past three years. Costs of property now range from around $1,000 to over $3,000 per square metre, depending on size of property and location.

Which Type of Property Should You Go For?

Apartments in Panama City and growth areas such as Balboa and the Colon region, will offer the possibility of rental yields and capital growth. New property offers tax breaks and is, therefore, more popular as a purchase. Panama City's old area, the Casco Viejo, attracts tourism and may well offer good possibilities if you can afford to renovate older property there. There are government incentives to help with this as well.

Beach property is highly popular but prices have escalated in the past few years, which may leave less room for further gains. If the object is to have a holiday property that is rented out to the international and local market, one of the newer, resort-style communities, preferably with beachfront access, would possibly be a better investment. Yields are currently 7–15% in the larger resorts.

Hotspots

Though still a relatively new market for international investors, Panama has moved quite fast and prices for both land and real estate are higher than many buyers might expect. Tax-free status for income earned overseas, beautiful beaches and a growing economy have all contributed to the country's success.

Panama City

Once an important point for trade between colonial powers, Panama City is still a bustling, commercial hub, situated on the Pacific coast and the Panama Canal. The city has a population of just under 500,000, with a large proportion of employment in international banking and other financial and services industries, in addition to the retail and hospitality sectors and, of course, the port with its shipping and trade. There are also plans for the local airport to be expanded into a global hub to rival Miami as a regional connection point for travellers.

There are two areas to the city: the modern district with its proliferation of high-rise condominiums, retail malls and office blocks, and the old town (*Casco Viejo*), a colonial gem. The government has offered financial incentives for those investors willing to renovate properties in the Casco Viejo district and some trendy bars and hotels are evidence that things are starting to change here. For investors who like a challenge, property in this area represents opportunity to earn in the long term with prices from under $100,000 for pretty, crumbling houses to over $350,000 for anything restored.

The area of **Balboa**, directly on the canal is already a large and important shipping port but is soon to be the centre of further economic growth. Two new mega-ports are planned in the area, in addition to the construction of a large oil refinery.

Much of the property in Panama City is apartments, often in apart-hotel complexes both in the city centre and suburbs, catering to either the local residential or ex-pat employees and retirees market. Prices are not as low as might be expected in a location that is still seen as something of an emerging market and range from around $50,000 for a one-bedroom property. More central property costs from around $120,000 to over $500,000 for something plush with ocean views or in an attractive rural location. And larger apartments or family villas with three bedrooms in exclusive estate locations can cost upwards of $350,000. Average rental returns of between 6.5% and 8% can be expected for an apartment in this area.

Colon

The province of Colon on the Caribbean coast has some of the country's most spectacular scenery and best beaches. It is also home to Colon City, Panama's second largest city and busy international commercial hub. Colon also has a free trade zone measuring around 400 hectares and is situated at the entrance of the Panama Canal on the Caribbean coast. The region is one of the most important trade centres in the world, second only to Hong Kong, with some of the best air, rail and road infrastructure in the country. Unfortunately, the city

The Americas

PANAMA

is in decline, crime-ridden, with 40% unemployment and large numbers of people living in slums. It is not a location that attracts many investors. However, the area also offers attractive coastal towns, such as Portobello and Isla Grande, and is the site of several new marina developments. Prices range from $50,000 for small apartments to around $250,000 for larger properties and from $350,000 for a family home with land.

> **INSIDER TIP**
>
> **Pacific beach resorts, such as Conorado, Gorgona and Punta Barco are around an hour from Panama City and have long been popular with both overseas visitors and Panamanians. Prices can be high here: $160,000 will get you a standard one-bed apartment in a new-build high-rise with beachfront access, whilst $190,000 will buy two-bedrooms or a small house in an inland location. Large villas with gardens or apartments in ritzier developments cost from around $250,000 up to over $600,000. However, rental returns average between 7% and 15% depending on whether the property is a villa or apartment and its proximity to the beach.**

Bocas del Toro

Bocas del Toro is an archipelago on the Caribbean side of the country. There are five main islands and many smaller and undeveloped ones. An area of unspoilt tropical forests, beaches and reefs, the location appeals to weekending locals and overseas tourists as well as investors. Homes on the main islands of Boca del Toro vary wildly from $80,000 to over $650,000 depending on size, amount of land and location. Land prices start at around $1,000 per square metre depending on proximity to waterfront or beach. Buyers should note that much of the land in this area, especially beachfront, is government owned and there is not necessarily any legal title to it. Vendors may attempt to sell with 'possession rights' (see Purchase Process) but this does not grant any legal ownership.

The Purchase Process

Non-nationals can buy anywhere in Panama except for some islands and within 10 kilometres of any border. Property is sold either with full title, which means the land and ownership of deeds are duly recorded with the Public Registry, or with what are known as possession rights (*derecho possessorio*). This means there is no direct ownership but a concessionary ownership akin to squatter's rights. Land sold this way is not legally transferred to the new owner though, in rare cases, it can be altered to titled land. However this is only likely if it is on the mainland and is rarely allowed for island property.

The safest way for a non-national to buy in Panama is to avoid property with possession rights and only buy titled land registered with the Public Registry. Your lawyer needs to check all documentation relating to the property, including deeds, boundaries, debts, covenants and encumbrances. There should also be checks on utilities such as water rights, sewage, electricity etc.

Once an offer has been accepted on a property the first stage of the sale is the drawing up of a preliminary contract, also known as a Promise to Purchase Agreement and a payment of a 10–20% deposit. All legal contracts in Panama must be in Spanish and must be signed before a public notary, then filed at the Public Registry. This gives the buyer time to arrange financing if needed and to perform due diligence on the title and land before pursuing the sale further. Any conditions of sale that must be met or issues that might release the buyer from obligation to buy, such as defects on the property or lack of clean title, are also included.

Once conditions of sale and all searches and checks have been completed the buyer and seller sign a second contract, the Purchase and Sale Agreement. This deed is registered at the Public Registry and the buyer is registered as the new owner.

The seller receives a letter of payment, usually issued by a bank, which comes into effect once the buyer has received clean title of ownership. Funds are released to the vendor once the new registration deeds are presented. The bank through which the buyer has a mortgage will supply one as part of the service, otherwise there will be an additional charge.

Properties that received a construction permit before 1 September 2005 have a 20-year period, during which no property tax has to be paid. Property that received permits after this date have reduced periods of exemption depending on the value: up to $100,000 has 15 years exemption; $100,000 to $250,000 has 10 years and over $250,000 has five years. The exemptions do not apply to land.

Mortgages

Finance is not usually a difficulty in Panama due to the presence of many international banks. It can be especially easy for American citizens to arrange, as mortgages can be issued in dollars. Rates also tend to be pegged to those of the US. You will not get a mortgage on land or property owned without clean title in Panama as anything owned via rights of possession is not legal ownership. Mortgages of up to 70% LTV are available over 15 year terms at interest rates from 6.5%.

Key Risks and Opportunities

Land issues are complex and ownership difficult to clarify in Panama. Coastal and island regions have areas that are government owned and one should exercise extreme caution and make thorough checks when offered any property or land for sale in this region. A purchaser could find there are future disputes over ownership of such untitled land or even have the land reclaimed by the government.

However, in order to minimise legal issues in areas of prime tourist appeal, the government has made provision for ownership of such lands for a maximum of 90 years. Often land is owned in this way by Panamanian corporations who will transfer rights to a new owner. This practice should be approached with caution as it is a complex issue.

That said, Panama has one of the most thorough title registration processes and buyers who have property with legally registered clean title should be secure.

Economically, Panama does not offer a risky market for purchasers. The government is stable and actively encouraging inward investment. Economic growth is steady and is set to continue based on the security of the profitable Panama Canal, international banking and the number of large-scale industrial and commercial ventures being established here. Corruption has been reported by some foreign businesses as being an issue and the government is being called on to tackle this.

Property price growth has been phenomenal over the past five years. Many local and overseas buyers are already priced out of the market and there is a feeling that property is becoming overvalued. However, as long as the economy remains strong and the government continues to attract investors via its package of tax breaks there appears to be no reason why a purchase here at this time would be an imminent risk.

The Americas

PANAMA

Opportunity Rating

Growth has been solid, if a little fast in recent years but there does not appear to be any signs so far that Panama could see a boom/bust scenario in the immediate future. The canal and associated shipping brings in a huge amount of investment, financial benefits and economic security. The government's encouragement of the financial services industry to establish trading arms here has proved sensible and increased the country's wealth. Though poverty is still an issue, Panama's continued industrial and commercial growth will need a larger local workforce and unemployment has been falling.

In addition, the natural wonders of Panama could prove a unique selling point for future tourism if properly managed. Based on this solid foundation, property here, even at current high prices, should remain a relatively sound investment for the foreseeable future.

Rating: $ $ $

Risk Rating

The Panamanian government has worked hard to attract development, new investment and commercial operations through beneficial tax regulations. As long as these remain in place the country will undoubtedly see an influx of wealth. However, the increased employment opportunities will not be available to the local population if better education is not provided. Some analysts are predicting a skills shortage for overseas companies and also local discontent as jobs remain out of reach of a poorly trained workforce which has also been priced out of the local property market.

Rapid development in industrial, commercial and property sectors may alter the fragile eco-system that is one of Panama's best assets. It may also disrupt local indigenous communities in both mountain and coastal areas whose way of life has remained unchanged for centuries. Panama's challenge is to manage its environment and, with crime and corruption still an issue, ensure that the increased wealth works its way down to all sectors of society.

Rating: ⚠

The Americas

PANAMA

Appendix: Contacts List

International Property Investment Advice
Property Frontiers: ☎+44 (0)1865-202700; www.propertyfrontiers.com

International Finance
HSBC: ☎+44 (0)20-7991 8888; www.hsbc.com
Frontiers Financial Services: 44 (0) 1865 202700; www.frontiersfs.com
Blevins Franks: ☎+44 (0)20-7336 1000; www.blevinsfranks.com

International Lawyers
John Howell and Co: ☎+44 (0)20-7420 0400; www.lawoverseas.com
Manzanares International Lawyers: +34 951273838;
www.manzanaresinternational.com
Max Gold Partnership: ☎+44 (0)870 800 4500; www.maxgold.com
Law Society: ☎+44 (0)20 7242 1222; www.lawsociety.org.uk

International Surveyors
Royal Institute of Chartered Surveyors (RICS): ☎+44 (0)20 7334 3811;
www.rics.org

Currency Services
HIFX: ☎+44 (0)1753-859159; www.hifx.co.uk
Currencies Direct: ☎+44 (0)20-7813 0332; www.currenciesdirect.com
Moneycorp: ☎+44 (0)20-7823 7400; www.moneycorp.com
XE.com: www.xe.com

General Country Information
United Nations: www.un.org
CIA World Factbook: www.cia.gov/cia/publications/factbook/
International Monetary Fund: www.imf.org
Organisation for Economic Cooperation and Development: www.oecd.org
Wikipedia: http://en.wikipedia.org
UNESCO: whc.unesco.org
UNDP: www.undp.org
United Nations Statistics Division: unstats.un.org/unsd/default.htm
UN Economic & Social Commission for Asia and Pacific: www.esa.un.org
UN Economic Policy analysis and Development Management: www.esa.un.org
UN Conference on Trade and Development: www.unctad.org
World Economic Forum: www.weforum.org
AON: www.aon.com
Control Risk: www.crg.com

European Bank for Reconstruction and Development: www.ebrd.com
Foreign & Commonwealth Office: www.fco.gov.uk
HM Revenue & Customs: www.hmrc.gov.uk/
World Tourism Organisation: www.world-tourism.org
World Trade Organisation: www.wto.org
The World Bank: www.worldbank.org

Investment and Property Magazines, Newspapers and Web Sites
The Economist: www.economist.com
Economist Intelligence Unit: www.eiu.com
Euro Monitor International: www.euromonitor.com
Doing Business: www.doingbusiness.org
The Financial Times: www.ft.com
The International Herald Tribune: www.iht.com
The Times: www.timesonline.co.uk
The Wall Street Journal: www.wsj.com
Forbes: www.forbes.com
Asia Times: www.atimes.com
Boomberg: www.boomberg.com
Moodys: www.moodys.com
ATKEARNEY: www.atkearney.com
Foreign Direct Investment: www.fdimagazine.com
International Construction Review: www.ciobinternational.org/en/home
Overseas Property Professional: www.opp.org.uk
Homes Overseas: www.homesoverseas.co.uk
International Property Investor: www.ipimagazine.com
A Place in the Sun: www.aplaceinthesunmag.co.uk
The Real Estate Journal: www.realestatejournal.com
Propertyinvestornews: www.property-investor-news.com
AME Info: www.Ameinfo.com
Channel 4 TV: www.Channel4.com

Global Property
Property Frontiers: ☎+44 (0)1865-202700; www.propertyfrontiers.com
E-quity: ☎+44 (0)20-7952 7650; www.e-quity.com
The Move Channel: www.themovechannel.com
Rightmove: www.rightmove.co.uk
Prime Location; www.primelocation.co.uk
Viviun: www.viviun.com
Escape Artist: www.escapeartist.com
Fly-2-let: wwww.Fly-2-let.co.uk
Buy Association: www.buyassociation.com
Skyscraper City: www.Skyscraptercity.com

Information by Country

Albania
Ministry of Foreign Affairs: www.mfa.gov.al/english
Institute of Statistics: www.instat.gov.al
ALBINVEST: www.albinvest.gov.al
Barrasford & Bird Worldwide: ☎+44 0845 600 1871: www.bandbw.co.uk

The Baltics
Ministry of Foreign Affairs of the Republic of Latvia: www.mfa.gov.lv/en/
Latvia Statistics Agency: http://www.csb.lv/avidus.cfm?lng=en
Estonian Ministry of Foreign Affairs: www.vm.ee/eng
Statistical Office of Estonia: www.stat.ee
Estonica: www.estonica.org
Government of the Republic of Lithuania: www.lrv.lt/main_en.php
Ministry of Foreign Affairs of the Republic of Lithuania: www.urm.lt
Someplaceelse: ☎+44 (0)20-7731 2200; www.someplaceelse.co.uk

Brazil
Federative Republic of Brazil: www.brasil.gov.br/ingles/
IBEG: www.ibge.gov.br/english/
Ministry of Tourism: www.braziltour.com/site/en/home/index.php
Property Frontiers: ☎+44 (0)1865-202700; www.propertyfrontiers.com

Bulgaria
Ministry of Foreign Affairs: www.mfa.government.bg/index.php?newlang=eng
Ministry of Economy and Energy: www.mi.government.bg/eng/
Ministry of Finance: www.minfin.government.bg/en/
Ministry of Interior: www.mvr.bg/en/default.htm
Ministry of Regional Development and Public Works: www.mrrb.government.bg/
indexen.php
State Agency of Tourism: www.bulgariatravel.org/eng/index.php
The Bulgarian Post: www.thebulgarianpost.com
Someplaceelse: ☎+44 (0)20-7731 2200; www.someplaceelse.co.uk

Canada
Government of Canada: www.gc.ca
Canadian Tourism Commission: www.corporate.canada.travel
Canada Studies: www.iccs-ciec.ca/blackwell.html
Property Frontiers: ☎+44 (0)1865-202700; www.propertyfrontiers.com

Cape Verde
Contact list of Government of Cape Verde: http://www.umassd.edu/specialpro-
grams/caboverde/cvgov.html
Cape Verde Property: ☎+44 01753 859233; www.capeverdeproperty.co.uk

Caribbean
Caribbean Tourism Organisation: www.doitcaribbean.com
Association of Caribbean States: www.acs-aec.org
Property Frontiers: ☎+44 (0)1865-202700; www.propertyfrontiers.com

China
Ministry of Foreign Affairs of the PRC: www.fmprc.gov.cn/eng/ljzg/zgjk/default.htm
Embassy of the PRC in the Great Britain and North Ireland: www.chinese-embassy.org.uk/eng/
The Peoples' Bank of China: www.pbc.gov.cn/english
Beijing 2008 Olympic: en.beijing2008.cn
Beijing Official Site: www.ebeijing.gov.cn
Shanghai Municipal Official Site: www.shanghai.gov.cn
Shanghai Vision: www.shanghaivision.ie

Croatia
Croatian Government: www.vlada.hr/en
Croatia Ministry of Foreign Affairs and European Integration: www.mfa.hr/MVP.asp?pcpid=1612
Croatia Properties: ☎+385 (0)98-310 773; www.croatiaproperties.biz

Cyprus
Cyprus Government: www.cyprus.gov.cy
Syprus Trade Centres: www.cyprustrade.info
The British Government's Foreign Affairs Committee report on Cyprus: http://www.publications.parliament.uk/pa/cm200405/cmselect/cmfaff/113/11302.htm
Peter Stephenson Properties: ☎+357 (0)25-812 084; www.peterstephenson.org

Denmark
Ministry of Foreign Affairs of Demark: www.denmark.dk/en
Statistics Denmark: www.statistikbanken.dk
Oline.dk: www.oline.dk

Dubai
Dubai Municipality: www.dm.gov.ae
The Official Portal of Dubai Government: www.dubai.ae/en.portal
Dubai Land: www.dubailand.ae
Dubai Sports City: www.dubaisportscity.ae
The Palm: www.thepalm.ae
The World: www.theworld.ae
AME: www.ameinfo.com. The best source of property news in the Middle East

France

Official site of the French public services: www.service-public.fr/etranger/english.html
French Tourism Office: www.francetourism.com
France Ministry of Foreign Affairs: www.diplomatie.gouv.fr/en/
Your French Property: www.your-french-property.co.uk
FrenchEntree.com: ☎+44 (0)1280-817 766; www.frenchentree.com

Germany

Official German Portal: www.deutschland.de
Germany Tourism: www.germany-tourism.de
Foreign Ministry of Economics and Technology: www.bmwi.de/English/Navigation/root.html

Greece

Ministry of Foreign Affairs: www.ypex.gov.gr/www.mfa.gr/en-US
Greek National Tourism Organisation: www.gnto.gr
National Statistical Service of Greece: www.statistics.gr/Main_eng.asp

Honduras

Embassy of Honduras, Washington DC: www.hondurasemb.org
Let's Go Honduras: www.letsgohonduras.com

India

The Government of India: www.goidirectory.nic.in/
Indian Government website official directors: indiaimage.nic.in
Ministry of Tourism: www.incredibleindia.org

Italy

Ministry of Foreign Affairs: www.esteri.it/MAE/EN/Home.htm
Ministry of Economic Development: www.sviluppoeconomico.gov.it
National Statistics Office: www.istat.it/english/
Italy Tourism: www.italia.it/wps/portal/en
Property Frontiers: ☎+44 (0)1865-202700; www.propertyfrontiers.com

Japan

Ministry of Foreign Affairs: www.mofa.go.jp
National Tourism Organization: www.jnto.go.jp/eng/
NHK Online: www.nhk.or.jp/english/

Malaysia

The Malaysia Government's Official Portal: www.gov.my
Ministry of Statistics: www.statistics.gov.my
Tourism Malaysia: www.tourism.gov.my
Inland Revenue Board of Malaysia: www.hasilnet.org.my/english/eng_index.asp
Property Frontiers: ☎+44 (0)1865-202700; www.propertyfrontiers.com

Mongolia

Mongolia Open Government: www.open-government.mn/phpgov/
UB Post: ubpost.mongolnews.mn
Embassy of Mongolia in the UK: www.embassyofmongolia.co.uk
Property Frontiers: ☎+44 (0)1865-202700; www.propertyfrontiers.com

Montenegro

Government of Montenegro: www.vlada.cg.yu/eng/
World Travel Tourism Council report: www.gom.cg.yu/files/1179413874.pdf
Someplaceelse: ☎+44 (0)20-7731 2200; www.someplaceelse.co.uk

Morocco

Government portal: www.maroc.ma/PortailInst/An/home
Ministry of Foreign Affairs and Cooperation: www.maec.gov.ma/EN/default.html
Official Morocco tourism website: www.visitmorocco.com
Atlas Immobilier: ☎+212 (0)44 42 26 72; www.atlasimmobilier.com

Panama

National Directorate of Immigration and Naturalization: www.migracion.gob.pa
Ministry of Exterior Relations: www.mire.gob.pa
Panama Tourism Bureau: www.ipat.gob.pa

Philippines

Government official website: www.gov.ph
The Department of Foreign Affairs: www.dfa.gov.ph

Poland

Government website: www.poland.gov.pl
Poland National Portal: www.poland.pl
Ministry of Foreign Affairs: www.msz.gov.pl
Warsaw: www.e-warsaw.pl
Gdansk: www.gdansk.pl
Lodz: www.uml.pl
Krakow: www.krakow.pl
Ober Haus Real Estate Company: ☎+48 (0)22-829 12 12; www.ober-haus.pl

Portugal

Official site of the Government Agency Investments, Trade and Tourism of Portugal: www.portugal.org

Romania

Government of Romania: www.gov.ro
Ministry of Foreign Affairs: www.mae.ro
Anglo-Romanian Development: ☎+44 (0)8701-453 853; www.anglo-romanian-development.co.uk

Slovakia
Slovakia Republic Government Office: www.government.gov.sk
Official travel guide: www.slovakia.travel
Statistical office of the Slovak Republic: www.statistics.sk
Slovakia Investment Property: ☎+44 (0)20-7152 4014; www.slovakiaproperty.net.

Slovenia
Government website: www.gov.si
Government Communication Office: www.ukom.gov.si
Official tourism website: www.slovenia.info
Ministry of Foreign Affairs: www.mzz.gov.si

South Africa
South Africa Government Online: *www.gov.za*
Department of Foreign Affairs: www.dfa.gov.za
Department of Trade and Industry: www.thedti.gov.za
Statistics South Africa: www.statssa.gov.za
Official Tourism website: www.southafrica.net
Pam Golding Properties: ☎+27 (0)21-797 5300; www.pamgolding.com

Spain
Cooperation and Foreign Office: www.mae.es
Spain Official Tourism Website: www.spain.info
National Statistics Institute: www.ine.es
Spanish Property Insight: www.spanishpropertyinsight.com

Turkey
Direct General of Press and Information: www.byegm.gov.tr
Turkish Statistical Institute: www.turkstat.gov.tr
Ministry of Culture and Tourism: www.tourism.gov.tr
The Turkish Property Centre: ☎+44 (0)20-7716 5767;
www.theturkishpropertycentre.com